The Rule of Racialization

Class, Identity, Governance

In the series

Labor in Crisis

edited by Stanley Aronowitz

The Rule of Racialization

Class, Identity, Governance

Steve Martinot

TEMPLE UNIVERSITY PRESS

PHILADELPHIA

Temple University Press, Philadelphia 19122
Copyright © 2003 by Temple University
All rights reserved
Published 2003

Printed in the United States of America

♾ The paper used in this publication meets the requirements of the American
National Standard for Information Sciences—Permanence of Paper for Printed
Library Materials, ANSI Z39.48-1984.

Library of Congress Cataloging-in-Publication Data

Martinot, Steve.
    The rule of racialization : class, identity, governance / Steve Martinot.
       p.   cm. — (Labor in crisis)
    Includes bibliographical references and index.
    ISBN 1-56639-981-5 (cloth : alk. paper) — ISBN 1-56639-982-3 (pbk. : alk. paper)
       1. United States—Race relations.   2. United States—Social conditions.
    3. Social classes—United States—History.   4. Slavery—Social aspects—United
    States—History.   5. Whites—Race identity—United States.   6. Racism—United
    States—History.   I. Title.   II. Series.

E184.A1 M3135 2002
305.8'00973–dc21

                                                                  2002020340

Dedicated to the memory of

Steven Harris Washington

(1959–1997)

for his friendship, intelligence, love, outrage, and dialogue

Contents

Acknowledgments

To the multitudes of people who have not only dreamt but walked, talked, envisioned, sweated, and organized to push this society toward a world in which a book like this would no longer be necessary or possible, and thus on whose shoulders we who believe in the many and varied human spirits and in human autonomy and freedom stand, I offer thanks from the depth of my being. In particular, I want to thank Carolyn Clark Shaw, Richard Busacca, Chela Sandoval, Sari Broner, Mike Hill, Mary Ann Brewin, Ruthie Gilmore, Kristin Eppler, and Theodore Allen, for having been in my life, whether for moments or epochs, and for having participated in the vast thinking of which this book is hopefully an echo. And most especially, I want to clasp hands in gratitude with Frank Wilderson, Jared Sexton, Norma Alarcón, and Dylan Rodríguez, in whose company and dialogue there has been a deep, strong, rare, and enduring search for insight, for genius, and for vision.

List of Abbreviations

The following is a guide to the shortened forms used throughout the text to refer to frequently cited sources.

BBN   Edgar McManus, *Black Bondage in the North* (Syracuse, NY: Syracuse Univ. Press, 1973).

BC   Daniel Mannix and Malcolm Cowley, *Black Cargoes: A History of the Atlantic Slave Trade* (New York: Viking, 1962).

BR   W.E.B. DuBois, *Black Reconstruction in America, 1860–1880* (New York: Atheneum, 1975).

BW   Winthrop Jordan, *White over Black: American Attitudes toward the Negro, 1550–1812* (New York: Norton, 1977).

CA   John R. Commons et al., *Documentary History of American Industrial Society* (A. H. Clark, 1910).

CCW   Howard Wiarda, *Corporatism and Comparative Politics* (Armonk, NY: Sharpe, 1997).

CIS   Norman Birnbaum, *Crisis of Industrial Society* (London: Oxford Univ. Press, 1969).

CR   Cedric Robinson, *Black Marxism: The Making of the Black Radical Tradition* (London: Zed Press, 1983).

CS   Eric Williams, *Capitalism and Slavery* (New York: Capricorn Books, 1966).

DSR   William J. Wilson, *The Declining Significance of Race* (Chicago: Univ. of Chicago Press, 1978).

FS   Eric Foner, *Free Soil, Free Labor, Free Men* (Ithaca, NY: Cornell Univ. Press, 1970).

HS   James Curtis Ballagh, *A History of Slavery in Virginia* (Baltimore: Johns Hopkins Press, 1902).

IE	Alexander Saxton, *The Indispensible Enemy* (Berkeley: Univ. of California Press, 1971).
IS	Joseph Boskin, *Into Slavery: Racial Decisions in the Virginia Colony* (Washington, DC: University Press of America, 1979).
ISS	Robert Starobin, *Industrial Slavery in the Old South* (Oxford: Oxford University Press, 1970).
IWR	Theodore Allen, *The Invention of the White Race* (New York: Verso, 1997), vol. 2.
LA	Christian Parenti, *Lockdown America: Police and Prisons in the Age of Crisis* (New York: Verso, 1999).
NP	Edward R. Turner, *The Negro in Pennsylvania* (Washington, DC: American Historical Assoc., 1912).
NS	Leon Litwack, *North of Slavery: The Negro in the Free States, 1790–1860* (Chicago: Univ. of Chicago Press, 1961).
OAP	Bernard Bailyn, *The Origins of American Politics* (New York: Knopf, 1968).
OW	Michelle Fine, Linda Powell, Lois Weis, and L. Mun Wong, eds., *Off White: Readings on Race, Power, and Society* (New York: Routledge, 1997).
PD	Toni Morrison, *Playing in the Dark: Whiteness and the Literary Imagination* (Cambridge, MA: Harvard Univ. Press, 1992).
PI	Kenneth Stampp, *The Peculiar Institution* (New York: Vintage Books, 1956).
PSR	David Brion Davis, *The Problem of Slavery in the Age of Revolution, 1770–1823* (Ithaca, NY: Cornell Univ. Press, 1975).
R	Albert Memmi, *Racism,* trans. Steve Martinot (Minneapolis: Univ. of Minnesota Press, 2000).
RAR	Alden T. Vaughan, *Roots of American Racism* (Oxford: Oxford Univ. Press, 1995).
RC	Charles Mills, *The Racial Contract* (Ithaca, NY: Cornell Univ. Press, 1997).
RFL	Tomás Almaguer, *Racial Fault Lines* (Berkeley: Univ. of California Press, 1994).
RJR	Eugene Genovese, *Roll, Jordan, Roll: The World the Slaves Made* (New York: Vintage Books, 1976).
RMD	Reginald Horsman, *Race and Manifest Destiny* (Cambridge, MA: Harvard Univ. Press, 1981).
RR	John Mayfield, *Rehearsal for Republicanism: Free Soil and the Politics of Antislavery* (Port Washington, NY: Kennikat Press, 1980).

RRR   J. Morgan Kousser and James M. McPherson, eds., *Region, Race, and Reconstruction* (Oxford: Oxford Univ. Press, 1982).

Saks   Eva Saks, "Representing Miscegenation Law," in *Raritan*, 8, 1988.

SL   William W. Hening, ed., *Statutes at Large: A Collection of All the Laws of Virginia . . .* (Richmond, 1809).

SLR   Martha Hodes, ed., *Sex, Love, Race* (New York: NYU Press, 1999).

SSS   T. H. Breen, ed., *Shaping Southern Society* (New York: Oxford Univ. Press, 1976).

Tise   Larry Tise, *Proslavery: A History of the Defense of Slavery in America, 1701–1840* (Athens: Univ. of Georgia Press, 1987).

Tracts   Peter Force, ed., *Tracts and Other Papers* (Washington, 1836).

VC   Peter J. Williamson, *Varieties of Corporatism: A Conceptual Discussion* (New York: Cambridge Univ. Press, 1985).

Wood   Betty Wood, *The Origins of American Slavery* (New York: Hill and Wang, 1997).

YI   Timothy Messer-Kruse, *The Yankee International* (Chapel Hill: Univ. of North Carolina Press, 1998).

Z   Arthur Zilversmit, *The First Emancipation: The Abolition of Slavery in the North* (Chicago: Univ. of Chicago Press, 1967).

The Rule of Racialization

Class, Identity, Governance

Introduction

The dispute over affirmative action is whether there is a history or not.[1] Those in favor of affirmative action want programs to compensate for the effects of past discrimination in hiring, housing, admissions policies, and political involvement until participation patterns roughly equal demographic distribution, overcoming a white-only past that had extremely traumatic effects on those excluded. Those against affirmative action want questions of hiring, admissions, etc., decided on present merits. Or, to put it a different way, the supporters of affirmative action want the stories of those who have suffered discrimination to be heard; those against affirmative action do not want to hear the stories. The latter's opposition to attempts to rectify the past has been catastrophic in many ways, not the least of which was to halt the effort of the civil rights movement to end institutional racism. One effect was to render discussion difficult if not impossible because the two sides ended up speaking different languages, grounded on different narrativities. This was what the white supremacists within the anti–affirmative action movement wanted, but the absence of a shared discourse highlighted a dilemma that even supportive whites could not get past, an incomprehensibility about racism's centrality to popular white thinking.

The Paradoxes of Discrimination

After affirmative action laws were implemented in the 1970s, some opponents charged that the policies constituted "reverse discrimination," since a few white people were not hired or not admitted to schools in some places in order to give people of color employment or participation where they had been previously excluded. When those formerly excluded responded to these charges by trying to explain about past and present racial discrimination, they were accused of being "racist" for having brought up the issue of race. The terms "discrimination" and "racism" lost their meaning, applying both to a structure of oppression and to a resistance and struggle against it. The danger was that in the conceptual vacuum and personal disorientation this created, only raw power would have presence.[2]

The white response to affirmative action, in calling it "reverse discrimination," which signified that white people were being discriminated against by minorities or their agents, carried the ethical implication that all discrimination was bad. On the face of it, as a purely ethical statement, in ideal circumstances, that is unexceptionable. But to ignore the question of what to do about past discrimination is unacceptable. To end past discrimination, those excluded by it must be included, and the obstructing deficits forced upon them by that past must be removed. From a democratic perspective, the monopoly on participation must be brought to an end. In a democratic context, in which avenues of participation should be guaranteed, any effects of historical discrimination which still bar participation would have to be eliminated. To diminish the white monopoly on social participation, and to dispel the inclusive control whites inherited from the past, the structures of discrimination would have to be dismantled, much as monopoly corporations were dismembered by antitrust legislation. Affirmative action laws attempt to do that.

The dismantling of the white monopoly may look like discrimination to those whose former control is brought to an end. But in the face of past discrimination, one either validates the crime by refusing to engage in de-monopolization, or one discriminates against the monopolizers to dissipate it. However, opponents argued that affirmative action ended their participation rather than their monopoly. By this shift in focus in calling the affirmative action project discriminatory, its opponents render the word "discrimination" meaningless and the issue undiscussable. If rectification is deemed as unjust as the injustice it is to remedy, then correction of the injustice becomes paralyzed, preserving the injustice; the claim to a superseding ethics perpetuates the unethical. To accept or give credence to the notion of "reverse discrimination" puts one in a double bind, able to go neither forward nor backward.

In other words, with the exclusion of history, the abstract political notion that all discrimination is bad becomes a dead-end street. The insistence on an abstract ethics leaves history out of the account; and the inclusion of that history renders an abstract ethics unethical. History and ethics get played against each other. Yet history and ethics are two inseparable dimensions of any consideration of justice. Under this double bind, justice becomes unthinkable.

This is a double bind into which racism places those whites who think discrimination is bad on ethical grounds. In order to oppose all discrimination as bad, they have to give some credence to the complaint of other whites that they are being discriminated against by affirmative action laws. Thus, they must become accessories to discrimination, either past or future, and their antidiscrimination project is turned against itself, rendered discriminatory. This is not a dilemma for black people, however, nor for Native Americans. For them, whites should just give up their monopoly and their need to control everything in the name of the democratic principles whites themselves advocate. Yet they too face a double bind. To call for an end to discrimination in the name of democratic principles means to put it to a vote, in which the majority wins. If the monopolizing majority (of whites) were willing to obey democratic principles, the question would not need to be voted on; democratic inclusion would simply occur in the absence of active exclusions. If ending discrimination has to be put to a vote, it means the white majority is not willing to end it and will vote it down. In other words, to put the question of democratic principles to a vote means democratic principles have already lost.

When in California in 1998 a majority of white people, along with a small number of minority people, voted for a proposition that ended affirmative action in the name of ending all discrimination, they represented a broad spectrum of positions on the issue. Some actually opposed equality for minorities; others thought all discrimination was bad. Some condemned affirmative action as insulting to the self-respect of the formerly excluded by providing an institutional crutch (oddly assuming that because it was provided, one had to use it). The proposition turned the process of equalization against itself; in the name of equality, it restored a situation known for its inequality.

What clinched this paradoxical situation was its valorization by the courts. During the civil rights upheaval, the courts recognized the need for affirmative action. Once the affirmative action laws were in place, whites complained about reverse discrimination and sought to get the laws overturned in the courts, and later repealed by legislation. The government claimed that it was colorblind, operating without consideration of race, and this became its methodological principle. Yet that principle assumed the effects of past discrimination had been dispelled, and that such equanimity was indeed possible; that is, on the basis of the passage and implementation of laws, the history of discrimination was over.[3] Yet the question of whether discriminatory structures were still in operation or not would seem to be a question of social investigation rather than juridical decision. To know this, the courts would have to hear the stories of racial oppression. But the exclusion of race from juridical discourse made that impermissible.

Furthermore, when the courts claim to be colorblind, to no longer recognize race, it is a way of saying that race does not exist—by definition, or fiat, or proclamation. Yet, to the extent that racial discrimination and segregation continue to exist in social reality, a blind eye or ear to that fact would contradict the court's decision. To ignore what still survives of the past is to preserve it. Thus, the courts are in a double bind. They must know the state of structural racial discrimination in order to make the decision they have, while they must make the decision they have in order not to be (reverse) discriminatory. To know if racial discrimination has been dismantled, they must listen to the stories of those who claim to be victims of racial discrimination, but the courts' claim to colorblindness means those stories are no longer admissible. Thus, in the name of antisegregation, the courts act to preserve the persistence of segregation, as told in the stories the court refuses to admit. Finally, those who seek justice against racial oppression are in a double bind; they are left without recourse. In engendering these double binds, those who favor racial segregation and oppression have brought the antisegregation process to a halt.

In every realm of social organization, the same problem is presented by racism to those who seek to confront and dispel it. They find themselves in a dead-end street, beset by an illogic that resists articulation, inverts ethics, rejects historical experience, and turns political principle against itself. And none of it is new. In 1866, Andrew Johnson vetoed the first civil rights bill. It was a bill that granted citizenship and the vote to black people and guaranteed them the same rights to make contracts, own property, serve on juries, bear witness, with full benefit of law and responsibility as held for whites. It established that no state law could abridge those rights. In effect, the law proposed federal safeguards of citizenship for black people, mainly freed slaves, against state governments that might attempt, within their recently curtailed tradition of holding African Americans in bondage, to abridge those rights. In vetoing the bill, Johnson said that the bill did for the freed slave what the government had never done for white people, and in that sense discriminated against the white race.[4] It was his, and the South's, way of saying that the United States owed the black freed slave nothing, neither payment for labor, nor citizenship, nor equality, and need take no special steps to provide those long withheld "inalienable rights," ignoring the fact (in a powerful act of amnesia) that the rights of whites already existed and had existed under original charter conditions, unbeset by an alien enslaving society. It was a way of using the fact that white people were the government, and that the government was white, to disguise that fact and bar others from inclusion in the same gesture.

Gerald Early (a black literature professor at Washington University) allegorized this inner paradox of white hegemony when he said, in speaking about Martin Luther King, that King was "a black leader in a society in which there are no white leaders." Recognition of King as a black leader signifies a white point of view that differentiated King from itself; it made a separation that no white leaders need undergo. In recognizing King, the white establishment assumed for itself the ability and power to grant such recognition, as a sign of status or special notice. It granted legitimacy, but in its own terms, from beyond King's relationship to his community. By exteriorizing him from itself, the white establishment relegated him only to his relation to his community. He is not a "leader" but a "black leader." At the same time, those granting legitimacy do not have to consider who they are in assuming that role. The legitimacy granted is assumed as part of white hegemony. That legitimacy thus belongs to the whites who grant it, rather than to King. The assumption of hegemony contained in the act of granting recognition thus withholds legitimacy as only its own to grant. The assumption of a hegemonic position from which to grant recognition thus withholds legitimacy and recognition in the very act of granting it, because it has appropriated that legitimacy as its own to grant.

This double gesture has long historical roots, going back to Jefferson himself, and the thinking of other "white" leaders of that time. In *Notes on the State of Virginia*, Jefferson reasons that the slaves should be freed, educated, sent back to Africa, and replaced by whites. Why carry black people to colonies elsewhere and not incorporate them into Virginia society? Jefferson says:

> Deep rooted prejudices entertained by the whites; ten thousand recollections, by the blacks, of the injuries they have sustained; new provocations; the real distinctions which nature has made; and many other circumstances, will divide us into parties, and produce convulsions which will probably never end but in the extermination of the one or the other race.

He compares the "beauty" of white women to black, and chooses white. To his expression of taste, he adds a generalizing psychology of the slave, speaking of a "them" that takes no account of their being slaves (as does the above quote), and thus speciates without species differences. He claims that "in memory they are equal to the whites," but inferior in reason or imagination. He goes on enumerating the accomplishments of white western society of which he declares black people to be incapable, such as poetry, mathematics, complex harmonies, or subtleties of sentiment, in short, all of the fineries of society made possible through the vast leisures and riches produced by working millions of people from dawn to dusk to support such an elite cultured style, without so much as a hint of gratitude. But in speaking of the improvement of "the blacks in body and mind," as opposed to their liberation (again in body and mind), he takes from them the very humanness he has granted and then found wanting in their circumstances.[5] That is, he must assume an inherent equality in order to assert an inherent inequality. Their mere associations with whites, for Jefferson, should have been enough to instill them with cultured refinements, of which he sees no evidence (refusing to countenance an imagination of freedom), and he ignores the fact that he lives in a society that murders imaginative slaves, those who demonstrate the autonomy that imagination requires, on the excuse that they don't know their place. But then he adds, to cap his musings about black inferiority, that it hinges on color ("this unfortunate difference"), as "a powerful obstacle to the emancipation of these people." When he debates the question of emancipation, he divides the field among, on the one hand, "Many of their advocates [who] wish to vindicate the liberty of human nature . . .", and on the other, "Some of these [who are] embarrassed by the question 'What further is to be done with them?' . . . ," as if these were polar positions subsuming the totality of the issue. In effect, he addresses only "their" advocates, and has these advocates respond with the same sense of "them" that characterizes his own thinking.

Jefferson demonstrates that the discussion about black people refuses to consider allowing black people to speak for themselves. The questions that pertain are to be decided by whites. Black people are to be denied entry into decisions that affect them, in order to accuse them of being incapable of entry, or inferior to participation. Denying black people entry into deliberations that concern them then constitutes limits that justify their denial of entry. Thus, power tells those in its power, "We know what is best for you." And oppression tells those it oppresses, "We know you better than you know yourselves" (as a variant of "We know you did it," that expresses the a priori criminalization at the foundation of lynch law or the witchburning Inquisition). Critical to these sentiments is not "what is best," nor the speaker's knowledge, but the "we," the power contained in that "we." It is the self-arrogated power to speak for another, which is always already discriminatory, exclusionary, and inferiorizing. When Jefferson speaks for the people he anthropologizes, he cannot help but make of them what his act of speaking for them makes them. Discrimination inherently speaks for those it discriminates against. Yet to speak for others in the name of a knowledge of them is at best an empty gesture, and at worst a wholly hypocritical act. It is a doubly duplicitous stance since the "we" is socially assumed by an individual in order not to speak as one, and to refuse responsibility for what is spoken. The space between individual and institutional racism is filled by this "we" and its desire to discriminate without being pinned down. It jumps from one side to the other, escaping between noninvolvement and nonresponsibility, masking itself as both institutional and individual.

Jefferson concludes his meditation by naming the strings attached to freedom: "Among the Romans emancipation required but one effort. The slave, when made free, might mix with, without staining the blood of his master. But with us a second is necessary, unknown to history. When freed, he is to be removed beyond the reach of mixture."

What is indeed unknown to history is the very notion of whiteness and the purity concept upon which Jefferson bases his arguments (unknown especially to the Romans), since that was invented in the very colony of which he was an ostensive leader. But in Jefferson's own logic, he has to set black people on a categorical par with whites in order to make the notion of "inferiority" meaningful, so that he can argue for their inferiority, and thus justify their extreme and absolute separation from whites as categorically different.

Under the surface of Jefferson's words is the final gesture of his thinking, the real reason for continuing slavery, withholding citizenship and franchise, instituting segregation, or sending emancipated slaves back to Africa. It is the problem of mastery, and the equation he cannot resist making between mastery and "purity." The assumption of mastery lurks throughout his proto-anthropological discourse on African American limits, his "reluctant" conclusions about black inferiority, based upon a reasoning that confirms mastery at the beginning in order to discover and affirm mastery at the end. The need to exclude black people as inferior in order to conceptualize racial mastery becomes precisely what warrants his "reasoned" descriptions of inferiority. "Mastery" must grant humanity in the very act of withholding it, in order to constitute itself as mastery in the first place.

This circular mode of discursive operation, with its triple gesture, threads its way through U.S. jurisprudence. For instance, in the 1856 Dred Scott decision, Justice Taney argued that the U.S. government was a white government in order to resolve the dilemma between the existence of slavery and the principle that "all men are created equal." Analyzing the history and tradition of citizenship in both colonial and U.S. society, he concluded that citizenship had been reserved only for native-born white people. Because native-born black people had previously been categorized as property, no citizenship was available to them. That is, black people could not escape their status as property through a claim to citizenship because the entire history of white settlement in America had considered them unable to make such a claim. It was immaterial to Taney that black people had been declared property or, if free, disfranchised by a society that had been overthrown. Taney's primary argument was simply that, regardless of the universality with which the revolution proclaimed its ideals and principles, they remained germane only to white prerogatives. That is, white people had established universal principles for themselves in order to withhold them from universality as ideals and principles. They were to mean only what white men had established for themselves that they would mean. In Taney's reasoning, the white male view of "all men" meant only what white men had shown "all men" would mean through the hegemony granted by universalizing "all men." "All" meant "not all."

Though an old society had been overthrown in order for a new society to begin, the new society could begin only by resurrecting the old society within itself. The English exclusionary principle, ostensibly overthrown, was nevertheless to be the governing principle. And we return to the double bind. Here was a case of a chief justice of the Supreme Court reasoning in the name of social justice against all social justice, and seeing no need to differentiate with respect to the social inferiority of black people between a judicial position having been produced by a transformation of a former society, and that former society remaining untransformed and ever present in his judicial reasoning. Blacks seeking to appeal to law to throw off their oppression were caught in a double bind between property status as the source of social inferiority and social inferiority as the source of their property status. Taney codified that double bind into law. In the process, he made the surreal argument that a black person from a foreign country could be naturalized as a citizen, while a black person born in the United States could not because naturalization was not a relevant procedure for someone born in the United States. Thus, an Africa American was not a citizen because property, entrapped within that property status because not a citizen, and ineligible for naturalization out of either of those states because not an alien.

We confront a number of structures here, and it is important to understand what they mean. The double binds that we have encountered here are the traps, deceits, and paradoxes into which racism leads those who oppose it, both white and black. The triple or triadic structure we have also encountered, with its circularities, is not just an extension of the double bind. It is part of the way racism constructs itself. It belongs to its inner mechanism, the manner in which it creates the double binds in which it traps those who oppose it. Something is granted, and withheld, and the act of doing the two things at the same time becomes both an expression of hegemony or power, and a direct reconstitution and rationalization (through a direct violation of one's own principles and basic assumptions) of that hegemony. This triple gesture, the withholding of legitimacy in the act of granting it as an appropriation of hegemony, is an act of power, or exclusion, of speaking for. These are thus different structures, operating at different levels of white supremacy. What is important to understand is that they are operative structures. They escape traditional logical systems or argument strategies.

In other words, to deal with racism, and to analyze it, we must think in terms of its structures, as a new form of thinking, beyond that of ordinary reasoning or logic. These structures perfuse and pervade the way in which racist thinking proceeds. Racism confounds attempts to use ordinary reasoning, or experience, or philosophical reasoning against it in argument because it obeys a different thought process. That means we must engage in a different kind of philosophical meditation. These structures are not stories whose unfolding we can follow; nor are they syllogisms or dialectics whose logical validity we can investigate. As structures, their different elements relate not through a process of moving from one logical moment to another, but in a spatial kind of conceptual relation to each other. These structures beset us in the world, but they become discernible only through articulations of their operation that reveal them in form.[6] When we can see these structures, it is because they appear in language—a language that appears to be "our" language—though as thought patterns that evade discourse because they evade traditional reasoning. That is why they call for new ways of thinking. If the sentences that describe racist thinking appear convoluted, it is because they are attempting to represent structures of (racist) thought that is itself convoluted, and whose convolutions appear only in the form of those sentences. It is this thought process, its historical origins and contemporary unfoldings, that we will attempt to approach through presentation of its structures in this book.

The same triple gesture characterizes the trajectory of affirmative action politics. Affirmative action programs were instituted to rectify centuries of exclusion and discrimination against large groups of people (rhetorically named "minorities" and "women"). Yet the institutions that promulgated these programs were the same institutions that sanctified and ratified the structures of exclusion and segregation throughout U.S. history. When they institutionally inscribed a recognition that discrimination had occurred, they were also withholding recognition that that discrimination remained at their own foundations as institutions—institutions through which that recognition had occurred. While the original structures of Jim Crow constituted an important dimension of governmental power and hegemony, the government's actions, through their recognition and nonrecognition with respect to Jim Crow, reconstituted that hegemony and power in the civil rights era. Confronted with a movement of the oppressed, of black and brown people suing for equality and participation, the government listened briefly out of a memory of democracy. But in obedience to an instinct other than democratic, it stopped listening, and backed away from further listening, heeding instead the charge of "reverse discrimination" that accorded with its pre–civil rights involvement. In recognizing past discrimination, the government acceded to its being white; in not recognizing it was white, it returned to its whiteness, forgetting (in another powerful act of amnesia) that past discrimination had been an injustice that required rectification. That the government was white was itself a paradox, expressed in this double movement; and the anti–affirmative action movement, in charging reverse discrimination, deployed this paradox of the government's whiteness against it—that is, in alliance with it, returning both to their positions of power and hegemony.

We see the inner workings of this triadic structure in the very notion of "reverse discrimination" itself. The charge of "reverse" discrimination added nothing to the issue. Affirmative action was not an exclusion of previous excluders (white people), neither in the name of a real political inclusion of black and brown people, nor in the name of encompassing democratic principles. If whites felt excluded by the equalization process of affirmative action, it was not in their existence as whites, but in their ability to exclude (that is, their hegemonic power). In other words, the exclusion they felt, as the historical excluders, was not of themselves but of their ability to actively continue to exclude. It was on this basis that the inclusion of the formerly excluded was rejected by whites as exclusionary, while their own re-exclusionary act of rejection was seen as inclusive (of themselves). This implies that whites who felt excluded (or victimized) by antidiscrimination measures would feel included only in their former role as excluders. Because whites were not included as excluders, with the ability to be discriminatory, they were therefore (in their own eyes) excluded as whites.

Here again, the triadic gesture recognizes the equalization process and disrecognizes it at the same time by appropriating it for the purposes of its own inability to cede power. In the actual debates on affirmative action, this triadic structure appeared as the false issue of quotas. The concept of quotas was familiar to whites in the sense that Jim Crow had established a quota system that was 100 percent white. The issue of affirmative action quotas in the anti–affirmative action arguments curtailed the ability to review the original history that was to be rectified, an absolute quota system. The quota argument rendered prior forms of discrimination by whites nonexistent—as nonexistent as "white leaders." Moreover, it provided the terms in which whites could adopt a stance of being victimized. It authorized the claim of victimization, and the resurrection of supremacy, by appropriating the civil rights project in order to reject it. Just as "all men" did not mean "all" for Justice Taney, "equality" did not mean "equality for all" for the opponents of affirmative action.

There is something sad and undignified when members of the white hegemonic majority go to court complaining of victimization, reverse discrimination, or racial oppression—undignified not because they should be more noble in their still assumed superiority, but because they should have recognized that their very assumption of superiority and historical hegemony (all but forgotten in the complaint) had already foreclosed any possibility of nobleness. Claiming to be a "victim" of a movement for equality seems unintelligible. Yet this sense of being a victim also has deep historical roots.

According to Bernard Bailyn, there is a strange syndrome in U.S. political thinking that considers it more subversive to "upset the apple cart" in favor of democratic principles than to leave undemocratic procedures intact as the status quo. That is, stasis is valorized over acting on the substance of issues if the latter leads to political contestation.[7] When the American colonists fought against the king, it was because the king appeared subversive to them in his use of unbridled power. His taxes and trade policies created hardships that led to urban mob upheavals of the poor and a threat of social chaos. To bring tranquillity back to colonial society, the elite acted against the king. It was not power they objected to but the sociopolitical upset produced by the king's policies. For instance, when Virginia and Carolina sought to curtail the slave trade in 1769 to maintain the capital values of the slave population, which were threatened at that time by oversupply, the king's veto threw their finances into turmoil. Thus, the revolutionaries did not see themselves as subversive, but as preservers of social values. Similarly, the police today are not seen as oppressive or subversive of freedom when suppressing political movements (Selma, Kent State, etc.) because they are standing as a line of defense against those creating upheaval, or upsetting the status quo. Affirmative action, regardless of how necessary its operations might be toward democratizing U.S. politics, or establishing a fundamental equality, was considered wholly subversive. It was in those terms that the demand for equal participation was seen as an intent to take over and dominate society.

Immersed in these paradoxes and a priori arguments, the meaning of racism gets lost in unrecognizable multiplicities. The resulting unintelligibility of the concept—the reliance of individual actions on institutional meanings, and institutional actions on individual sentiments—is the secret of its tenacity. Unintelligibility does not make a problem go away; indeed, it enhances a social problem's tenacity, while its tenacity enhances its unintelligibility.

Today, against the dents made in white supremacy by the civil rights movements, the nation slowly reconfigures a system of racial discrimination. The police arrest a disproportionate number of black and brown men, which they legitimize based on suspect profiles, though those profiles are constructed from their own statistics. Black people are routinely charged with felonies for crimes that are considered misdemeanors for whites.[8] Longer sentences are given black and brown people in court; for instance, ghetto-targeted drugs like crack draw longer sentences than the powder cocaine used primarily by the white middle class. Four times the number of black men as white go to death row for only a proportional number of murders. Housing and loan discrimination, redlining by banks, and job promotion disparities favoring whites over blacks persist. White people fight for the survival of their purity in survivalist societies and fortress (gated) communities based on political attacks against blacks who attack nothing.[9]

In other words, the reconstruction of white hegemony goes beyond countermanding a democratic demand. But let us look briefly at what is being countermanded by the processes that are reconfiguring racial discrimination.

The Paradoxes of Antidiscrimination Movements

Four major trends of antidiscrimination inscribed themselves into U.S. politics during the civil rights era, two white and two not white. African Americans took the lead in confronting the white supremacist structure, establishing a tradition of oppositional cultural thought that brought the concepts of identity and cultural autonomy into common political parlance. In its wake, there rapidly grew movements of Chicano/Latino consciousness and a Native American traditionalism that made varying land claims based on pre-colonial and treaty sovereignty. These latter two movements harkened back to a cultural past and sought to recuperate certain foundational mythologies that had been appropriated by white conquest to serve as ingredients of its mainstream "American" identity. All three saw themselves as in some sense liberation movements against the internal colonialism of white supremacy. Though their respective forms of "nationalism" differed according to varying political contexts, they were alike in being incommensurable with what Euro-American tradition understood as nationalism. The internal "nationalism" of U.S. "minorities" was neither power oriented (in the sense of seeking to take over a government) nor secessionist, but land oriented: land as a place of being rather than as property. Each invoked a conceptual relation to the land and to the continent as a cultural consciousness. For Native Americans, land constituted sacred space, the place of cultural autonomy; for Chicanos, the land was ancestral, granted by the first liberation of a nation from Spanish colonialism, before its usurpation by the United States in the Southwest; for African Americans, the land meant a claim to respect and recognition as being at the center of American society, the source (in the bodies and labor of African slaves) of its wealth and its historical survival.

Such movements are always seen by hegemony as disruptive, regardless of the ethical or democratic nature of their goals. As Simone de Beauvoir says, when oppression condemns a group of people to "mark time hopelessly in order merely to support the [overlording] collectivity," they have only one option, and that is to deny the tranquillity of the socius from which they have been excluded.[10] Fanon adds that, whatever the nature or justice of their challenge, it will be seen by the elite it confronts, in an inverted double bind, as either terrorism or insanity.[11] These movements are not the focus of this book. However, they highlight and contextualize many aspects of what we will be looking at.

The two major white antidiscrimination movements have been the Marxist and the humanist or liberal. Humanism and liberalism address the effects of white supremacist discrimination and call for inclusion of people of color at all levels of social participation. As active ideological formations in all arenas of civil rights based on all people being free and equal, they push for authentic guarantees of democratic participation. They argue with the personal prejudices of whites that effectively constitute the daily operations of racial discrimination, and they seek to defeat them through reason.

Yet the irony of Euro-American humanism is that it succumbs to the unspeakable double bind that we have discussed. Positing a concept of the universal human—which it derives from eighteenth-century liberalism's uprising against the arbitrary social stratifications and superiorities of medieval feudalism—humanism produces for itself a standard or norm as the measure of human being. The universalized human it produces, however, and exhibits as a standard, derives from European society; it understands itself and its normativity as white. Europeans find themselves thereby empowered to judge others, and to abjure those who don't measure up. The universal human, by suppressing its recognition of differences, concretely devalues what differs. In their humanist insistence on universality, Europeans became exclusionary. In effect, Euro-American humanism incorporated white supremacy and the white racialized identity incumbent upon it.

For humanism, the generalization of humanity to a European standard, and the exclusion from that standard of those categorized as inferior (or inferiorized as categories), were part of a political program. It sought to "raise the level" of "those" people victimized by colonialism and racism, to alleviate the effects of their oppression or their assumed "natural" inferiority. Its universalism blinded it to its complicity with the situation it sought to assuage, and to its stance as a white hegemonic stance. Its own notion of the political, and of the state, hid this from itself. The humanist concept of the state is not just that governmental structures are a social contract, or that the state is constructed by people to govern their affairs in the fairest fashion. The "social contract" of Rousseau does not occur in a vacuum but in a European landscape. While its mythic origin is a state of nature, its real origin, its historical parentage, is the specifically European feudal system, which did not obtain in other parts of the world. In the process of deriving a solution to their problem of medievalism, Europeans decided they had derived the solution to everyone else's medieval problem, whether it existed or not.

Ironically, Rousseau's *Social Contract* (1762) was wholly contemporary with Linnaeus's system of taxonomic classification and Buffon's treatise on natural history, which marked the first steps toward a theorization of racial biology. Political humanism and the white biological theorization of race appeared during the same quarter century, authored by men belonging to the same generation of European thinkers; that is, they occurred in tandem and conditioned each other culturally. While one established the "human" as an ideological standard for itself, the other hierarchized that standard within and against its pretense to universality. In other words, humanism differed from white supremacy only in what the human standard was to be, and what it was designed to accomplish. Neither questioned the social role of universality as such, nor of a universal standard, nor its necessity to set limits, to exclude what might de-universalize it by being different. In leaving unquestioned the idea of having a standard in the first place, neither humanism nor the theories of racial biology wholly dispensed with the medievalism they had contested as worldview.

Marxism takes a different tack toward racism. For Marxism, society and all social processes are to be analyzed on a class basis. In particular, class politics were to bring the industrial working class to an awareness of its historical task of finally eliminating social classes altogether by overthrowing capitalism. In Europe, because capitalism functioned across national boundaries at will, Marx called for an international conjunction of working-class efforts. To this idea, the national chauvinism of workers from different countries became an obstacle. Working-class politics more naturally developed on a national basis, and Marx's "internationalism" has always been a programmatic idea rather than a "natural" emanation of working-class experience. In the United States, racism was addressed in an analogous fashion. Slavery and segregation were understood as problems of class struggle. The focus was on the growing industrial working class, exploited and impoverished in its own right. On that basis, Marxism posited racism as a capitalist tactic to divide the working class by turning white workers against black people in general, distracting them from organizing and realizing their objective class interests. This view has had greatest currency for the twentieth-century labor movement, particularly in industrial union organizing. Against white racism, Jim Crow, and union segregation inherited from the nineteenth century, Marxism described black workers as a "super-exploited" sector of the working class with whom to make common cause in class organizing. The corollary to this, however, was that civil rights and black liberation movements were to be seen as adjuncts to the labor movement.

Unfortunately, by pushing the issue of racism into the mold of class relationships, Marxism ignored the profundity and the complexity of the processes of racialization in the United States. The easy programmatics of Marxism have not worked, and the tenacity of white racism has remained incomprehensible. While labor history provides examples of black and white workers uniting in union organizing campaigns prior to the civil rights movement, they are the exceptions. For the most part, white workers refused multiracial organization, choosing economic deprivation rather than join black workers in a common effort. Marxism could not see that a cultural identity such as white supremacy could not be addressed through programmatics. It has to be understood as a social structure. For that, class analysis is insufficient.

The Marxists were right, of course, that racism was a means of dividing people in order to better dominate them, whether as classes or communities, or as an electorate. But to leave that as an element of theoretical understanding is to avoid the question of why it works so well. The central question rarely asked and never fully addressed was from what social foundation, and on what cultural structures, did racism grow, and on what foundation did capitalism rely in its use of racism. Where did racism and white supremacy get the power and tenacity to so consistently supersede the alleged strength of class interest and of the class programmatic?

On the other hand, suppose race and class are not as separable as the "divide and conquer" paradigm would imply, and that class is as dependent on structures of racialization in the United States as it is on nation and nationality in Europe. (By *racialization*, I mean the way race is produced and bestowed on people by institutional social actions, and not simply as a condition found in people as their racial category. Racialization means that race is something people do, rather than what they are.) It is possible that Marxism does not look long and hard at race because it might find that the foundations of class relations in the United States are different from those in Europe; that would undermine the notion of class and class structure as being primary to political event and process. Or worse, Marxism might find itself to be in some sense a racialized (white) ideology.

This point has been made by a number of black thinkers. Cedric Robinson, for instance, argues that black radicalism has largely gone unnoticed by Marxism because it did not follow the organizational forms or promulgate programmatic goals familiar to Marxism from its European origins. Robinson extends the notion of black resistance and radicalism to include mutinies aboard slave ships, the collective suicides of those enslaved, the Quilombos, Palenques, Maroon and Seminole communities of runaway slaves, and the many "terminals" of the Underground Railroad. Black radicalism embraces what DuBois called the largest general strike up to that time when, during the Civil War, millions of slaves left the plantations and moved overtly and covertly to the Union army lines (BR, 57)—though in so saying, DuBois is perhaps only metaphorically acceding to a Marxist language; flight from the place of slavery reveals a mode of psychic survival very different from a traditional strike. This difference re-expresses itself in the present through a variety of alternate antiracist organizational forms: national liberation movements, the mass civil rights actions that shook the United States to its foundations, and the cultural movements of the many third-world communities inside the United States. In other words, black resistance to slavery and segregation cannot be understood through a few recognizable uprisings such as those of Gabriel or Nat Turner. Even the polite and respectable petition for redress, for release, for freedom, for the franchise, and for a sense of humanity were aspects of black resistance; indeed, during the first half of the nineteenth century, the existence of such petitions was routinely used as a reason to refuse them by white state governing bodies, precisely because they represented organized black opinion and expression.[12] The underground black churches that formed in the midst of slavery later flourished and played a significant role in attempting to stem the tide of Jim Crow as it rose in the wake of Reconstruction—and still later formed a core network for civil rights actions in the 1950s. All this is today being recognized as manifesting a tradition which had been left out of the account by European categories of resistance.[13]

In these terms, Robinson addresses Marxism as a European construction whose view of itself as world-historical partakes of a certain European conceit (CR, 2). It presents its Eurocentric historiography as the necessary developmental process other cultures must undergo. That is, it conceptualizes historical development in terms of a European template. For instance, Marx supported British economic domination of India, with all the suffering that entailed, because it "advanced" India toward a capitalism from which a working class could emerge that would make possible a classless society. This assumed that the Indian people, or the Indian working classes, needed developed capitalism (à la Europe) to take India closer to classlessness. Like bourgeois European historiography, it saw other traditions as backward or primitive in order to see its own as advanced or superior. In other words, Marx used the European trajectory, interpreted his own way, as a standard to measure the historical stage other countries had attained in terms of social structure. By requiring developed capitalism as the foundation for Indian or any other liberation, Marx established European working-class consciousness as the world-historical form. In effect, Marx made assumptions similar to European colonialism's, and his argument becomes a rationalization for imperialism.

As Robinson puts it, all this relieves "European Marxists from the obligation of investigating the profound effects of culture and historical experience" on social and economic processes (CR, 2). While eighteenth-century imperial white supremacy and social racialization could never emerge as a developmental possibility for other colonized cultures, those cultures were nevertheless analyzed and narrativized by both Marxism and colonialism as subordinate cultures that required industrialization, both to escape white supremacy and its colonialism and, by abjured implication, to duplicate it. In that sense, even for Marx, the answer to European colonialism for the colonized was to become their own colonialism.

The colorblindness in Marxism's self-universalization is a white colorblindness. Marx's theorization of primitive accumulation is a case in point. Marx labels capitalism's ostensible first step toward accumulation of capital as "primitive" accumulation in order to differentiate it from the ongoing accumulation process that is capitalism's driving force. It occurs in the form of the expropriation of the independent peasantry in Scotland and England, and thus as an internal affair in sixteenth-century British economics.[14] But Marx leaves out that it also relied on early colonialism, and the despoliation of new areas (Africa and the Americas) during the sixteenth and seventeenth centuries. The British began their industrialization in large part with shipping, and developed their shipping industry through the enormous profits to be made in the slave trade. The slave trade laid the basis for industrialization in Liverpool, London, and Birmingham, as well as in New England.[15] The plantations in the Americas then provided a form of mass production also at high profit. Thus, the slave trade and plantation slavery both served to kickstart capitalism's operations. In noting this, Oliver Cox argues that what Marx posits as the beginning of the capitalist system was already only its normal functioning, and primitive accumulation is in reality ordinary capitalist accumulation as the theft of labor.[16]

For Robinson, white Marxism leaves its own implicit racialization as white out of the account, rendering racism and the struggle against it an adjunct to the class struggle. It creates a hiatus between itself and black radical thinking, and Marxism's self-universalization becomes its own implicit self-deracialization—that is, it ignores its own racialized character. To the extent Marxism considers class politics and class ideology above race and color, and thus colorblind, it misreads black radical, anticolonialist, and antiracist thinking as well as its own.

Charles Mills raises the same question in his book, *The Racial Contract.* For Mills, the "racial contract" is an actual though tacit and unwritten, thoroughly methodological agreement "between members of one subset of humans" designated by various "racial" criteria as "white" to "categorize the remaining subset of humans as 'nonwhite.'"[17] It is a contract to which all whites are beneficiaries and principles, and to which no nonwhites are "consenting parties" as the objects of the agreement. Mills argues that the various theories of liberal state organization from Locke to Marx all function within this racial contract; that is, they concern the "white state." For Mills, Marx ensconced himself in the whiteness of his own critique of the capitalist state by never venturing into a critique of slavery as it functioned in the capitalist world from the dawn of colonialism onward (RC, 94). He further asserts that an alternative (to the liberal and Marxist accounts of the state) is needed once the existence of the racial contract is recognized (RC, 82).

Anticolonialism and Marxist Theory

Robinson, Mills, Cox, DuBois, and other writers on black radicalism are all part of a broader critique of European humanism that emerged in its fullest form in the thinking of national liberation movements in Africa. Following World War II, with the image of Nazism looming behind European society, African anticolonial movements began re-analyzing the bases of European culture. They called in question its humanism by counterposing their own experience with Euro-American colonialism. Embracing aspects of their own traditional thinking, not as below standard but as other than the pretended white western standard, anticolonial theorists from many areas of the third world deconstructed Euro-American pretensions to universality and the project of discovering universals in the first place.[18] The realization that European humanism was neither generalizable to all people, nor that humanism would prevent the extreme dehumanizations of which Europe and its capitalism were capable, imparted a new sense of cultural and political sovereignty to anticolonialist politics and cultures. A general critique of the foundations of white western philosophy and its place in the world emerged. From that basis, the universal human, the western notion of consciousness and subjectivity, and the industrial foundation of culture were rearticulated as the effects of imposed power rather than of natural social superiority.

In the United States, black radical movements (followed swiftly by Native American and Latino) embraced the new ideas and questions emanating from Africa, Latin America, and Asia. In their several ways, they threw themselves against the cultural structure that had racialized and ostracized them. The combined efforts of people on all continents to dismantle the structures of oppression everywhere during the 1960s made that period internationally spectacular. Anticolonial liberation and civil rights movements fought against forms of oppression that differed from the class relations Marx had described, and in fact contained and defined those relations. New modes of organizing and oppositional action, new modes of critique of the nature of oppression, new modes of contesting the power of hierarchy, racism, or colonialism emerged everywhere. They reflected the ways that national liberation revolution implied a change in global class relations. Power was no longer seen simply as aligned in struggle across the means of production, as in Marx's paradigm, but now across national and continental boundaries—struggles between cultures took the form of struggles between national formations, though they often got articulated as struggles between classes in a colonialist context.

For Marx, class relations were fundamental, and a critique of their foundationality would appear unintelligible. But class-oriented thinking distorted the counter-hegemonic focus of African, Native American, and Afro-American thinkers.[19] The propensity to understand African "nationalism" on the European model is an example. In European eyes, the anticolonialist movements for national sovereignty seemed to embrace a familiar sense of nationalism, though that was in part an artifact of how Europe articulated their politics to itself. Some national liberation movements understood themselves through alternate forms of political autonomy, however, and their thinking was more in terms of a "land question" rather than state power.

The "land question," beyond the categories of both colonialism and anticolonialism, is a question of how to live on the land socially, cooperatively, collectively, rather than through its commodification or the eminent domain of the nation state. As an alternative to capitalism, rather than in confrontation with it, the land question posed a concept of national liberation that did not fit the European notion of nationalism. In many pre-colonized areas, the marketing of land as a commodity for profit had been anathema. Liberation movements from Guatemala to Congo to Laos sought to abandon land commodification in order to retrieve an ability to live the land rather than live off it. In the process, rural movements of farmers brought themselves to prominence as armies of cultural liberation and land reform. In the writings of Zamora Machel of Mozambique, or Amilcar Cabral of Guinea-Bissau, the literature of Achebe of Nigeria or Ngugi of Kenya, these questions are broached and critiqued. While these movements called themselves nationalist, as a reference to the territory they sought to reclaim from European colonial definition, what they envisioned was a cultural retransformation. This did not mean abandoning all commodity production or technology, but it meant establishing a relation to the land, and to the planet, that was incommensurable with the European model of national governance.

On the other hand, European and American capitalism strove to construct nation states with which they could do business. Colonialism has always functioned by invading an indigenous local economy and dissolving it through commodification and the formation of overriding markets. From the sixteenth century to the present, in the African, Asian, and American colonies, starvation and proletarianization were produced among masses of people by disrupting their relation to the land and the local land economy that supported them. Commodification of land left whole areas destitute, and that condition met capitalism's needs.[20] Military power has always been thrown not only against popular organization but against antiuniversalist thinking and indigenous cultural traditions. Contemporary Euro-American colonialism, however, attempts to denature national liberation movements by deploying the power of commodification against them. Revolutions have been culturally defeated by negotiating a European form of independence that compromised the land question in favor of European models of political organization and economic production. European and U.S. support for military dictators and corrupt bureaucracies in Africa and Latin America defeated the cultural concept of sovereignty and acted against the logic of socialization of the nation's resources. The latest form of Euro-American colonialism is the Structural Adjustment Programs imposed by the IMF through coerced loans.[21] Debt has long been a traditional means of subordination of the impoverished by the rich.

Unfortunately, European Marxists and radicals too often translated third-world nationalism into terms of western thought and philosophy, and then saw the anti-colonialist movements as backward, as bourgeois or reactionary because nationalist. They often accused such movements of having fallen short of understanding the class categories of the nation state and state power. In prioritizing the European sense of the nation state, they became ideologically complicit with capitalism in suppressing alternate or indigenous forms of political organization, and sometimes complicit in practice through misunderstanding, nonsupport, or uncritical accession to the role of commodification. Capitalism always found plenty of colonized people who would accept the promise of wealth and promulgate a form of independence that did not provide real autonomy or sovereignty. Those who sought sovereignty through alternatives to that form of corruption fought not only armies, but the rhetoric of western philosophy, the UN, and too often western radical thinking as well.

It is with this complex process of anticolonialism as a background that Cedric Robinson levies an extensive critique of Marxism. He begins by pointing out that Marx regarded black slavery as simply an economic category rather than as labor productive of value. In a letter of 1846, Marx explains that slave labor is to be considered a factor of production like machinery or credit (CR, 105). He recognizes that the "triangle trade" did more than simply encourage British industry because the profit rate from the slave trade was the highest of any Atlantic industry. Beyond providing the stimulus for industrialization, that profit made from the body of the African slave constituted the very body of capital for investment. But for Marx to reduce the Africans to the status of "factor of production" means withholding from them the humanity that, as laborers, would produce surplus value. It is not amenable to Marxist historiography to consider slavery productive of surplus value if slavery is already relegated to a pre-capitalist form. Marx in effect primitivizes the slave system and the slave (in unfortunate conjunction with the western economy's "creation of the negro") by categorizing the African not as a source of accumulation but as part of the very capital accumulated.

Robinson criticizes Marxist historiography by showing that slave and feudal forms of labor coexisted in Europe during the medieval period at the dawn of capitalism, which imparts an indistinctness to Marx's categories of labor (CR, 12). That indistinctness then undermines the idea that slave labor and wage labor are in opposition and could not both function as value producing. Robinson cites DuBois as understanding that "American slavery was a subsystem of world capitalism" (CR, 281). He adds, wryly, that "it is difficult to understand how capitalism might 'create' precapitalist forms of labor" (CR, 136, n48).

What is at stake here is not the mode of exploitation in which slave labor is to be considered, but the racialization of the Marxian framework that makes the distinctions it does. Robinson suggests that the socioeconomic structure around the body of the African slave as both wealth and labor—that is, as person, object, cargo, commodity, accumulated capital, real estate value, source of hyper-profit, labor, and producer of surplus value all at once—is too complex for Marxism to incorporate (CR, 153ff). Moreover, Marx's reduction of the African slave to the level of a "factor of production" only occurs because of a single absence from the above list, that of "consumer."[22] It is as non-consumer that the slave ceases to be a human laborer in the Marxian ontology of production. But if the item of non-consumption is all that stands between the categories of slavery and wage labor, then it is not a distinction that can be made clear simply on an economic basis. White wage workers, for instance, do not lose their value-producing capacity for Marx when forced to "purchase" their goods at a company store with scrip, yet African slaves lose theirs, though the weekly provisions given them on a plantation function similarly, without the intermediary of scrip. In effect, the distinction appears racial rather than economic.

The fact that Marxism categorizes labor forms differently in the face of an historiographic indistinctness marks, for Robinson, a real "colorblindness." The problem it raises is whether this colorblindness is different from that of contemporary U.S. jurisprudence. Since its inception in nineteenth-century class struggles, socialism has considered class to be without color. Socialism assures us that it seeks to liberate all the oppressed in its march toward classless society. But does that mean a mode of liberation decided upon by the oppressed, or a mode of liberation previously decided for them? This becomes a dire question when we remember that in the nineteenth century, many socialists (like Fourier) were also rabidly anti-Semitic. To ontologically devalue the African slave through an ostensibly structural disparity signifies that Marxism has made no provision for the slave's personal integrity (CR, 173ff). For Robinson, the personal integrity of the kidnapped and enslaved African (as a person from a culture, with a past, with its own philosophies, undergoing present suffering and responding in complex ways to dislocation, etc.) becomes an element that neither the slaveholders, nor industrial capital, nor Marxist economy could grant credence of being.

Inverting Marx, W.E.B. DuBois considered slavery to be the real archetype of capitalism insofar as the extremity of capitalist exploitation of labor is exposed in raw form. Slavery revealed the extent to which that exploitation will go for commodity production, as well as the dimension of force that underlies it. In these terms, DuBois considered white workers to be petty-bourgeois because in white society whiteness constituted a property that they could cash in, as a specific privilege and advantage (BR, 17). Against this, as coerced labor, black workers constitute the archetype of working-class proletarianization, rather than an element of a precapitalist formation (CR, 323).

For Richard Wright, on the other hand, Marxism itself is petty-bourgeois because it diminishes the importance of black proletarianization as well as the fascist nature of white society. Wright argues that white supremacy reveals a populist mode of operation with respect to black people that is congruent to the fascist petty-bourgeois populisms of Europe (CR, 432). Marxism isn't fascist, for Wright, but it doesn't admit to the larger contextualization of class relations or its own concepts of class distinction that he sees emerging from the history of racialization in the United States. In blurring the distinction between racialization and class relations, Marxism reduces racialization to relative privilege. But the concept of social privilege signified by the proletarianization of black workers against the nonproletarianization of white is not something that Marxism can grasp critically. In its white-oriented way of distinguishing between white workers and black, it reduces its own concept of race-class relations to an economist one.

In general, Robinson agrees with Wright that Marxism is insufficiently radical to get to the racialized core of the capitalist order in the United States, or to recognize the forms of oppression that emerge from that core (CR, 451). He agrees with DuBois that Marxism is not a "total theory of liberation" yet retains a certain usefulness for analyzing questions of class formations and class oppression in white society. That is, Marxism can serve as a grammar for articulating the alienation of people and the degradation of production workers in capitalist society (CR, 416). While Robinson understands its attractions, its "alternative mapping" of history, its intellectual and confrontational power, its "identification with the underclasses," and "its promise of a hidden truth," in his view Marxism remains limited insofar as it is unable to conceive of itself as racialized—that is, as white.

The Structure of Racialization

For both humanism and Marxism, then, the paradoxical attitudes of the white hegemonic mind re-assert themselves within their efforts at antiracism. The central double bind into which much white antiracism gets trapped is thinking the source is the effect and the effect is the source. Without questioning or dismantling their own hegemonic relations to black or brown people, humanism and Marxism fail as modes of antiracism. The form that failure takes is an inability to read and engage the alternate projects of black thinkers, or to understand what disables those projects from entering into dialogue with the cultural foundations of U.S. society. Through that nonengagement, Marxism and humanism remain complicit with the silencing of those projects inherent in white supremacy.

How racism can be such a potent force against liberatory thinking, such a tenacious tool for the sculpting of political amnesia, consensus, and triple thinking, becomes a central question. Unless they critique their own white hegemony, antiracist whites fall into the same triadic trap of granting equality in order to withhold it, under the assumption of their self-defined hegemonic role in struggling against inequality. What makes the triadic conditions of white hegemony work? Though these structures express themselves clearly on the surface of U.S. history, they clothe reason in irrationality, and irrationality in reason, camouflaging themselves so that, even when whites look at them, they do not see them, or know what they are seeing. The double bind, for antiracist whites, lies in the fact that one cannot see racism if one simply looks at its effects, at the prejudices and privileges of one side and the harassments and impoverishments heaped on the other. The effects must be the reason one looks, but one must look more deeply into racism's histories, institutions, and identity structures to see where those triadic structures and double binds come from.

Two ideas must be clarified before we begin this investigation. The first is the idea of race, and the second is what we are referring to when we use the term "white" with respect to an institution, as in understanding the government or the law as "white."

The first thing to understand about "race" is that it does not refer to something internal or inherent in people. To be inherent in a person, race would have to be biological, and enough has been argued over the whole twentieth century concerning its nonbiological character. But let us go over the main points. Race would first of all reveal an objective homogeneity across different cultures. Yet different cultures define race differently, and hierarchize racialized groups in different ways. Brazil and Mexico stratify races differently than does the United States. What is constant in all cases is the fact of racial hierarchy. Social hierarchy is not a biological notion; it is socially constructed. This implies that race and racial differences are defined through social hierarchy, rather than social hierarchy expressing racial differences. In other words, to paraphrase de Beauvoir, one is not born into a race, but given it by the society into which one is born. "Race" then refers to a system of social categorization.[23] That is, the color terms by which racial designations are shorthanded are the names of social categories and not body-descriptive terms.

Furthermore, human traits (physical features) vary over continuous spectra. This is especially true for human coloration, which varies continuously from black to very pale. There are no natural divisions in it. Between any two people of differing color, one can always find another individual whose color will be between them. On what basis, then, did color become the shorthand or code for race? Or, to ask this question a different way, what social forces transformed terms for color from being descriptive to being racializing, that is, socially categorizing. One could add that no two human traits necessarily go together; there is no constellation of necessarily associated traits through which to biologically define a racial group. The group has to be defined first—for instance, as inhabitants of a particular region, in terms of which descendents of that group are then racialized. But that is geopolitics, not biology. Biology is only called to account after the fact (of racialization).

The politics of biologization reaches its highest level in the United States as a politics of parentage conditions. In the United States, a person is white if both parents are white.[24] This means that a white woman can give birth to a black child, but a black woman cannot give birth to a white child. To say this another way, a person is said to be black if she or he has one black foreparent in the preceding four (or eight, or one hundred) generations, but is not white if there is one white foreparent in the preceding four generations; white ancestry is cancelled by a single black foreparent, while black ancestry is not cancelled by a white foreparent.[25] This absence of parity is evaluative, definitional. Biology makes no such associative value distinctions; the color of the offspring of parents of different color would simply be a third color. The absence of parity in the definition of race means race does not derive from natural occurrence.

In short, the absence of parity signifies a purity condition for whiteness (one is white if one's ancestry is purely white). A purity condition is conceptual, however; it is an ideological proposition, a discursive construct artificially and gratuitously imposed on social relations. When the child of a black person and a white person is proclaimed to be not white rather than not black, it expresses a power to define rather than an observation.

It is this purity condition that first defines and conceptualizes a division in the continuous spectrum of human colorations. It discursively defines a whiteness of parentage that separates it from all others. Since race constitutes a system of separations of human beings, this purity condition, as the first separation, the foundation for the existence of white people, becomes the necessary condition for the existence of "race" itself. Without it, the concept of race to which "white supremacy" refers could not exist. Through this purity condition, whites assessed for themselves the power to define other races as they then saw them—that is, as they saw fit. In other words, "race" is the invention of "whites."[26]

The initial emergence of a purity condition was a response to a particular problem of colonial administration. When the first children were produced by unions of Africans or Native Americans with the Europeans, it was noticed that the color of the children (understanding "color" descriptively) matched neither of the parents. They were not simply lighter than the African or Native American parent, but also darker than the European parent. Whether this bothered anyone but the Europeans is not recorded; but it bothered the Europeans. There was a religious objection; these children were evidence that a Christian had "sinned" with a pagan (for which the "color" of the child was the immediate signifier). But the real problem was political. Colonialist administration, and colonialist ideology, depended on maintaining a boundary between the colonizer and the colonized (a boundary necessary to colonial identity, but one to be transgressed by the colonizer whenever desirable). The colonizers (men, mostly, at the beginning) had to choose between adopting their "mixed" children as members of the colonizing group, blurring or shifting that boundary, or rejecting them as members of the colonized, though that would diminish the population ratio of colonizer to colonized.

In an effort to keep the colonial boundary in place in the English colonies, intermarriage was prohibited, and the purity condition was invented as part of the politics of that prohibition. In the Spanish colonies, this did not happen at the beginning because the occupation of land was essentially a military operation (more definitively male) and colonial administration was handled by military force rather than civilian organization for a period of time. Intermarriage was not prohibited because the "mixed" offspring presented no military problem. Some of the children were conscripted as soldiers, and others were enslaved. This is one reason race is defined differently in Latin America today than in the United States.

Adopting this purity condition as a dimension of colonialist administration, Europeans initiated a process of separating people, and in particular themselves, from the colonized, on a color-coded basis, leading ultimately to politically categorizing all others outside the purity condition through various uses of color terminology. (It wasn't the only possible way of categorizing people, but the one that emerged from the colonial enterprise, with its outer boundaries and its inner religious fixations.) The purity concept, as the first (artificial) separation in the continuum of human coloration, marks the inception of all other forms of racialization.

The purity condition, as a social meaning, is at once ideological, hierarchical, and denigratory in its implications. It is ideological as an artificial conception imposed upon a world of human variation it then interprets and regulates. It is hierarchical in reflecting the arrogated power to define in the first place on the part of whites. Conceptually, it is self-superiorizing in the sense that its exercise of hierarchical power produces a stratification that inferiorizes (again, as something some do to others, rather than a condition found in people). But a purity condition is wholly dependent on those it abjures as not pure; excluded by definition, they reside nevertheless at the center of purity's conception of itself, while being ejected from it. In this sense, violence is inherent in the purity concept. It must continually reaffirm itself in order to preserve its hegemony against those it defines as not pure, yet through whom it defines itself. It must initiate violence as indispensable to its being. Its violence becomes paradigmatic for the paradoxes and incomprehensibilities encountered in the concept of race.

The process can be summarized as follows. In order for colors to be racialized (that is, given a social meaning beyond the descriptive), a concept of race had to exist. In order for a concept of race to exist, divisions had to be discoverable between people for which definable boundaries could be authorized. In the face of continuous spectra of human characteristics, those divisions had to be invented. To invent those divisions, a first division was necessary. The first division invented was that between whites and all other shades. And the purity condition for whiteness was the essential concept that produced that first division. Thus, all concepts of race, and all racializations of people, derive from the European invention of whiteness through the assumption of a purity condition for themselves in the context of a colonial relation with other peoples of different shades.

This outlines the social construction of the concept of whiteness, and of the system of conceptualizations that underlies contemporary structures of racialization. In this system, the terms "black" and "white" (for instance), while they refer to bodies, do not describe bodies. They name socially constituted human groups without being descriptive of them. They remain terms of color, but function to categorize rather than describe. They have become social signifiers whose role is to engender a perception of the "racial," to produce a social distinction that is seen racially because described as such, that is, as racial rather than perceptual, and for which the racializing description is actually an act of naming (signifying). These signifiers generate raciality by providing the means of noticing it. Yet they are themselves produced politically, producing what they provide to be noticed as a social importance. "Race" is not discovered through a process of perception; instead, people are racialized by a social process of categorization and stratification through which race is then "perceived." One imposes the concept of race on the world in order to discover it there.

If "black" and "white" (for instance) are racialized rather than descriptive terms— social rather than biological concepts—produced by a purity concept, then "racism" becomes the instituted and institutional means of social stratification pursuant to that white purity concept. That is, racism is the source of race itself; it is what produces racialization and preserves racial categorization. One is not born white; one becomes white as a condition given by a white society. One is not born black or brown; one becomes black or brown in being categorized as such by a white society that refuses or denies one full participation or membership through the imposition of that "trait." This would not work the other way, because no other racialized group is founded on a purity concept. Thus, no other racialized group needs to either exclude nor engage in violence. It is the white milieu, and the concept of whiteness, that creates the paradigm for violent racialized exclusivities.

Ironically, the idea that race is a social construct leads some people to assert that it doesn't exist (and thus, that racism does not exist either). For them, if race has no biological existence, it has no existence at all. But the imposition of a concept on the world in order to discover it there engenders the existence of something. The "something" that emerges from the imposition of the purity condition is the existence of race as a social structure, a system of social categorizations, for which the biological is only a disguise. Though racism pretends to refer to biology in order to establish social categories on the basis of the visible, it establishes the visual on the basis of social categorization. The claim that race does not exist is then a disguised insistence that race can only have biological existence and cannot be a social construct. In its Manichean reification of the biological, it is an attempt to render race unintelligible. And it is often used against people subjugated by racial hierarchy, who have attempted to construct a form of "race consciousness" for themselves as a mode of resistance to white supremacy. To proclaim race nonexistent is disrespectful to those people who, having been racialized, have constructed a sense of identity and resistance as a group out of the terms and conditions of that racialization. Their struggle against what had been (socially and politically) imposed gives their oppositional sense of race a new and oppositional sense of social and political reality for them. To ignore that is to ignore the effects of social racialization rather than rectify them. It buttresses racism's tenacity in the same way that judicial colorblindness does.

Racism's tenacity and blindness are inseparable, precisely because they depend on the visible being given a social importance that is lived rather than seen. An insistence on biology reflects this confluence of tenacity and blindness, insofar as biology naturalizes race, meaning it can be lived as part of the world rather than as conceptually imposed—a pretense of permanence upon which to seem reasonable. But it is the disparagement implicit in imposing a social importance on somatic differences that otherwise would have had no importance that is made to seem reasonable, as are the denigrations and ostracisms that are the content of that importance. Thus, racism is doubly blind, first to its social arbitrariness, and second to its artificial production of social categorization.

If racism is a mode of social structuring, then it does not arise out of personal feelings. The personal feelings associated with racism and racial prejudice are contingent on a structuring of society. The existence of social categorization and its attendant oppression produce and use personal prejudicial feelings as their manifestation and mask. When white people express personal prejudicial feelings, they are acting as conduits of a social mechanism, rather than as autonomous beings, though they have wholly internalized and hidden their being a conduit within their white racialized identity. They have become cogs in a social machine, in a social institution without which what they feel would make no sense. To eliminate racism, its institutions must be supplanted by alternate social structures that do not rely on hierarchy or hegemony, and do not disguise themselves behind personal feelings.

Because whiteness and racism are social structures, it is possible to speak of other structures, such as government or law, as being white as well. They are the constituted institutions that preserve and facilitate the continual reconstruction of white racialized identity, whiteness, and white supremacy. This goes beyond white supremacy being a constant factor in U.S. history, or the content of many Supreme Court decisions (Dred Scott, Plessy, Fugitive Act, etc.). The very necessity to pass a Voting Rights Act in 1965 confirmed that the government was white.

But if the political structure is white, does that mean that even the Civil Rights Act of 1964 and the Voting Rights Act function to buttress white hegemony? To respond to such a question, we would have to understand that a government's being "white" is not just an historical observation. Our response would have to be a different kind of statement that goes beyond political and administrative issues or positions. We would have to investigate the cultural underpinning to government, law, and so forth. That structure will be the prevailing thematic of this book.

It is not just that the "founding fathers" proclaimed the United States a "white nation,"[27] and it is not just that this nation was materially founded on the seizure of inhabited land and the forced labor of kidnapped Africans. The seizure of labor and land was made historically moral by mythologizing it as a legitimate destiny. Why that required structures of cultural separation, the annihilation of whole societies, the imprisonment on reservations of others, and the construction of juridical systems of enslavement are questions integral to understanding the structures of white supremacy—upon which both the history and the mythology depend. But the "whiteness" of the United States as a society and a governing structure is more directly brought in focus by its self-proclamation as "colorblind."

What renders social and political structures white is more than their use of chromatic terms ("white") to designate themselves. If the United States proclaimed itself a white nation at the beginning but was not that now, is there an identifiable moment in history when it stopped being a white nation? No such moment can be identified, since after that moment the government would have no necessity to proclaim itself colorblind, nor to repeal affirmative action laws—let alone pass them in the first place. The claim to be colorblind poses the question not of what colors the law does not see, but to which racialized color the law has reduced all other colors. The claim of colorblindness does not mean the law treats all people as white; it means it operates judicially as white, constituting that racialized domain as the source of its vision. As colorblind, the judiciary continues white hegemony. Racism's tenacity resides in a refusal to see the social categorizations it produces behind concocted color designations. Colorblindness does not render race or racism nonexistent, but rather, grounded in white supremacy.

One reason the idea of government or law being "white" presents certain conceptual difficulties is that traditionally, in the Euro-American world, government and law, or political structures in general, are understood in partisan class terms, or in neutralized humanist terms. Marxism understands the state as the agent of the ruling class and the repository of ruling-class ideas; thus, while Marxism understands that the state will act to preserve white supremacy (the dominance of the white race over others), it cannot understand whiteness as a social structure that conditions the structure of the ruling class itself. The idea that the state is white has no meaning for it. Liberalism, on the other hand, sees democracy as a political arena of middle-class involvement, where popular contestation of capitalist class hegemony is possible, and thus where white hegemony need not be countenanced. Education and voter registration should solve the problem of white supremacy for the liberal. The Marxist calls for class unity as the answer to racism; the liberal calls for guaranteed civil rights for the same purpose. But if Marxism and liberalism, as well as the class relations and the governmental structures that they address, are themselves "white," then how are they going to deal with the question of white supremacy? How are their respective modes of contestation of racism to traverse the boundaries of that supremacism? If the government, with its legal and political structure, is white, and if Marxism and liberalism, unable to see their own racialization as a Euro-American ideological structures, are also white, then where does one go to deal with the problem of racialization?

What recourse the racially oppressed have against that dehumanization, that distortion of all democratic principles in American society, is the ongoing problem, unresolvable even after centuries of resistance and opposition. We generally tend to think of the government as the "people's" political sphere (though this may be wholly vestigial in the era of corporate globalization[28]). Opposition to racism has traditionally turned to the government for resolution and representation against the problem of racism, given that discrimination and segregation are antithetical to the principles of democracy. The civil rights movements saw no alternative than to go to the government, which pretended to be democratic. To petition the government, however, they had first to create the ability to petition it by directly confronting governmental power; that is, they had to transform governmental perspective in order to open the government to their perspective. What happens when opposition to racism and white supremacy must go to a government that is itself white supremacist to meet its demands? Recognition is given and withheld in a double gesture that preserves white supremacy while transforming its terms in which that preservation is indistinctly seen.

How to understand this is a large part of what this book addresses. This book is neither an argument with racism, nor with the government. If racism is the source of race, then one can argue endlessly against racism, about the equality of races, or that they have no foundation in reality, but it is wasted time. Racism simply reinvents race and racism through its appropriated power to legitimize, to grant or withhold legitimacy, effectively reproducing the double binds that are the hallmarks of the power to negatively racialize. Therefore, this book examines what it means that racism and white supremacy exist, and persist, and it analyzes the social and cultural structures that they express. The hope is to open a conceptual space in which to address these issues.

The first chapter of the book examines the history of the invention of race and whiteness in the Virginia colony during the seventeenth century. The second chapter extends the investigation of the structures of racialization to the question of class relations and class struggle as they emerged during the nineteenth century in the United States. The third chapter then examines how the racialized class structures that emerged from the industrialization processes of the nineteenth century continued to express themselves, as seen in the issue of affirmative action and the structures of the two-party system and racial profiling. The last chapter explores what this history portends for the inner structure of white identity, focusing on what it means to identify oneself as white.

CHAPTER 1

The History and Construction of Slavery and Race

The Problem of History

Did the social invention of race bring racism into existence, or did racism create race? If the former, why invent race in the first place? Without the hierarchical perspectives that racism provides in its sense of superiority and inferiority, what purpose would the invention of race possibly serve? And how would the social agency implicit in the notion of an impersonal "invention" have to be understood? If the latter, then the term "racism" becomes a misnomer, since it presumes the existence of races to which to apply itself, while still having to invent them.

A history of race and racism must somehow escape this rhetorical circularity. If the concept of race was invented through a social process, then there had to be a time when it did not exist, a time before people were noticed, classified, and categorized as belonging to one race or another. The problem of such a history would be how to examine that time before the concepts of race or racism had emerged into social thinking. What concepts would one use to describe the process of their emergence? How would one understand what the people involved in this process of invention were thinking if they did not know to what they were giving birth until after it happened? What language could we use to describe that process? After all, we know from our position in its future what the outcome has been. And our language, the language we would have to use, already contains the terminologies of race threaded through it, in words for features, characteristics, traits, and a small but complex vocabulary of chromatic terms. Historical investigations of race racialize themselves when the language of the investigation is already racialized, and they end by imposing that racialization on what the investigation "sees" and refers to historically. Will not the difference between our language and that of a pre-race past make that past unintelligible to us?

Still, there had to be a time when racism or white supremacy as we know it in the United States did not exist. It should be possible to conceptually return to that time and examine it as the process of invention unfolds. It will mean trying to see that past situation without imposing on it the conceptions that inhabit our own background. But avoiding this pitfall will be doubly difficult with respect to the question of race, since most contemporary reference to race implies it is an inherent aspect of a human body, and of human being. It will mean examining a time when something many people today consider inherent in humans had not yet been brought into social existence, let alone conceived of as inherent. Given that human bodies have coloration, or shades of a color varying from very light to very dark, will it be possible to see the human colors of the past as not yet racialized as they are today? Will it be possible to speak of the thinking of a former time in which people did not see differences of human coloration as racially distinguishing without changing that thinking by articulating it? In sum, if we return to a pre-racial time, then we must see the people of that time as not seeing each other as racialized by color. Can an investigating eye that already insists that race be associated with color contemplate bodily features as meaning nothing racial? If the answer is no, we are stymied. We confront a concept of race that has a beginning, but that makes that beginning impossible for us to see. It will become invisible through our very attempt to see it.[1]

The problem of history with respect to race is thus threefold: (1) how to conceive the social process of invention of something that could not be taken as a goal, a concept, or a motivation beforehand (if it were already known what was being invented, the process would have already occurred); (2) how to understand what individuals thought at that time as they entered this process of invention without imposing upon them our understanding of what they eventually brought into existence; (3) how to see that pre-racialized time without imposing our concept of race upon it in the very language we use to describe it.

Historians of race have not been able to avoid these problems. For example, Alden Vaughan, a well-known historian of colonial Virginia, succumbs to them in quite innocent ways. In *The Roots of American Racism,* he says that colonial law in seventeenth-century Virginia "pertained to whites (assumed to be synonymous with Christians by the seventeenth century)."[2] But the colonial statutes of Virginia refer to Christians, not to whites, and seventeenth-century English settlers identified themselves as Christians, not as whites. They did not refer to themselves as "white" until the end of the seventeenth century. It is the twentieth century that assumes that when they referred to themselves as Christians, they were actually referring to themselves synonymously as whites.

Not to bear this in mind creates problems for the historical project. In seventeenth-century Virginia, there were Africans who had become Christians.[3] They remain unaccounted for in Vaughan's assumption about the seventeenth century. The question is, for colonial Virginians, if black Christians were not to be included in the law, on what basis had they been converted? Suppose that Vaughan is partially right, that by the late seventeenth century the term "Christian" did not include those Africans who had converted. If conversion had originally been intended as a form of inclusion (in the early seventeenth century), what process was at work that later excluded the black converts? To assume "Christian" is synonymous with "white" is to obviate any examination of that question (this is the problem of language). Yet it must lie at the heart of any investigation of English racism.

Similarly, Vaughan hesitates to use the term "Negro" (by which the English referred to all people of African descent) as an economic term or category (RAR, 158). After 1662, the term "Negro" begins to appear in the Virginia statutes as a synonym for "slave," as in "Negroes and other slaves." That is, it was an economic term; "Negroes" were placed in an economic category in the colony. Not all Africans could easily be placed in it, however; some were free, landholders, and employed bond-laborers, though the statutes of 1662 were steps toward taking this away from them by the colonial elite. Thus, even the economic use of the term is imperfect, something in flux. But Vaughan uses "Negro" as synonymous with "black," giving it racialized meaning (RAR, 160). To use the terms "black" and "white" to refer to races would imply already understanding how the people in question ("Negroes" and "English"—referring to their geopolitical origin) got racialized and categorized under the signs of "black" and "white." To refer to Virginia through the use of racialized terms means the question of how they got racialized cannot even be asked, let alone answered. While, for Vaughan, the Christians and the Negroes of seventeenth-century Virginia were already races, when the term "Negro" is used as an economic term, it is conceptually and descriptively other than racialized (and this is the problem of social conception).

The question of how and why the one social distinction between "English" and "Negro" got transformed to a different distinction between "white" and "black" is at the center of the invention of race. Before we approach the history itself, perhaps two objections could be addressed, to elaborate the character of the problem. There are two grounds on which one could say, "What's the problem?" The first is the assumption that race is empirical, that one can see people belong to differently appearing groups, just on the basis of observation. Race, they would affirm, is not a question of invention but of discovery. The second is that race is conceptual and was invented in order to meet certain political needs—of power, of hierarchy, of the division of people against each other.

Regarding the first ground for discounting the problem of the historical invention of race, the argument that race is empirical, one would answer that it is not possible to maintain a separation between appearance and concept; they interact and condition each other. "Appearance" with respect to race refers not to looks or comportment but to a knowledge of "who they are," to a primacy of a certain conception of person over bodily realities (which do not mean anything on their own). Appearance (including color, hair, facial features, stature, etc.) remains the main signifier for racial membership while, conceptually, race adjoins a condition of ancestry. Appearance signifies ancestry, and ancestry places one in a racial category. But the empirical is sufficiently variable that sometimes appearance does not reveal ancestry. One cannot pin it down. One gets the phenomenon called "passing."

Passing means that one assigns one's own body a different meaning than society has assigned it, and is able to convince others of this alternate assignment. This is done to evade or refuse the stratification that accompanies a social assignment, to move to a different level of the hierarchy established by the system of such assignments. The hierarchies in question are familiar to all. With respect to race, sexuality, gender, ethnicity, and class, for example, social boundaries exists such that people are socially valued unequally across them, and those boundaries represent forms of social domination for which the differential in valuation is the effect and the justification. A person who appears white, but two of whose grandparents are Native American, can "pass" to the extent that others think s/he is white by appearance. The person will be conceptually transferred from one race to another as soon as his or her parentage becomes known. The person will still appear white, but will be "noticed" as Native American—that is, no longer "unnoticed" as white. Conceptually, the person's "appearance" will "change." In such a case, ancestry not only signifies but determines one's appearance to others.

Indeed, the notion of "noticing" includes within it a confluence of appearance and concept. A person "notices" another's race because conceptually the other's raciality is established in and as the other's appearance, for the one noticing. This is at the level of the individual, while the concept is given socially (as an institutionality). For the individual, appearances are conceptually conditioned, they become interactive, mutually conditioning, inseparable at the heart of a person's consciousness of race. But at the level of social structure, if race exists only through socially invented concepts (emergent as opposed to derived), and concepts actually direct acts of noticing by providing their content, then those racialized by those concepts would go unnoticed without those concepts directing another's attention. If race went uniformly unnoticed, it would cease to exist as a social phenomenon. Thus, the mutual conditioning of appearance and social concept is not a simple thing; the forms of their interaction fill the space between the individual and the institutional aspects of racism. The history of the social invention of race and white supremacy must focus on the emergence of a separation between bodily appearance and racializing concept, for it is across that separation that the social institutionalization of racializing concepts becomes concretely determinative of appearance in order to be discovered there, as if empirical.

This circularity reappears with respect to the second ground for discounting the problem of history, the argument that race is a concept invented for certain political needs or ends. Since neither race nor racism can play a role in the emergence or invention of race or racism without that implying they had already invented themselves, the notion of motivation or intention with respect to the historical process of invention must itself be empty. For instance, if Europeans constructed whiteness as racially superior, in the guise of what concept of race did they do so? If whites constructed race as hierarchical, then did not a white racism have to already exist to express itself through such a stratification? If white racism constructed race, on what pre-racial grounds had it been a racism? If the colonial process of racialization was driven by the construction of colonial dominance, from whence arose the notion of race that drove dominance to construct itself as white? These are rhetorical questions that leave something in their midst unreachable. As colonial society was giving birth to race and white supremacy, the real political exigencies it sought to meet by doing so could not have contained a vision of race or racism, as such, which could meet those needs. From colonial administration there emerged a structure of racialization that could not be couched in terms of race (or white as opposed to English superiority) without assuming their prior existence.

This points to a contingency between colonial domination and the structures of racialization, the gratuitousness of which makes its outcome all the more horrible. That contingency conditions the way the social, cultural, and political aspects of colonial Virginia unfolded and ultimately organized themselves. If race is a gratuitous result of other processes, then race will not be the point of the story to be told, though it will nevertheless be its utter and unutterable outcome. A clear motivation, an intentionality of invention, will have to remain absent, a future shadow, in order for the historical question of how race and white supremacy were invented to even exist. That is, the social and political processes we must look at can only function to silhouette the process from which race and white supremacy emerged. No linear or developmental process will reveal itself; the surrounding social events will only form an outline, without providing the detail that goes on inside it. Inside the silhouette, the shadow of a structure which racializes people will begin to become discernible, to emerge from the shadows of other endeavors and, over the course of one hundred years, take over. But the story we are going to look at here extends over that great a length of time, and it takes place within a tangle of political, economic, and juridical processes that will gradually coagulate into a discernible form, that of race and white supremacy.

Nevertheless, in an abstract sense, as suggested in the introduction to this book, a certain number of discursive elements can be seen operating in the course of this historical invention. On a theoretical level, race exists because one group, the European colonists in the Americas, conceptualized a purity condition for themselves within certain practical problems encountered administratively with respect to colonial conquest and, by inferiorizing and excluding all those who did not meet the purity condition, defined themselves as white.

Whites concede the purity condition as they understand it to no other race. It is not that someone cannot be "pure Ibo," or "pure Cheyenne." That would abstract from the difference between ancestry and a racial conception of ancestry, in which the first determines one's physical appearance while the second transforms one's racial appearance. This can be seen most easily in the negative. A mixture of white and nonwhite is designated nonwhite, under the white purity condition. Were there such a thing as "pure black," then a mixture of white and black would be nonblack. But that is not the case under the racial system that whites have generated through the imposition of their purity condition. It is not that a parallel purity condition within another group would have no basis in their conception of themselves; it is that no other group faced the colonial necessity for a purity condition. No other group seized land and labor in the way the Europeans did.

Though in actual practice, the purity condition itself may never have been conclusively established, it constituted a general ethos if not an explicit proposition by which whites rendered themselves and their racial self-identification homogeneous. That is, they racialized themselves as white by constructing an abstract racial identity through others to which to adhere. How they did this is the question that will concern us in this chapter.

If what we are speaking about here is an origin of race and white supremacy, we must recognize that an origin can only be understood in retrospect, as a moment of self-repetition (or self-mythologization) backward, by that which claims to have been given origin by it. If "America" proclaims its origin in the colonies, it is because, as "America," it looks back at that moment and recasts it in the language that now assumes it as an origin for itself, rendering it a cause of which it then claims to be the effect. In other words, what it sees when it looks back is only its own shadow, what it makes for itself and not what made it what it is. It looks back and sees something that is not itself; in calling that its origin, it is naming something that is not there as such. What could be called an "origin" or "invention" of race and white supremacy extends this to the extreme, since it cannot be located in a moment; it emerges from a century-long process.

Racism has its own account of its origin. It claims that mere chromatic difference (and the many stereotyped cultural and dispositional characteristics associated with color) is sufficient to generate complex prejudices requiring social constraints and hierarchical structures.[4] If chromatic difference presents itself as "strange," racism asserts, this strangeness itself is enough to produce rejection and fear of the alien other. But it is racism that makes chromatic difference strange and fearful, rather than esthetic or something to be noticed as attractive—let alone dispensing with the need to notice altogether and allow encounters to occur simply between individuals. Racism's self-proclaimed origin is only a reflective repetition of itself, while at the same time rendering the other "alien" as one of its central meanings. Thus, racism's assertions remain part of its own mystification.

Other explanations of the emergence of racism and white supremacy in the Atlantic colonies have also been generally insufficient. In the Marxist view, for instance, the necessities of class domination set the racialization of labor in motion (as white vs. black, dominant vs. marginal) in order to divide and control the labor force. In other words, the political necessities of slavery or of capitalism brought racism into existence. Racism occurs, on this account, as a ploy, a tactic, a capitalist-imposed ideology. Marxism does not ask where the idea of race came from to which an ideology of racism could be applied, nor why it works so well politically in the face of countermanding economic working-class necessities or interests. It tacitly accepts the idea that race has objective physical existence, signaled by chromatic difference, which racism then simply stratifies.

Winthrop Jordan, on the other hand, assumes the prior existence of racism itself. In his still influential historical studies, he argues that racism and racial prejudice accompanied the colonists to the Americas, as a common social perspective toward

Africans and Native Americans.[5] He accepts the "chromatic" account of racism, in which difference in color produces fear, rejection, and social ostracism through psychological associations with particular colors. He uses literary examples from the fifteenth and sixteenth centuries to depict the English psychological associations of the color black with evil and the color white with good. His claim is then that the English came to the Americas with their prowhite and antiblack paradigm well established, and he concludes that the colonists built the kind of slavery they did as an expression of that racism.

Jordan's use of the literary is an interesting way to approach the question of prejudice—especially of an historically distant time for which the literary work may be the only "documentation." But it is undecidable whether the "author" (since the work is literary) is reflecting a cultural norm or representing (literarily) a purely individual, or even experimental, perspective—especially if that perspective later shows up in a future cultural norm. While Jordan presents the particular writings of specific authors, he assumes the attitude or prejudice they express to be general among the English; that is, he assumes a social homogeneity of opinion, feeling, and operation for the English of the seventeenth century, which is precisely what the use of literary works makes undecidable. In transforming a specific literarily expressed value to a general social opinion—from artistic particularity to social generality—he is generalizing the English and treating their prejudices as uniform across class, gender, or occupational lines (and thus perhaps expressive of his own). He leaves no room for a spectrum of attitudes, class differences of approach, divergences of opinions, nor for social contestation of the issues in question. As we shall see, his assumptions are not warranted.

Jordan exemplifies the problem of racism itself. To see a sixteenth-century literary treatment of color as exemplary of social prejudice is to see it through a prior (on the part of the critic) generalization which one brings to it. One assumes something about others in order to discover it there. Ultimately, in the literary use of color terms, the terms remain descriptive because literary—whether descriptive of the author's subject or of the author's own thoughts. Meaning is added to the author's subject, but only as a literary image. For a negative literary image of a person to be interpretable as exemplary of a cultural milieu, or a structure of social categorizing, a different trajectory for the image would be required, one that already pertains to a system of social categorization of people in that society. A novel's disparaging images of police officers or church ministers will not set those occupations aside for cultural disparagement, nor will they necessarily reflect that, though the corruption portrayed be real and related to extant examples. For a union movement that has faced continual police harassment, disparaging images of the police in its literature will reflect a concrete prejudice but mainly for that movement. To claim that a literary image is reflective of a social prejudice requires a different nonliterary argument. In the case of an historical racial prejudice, one has to show that the terms used have already been racialized. The historical question becomes precisely an account of the transformations between description (of an individual) and the use of the same language to reflect social categorization. That is, what functional transformation within the apparatus of colonial administration occurred that transformed the substance or meaning of an entire (body-related) vocabulary? A history of race must discover and include how that transformation came about.[6]

Theodore Allen provides an interesting response to both Jordan and Marxism.[7] He addresses the construction of colonial domination in both Ireland and the Virginia colony. By mapping the structural topography of colonization as a confluence of social, economic, and political oppressions, he shows the process by which both evolved similar structures of social categorization, understood as forms of racialization. The general account of racialization he derives by comparing the two specific situations is then independent of color and color differences. Allen argues that processes of racialization conditioned the initial structuring of class, as a predominant way of organizing rather than merely maintaining capitalist control and hegemony. The stages he describes did not begin as a racially motivated exploitation of African workers. Instead, they expressed a drive for absolute profitability through the absolute impoverishment of the worker which was then codified as the slave system in the American colonies, where it was shifted to the African laborers.

But Allen remains too much in the realm of class structure, and thus relies too much on terms of economic relations to trace the development of the social ground on which a concept of race and white supremacy grew. He does not explain the source of whites' obsessiveness that seems so essential to their racialization of others (which neither Jordan nor Marxism accounts for either), and that gratuitously erupts in so many forms of violence. While he answers the psychological argument that Jordan develops, Allen offers no alternate description of the "cultural psychology" of whiteness or its insistence on supremacy. If anything needs to be understood from the history, it is racism's tenacity, which is inextricably linked to the obsessiveness that seems so firmly in command of the thinking of white people.

Other contemporary thinkers have begun to plumb the cultural depths of whiteness, to explain its obsessions and compulsions. Michelle Fine, for instance, provides a paradigm of how U.S. social institutions continually produce and reproduce whiteness.[8] She argues that whiteness does not come into existence simply in parallel with what whites characterize by means of colors, but rather through them. That is, white identity (as a racialized identity) defines the idea of being nonwhite for itself in order to bring itself into existence as white. Ensconced within the assumed power to define, whites render themselves privileged as hegemonic, and see themselves as neither. The resulting construction of exclusionary boundaries concerning jobs, welfare, sexuality, etc., that people of color then face constitutes a "fix," as she says, giving white people a sense of being and belonging. Social institutions are thus designed as if hierarchy, stratification, and scarcity were inevitable rather than contrived, and their self-projected aura of inevitability becomes a disguise for the fact that whiteness, and therefore the entire concept of race, is fundamentally relational. "Whiteness is actually co-produced with other colors" (OW, 58). White obsessiveness then emerges from a necessity to continually reconstruct that production through others, in dependence on those others as the source of its own existence as not them. To ventriloquize the English in their prejudice toward Africans, as Vaughan does in equating Christian with "white" without showing that they spoke for themselves in this way,[9] is to ignore the relational nature of racialization.

Toni Morrison would add that if white is constructed through black, and finds the center of its being and identity in that elsewhere, then whites should really refer to themselves as nonblacks rather than as whites, given that they have set black people at the center of their identity in order to be white. To center whiteness, to see whiteness as other than in dependency relation to black, is then the real and vain proclamation of white supremacy.[10]

A number of considerations need to be kept in mind in this re-examination of the history of race and racialization. First, if race is produced through a process of social invention, then careful attention must be given to the participation of social institutions and, in particular, the operations of the state in the guise of its political enactments. Second, we must consider what (if any) other social structures were being built (such as slavery itself, in which both English and African labor participated, whether reactively or proactively, for autonomy or survival) for which the process of racialization was essential rather than tactical or ancillary. Third, racism's logical circles, ambiguities, and contradictions must be included, even as a way of thinking about this subject, insofar as they signify that the heart of the matter lies in social structures, whether lived individually or collectively.

The fact that, when the Virginia colony was first founded, there was among the English no tradition or juridical structure of slavery (though the social concept was well-known) testifies to the importance of these considerations. According to Kenneth Stampp, the kind of slavery eventually developed in Virginia had been previously "unknown to English law."[11] Did slavery evolve as a blind, callous process? Was it invented through identifiable events? Or was the social invention of racialization the way in which a slave system constructed itself around and in transcendence of the intentions of the people involved, whose contestations with each other over daily life, property, law, and rights amounted to the moments of that process of construction?

In other words, we are not just going to be looking at the development of a structure of slavery, the growth of an Atlantic economy around it, the evolution of a corporate structure of governance, or the role of antimiscegenation laws, all of which constitute "events" of interest to this investigation. To simply recognize that tobacco plantations and the slave trade existed and played a role in the racialization of the colony would be inadequate. The forms they took are inseparable from the transformations each went through in their concomitant production of colonial culture, and which in turn empowered them.

The Question of Allegiance

The Virginia colony was founded (1606) by the English for two reasons: to discover a source of wealth in the Americas in emulation of the Spanish and Portuguese, and to stake a claim in the distant continents in competition with them. (This study concentrates on Virginia, since it constituted the vanguard of the continental plantation colonies, generally instituting policies and undergoing transformations ahead of the other neighboring colonies.) While its original vision was of amassing riches from precious metals and fur trading, neither "panned out"; the colony did not hit "paydirt" until it started to grow tobacco.

At the beginning, the colony was a form of joint-stock corporation, called the Virginia Company, chartered to establish a settlement. All the settlers were employees of the corporation. Some held stock, others were under contract as labor, but all were attached to a corporate structure that reserved the right, from afar, to set goals and determine social standards. The on-site representative of the corporation was a small elite council that governed social relations inside the colony. Its job was first to secure the settlement, to plan its development, and to guide the enterprise toward profitability. After tobacco became the cash crop, the council's charge was to regulate production, guarantee a supply of tools and resources, maintain labor discipline, and facilitate marketing the product. The first Africans brought to Virginia in 1619 were paid for by the Virginia Company itself, through the Colonial Council, which then distributed them to different plantations (RAR, 129). Though they arrived as "cargo" rather than as contract employees, they essentially joined the ranks of corporate personnel within the stratum of contract labor.

Before it discovered tobacco production (1614), the colony found itself in serious trouble. During its first few years, it was organizationally unprepared to cope with the wilderness. As a corporate body, it had little incentive to imagine alternate communal forms focused on subsistence rather than quick wealth. Instead, the colony's leadership thought in terms of logistics, and a militaristic social order. It sought to provision the colony by trading with the Native Americans (a number of Algonquin peoples) but maintained a dependence on England for supplies. It also insisted on imposing an English social architecture, a facsimile of an English lifestyle, rather than permit a social organization to evolve through direct interaction with the new environment and land to which it was alien. The colony also attempted to conscript the native peoples as labor. Yet, for the indigenous, the colony had only captivity and Christianity to offer in exchange, which they refused.[12] The colony responded to this refusal through arrogant demands and took to trading by force, which meant sending out militia units to take supplies from the indigenous, leaving what they thought the supplies were worth. Relations became quite strained, and the colony quickly faced rampant starvation.

Because the native peoples were able to live quite well on the land, many English sought to escape to nearby indigenous communities. This threatened the colony's corporate social fabric, however, and was considered desertion. Those who fled the colony were recaptured and publicly tortured in the settlement, often to death.[13] The public punishment was not only to enforce an ethic of obedience to the colony, but an imperative of allegiance to Christian origins and English society. The enforcement of allegiance was the colony's primary response to internal crisis.

Its necessary concomitant was the demonization of the native peoples. Consorting with them was rendered punishable. In response to their refusal to work for the settlers, the colonial elite proclaimed them shiftless, treacherous, hostile, and hypocritical. They became people who were not to be trusted, primarily because they would not accept subservience to the new settlers' governance or faith.[14] Their resistance to being controlled was renarrativized as warlike. John Smith declared that the Algonquin were to be distrusted most in their simplest acts of friendship, compassion, or generosity. Though Smith promoted himself to both the Indians and the English alike as a great friend of the Indians, he wrote in 1612—after he had been withdrawn from the colony for political reasons—that the Indians were "inconstant in everything" and that the only things they understood were "force and fear."[15] Colonists from England who read John Smith would arrive in the colony with the authority of his prejudices in mind.

Smith's statement is revealing. One advocates "force or fear" to induce a response that is not otherwise forthcoming. Smith implies that the Indians did not respond as the English expected or demanded (euphemized as "inconstancy"). Implicit in a demand for a desired response lies a more essential demand for obeisance, and obedience. The attitude of obeisance or obedience can only be brought about by force. The charge of inconstancy would then refer to the Indians' resistance to the English demand for obeisance—that is, the Native American's sense of their own dignity.

This is the context for understanding the nature of allegiance as a critical aspect of the colonial culture. In the colony, allegiance was established as primary over subsistence, environmental integration, or human freedom; it was designed to prohibit individual independence and autonomy. The demand for allegiance provided the administrative platform upon which the English as "Christian" and "civilized" were to be valorized by being set against the Algonquin as "heathen" and "savage."[16] The inherent function of the structure of allegiance, as the institutional enforcement of loyalty and the renarrativization of the outsider's personality and intention, is internal organizational consolidation. The mythology of allegiance proclaims that it is given voluntarily, as befits those both Christian and English; however, it relies on real or potential violence, as a defensive solidarity against a self-engendered environmental hostility. As Michelle Fine points out, hierarchy rationalizes its inferiorization of other groups by regarding that act as inevitable. Social interaction was restricted in the Virginia colony by fictionalizing (renarrativizing) the Algonquin as if to do so were preordained.

Crèvecoeur provides further insight into the ultimate and implicit effects of such a cultural paradigm when he claims, writing in 1782 from upstate New York, that thousands of colonists had left the colonies voluntarily to live with various indigenous societies, while not a single indigenous person was known to have left his or her society *voluntarily* to live with the Europeans.[17] Crèvecoeur then meditates that, "there must be something more congenial [in the indigenous societies] to our native dispositions than the fictitious society in which we live." He is implicitly suggesting that the denigration of native peoples (as understanding only force and fear) had indispensable ideological (fictional) meaning for the colonial elite and colonial society—meaning that did not arise from experience but was inherent in the project of colonizing.[18]

Benjamin Franklin embellishes this idea when he speaks, in 1753, of the closeness to the land (which he calls "idleness") that enables the native peoples to survive without "arts and sciences." Children raised in the colonial society, he notes, once they return to the tribe, stay with it. On the other hand, the Indians complained that children raised too long in English schools returned to the tribe useless for native society, unable to hunt or engage in daily events (IS, 75). Of course, Franklin considered the arts and sciences he invoked to be superior, perhaps because they too were fictional and not derivable from real experience with environment, land, or the people living there. By counterposing the "fictitious society" of arts and sciences to "our native dispositions," Crèvecoeur is illuminating the character of allegiance; it is a discursive connection to a fictional inevitability of superiority.

If "superior" society required force to keep people in place, ideologically locked in, as it were—while many individuals, even children, saw a superiority in the unfictitious, which they found more attractive—then one can detect a crisis in values lurking beneath the surface of the colony, whose effect could be kept at bay only through greater ideational constraints. Throughout the seventeenth century, that crisis of values was continually encountered and countered by further demands for allegiance. New arrivals had first to swear allegiance to the king and to Englishness, pursuant to a standard clause in the royal charters reissued for the colony (SL, II: 485). Oddly enough, new arrivals from England had also to swear allegiance to the colony. To what were such persons swearing allegiance if they had already sworn allegiance to the king and to the state of England as a condition for going to the colony in the first place? What was the threat against which such exorbitant oaths were required? Was it the native warrior, who was no match for English guns? Or merely the alternative existence of native society? The French and Dutch were not a threat, and the Spanish had become trading partners between Virginia and the Caribbean. Flight to the native societies had been the first threat to the colony and its organizational sanctity. If the members of the colony had already sworn allegiance to membership, the only thing left to which to pay obeisance was the colony's idea of itself as "civilized" against the native people as "uncivilized," savage, or evil. In other words, it was allegiance to an ideological proposition, against empirical evidence which might falsify it.

This arcane crisis in colonial society is again detected in the central role that the concept of allegiance plays as a thread woven through the fabric of U.S. society, even up to our time. The United States is alone among industrial countries in requiring school children to pledge allegiance. Other European nations assume nationality as unquestionable; its irrevocability renders a pledge of allegiance absurd. But in the United States, both nationality and allegiance have a more tenuous character, grounded elsewhere than mere birth or citizenship.

Bernard Bailyn generalizes this to an insight into the conservative political style that characterizes political thinking in the United States. He looks at the eighteenth century, when the question of factionalism had become an issue. A plethora of parties and political groupings had formed at the time, leading to great instability in administration. The effect was to valorize a notion of authenticity within the context of allegiance to the colony. The enemy became those who subverted government stability and by that means enslaved the people to despotism while making them think they were being protected (OAP, 136). He argued that this paradox or malaise of colonial government arose within the space between an elected assembly and a governor appointed from England, causing an ambiguity of power base that allowed each to function subversively toward the other. What could be articulated clearly in such a situation was only the necessity to "nip arbitrary power in the bud" (OAP, 152). To the crown, that looked like an "undiscriminating democracy," while to the colonists the power of the crown itself became subversive in opposing that. This dual destabilization became a force for great conservatism, even in the midst of revolution, since the revolutionists conceived of themselves as attempting to rid their society of such subversive elements.

The effect of the emphasis on allegiance was twofold. It produced an organizational standard whose effect was an unquestionable oppositional binary between being English, Christian, and civilized on the one hand, and being non-English, non-Christian, and uncivilized on the other. Regardless of how murderous or barbaric the English were in enforcing that binary, the force of the binary itself determined that any association of wanton violence and torture with the English would be overlooked, since such actions were by definition relevant only to the categories imposed on the other side. As Pierre Bourdieu says, the function of "the act of institution . . . [which] signifies to someone what his identity is . . . [is] to discourage permanently any attempt to cross the line, to transgress, desert, or quit."[19] The enforcement of allegiance and the organizational regulation of both activity and identity are two sides of the same coin.

The Colonial Labor Problem

Tobacco cultivation provided the Virginia colony with its first source of wealth. Tobacco was a drug whose market in Europe grew rapidly and whose profitability was thus assured. As a cash crop amenable to mass production, it redirected the colony's focus toward international markets rather than toward precious metal extraction, as in the Spanish colonies. Tobacco not only became the colony's chief source of wealth but served as currency as well, by which commodity exchanges, wages, and the calculation of human value came to be measured. As such, it conditioned a different form of internal colonial organization from that of the Spanish colonies. Where the Spanish relied on military conquest and occupation, the English elaborated the corporate structure of their original settlement—even after the Virginia Company dissolved in 1624—and governed along a different axis of brutality. The exigencies of corporatized agricultural production, and in particular the concentration on tobacco, required a more carefully administered social economy and labor supply. The primary focus was toward large-scale capitalist agriculture (or agro-business) based on a stable unskilled labor force—as opposed to the non-survival exploitation of labor in the Caribbean colonies. Though subsistence agriculture developed on the margins, the concentration on tobacco kept it a secondary concern, and obviated the development of cooperative agriculture. In short, Virginia pioneered in a new corporate form of plantation system.

The critical problem of tobacco cultivation is labor. It was eventually solved through a system of mass-production slavery which developed only over an extended period of time. Up to 1650, English bond-laborers (called indentured "servants") constituted the main source of plantation labor. They accounted for over half the arrivals to the colony.[20] While many bound themselves to the colony voluntarily, with the promise of independence and land after their service was over, others were prison transfers or kidnap victims off the streets of English cities (a thriving industry for a while). English laborers came with written contracts providing for length of service, a release date, and sometimes a specified grant of land upon release. While under contract, the laborer was legally bound to the owner of the contract. Any infraction of duty through neglect, resistance, or attempted escape was punishable by law. Generally, the punishment was time added to the term of service; more serious crimes incurred beatings. In severe cases, branding or other forms of torture were ordered.

The fact that disobedient laborers could have time added to their contract signified that labor status was under the administrative control of colony government, not just the contract owner.[21] While the contract itself was a civil matter between the laborer and the contract owner, violation of the labor contract was a criminal matter that the colony enforced juridically. This meant that the Colonial Council (as a political body) took corporate responsibility for the regulation of labor in the colony (as in any corporation). In most circumstances, English laborers who had fulfilled their contract had to have council certification of having been freed to guarantee social recognition of their status as released from servitude (HS, 81). At that point, they moved to a different stratum of corporate society.

This juridical regulation of labor meant, as Theodore Allen argues, that indenture constituted a prototypical form of chattel. Through the contract, the laborer could be sold, transferred, inherited, assigned to heirs, accounted as wealth, and used to pay debts. When the contract was transferred or sold, the laborer went with it (HS, 47). Boskin concurs in suggesting that even when the predominant form of bond-labor was English (well into the 1660s), labor was considered wealth, and wealth was the lever toward status and power in the colony (IS, 15). Though contractually temporary, English bond-labor was a form of commodity that presaged what the African slaves were later to be. The eventual codification of slavery in Virginia relied on juridical precedents established first with respect to English labor.

For the English indenturees, servitude was a hardship. The work was hard and the term of servitude long. Many sought to escape. Flight became easier as the English colonies grew and established different sites along the Atlantic seaboard. As the plantation economy grew, the "labor problem" ceased being one of availability and became one of enforcement: how to keep the laborers in place and hard at work, doing what they had been told to do.[22] One of the motives for eventually shifting to the use of African labor was that those Africans who escaped did not blend in, whereas the English did.

Before examining the evolution of slavery in Virginia, some historiographical questions or preconceptions should perhaps be addressed. One such question is whether slavery signifies a pre-capitalist form of production. Marxism, for instance, understands slavery to have preceded feudalism, which in turn preceded capitalism. For Marx (from Hegel), the stages of economic development from slavery, through feudalism and capitalism, to socialism represented the progressive liberation of the worker and the humanization of labor. In a structural sense, the plantation system, characterized by labor's absolute bondage, represented a return to an earlier form. But there are some problems with this.

The Marxian account might reason as follows. Insofar as slavery directly preceded the rise of industrial capitalism in the United States, it would serve as a pre-capitalist analogue to the European feudal system. The plantation elite could then be seen as an ersatz aristocracy, and the Civil War, which extended industry and a generalized wages system into the South, would then count as the American bourgeois revolution (comparable to the French Revolution in being an overthrow of feudalism). If slavery flourished in the western hemisphere at the same time that industrial capitalism was being born in Europe, it simply meant that the two developmental processes were out of phase (though controlled by the same colonialist interests). But the Civil War would be somewhat anomalous as a revolution. It transformed southern society by a force from beyond its borders; thus, it would more aptly be construed as a first act of northern capitalist colonialism. Furthermore, the Civil War left the southern landowning system intact. If the southern economy was pre-capitalist before the Civil War, what does it become when the plantation owners are given back their land and work it to the same effect, substituting tenant farming and debt-slavery for the chattel system? How is slavery in the North to be understood, coexisting with capitalism until well after the American Revolution? Frederick Douglass gives an account of working as both a slave and a wage earner at the same time in Baltimore. Moreover, as many historians have recognized, much of the capital to industrialize Europe and New England during the eighteenth century was generated by the slave trade, which was in turn fostered for that purpose.[23] That is, the slave trade was itself an industry, the most profitable of all in the Atlantic economy. Finally, commodity production for an international market by a joint-stock corporate venture with a board of directors that functioned as an absolute governing body (which correctly describes the Virginia colony and its governance of plantation production) is not characteristic of feudalism or any other pre-capitalist form of production. In other words, the categories of Marxist historiography do not seem all that useful.

Indeed, the arguments for southern plantation slavery being pre-capitalist are often somewhat forced. Eugene Genovese, in *The Political Economy of Slavery*, argues that the plantation system could not be capitalist because it did not engage in the kind of capital accumulation characteristic of capitalism.[24] He presents data that indicate a process of accumulation, but one which occurred very slowly, too slowly to compete with the process of opening new land and starting agricultural production anew elsewhere (in other words, useless accumulation). The result was broad stagnation in development and technology, an inflexibility of operations, and a politically governed local commodity market. While all this would explain why the plantation economy was unable to compete with industrial capitalism, it does not demonstrate that it was not capitalist. Indeed, each argument Genovese uses actually assumes a capitalist category, which he then shows to be either inefficient or insufficiently fulfilled. In point of fact, accumulation was very much a concern for the inner workings of plantation wealth, but it had a different character from that of industry, as we shall see below.

Marxists are not the only ones who see southern plantation slavery as pre-capitalist, however. W. J. Cash in his long, historical, and often self-valorizing critique, *The Mind of the South,* refers to its economic system as feudal.[25] Eva Saks, in an analysis and critique of antimiscegenation law and its categorization of the body as a form of property through racialization, concludes that this represents an internalization of a feudal economy and social ethos.[26] Even the eminent sociologist W. J. Wilson, in *The Declining Significance of Race,* understands the colonies as pre-capitalist.[27]

Wilson's project is to derive an account of oligarchy from a historiography of racism. For this purpose, he divides U.S. history into three stages: the period of slavery up to the Civil War, the industrial period characterized by forms of segregation (Civil War to World War II), and the modern period of mass resistance to segregation, the passage of civil rights laws, and the opening of economic opportunities to black people. Because he characterizes the period of industrial growth and expansion as the "capitalist period," he implies that the pre-industrial period of plantation slavery was perforce pre-capitalist, and as such instrumental in defining the basis for the oligarchic political tradition that is his focus: "One of slavery's most direct and obvious institutional effects was that it provided the basis for the enormous accumulation of public power by a small elite, power that was used to shape the economic structure of the South and the political structure of the nation" (DSR, 24).

This is a very important observation, often neglected by liberal political critiques of the United States. Yet even this ignores the fact that the Virginia colony's original form of internal organization emanated from an oligarchical council, a small elite exercising great public power, and focused on corporate profitability. That original oligarchy engendered a slave system in the colony as the most efficient way to realize *its* goals. This would invert Wilson's account. Oligarchy was not an effect of slavery; though they both fed off each other, slavery was essentially an effect of oligarchy, and the consolidation of the slave system served to transform one form of corporate elite into another.

Wilson also appears to be equating capitalism with technological industry. The plantation system was clearly pre-technological, but that does not render it pre-industrial. In mass producing certain commodities (tobacco, rice, indigo, cotton) for an international market, focusing on profitability, and employing large masses of workers doing the same, endless, unskilled labor, it actually exemplified industrial production. Though Wilson focuses on the slave relation rather than production, each plantation constituted an industrial enterprise whose primary class relation was between the landowner and a stratified aggregate of bond-laborers. Again, to the extent that overall organization and responsibility for the functioning of this system, including the regulation of labor conditions, were in the hands of an elite, then oligarchy and slavery were two sides of the same socioeconomic coin.

One could speculate that had there been no elite Colonial Council to organize and guarantee the marketing and profitability of the plantation cash crop, agriculture would have naturally evolved toward subsistence instead, with greater diversification. Landholdings would presumably have been smaller and more equitably distributed, with a less rigid, more cooperativist class structure (if any). Power also would have been more diffused. But the pre-existence of a corporate structure dedicated to profitable mass production based on cheap labor obviated an economy adapted to communal rather than capital needs. Such historical speculation, of course, sidesteps the nature of colonial enterprise, the existence of slavery in the Caribbean, and the slave trade which itself grew as it fostered the plantation system throughout the Americas, enhancing that system as it grew.

Indeed, the slave trade was the most profitable industry in the entire Atlantic economy, so much so that most slave-trading ships could lose a third to a half of the people imprisoned in their holds to disease, starvation, or mutiny and still make more profit than most other enterprises.[28] Not only did the tobacco plantations need labor, enhancing the profitability of the slave trade, but the enormous profit attainable from the slave trade created pressure for plantation expansion. While slavery was not adaptable to New England conditions because the land did not lend itself to plantation production, the slave trade was (BC, 66). From New England there grew a second triangle in the triangular trade. Africans were brought to the islands and the continent, sugar and molasses were then carried to New England, and rum from New England was taken to Africa to exchange for more Africans to enslave. Here too (as with tobacco), it was a drug (alcohol) that constituted an essential element of an industry of highest profitability. The capital accumulated through the rate of profit from the slave trade and its ancillary industries formed the basis for the industrialization of both England and New England.

But let us leave aside the doctrinal definitions involved in debating pre-capitalist historiography. The real question concerning slavery, as the underlying condition for the capitalist vs. pre-capitalist debate, is can a human being be owned? What does ownership mean for the recipient (called the "owner") of the labor of another human being, whether on a temporary or permanent basis, whether industrial or domestic, if the laborer confronts the "owner" with the ongoing problem of extracting labor? There may be a market system in which human bodies are exchanged for money. There may be laws that juridically define a category of "ownership" of a person. But would ownership not mean that the laborer's thinking was owned also by the thinking of the owner? Why would the owner of persons still have to employ force, continually reterrorize the laborer into obedience, and constantly guard against runaways? All "owners" of laborers have had to do those things, implying that, from the laborers' point of view, the concept of their being owned falls somewhat short of being convincing.

If one has the power, one can kidnap people, hold them in captivity, physically pun-ish them if they do not work, or torture them into dementia and blind obedience. All this is possible. And each step is today considered criminal in substance. But the con-cept of ownership implies nothing less than a merging together of all these crimes. The notion that people can be owned becomes a juridical metaphor for the crimes commit-ted and forces used to make people work. It marks a juridical act that renders these crimes legal. In other words, a political structure has rendered a juridical metaphor material and systematic in order to bring a concept of ownership, with its legitimation of criminal activity, into existence. That structure became the basis on which so-called owners could govern their affairs, transfer persons from one "owner" to another in exchange for money, and constitute economically meaningful relationships between themselves in that way. In sum, the juridical idea of ownership is meaningful not in relation to the domination of a laborer by a landowner (which is based on violence beyond the juridical), but rather as a relation between owners, a way they understand their relation to each other.

Ultimately, the notion of owning a person belongs only to the language of the landowner. The "property" euphemism constitutes a disguise both for the crimes committed in enslavement and for erasing from consideration the intentions and feel-ings of the African or African American, which are thereby transferred to a discourse of things. But the laborers were never property, because they always resisted, while doing what they needed to do to survive physically and psychically (not always suc-cessfully). Ownership does not belong to the language of the laborer. Despite the fact that numbers were written in ledgers, they constituted a language by which only landowners communicated with each other. A similar disparity would characterize the situation of the wage worker in capitalism. The power to enforce labor directives is culturally located within the ethics of the supposed bargain made upon hiring the worker. This bargain functions as the cultural standard conducing the wage worker to do the task directed. Yet even the wage worker's time cannot be owned any more than the slave's body. Force always lies behind the bargain made at hiring time. The juridical recourse enforcing the bargain is the employer's ability to fire the worker if s/he does not do as commanded (which, in a wholly commodified society, in which everything must be purchased for money, is an imminent threat to life and health).

Yet wage workers are not slaves. The wage worker places his or her labor on the market, is hired for a period of time, and paid. For Marx, this freedom to sell or not to sell on the labor market is the key to understanding surplus value, and thus the entire functioning of the capitalist system (profit, accumulation, growth, crisis, and the worker's ability to strike). But the freedom of the wage worker is just another the-oretical nicety. In a society that requires a person to have a monetary income in order to live (unless one has investments), there is no alternative. One is enslaved to that system—and cannot even "run" away. The acts of kidnapping, captivity, and torture may occur in the more subtle forms of poverty, class repression, and job stress, but they occur nevertheless.

On the other hand, slaves are not wage workers. What the slave receives to keep him or her from perishing is (generally) not money. It can be neither saved nor invested, nor used to buy things in a store. A slave is paid a bare subsistence of food, clothes, and shelter. Survival for the slave means the ability not to be beaten on any particular day. This is analogous to the wage worker's ability not to starve or lose his or her lodging in any particular month by getting fired. The time scale is simply different between them. But there is more than time scale involved. The wage worker is not a commodity either. The worker may "sell" his or her labor power, but the real task of the "buyer" (owner) begins at that moment in still having to make the worker actually do the task directed. The slave system reveals this relation in its raw unmediated violent form; the slave is paid nothing, cannot be fired, but can be injured or killed. The wage worker may be socially at large, and the slave a captive, but a structure of coercion exists for both. These structures differ greatly in substance, but as coercion they have the same form. As DuBois puts it, slavery is an "exploitation of labor reduced to a wage so low and a standard of living so pitiable that no modern industry in agriculture or trade or manufacture could build upon it" (BR, 52).

In other words, to distinguish between the wage worker and the slave on the basis of the kind of payment each receives is to make a political rather than an economic distinction. Slavery is a political as well as an economic concept. Its euphemization as "ownership" constitutes a political act. It means defining a person as a captive laborer for life, whose every thought and desire is suppressed or superseded by the commands of an "owner." It defines a social status of noncitizen, or alien, whose social being is kept outside political and civil society. Thus, slavery means more than pressing the unwilling into service as labor, in exchange for which they are given sub-subsistence; the crimes of kidnapping and captivity, their political legitimation through the concept of "ownership," and the political exclusion from citizenship cannot be left out of the account.

In sum, while the slave is excluded from the money economy, and the wage worker is placed at the center of it, economically both engage in commodity-oriented production for a market whose sole purpose is profit on investment generated through similar exploitation of labor. It looks like capitalist production either way. To question the idea that people can be owned (in general) is only to affirm that a difference in the kind of wage, whether money or subsistence, does not make it less a wage. Plantation slavery is wage labor by overtly criminal means, which inversely covers up the full extent to which wage labor is really slavery by covert means. In effect, the conclusion that plantation slavery was a different system of labor from capitalism represents a political perspective. Indeed, it involves acceptance of the landowner's language (rather than the laborer's), a language in which ownership of humans is possible.

Many white workers during the nineteenth century opposed emancipation, claiming that, as wage workers, they lived under worse conditions than did plantation slaves. The significance of this claim is that it was not seen as a reason to emancipate both, or as a reason for unity with the slaves against the two systems. One could say that because whites could not see slaves as wage workers, those workers could not see their own wage labor as slavery (BR, 52). Yet in responding to a call to support emancipation by claiming more dire exploitation, white workers were actually demanding that the slaves act first to support wage workers in their struggles. If that referred to the organization of unions, then its absurdity becomes clear, as a primacy of racism over economic relation. Ultimately, though formally congruent, the distinction between slavery and wage labor seems real because, as forms of labor, they have been racialized—wage labor as white, and slavery as black. But that is getting ahead of our story.

The Evolution of the Slave System

In Virginia, the simple procurement of the labor demanded by the cultivation of tobacco was from the first a problem. When the ordinary means of enticing English laborers to voluntarily join the colony proved insufficient, many were brought under duress through debt, prison transportation, kidnapping, and other means. And the means of extracting forced labor were developed in tandem with the hijacking of persons. Before the 1650s, few African laborers supplemented the English labor force; in 1650, there were 300 Africans in the colony (out of a total population of 15,000). Only after 1650, as the slave trade grew, did the work force's center of gravity shift.

One could not say that the Africans were fully accepted into the colony's civil society during the early days; they were more or less grafted onto it. At first, the Africans were employed under the same conditions as English laborers. Stampp confirms that many Africans were released at the end of a standard period of servitude, like English laborers, and given both freedom and land (PI, 21). Some entered the colony's gentry through their landholding, bought more land, and participated in the community's social life. Up to the 1660s, for those still in servitude, little distinction in legal status was made between them and English bond-laborers (IS, 38). Black Christians could bring suit in court while non-Christians could not (IS, 41). No steps were taken during this time to provide education for African children, though it was guaranteed to English children. But education was not prohibited to African children, and those who did go to school attended integrated schools (IS, 24). DuBois records that free Africans had the right to vote in the colonies (and did so even as late as 1723 in Virginia), though in 1648 they were barred from bearing arms. In 1723, their right to vote was eliminated, as it had been in South Carolina in 1716. In other areas, free African Americans were only disfranchised after the Revolution (BR, 6–7).

The Africans, however, were not put under contract. One of the excuses given was that they did not come from England, and thus could not claim status under English law (IS, 38). Without a written contract, an African's period of servitude was at the whim of the landowner. Different planters adopted different practices, some granting freedom after a standard period, others holding the laborer in service beyond that. The issue was debated and contested among the English, with some landowners arguing that indefinite servitude was unchristian. But those laborers without contract whose time was arbitrarily extended had no statutory recourse.

Gradually, the issue came to the attention of colonial jurisprudence. Transfers ("sales") of African laborers occurred in which the conditions of servitude were set in the transfer agreement, rather than as a relation to the laborer. In one case, a man "bought" an African laborer on the condition that it was for life, as stipulated in the transfer agreement. The laborer brought suit against this condition, and it was overturned by the court. As a result, the buyer then sued the seller (for loss of a "servant") (IS, 41). To regulate such affairs, the elite began to legislate a differential in status for Africans, based on the absence of a contract. The first measures in this regard, during the 1650s, provided for levying heavier penalties for escape attempts on African than English laborers—corporal punishment and greater additional servitude time. This was eventually to include statutory lifetime servitude for repeated attempts.

The extension of lifetime servitude to more and more Africans gradually produced an economic distinction between African and English bond-laborers. To the extent both could be transferred, assigned, or "sold" as property, the English laborers lost value as they approached the contract's release date, while African laborers lost no value to the extent they had no release date specified, or the possibility of release had been juridically abrogated. The African laborers thereby became a more stable form of "capital value" than the English laborers. This was a distinction that had meaning for the elite, and not for laborers themselves—that is, the earliest social distinction between English and African was class based, in the sense that it emerged from the interests and the economic consciousness of the elite rather than from any general sentiments among the English (IWR, 161). The elite then sought to inculcate a similar sense of distinction in English laborers through differential punishments for escape. That the elite felt the need to differentiate African juridical status in the colony through differential punishments between African and English laborers testifies, in large part, to the degree to which those laborers made common cause, especially in escaping. Mass escapes were organized in common as the only form of organization or strike for better conditions open to the indenturees. Ballagh reports that by the 1660s, as African laborers were becoming predominant in the labor force, English escapees specifically sought to induce Africans to escape with them in order to hamstring the plantation they were leaving, thus increasing their chances of succeeding (HS, 55). The elite's response was to create a third category of punishment. English laborers who aided Africans in escaping were punished more severely than English who escaped alone. One 1661 statute established that if the black laborer was unable to make restitution for running away by the addition of time (because already under lifetime servitude), then the English runaway had to make compensation for this. If the black laborer was injured or killed, then specific additional time and fines were to be provided by the English runaway. Interestingly, the conditional syntax of the statute indicates that although some Africans were held in perpetual servitude, not all were (IS, 43).

In the face of the complexity of this evolving structure, it would seem Winthrop Jordan's hypothesis of a generalized antiblack prejudice among the earliest English settlers (as the source of the slave system) is unfounded. Had it existed, there would have been no need for legislation to turn one against the other, nor even to codify African status. Common practice would have already accomplished the task. Stampp makes specific mention of the fact that for bond-laborers, differences of appearance were not of importance, nor given special notice, in those early days (PI, 22). Only in estate inventories, bills of lading, population counts, and bills of sale were the Africans identified as such, possibly because they did not have contracts, and because their English names were necessarily nicknames (IS, 29). If the search for a means of social separation was a concern of the elite, rather than the English laborers, one would have to deduce, for the period before 1660, that no uniform discriminatory hostility by the English toward Africans existed, nor a prejudicial desire to consider the Africans' social status reduced in advance.

This does not mean that prejudice against Africans did not exist during the seventeenth century. Instances could of course be found. There was profound prejudice against the native population (for their "ingratitude" in refusing the golden opportunity to become Christians and enslave themselves to the colonists). But color (as opposed to religion) had not yet been made "a badge of degradation" (PI, 23). That is, reduction of African social status, as a differential categorization, was not endemic to the colony. Instead, as Stampp puts it, the statutes that created distinctions between English and African bond-laborers "evolved piecemeal" (PI, 22). The Virginia government groped slowly toward recodification of African labor, in response to varied landholder practices and interests—and always to enhance the landholders' wealth. Ultimate reduction of African social status, for the purposes of establishing boundaries, occurred fundamentally in obedience to juridical treatment of economic issues. However, it did not work at this level; labor solidarity remained an ethos of resistance until after Bacon's Rebellion.

Structurally, the road to plantation slavery in Virginia was prefigured by the nature of indentured servitude itself, which, as Allen argues, constituted the first form of chattel (IWR, 98ff). As chattel, English indenturees constituted an economic resource rather than a class. Politically, they would know themselves as a class primarily through the forms of resistance they could mount against the landowners' oppression. Yet chattel status tended to atomize the laborers socially; each had a different contractual relation to the landowner, different release dates, and the possibility of being transferred to another "owner." As bond-laborers, they had no legal means of resistance, and the punishment for strikes or unions was severe. Under colonial statute, these forms of resistance constituted sedition. The least dangerous form of resistance was escape.

Allen points out that a depression in the 1620s established certain precedents toward slavery by playing debt against tenancy to drive labor costs to zero. Freed farmers went into debt and were conscripted into plantation work forces to pay it off. The plantation economy began to accustom itself to the economic practice of employing labor at its bare minimum cost, as close to zero compensation as possible (IWR, 79ff). When, after the 1650s, Africans were brought to the colony in increasing numbers, they entered a society for which labor was already assumed to be for the most part uncompensated as part of the culture. This, too, militated toward greater use of African labor, insofar as the absence of a contract made such reductions in status easier.

But two specific conditions pushed the Virginia colony's economic development directly toward slavery as a far-reaching extension of conscript labor. These would play singular roles in the accompanying invention of whiteness, white supremacy, and racialization. The first was the existence of the auction market in African laborers; the second was the legislation of matrilineal servitude status. Both assumed a special significance in the context of the colony's corporate structure.

The existence of an auction market for African laborers was predicated on the fact that they were not given contracts. The principle means of redistributing the labor force was through transfer agreements, or purchase and sale of a laborer's contract. When an English bond-laborer was transferred, the terms of the contract remained the same, enumerating the person's rights and the conditions to be fulfilled upon release (though they could be judicially abrogated if the laborer failed to fulfill the contract, ran away, was insubordinate, etc.). But African laborers, without contracts, had to be transferred directly, in person. Since future conditions (of release) were not predefined or transferable, the person's present (bodily) condition was of primary concern. The bodily presence of the bond-laborer was therefore required in the market. The laborer's body thus substituted itself for the juridical instrument, the contract, in the market. A multilayered system of labor marketing grew and institutionalized itself, eventually perfusing colonial society, composed of trade centers, systems of bond-laborer transportation, regularized auctions, and decentered extemporaneous auction events. Though "trading" was not always done through formal auction, bargaining between parties was generally done in public. The public nature of these transactions rendered the market in all its aspects an ongoing site of value determination. That is, an institutionalized auction marketing system served to standardize prices and provided continuing quotations of the monetary value associated with different categories of workers. Price levels on the market became a way a landowner holding African laborers could calculate his wealth—just as one determines one's wealth in corporate stock by its price on the stock market. The market price for bond-laborers became a factor in assessing a plantation's value, whether for sale, or inheritance, or simply as an audit of personal wealth.

Through the market, bond-laborers acquired an economic meaning and value beyond that of labor. When their price fluctuated upwards, the estate value did also, and vice versa. Because a plantation constituted real estate, that which contributed value to it took on the same economic character. The social status of African bond-laborers was transformed from worker to commodity, then to wealth, and finally to a socio-juridical category of "real estate" (HS, 40). As this occurred, the concept of a release date for the African bond-laborer became inimical to economic interests. Thus, the institutionalization of the auction market became a prominent factor militating for permanent enslavement status for Africans. The political power that wealth gave a landowner caused those who resisted the concept of perpetual servitude to relent. It also called in question the freedom of those Africans already released. It was thought that a community of free Africans, if it became too large, would undermine the definitude of the slave market, destabilizing its economic role, and thus the social wealth and political power it grounded.

It was in pursuit of stable real estate values that the Virginia colony attempted, at various times, to ban or curtail the slave trade, without ever contemplating eliminating slavery. In 1769, the Virginia House of Burgesses banned further slave importation, in order to maintain market price by restricting supply. It was simply an attempt to preserve and enhance the planters' wealth. At the time, it was overruled by the king, who was more interested in commodity production (tobacco, rice, indigo, cotton) than in the value of a settler's real estate. This conflict became one of the factors honing the Virginians' desire for independence. For them, as for others, independence would mean the ability to regulate their own wealth. The first Continental Congress, as soon as it could in 1774, barred new slave importation (though not internal trade), an act that was ratified by each of the slave colonies (PI, 25). South Carolina reopened the slave trade in 1803, as westward expansion created unignorable demand. Though external trade was officially banned by the federal government in 1808, the wealth involved in supplying western extension of the economy kept clandestine external trade in operation up to the Civil War.

This process of development strongly differentiated the form of slavery in Virginia from that in the Caribbean. For the Spanish, and for the English sugar plantations in Barbados and Jamaica, colonization meant conquest and the direct extraction of wealth (whether as gold or sugar). Their occupation of the islands relied on overt and unceasing brutality. In Hispaniola and Cuba, the Spanish established gold quotas for the conscripted indigenous, failure in which meant death (whether there was extant gold or not was immaterial to the Spanish). The indigenous populations were quickly decimated, and the slave trade rapidly developed to fill the vacuum (BC, 6). The sugar plantations were organized similarly for the purposes of extraction rather than settlement (CS, 85). The imported Africans were placed in a nonsurvival labor situation; the slave trade had grown to the point that it was cheaper to work laborers to death and get replacements than to maintain the laborers in health. Thus, the slave markets on the islands served mainly for distribution of newly imported laborers and not for capital value determination.

This nonsurvival attitude toward laborers would not have worked in Virginia. African labor initially was not as available; slave traders went to the Caribbean first, where they got higher prices for their captives, owing to the inordinate demand. Further, the English tobacco colonies on the mainland had not adopted as extreme an exterminationist attitude toward the native population, since they depended on them in part for food. Moreover, prior to the 1650s, English bond-labor had predominated. Though chattel, these laborers had recourse to English law, through the same commerce with England that motivated the landowners to overexploit them. As mentioned above, the English bond-laborer decreased in capital value as time went on, owing to the contract's release date. This impelled the colony's economic focus toward permanent (African) servitude. A prodigal use of labor was by then counterproductive from the landowner's point of view; the capital values that the Africans began to represent implied a different response to their presence than pure force. Their centrality to economic stability meant the white elite had to judge labor differently, or vitiate the economy.

Eventually, the system of slavery reflected the Virginia colony's focus on a stable labor system based on mass commodity production rather than raw material extraction.

For the elite, this initiated a sense of greater economic autonomy than in the Caribbean economies, which remained more dependent on Europe (CS, 111).

The multiple categories into which the African laborers were thrust, as labor, as commodity, and as an item of estate value, meant that they resided at the center of two social structures. First, as laborers, they had a production relation to the landowners within the general plantation economy. Second, as an incarnation of wealth, they became a socioeconomic mediation between English landowners, and ultimately between all the English, whether slaveholders or not. To the extent that wealth functioned as a measure of status, both social and political, the African and African American slave occupied the central space in the colony's social dynamics.

The idea that labor, and in particular African slave labor, is a relation between people (in two senses) is something that Winthrop Jordan (for instance) is far from understanding (BW, 52–54). Speaking about the concept the English had of slavery in the sixteenth century, Jordan says:

> At law, much more clearly than in literary usage, "bond slavery" implied utter deprivation of liberty. . . . Slavery was also thought of as a perpetual condition. . . . Slavery was open ended; in contrast to servitude, it did not involve a definite term of years. . . . So much was slavery a complete loss of liberty that it seemed to Englishmen somehow akin to loss of humanity. . . . to treat a man as a slave was to treat him as a beast. . . . John Smith was moaning about being captured by the Turks and "all sold for slaves, like beasts in the market-place." (BW, 53–4)

What Jordan understands by this, without giving attribution to any but Smith, is a prison condition rather than one of forced labor. He approaches the question of "liberty" as if it meant "not in prison," and he sums up slavery as a certain brutality of individual treatment. Brutal it was, but a bond-laborer's ability to survive (and to escape or resist) depended entirely on understanding his or her labor as a relation to others, and not just constraint. In that sense, the difference between a domestic servant and a plantation production bond-laborer, between skilled bond-laborers in New England and Virginia plantation slavery, in which bond-laborers faced widely varying degrees of brutality, placed them in significantly different social roles in continental colonial culture.

These differences seem to have no meaning for Jordan (BW, 67). He uses the words that express these relationships but, in a bizarre way, fails to make sense of them. He gets lost in his own need to generalize and categorize the people he is considering (both Africans and English), to render them semimathematical entities in order to reason about them as categories. "Contact with the West Indies could [not] have by itself created Negro slavery in New England; settlers there had to be willing to accept the proposition. Because they were Englishmen, they were so prepared" (BW, 67). He thinks of each ethnos as homogeneous and discusses it as a thing with immutable properties, attributing a uniformity of thought to the group through which to "understand" it (BW, 54). Its "creation" of slavery was one of the attributes to "understand."

Racism uses similar disguises. It pretends there are sets of conditions that precede the racist relation, an objective reality to which opinions and beliefs then attach themselves and make themselves relevant. The victim is implicated as a cause of this relevance, rather than its effect, since the victim's "reality" is supposed by racism to precede racism's effects; the victim is seen, and recognized, through the racist's description, and racist descriptions are thus made to seem to precede the racist relation. The victim's victimization, because known through a generalization, is seen as "natural," rather than as a relation. Racism becomes a combination of the precedent description, the victim as a priori "cause," and a discourse of the "natural." This combination of inverted reasoning and essentialization allows lynch law to look like justice, and discrimination like equality.

Such a structure of inverted (and perverted) thinking also conditioned the transformation of the African slave, as wealth, into a relation between English owners. The absence of a labor contract for Africans, for which the African bond-laborer's body became the social and juridical substitute, slowly but inexorably gave rise to a further social distinction (IS, 38). Because the African bond-laborer was by *definition* without title or "papers," the African body became the labor contract and signified the contract's absence. That is, it marked the person as essentially outside or beyond the law, a mode of de facto and de jure categorization that attached itself to the African laborer's being, a tacit criminalization that presented itself as an originary condition. The absence of juridical standing or recourse, as understood by the elite and the landowning class, rendered the African's color iconic, after the fact, for an a priori social otherness and exclusion. Though this inversion was more significant for the landowning class than for English laborers in mid-century, since the former traded in law and legal distinctions, by the end of the century it had become generalized throughout the colonial culture. That is, a criminalization based not on the person having violated any laws whatsoever, but in having been rendered outside the law before the fact (any fact), wove itself through Virginia social thought and established itself as an aura around any African's body. The African and African American became the victims of a massive criminality that criminalized them for who they were, and that victimized them for having been the victim in the first place.

In sum, a step at a time, through an accretion of structural elements, the colony built a mode of social differentiation between English and Africans that mediated the ongoing process of constructing and conceptualizing slavery. The common element of all these stages was the preservation and enhancement of the planters' wealth. In its early phases, prior to 1690, this social differentiation was not designed to divide laborers in order to consolidate the planters' political power over the labor force, nor the planters' consciousness of that power; that was not in question. But planter interest is not the same as planter class consciousness. The process of constructing a slave system responded to planter interest in amassing a new form of wealth in the form of the enslaved African laborers. Planter consciousness, and the need or ability to further capitalize on the growing phenomenon of bond-labor, grew out of the moments of social and political transformation that answered to planter interest. The Virginia colony, for its first sixty years, slowly groped toward a concept and a system of slavery by addressing issues that arose from its gradual aggrandizement of wealth: the

regulation of labor supply, the adjudication of labor relations, economic claims, debt payment, inheritance. The slow rate at which this occurred testifies to the contested character of this process in the colony. Slavery was not established full-blown (or "created," as Jordan would have it) but emerged gradually, over the course of a century, out of the economic pragmatics of a profit-oriented plantation society. What eventually came to be known as slavery in the eighteenth century was in partial and unofficial practice by 1640, became socially recognized as a common practice in the 1660s, and was ultimately codified as a system in 1682 and 1705.

Throughout the seventeenth century, many Africans, both those in bondage and those who had been freed, made individual and concerted efforts to halt the process toward enslavement. They attempted to do this through whatever channels were available, including political petition, grievance procedures, court suits, and defense in court actions. While some freed Africans became landholders and sought to participate as equals in the politics of the colony, their success in doing so was essentially at the whim of the English elite in whose midst they found themselves. The bond-laborers had no political rights at all. Because the punishment for protest, strikes, or organization of resistance was so severe, what "respectable" uses of legal political channels existed had little effect or weight. Though many cases or arguments were actually won, it was to no avail against the juggernaut of wealth accumulation. Ultimately, the main mode of resistance available to African as well as English bond-laborers was escape. The overall historical process set in motion by the plantation system and fed by the slave trade led the colony unwaveringly, if blindly, toward systematized enslavement of the Africans and their eventual racialization.

It should also be pointed out that the existence of the slave trade was itself insufficient to generate the concept of race. The slave trade had a longer history than the use of slaves for mass production purposes in Virginia. Early ventures into colonization had been financed in large part by the capital realized from it. But racialization requires other kinds of social constructions. Indeed, the Virginia plantation economy did not originate with the slave trade, as did the Caribbean economies. If it later utilized the slave trade to facilitate its construction of a racialized system, it was as an instrumentality, while the concept of race was far more developed in the Virginia colony than in the Caribbean.

A Turning Point: The Legislation of Gender

In 1662, the first antimiscegenation law was passed in Virginia, and with it, a law establishing matrilineal servitude status. (This is the only issue on which another colony did not simply follow in the wake of Virginia; Maryland passed its first antimiscegenation statute in 1661.) "Miscegenation" (a term first coined around the time of the Civil War) is actually a misnomer here; it generally refers to mixed-race marriage, and we are attempting to discuss a time before the English, indigenous, or Africans had been racialized. Mixed marriage had previously been prohibited on religious grounds and punished under religious auspices.[29] During the 1640s, the ability of bond-laborers to marry at all was codified within a more general imposition of controls on the work force. Marriages between English and African bond-laborers were permitted, but only under conditions that reduced both partners to greater servitude.

In 1662, however, the Virginia colony passed statutes banning all sexual relations between "negroes" and "Christians." Strict fines were levied, and mixed marriage was made a crime. The implication of such legislation is that, for the elite, mixed marriage had become too prevalent in the colony. The colony, after all, was not a democracy and did not act to express the will of the people. Colonial statutes did not express a popular anxiety (about mixed marriage, or anything else), but an elite desire to curtail something. Had there been general antipathy to mixed marriage, its occurrence would have been minimal, requiring little or no official prohibition. Indeed, in Maryland, an act of 1664 (that is, a second enactment on the issue) denounced "freeborn English women" who "forgetful of their free condition and to the disgrace of our nation do intermarry with Negro slaves."[30] In the Virginia statute in question, the English woman who does so marry is punished. But even this did not stop the practice. In 1681, a statute was passed shifting the punishment from the woman to the slave-masters who allowed such marriages (that is, increasing the pressure against it by going higher on the social scale). Evidently, mixed marriages were all too acceptable to the people, Jordan's estimate of the English temper notwithstanding.

Why would the elite need such a statute? In what way would it enhance their wealth or political control? If such a statute was not to express an existing antipathy among the people (which would have obviated its necessity anyway), then its purpose would seem most probably to be to engender such an antipathy. In an oligarchic or nondemocratic social environment, legislation, far from expressing opinion, is a mode of creating it. This would be consistent with hostility to Africans being class based, and of elite origin. Diffusion of such an antipathy among all the English would be politically desirable for the elite, as an adjunct to their transformation of black people as laborers into wealth.[31]

The issue was more complex, however. A suggestion of how complex it was is given by a small event that occurred in 1630. An Englishman named Hugh Davis was reported in the Colonial Council proceedings to have been whipped for having sexual relations with a "negro" (SL, I: 146). Yet there had been no prohibitory laws passed up to that time. That absence is consistent with the fact that the number of African laborers in the colony was still small. But the council records that Davis was whipped "before an assembly of Negroes and others" for the offense of "lying with a negro woman." Why prioritize the "Negro" contingent of the audience? Where punishment was generally seen to be a deterrent, the target of this deterrence appears to have been the African bond-laborers. But how is that to be facilitated by punishing the Englishman? Perhaps the Africans were using sexuality as a way of transforming or alleviating their condition, as the settlers had told them they should use baptism and conversion to Christianity. But if the purpose of punishing Davis was to create a fear among the Africans against sleeping with the English, why then whip the English partner? Another possibility is that Davis raped the woman in question, and it is her compatriots who filled the audience at his punishment. But the account says nothing to suggests that eventuality, and in the seventeenth century, it was generally the assaulted woman who was punished for having misused her sexuality. One is left to conclude that the punishment was designed to create a fear among the English of sleeping with the Africans, and that the "Negro" audience was prioritized in the report in order to disguise this focus and make it look as if the problem (or the social target) was really somewhere else. Whatever the arcane politics behind this event, the punishment went beyond what was established by law. Evidently it did not work, since antimiscegenation laws subsequently became necessary.

Apropos of bans on mixed marriages, Eva Saks argues that antimiscegenation law represents the "power of legal language to construct, criminalize, and appropriate the human body itself" (Saks, 39). In those terms, antimiscegenation law is not only consistent with the ethos of slavery, as a concomitant of it, but is in essence a commitment to it, as an extension of that appropriation into the realm of gender. Antimiscegenation law establishes the principle that having a certain heritage, as measured or evaluated according to specific statutory conditions, constituted either a form of entitlement to property or disentitlement as property (Saks, 41). It signifies that before race could become race (as a function of an arbitrary parentage condition), it had first to become a property of property (Saks, 50).

In other words, the banning of mixed marriages, rather than a function of racism, reveals itself to be one of the preconditions for racialization.[32] It served to enhance plantation wealth through its corollary, a statute on matrilineal servitude status. Pursuant to the property principle contained in antimiscegenation law (the "appropriation of the human body itself"), the matrilinearity statute established that the children of a mixed couple would have the servitude status of the mother rather than the father.[33] Under the statute, the children of bond-labor women were to become wealth as future bond-laborers. The children of free women were to be free, so the statute added that the English mothers of mixed children were to be punished. Though this statute inverted patriarchy's central tenet of patrilineal descent, and broke with English common law, in which the status of a child was determined by that of the father (SLR, 115), it was a direct extension of the colonial purity condition. The matrilinearity statute engendered what was perhaps the most severe dissociation between the English and the Africans.

Its immediate effect was to turn all women (English and African) into breeding stock. The childbearing capacity of those in permanent servitude (African) became a direct enhancement of real estate value. Indeed, breeding farms were instituted that, according to Stampp, were quite profitable (PI, 245). English women were limited to bearing the heirs to that real estate, on pain of severe penalty. As a rearticulation of motherhood and sexuality, the statute created profound distinctions between English women and African women, and thus between English and Africans in general, through the women's personal relations and marriages. On the one hand, the Colonial Council put the onus on free English women for bringing into existence the pos-

sibility of a free African (mulatto); at the same time, it legislated landowner ownership of any progeny of women bond-laborers that they owned. African women were
set up for endless sexual assault, without recourse. As women, they were legally
renarrativized, or sexually fictionalized, for the purposes of planter wealth, through
robbing their very womanness as persons. Though English women were nominally
free, with the ability to aspire to a certain social status through their sexual discretion
and comportment, they were to be watched very carefully. Their social value accrued
to their not being sexual beings. The basis on which an English woman could be considered to have been raped was shifted from the question of her sexuality to that of
her purity, not as a woman, but as an English Christian (and later as white).

In effect, the statute opposed African women and English women to each other
through inverse renarrativizations, to be used in different opportunistic ways by the
male elite of the plantation economy for the sake, in both cases, of profitability and
property. It recalls a notion from Simone de Beauvoir, that marriage is a relation
between men, for which women are the means. In the English colonies, all Africans
and African Americans participated in the property relations between English men,
and all women were conscripted to the relation of those men to their property.

Ultimately, the matrilinearity measure was an important step toward the biologization of an English/African difference. With this statute, women and womanly
being were deployed to shift prior juridical distinctions to a different plane. It produced a "color coding" of sexuality, and further socialized the already growing color
coding of labor.[34] Where sexuality had already been made an extension of the market, and regulated generally according to servitude status, the matrilinearity statute
rendered the bond-labor market an extension of sexuality. It reduced all Africans,
through the reduction of African women, further into the pall of being wealth-producing property. And all women found themselves held in greater thrall, juridically
and socially. It reduced English women to their function as bearers of the heirs of the
property that the African women had been reduced to, and it forced them into the
position of incarnating (or housing) the concept of purity through which Africans and
English would ultimately be racialized. The matrilinearity statute, and its contextu-
alizing antimiscegenation law, marks the moment of embodiment of the purity concept without which the concept of race would be impossible.

This returns us to the "origins" question. Did slavery produce racism or did racism
produce slavery? It will be worthwhile pursuing this question briefly as a way of
expanding and (hopefully) clarifying what some of the issues were. Some historians
have seen the passage of the matrilinearity laws as a reflection of prejudice, rather
than as an elite measure to create such a prejudice in the interests of landed wealth
(RAR, 161). Vaughan takes issue with the idea that the statutes are designed to create difference rather than express it. His lens is not race in such a case, but rather, his
habit of thinking in terms of democratic process. Only in the presence of general democratic process can one presume a legislated enactment to express a social sentiment
rather than engender it. Without democratic process, a statute represents what the
upper classes want the lower class to do. In 1660 Virginia, democratic participation

was restricted to the elite. Vaughan thus attributes a homogeneity of feeling to the English, as a community, that is belied by the extant social hierarchy and by what the elite felt constrained to outlaw.[35] Boskin argues that slavery arose out of prejudice, but a prejudice generated only after the Africans arrived. He argues that differential punishment statutes passed in 1661 represented a racial distinction, rather than a difference in juridical status as a step toward racial distinction; that is, that racial division already existed in order to produce such a statute. He concludes that a codification of slavery for Africans was implicit in the legislation, though the wording of the statute does not go that far (IS, 43–45). Yet well into the 1670s, African bond-laborers were being freed, and given land upon release. What the statutes of the early 1660s do is recognize that perpetual servitude, a de facto slavery not yet codified, did exist for some Africans, though not for all. Indeed, "Negro slavery" as a term first appears in the statutes in the 1660s. But slavery as such was not yet systematized.

What of cultural difference? Would not cultural clashes produce prejudice and racism? Boskin quotes Brewton Berry (an historian of race and ethnic groups), who posits that conflict between two cultures is always inevitable, involving "subtle" forms of aggression designed to "reduce one's opponent, but not eliminate him altogether" (IS, 7). This is a clear recognition of the dependency relation mentioned above. For Berry, where conflict arises between cultures, it suggests that each group has a certain conception of itself, or as Berry puts it, an inbornness. But one then has to ask what that conception is. What the English proclaimed for themselves as colonists was Englishness and Christianity, which counterposed itself to paganism. In the English conception of themselves as Christian, the Indians were to be captured or kidnapped in order to convert them, as part of an English self-conception. The thought was to take the indigenous from their homes, imprison them in the colony, and put them to work, to the effect of winning them over to the faith. It was to establish a false and forced proximity with the indigenous in order to exhibit the superiority of the English civilization; one enslaves him to convert him, and one converts him to make him work voluntarily.

The (ethnocentric) assumption in this paradigm is of Christian infallibility, against which the Indian is a priori wrong. At the same time, it assumes the Indians to be too ignorant to see through the contradictory and criminal ethics by which the English approached them. But it was the English who could not see that the crimes and barbarisms committed in the name of civilization and superiority, by considering the other savage and barbaric, were in fact crimes and barbarisms. Boskin recognizes this paradigm in the thinkers of the sixteenth century (IS, 9), but he does not apply its logic to the differential punishments for escape. Boskin represents them instead as racial prejudice and differentiation (IS, 39), while the logic of dependency would interpret the same statutes as constituting a means of forcible integration of Africans into a cultural framework of Christianity. Similarly, the matrilinearity statute would also constitute a mode of forcible integration of Africans into the colonial structure whose form was a differentiation between English and African women and whose content was the self-enhancement and accumulation by the English elite of plantation (landed and financial) wealth.

The pigmentation theory of racism, which Vaughan invokes, is at the core of the racist mythology in the United States, in its undying attempt to explain white supremacy in terms other than its own systematic oppression; it does not, however, explain the compulsion to consider others to be lesser humans, or of an inferior social category. Both Jordan and Vaughan list factors such as strangeness, numbers, antipathy to blackness, and fear of rebellion (actually a form of guilt at having created a system against which rebellion would be wholly reasonable). While these may be actual aspects of prejudice, listing them does not explain how the English transformed these "fears" into a structure of racialization, which implies racializing themselves through their racialization of the Africans. If the English had not yet racialized themselves as white, then by the same token they had not yet racialized the Africans as black, though they differentiated all Africans descriptively as "Negroes."

This recalls Albert Memmi's definition of racism. For Memmi, racism begins with the attribution of a negative valuation to a (real or imagined) difference between people in order to produce a hostility toward them, whose end is to prepare an aggression.[36] It is in this way that the English "racialized" the Irish in colonizing Ireland, as Allen demonstrates, though the main differences through which the English could devalue the Irish were language, religion, and cultural traditions. According to Memmi, the importance of a negative valuation of the other is not that it constitutes prejudice, but that it grounds and valorizes a positive valuation for oneself. It must concretize a system of hierarchy (meaning a structure of oppression) through a renarrativization of both the dominant and the dominated—that is, a renarrativization of the dominant through a renarrativization of the dominated—the effect of which is to provide a basis for prejudice. As he says, concerning Arab anti-Semitism in the Maghreb (from which he comes): "The Arabs do not oppress the Jews because they are anti-Jewish; they are anti-Jewish because they oppressed the Jews" (R, 75). In short, prejudice is socially engendered through the construction of a social importance for differences that would otherwise be unimportant outside a structure of oppression and hierarchy.

The notion of race is always relational, rather than an objective characteristic. A group can racialize itself only by racializing another group; it inferiorizes another group in order to superiorize itself. Its dependence on those inferiorized—through whom this is accomplished—is absolute. What miscegenation law reveals about the process is that race and the construction of socially required difference is based on a juridical process through which these relations are institutionalized (Saks, 63). If the colony called upon patriarchal hierarchy to do so, it also saw fit to violate it juridically in the interest of capital values. To disguise this complex relationality, and the dependency of the defining group on those it inferiorizes for itself, biology was eventually called into play, to cover the relationality of racialization with a pretense of scientific objectivity.

In terms of Memmi's structural paradigm, the English could only racialize the Africans (and African Americans) by superiorizing themselves with respect to an inferiorization of Africans—that is, by racializing themselves with respect to a racialization of Africans. If they called upon patriarchy to provide a model of self-superiorization, they had still to derive a language through which to engender a structure of racialization. Ultimately, such a language was built on signifiers for color. But the English did not begin to refer to themselves as white in any social or racialized sense until the 1690s.

In point of fact, the term "white" first appears in the colonial statutes in 1691, in an antimiscegenation law. The council established that for interracial relations between a white woman and a black man, both partners would be punished; where the "color" of the partners was reversed, the white man would not be punished. The overall purpose of the legislation, of which this statute was a part, was to eliminate the possibility of a freed black population in the midst of the colony, and to create conditions making it difficult for slaveowners to free their slaves. (Up to that time, freed Africans lived in the colony.) The statute provided that, should a freed African bond-laborer marry an English person, the couple had three months to get out of the colony and go elsewhere, otherwise they would be conscripted into bond-servitude. A white woman giving birth to a mulatto child had to pay a fine and leave the colony. After 1691, no African bond-laborer could be given freedom unless the landowner freeing him or her provided enough money within six months to transport the person out of the colony. To the extent that those statutes were steps toward the codification of slavery, they were at the same time political constructions of the purity condition for whiteness at the foundation of the concept of race.

Thus, it was only slowly, over the course of almost a century, that slavery and the concept of race mutually conditioned each other, and that the English coalesced around the notion of whiteness, arriving at seeing themselves as white in a formalized way. But one more turning point occurs before 1691 and the institutionalization of the purity condition: Bacon's Rebellion of 1676.

Bacon's Rebellion

Bacon's Rebellion erupted from a geopolitical contradiction in the agricultural structure of the Virginia colony. Newly arrived English farmers or newly freed indenturees were granted small landholdings on the western periphery of the colony. They then functioned as a buffer between the colony's center (its main plantations) and the Algonquin. Set at a distance from the center, they had little influence or representation. Thus, they were geographically, economically, and politically marginalized. They could advance in the social structure only through augmented wealth, and the avenue to wealth was by the acquisition of more land. But the acquisition of land meant taking it from the indigenous, against which there were royal restrictions. The king and the Colonial Council curtailed land claims beyond the colony's boundary in order to maintain minimal trade and diplomatic relations with the Algonquin. Any independent attempt to take more land would put the outlying small farmers at great risk, since they would bear the brunt of Algonquin counterattacks.

Nathaniel Bacon, a newly arrived large landholder, organized these outlying marginalized farmers against the Algonquin and led them in a number of military adventures whose stated aim was to open new lands for acquisition (their real aim simply may have been to stir up hostilities).[37] When the Algonquin retaliated, the Colonial Council offered only reticent and minimal assistance. Bacon in turn accused the council of insufficiently defending the colony, and marched against it. For the council, Bacon's adventures against the Indians had abrogated stabilized boundaries (SSS, 205) and constituted rebellion (SSS, 203). Bacon accused the council of corruption in dealing with the small farmers and proclaimed himself to be simply demonstrating that fact. In June 1676, Bacon confronted the council and sought to transform it, to make it more representative. There was a standoff; the elite leadership fled across the Chesapeake, called on England for help, and somehow managed to survive. The rebellion was defeated after several months of fighting. Bacon died of illness while fighting was still going on.

The council may have been his real target all along (the record is ambiguous on his motives). According to Bailyn, the elite of the colony was a fairly entrenched group, a self-reproducing and largely absentee political leadership that did not represent the colony, but rather the English merchant families who had investments in the colony and determined its policies (OAP, 90, 97). A secondary target was the House of Burgesses, or county leadership assembly (SSS, 200). A conflict existed between it and the Colonial Council, to the extent that the former were excluded from the privileges of officialdom (SSS, 204). Bacon used these political contradictions to transform the issue of land acquisition into a call for democracy. He developed a program for voting rights for all freemen at the county level, which would dilute the political control of the county freeholders (land-grant planters), and he demanded county representation within the council itself (SSS, 206).

Ultimately, his campaign had three political components: (1) a struggle of (outlying) county farmers against the central Colonial Council for greater representation; (2) a struggle of small county farmers for greater representation at the county level; and (3) a chauvinist campaign against the indigenous proclaimed to be the real enemy. In calling for greater representation for the small farmers, along with new land settlement, Bacon's movement was the first to demand popular representation in colonial and county governance in the Virginia colony. His movement was seen as a rebellion not because Bacon wanted to feather his own nest, gain greater political power, or do autonomous battle against the Indians, but because he organized the poor rural population in order to do all that (SSS, 124). The last element is significant in that this first democratic movement of marginalized Euro-Americans occurred in terms of a dissimulated crusade against a demonized non-European people.

In this sense, Bacon's rebellion revealed the major characteristics of all subsequent white populism, such as the Farmer's Alliance in the 1880s and Tom Watson's People's Party of the 1890s. Populism has revealed itself to be a conjunction of democratic pretensions (a rhetorical class struggle against the rich) and an opportunistically machinated chauvinist campaign against a nonwhite group (the Algonquin, in Bacon's case). Not only did Bacon accuse the indigenous of aggression in their retaliations against the colonists, but he led the colonists in assuming that the English had a higher right to the land.

The rebellion was itself spectacular in embodying a totally unforeseen degree of common cause between English and African laborers. When Bacon's movement was defeated, many African bond-laborers were found in its ranks, under arms. Beyond this expression of common cause, the simple fact that armed Africans were welcomed by the English rebels defied long-standing (since 1648) prohibitions against it (SI, 39). It meant that the division and alienation the elite had sought to inculcate between the two groups through various juridical measures had been far from effective. According to Zinn, the rebellion convinced the colonial elite to take more serious measures to foreclose further concerted action against them.

Bacon's sin, as far as the elite were concerned, lay in initiating a social process that had the potential, through civil war, of engendering class divisions based on consciously realized interests and processes of political self-definition (SSS, 124ff). As Bailyn suggests, prior to 1676, there were no "classes" in the colony in the sense of stable interest positions (OAP, 100). The difference in economic status between planters and small farmers accounted for the main social distinction, while bond-laborers remained outside the ken of social participation. Though the disparities in former status clearly contained a political contradiction, the elite did not want that to develop into a class division. To that end, the elite attempted to maintain a coherence along administrative (hierarchical) lines. The council was essentially reserving for itself the power to define class status and class relations, and the unity of bond-laborers in the rebellion clearly reflected a political consciousness that would undermine that power.

Social unrest persisted in the colony until 1680. There were a variety of local rebellions, mostly in response to depressed economic conditions. In 1680, however, the tobacco market recovered, providing the Virginia economy with a sense of stability. The increase in the price of tobacco on the English market rendered even small tobacco farmers viable. This meant that freed English indenturees had the chance to consolidate themselves as farmers, and enabled more to escape the labor domain (SSS, 129). A militia had been established in the wake of Bacon's rebellion to suppress further labor unrest, given an ongoing solidarity between English and African laborers and small farmers (SSS, 128); this force was now turned to clearing the indigenous off outlying land and opening it for settlement, giving small farmers access to economic expansion (SSS, 131). At the same time, the plantation system was extended to these newly seized lands, greatly increasing the demand for labor. In this more salutary economic environment, the measures the council took to engender a real social separation between English and African bond-laborers began to take hold.

The Colonial Council took steps to definitively shift the labor force from English to African bond-laborers. In 1682, it first codified African slavery and increased the direct importation of Africans from Africa. Previously, the African captives destined for the continent, after the island plantation demand had been met, were first taken to Barbados or other islands, taught English, and "broken in" to being laborers. By 1680, there were an estimated 4,000 Africans in Virginia, integrated to some extent into the colony (SSS, 132). Importation direct from Africa changed the way Africans were subsequently perceived, however. The Africans arrived on the docks of Virginia in terrible, dehumanized condition, terrorized, in shock, naked and in poor health, and speaking no English (SSS, 133). Breen gives this description.

> They were simply dumped on the wharves of the river plantations in a state of shock, barely alive after the ocean crossing. Conditions on the slave ships were terrible.... No white servant in this period, no matter how poor, how bitter or badly treated, could identify with these frightened Africans. The terrors they had so recently faced were beyond comprehension.... Language became a major barrier between white laborers and the thousands of new black immigrants. (SSS, 133)

The people "dumped on the wharves" were hardly "immigrants." Yet there they were, without cover or consolation. Even the meanest of English, in comparison to the condition in which Africans arrived on the docks, would appear well off. The colonists saw the people on those docks not as kidnap victims but as creatures devoid of humanity, and the reaction became one of hostility and contempt rather than compassion. Perhaps the most appropriate modern analogy to this is the effect concentration camp life had on the Jews and political prisoners in Nazi Germany. The camps were designed to totally degrade, dehumanize, and humiliate the prisoners. When Germans (having accepted the denigrations of anti-Semitism) saw them in that state, the effect was to turn them against the prisoners as being subhuman.

The institutionalization of slavery built upon the conditions of the new arrivals; the reduced state and status of the slave seemed to explain enslavement itself. Such is the modus operandi of all racism. It functions to reduce those racialized as inferior to a social condition that then explains their racialization and inferiorization. For those caught in that trap, only harsh rebellion provides a way out. Respectable modes of addressing the inferiorization process (political petitioning, electoral campaigns, a demand for fairness) go unheard. More to the point, they are turned against the petitioners; political activity is predicated on being recognized as equally human, and that is precisely what racism systematically withholds.

The council's codification of slavery was accompanied by a campaign of propaganda that played on the memory of the adversity and social dislocations of Bacon's Rebellion. It used that experience to engender fear of an African uprising in the mind of poor English farmers and laborers, who now were living better in post-depression conditions. The council (in 1682) made note of the "danger" attendant upon slave meetings for such things as feasts and funerals (IS, 47) and enacted statutes providing warnings against the special danger of "Negro insurrection" (SL, II: 492). As the ranks of African bond-laborers swelled, many unable to speak English, the very concept of rebellion was slowly rearticulated and politically situated within the slave population. In addition, slaves escaped and became an alien, unseen presence in the hinterlands; stories of marauding bands reinforced the aura of threat and danger the council sought to create. In short, the council politically co-opted the idea of rebellion for its own purposes; rebellion was, in a word, "Africanized." The African laborers became an icon in the language of the English colony for all the privations and miseries previously experienced during Bacon's Rebellion, as well as the primary sign of new social upheavals.[38]

The Colonial Council's endeavors, however, actually serve to confirm that the process of racialization had not yet occurred. In the inquest following the rebellion, the composition of Bacon's army was given simply as "freemen, servants, and slaves" (Tracts, 44). By this time, only Africans were held as slaves (for life), while not all Africans were slaves. In the writings of the period, both for and against, Bacon's army is spoken of without mentioning color, though the social status of his troops was generally included (Tracts, 46). (Those opposing the rebellion tend to mention as scandalous that one of the leaders replacing Bacon after his death had a "Negro woman" as a mistress, though this did not seem to put his leadership in question.)

The council's project would eventually change all that, though it took time. Working at three levels at once in codifying slavery, engendering a generalized fear of the African bond-labor force, and bringing in more Africans in a state of desperation to exacerbate those fears, the council essentially went about the job of constituting a class structure. It was not a classical (capitalist) class structure. On one side stood the African bond-laborers, doing the mass production work; on the other side were all the English colonists, brought together in solidarity against the politically defined threat of "Negro rebellion." As Breen points out, the elite ideological warning against "Negro rebellion" not only reconceptualized the labor situation, but also constituted an enhancement of the original de facto "criminalization" of Africans that accompanied the absence of a contract. Ultimately, the council's warning became a call for social cohesion against what it wanted perceived as an alien entity (the class of African laborers that the plantation system had brought into existence). It focused on including all English against this internal danger as a form of political participation. In making its call, the elite co-opted the modus operandi of Bacon's Rebellion (an attack on the center in the name of democracy for the margins) and transformed it into a new unity of the expanded (English) center against its (African) margins.

The Beginnings of Racialization

The effect of setting aside the African population as a juridically ostracized category was to construct a social consciousness on the part of all English of a commonality against the Africans (that is, one can see the enactment of social categorization preceding the invention of the concept of race used subsequently to categorize). Where Bacon had "racialized" his rebellion through attacks on the indigenous, the council "racialized" rebellion itself by generating an official and juridical paranoia against the African bond-laborers, who were rendered wholly alien in the process.[39] From its beginnings, racialization has depended on augmenting a juridical and paranoid hostility to a group it criminalized for the purpose, against which a new allegiance and unity could be constructed. The concrete social separation of the English and African bond-laborers depended on the generation of a massive social paranoia.

Paranoia, as Richard Hofstadter and David Brion Davis use the term, does not refer to psychosis in a strictly psychiatric sense, nor does it have to do with the reality or truth of a possible conspiracy. It refers to the way events are perceived, and the way things are believed and advocated.[40] The possibility and appropriateness of rebellion by the oppressed and the rationales (and valorization) of preemptive suppression by the English are the two sides of this question. If one side is the recognition of the reality of uprising against oppression, the other entails imagining a forbidden rebellion against which all countermeasures are appropriate a priori. The notion of paranoia substitutes the demonic for what would have been supported in terms of social justice (or class interests), within an alternate paradigm of solidarity (English). It is from within the convoluted thinking of this structure that race and white supremacy evolve.

But in reconstructing social allegiance on the basis of paranoia, the colony was also constituting a class relation between the slaves and the nonslave community. That is, racism, at its inception, was not a division in the working class but a division of society into prototype classes, one a source of rebellion and the other an allegiance to counterrebellion. As paranoid, it obeys Memmi's insight that the dominant group does not oppress the dominated group because it fears and hates them; it fears and hates the dominated group because it oppresses them.

It was in terms of this sociocultural recategorization of the Africans that the English began to look at themselves as white, as a cultural group. One can mark the stages of their trajectory toward this identification in the terminology for group distinctions over the course of the seventeenth century. It presents itself as a sequence of binary distinctions between the English and the Africans, which can be read in the colonial statutes. The first binary, early in the seventeenth century, was an echo of the religious distinction proclaimed between the English as "Christians" and the Native Americans as "heathens." The Africans were held at a social distance from the settlers as long as that religious disparity obtained, and the Christian/heathen binary was used. But the English saw themselves as agents of Christianity and, having the Africans already captive, thought to convert them (captivity having been one of the steps envisioned originally for converting the indigenous [see note 12]). Though the English colonists never made a concerted attempt to convert the Indians, the Indians also refused conversion, perceiving the doctrine of Christianity as hypocritical in the face of the brutality of the colonists and their land seizures. For the indigenous, colonialism was a serious obstacle to believing what the English believed. While the Christian project vaguely rationalized colonial land seizure, it more directly rationalized the enslavement of African bond-laborers in the colony, as an avenue toward conversion. The promise was made to the Africans that baptism would enable a person to attain civil status and eventual freedom, so many converted. As a result, the social binary shifted away from "Christian" and "heathen" during the 1630s to "English" and "Negro."

But the gradual commodification of the Africans and the process of conversion were in contradiction. The latter, to the extent the promise of freedom was kept, began to threaten the planters' wealth in total, not simply in the freeing of some bond-laborers, but because it would also establish a social sector of free Africans to which all could aspire, and which spoke out for the promise to be kept generally. In stages, in 1644 and again in 1667, Christianity as an avenue to freedom was closed by statute (IS, 45). The council ruled that baptism would no longer change one's servitude status. Concomitantly, the referential binary again shifted, this time from English and Negro to Christian and Negro. That is, after the 1660s the term "Christian" became more prevalent in opposition to "Negro," in order to refuse recognition to the Christianity of converted Africans, thereby disabusing them of the illusion that baptism might bring eventual freedom.

Nevertheless, how the English referred to themselves in the council proceedings depended on context. If the question at issue was one of African labor as such, or African conversion to Christianity, the binary would be English and Negro. If it was instead an attempt to rationalize the institution of perpetual servitude, as it gradually evolved and gained juridical status, the binary used would be Christian and Negro. While the designation of the other (the African) was the same, English self-designation changed according to the social role at stake. Slowly, as the latter binary came to predominate, the term "Christian" came to connote "non-Negro" for the English; that is, it was used with a rhetorical force that the term "English" had not generally had in earlier times. In other words, "Christian" occurred in those rhetorical roles that later would be filled by the word "white."[41] It was as an effect of this extended process that the terms "black" and "white" were transformed from descriptive terms to racializing terms, from literary references to signifiers for forms of social categorization.

Some historians (for instance, Ballagh) argue that racialization, as the categorical designation of people as white or black, directly substituted itself for the original religious differential. But that view overlooks the fact that the English did not generally refer to themselves as whites until the 1690s (though individual Europeans may have done so earlier in letters and literary texts). Thus, it ignores the conceptual evolution racialization required, involving a commodification of people, juridical regulation, a purity condition, and the structuring of labor as a system of perpetual bondage. Racialization marked the extensive socialization of an idea that emerged from a political process, the political centrality of allegiance (in part to Christianity, but also to England, and finally to whiteness), and a cultural structuring of social categorizations which eventually came to be called "race." In other words, the ethos of allegiance played a stronger role than the religious creed. Ultimately, if the foundation for whiteness and white supremacy was the codification of slavery, the legislation of gender provided the machinery for a social coalescence (around being white), for which the African was the marker, labor the terrain, juridical enactment the discourse, and biologization the ultimate theorization.

A corollary to the English eventually conceiving of (i.e., racializing) themselves as white (and thus racializing the Africans as "black" or "Negro") was a certain decentering and shift in their self-conception as English. Insofar as this induced an eventual partial abandonment of allegiance to "being English," the process of becoming "white" involved a concomitant sense of independence from England. It was not that a sense of independence would provide an alternate sense of allegiance; rather an alternate sense of allegiance to being white imparted a cultural value to a politics of independence. This is confirmed by the fact that, for the "founding fathers," the revolution was proclaimed to have established a "white nation"—a claim no other nation had made (including England). Insofar as plantation slavery for Africans was not established full-blown at one stroke in Virginia, its gradual construction and definition in obedience to the pragmatics of a corporate, profit-oriented society functions not as a cause of race but as a social interface between an earlier English cultural politics, an English Christian ethnocentrism, and a culture of racialization.

One more step was required to bring about the alternate sense of social solidarity that would envelop the Virginia colony in such a shift in allegiance. That step was the organization of the patrols in 1727 as a mode of police force, or what Allen calls an intermediary control stratum, for the slave system (IWR, 252). The job of the patrols was to maintain bond-laborer discipline around the plantations and enforce the slave codes. This meant watching for and capturing runaways, suppressing any appearance of personal autonomy in a slave, and watching over or suppressing group activity by slaves. Before the patrols, the militias organized in the wake of Bacon's Rebellion played that role, though inefficiently because it was not defined for them as an official function. The functions of the patrols were defined, and small farmers and laborers were conscripted to them. Negligence in their duty was punishable. Through the patrols, poorer whites acted as shock troops and commandos under elite leadership to guard and protect white society against the elite-proclaimed threat of "Negro rebellion." The social paranoia engendered in the English toward African laborers by that proclamation was enhanced through the alarm signified by the patrols' existence and operations. In the face of increased slave importation, this paranoia was transformed into a call to overall English solidarity against this internally generated danger to the colony. The patrols became the material practice of social paranoia in concrete organizational immediacy.

The patrols were ironic in the context of an overall response by the elite to the social exigencies raised by Bacon's Rebellion and its democratizing demands. Though the poorer whites remained economically marginal and politically disfranchised, their enrollment in the patrols provided an avenue of participation, a limited citizen franchise with respect to governance, a role of policing rather than making policy. As an institutionalization of the power of paranoia, the patrols kept powerless whites constrained to the colony and hard at work by giving them that role, if not rule. Elite control was exercised through granting the power to control, and planter hegemony took the form of white solidarity.

This solidarity had the effect of diminishing a sense of economic competition between white agricultural strata (poor and rich farmers), or at least preventing that competition from expressing itself as a class distinction. Rather than see the plantation owner as their main adversary, the poor whites on patrol were made to see the slaves as their social nemesis. The violent abuse of slaves that quickly came to characterize the operation of these patrols provided the poor whites with a way of discharging frustration and anger at the elite. Further, the violence of the patrols became a means of increasing the level of social paranoia, which in turn the elite used to legitimize the violence of the patrols. In general, as the brutality with which the Africans were treated increased, so did the claim for its necessity from the patrols. In effect, the patrols transformed both paranoia and institutionalized allegiance into the production of terror. A diabolical cycle was generated in which white paranoia and the Africans' real need to resist or rebel fed off and enhanced each other.

Essentially, the intermediary control stratum was both independent of the economic structure and constitutive of it insofar as it functioned as a mechanism for the construction of class relations between the mass of plantation bond-laborers and the elite. Conversely, through its operations, the socioeconomic differences between the elite and other white intermediary strata were attenuated and rendered administrative within an encompassing corporate state.

What is important, however, is not only the forms of domination the patrols engendered but their profound sociopolitical materialization as white solidarity. Paranoia reached into the heart of personal identity and conflated the individual with communal self-defense, identity with sacrosanct identification. All three elements—allegiance, violence, and paranoia—operated in tandem to define a white identity on the one hand, and on the other a political antagonism between planters and slaves as the fundamental class system. The patrols can be said to have brought into existence for the first time a real class politics between an elite nourished by white social solidarity and a black bond-laborer class whose concerns were survival and resistance against gratuitous violence, on the terrain of patrol impunity.[42]

For Allen, the organization of this intermediary control stratum was an essential moment in the process of constituting "race" and consolidating the slave system. It added the critical social ingredient. As Allen theorizes it, the process of inventing "race" had three dimensions. The first was that the group to be dominated (through some difference) be given undifferentiated status, that is, generalized, and inferiorized insofar as an act of generalization always implies an inferiorization. The dominated group is made homogeneous, and massified, so that intragroup class, gender, and religious or ethnic differences no longer count for the dominant group. Each individual becomes an example of the group, and the group becomes composed of examples and ciphers rather than people.

The second dimension in the invention of race is the totalitarian enforcement of social control, through the intermediary control stratum, manifesting the power relation symbolized by generalization. For American slavery, that stratum was both judicial and paramilitary, and its eventual terrorism toward all Africans and African Americans signified that racism relies on a process of paramilitary activity. The third dimension is that the dominated group is accused of lacking something, which specifies its inferiority, and is simultaneously prevented from becoming or acquiring what is lacking by social or juridical means. That is, the intermediary control stratum acts to reduce the group in status and mobility, producing an appearance of inferiority that is then held against it. This self-fulfilling proposition further enforces the inferiorization, preventing escape from the imposed social condition. Concomitant with the demand that the inferiorized group transform itself and integrate itself into the culture of the dominant is the juridical and social prohibition against doing so.

Because an intermediary control stratum constitutes the primary form of social control, after administrative law enforcement, its founding would mark the initial appearance of class as a sociopolitical division in the colony. Class structures, as political systems of economic relations, express themselves in any social context through available means of resistance to oppression (whether real or imagined) and the means of repression of that resistance (whether extant or potential). That is, class relations and class consciousness occur on the political plane, as functions of, but not identical to, class interests. Prior to the founding of the intermediary control stratum, it would have been difficult to clearly define classes at all. Though plantation and small-farmer economic interests may have differed (prior to 1680, for instance), class disputes on the basis of conscious political interest would have required a degree of political organization. But the intermediary control stratum, the patrols, constituted the first form of nonelite organization functioning as a political entity in the colony. Previous to that, class disputes, based on class contradictions between class-conscious groups, would not have been a relevant political concept.

In the transformation of class interest to class-conscious organization, there is always a factor of violence. The formation of classes, as of states, is always founded on the performance of real or potential violence, aimed at bodily harm or deprivation. The plantation elite came into existence through a seizure of land from the indigenous, paralleling the violence by which the capitalist class gave birth to itself in England through the expropriation of rural farmers and common village lands.[43] Both brought a working class into existence for themselves through impoverishment, indenture, kidnapping, captivity, and partial or total enslavement. But with respect to Virginia, the question is how an amorphous population of laborers under extreme conditions of repression, yet with widely differing relations to the planter elite, could have defined themselves as a class. Escape does not do that. The rebellions of 1663 and 1676 (Bacon's) began the process but did not complete it. In response to the latter, the elite instituted new forms of social and cultural violence. The forms this took constituted the foundation for the racialization of the colony, as well as the beginning of a structure of class relations both among whites and between whites and the African and African American bond-laborers.

Rather than preserve a class hierarchy, racialization was a means of defining it. Insofar as the racialized division of colonial society between black and white structured the plantation economy as a class relation between an African work force and the plantation elite, it also marked a class difference between African and English labor to the extent it absorbed English labor into the white socius standing over the black laboring class (slave). But the logic of this rearrangement of allegiances and solidarities was that the chattel status of the English laborers had first to be eliminated. This additional factor positions the process of class construction and racialization historically. Although the elimination of chattel status for English laborers became economically feasible after the 1680s with an increase in the slave trade and a rise in tobacco prices, that was not the case in the 1660s. "White unity" as a political concept would have had no fertile ground in which to germinate until the 1690s. The institution of the patrols and its foregrounding the process of racialization marked the core of a process of class construction.[44]

In effect, racialization was not a divide-and-conquer strategy to govern previously constructed class antagonisms. To argue that it was, one would have to ask which class the council was attempting to divide by engineering a paranoid social unity that took the form of racism. If it were an unracialized class of bond-laborers, then against whom or what would white social unity be forged? If a class of bond-laborers as chattel were racialized, what would it have meant to build a unity between white landowners and white chattel? If the bond-laborers were not a class, because they constituted a material resource, what was the elite doing by racializing them? Rather, a social unity reconfiguring a sense of allegiance is the predominant moment in white self-racialization through the racialization of the Africans as a working class. This renders the division between white and black originary, not tactical with respect to class divisions.

Essentially, the notion of racialization as fundamental to class organization itself, rather than as an attempt to divide a working class and dominate it, begins to explain why racism has been as successful as it has in that divisiveness, what has made racist strategies of division so fruitful. Rather than the class nature of race, it is the racialized nature of class that needs to be understood.

In sum, the nature and structure of the intermediary control stratum marks the consolidation of a politics of white supremacy and race. It represents the function of allegiance in a diverse and stratified society, and institutes it as a culture of allegiance (of social solidarity) built upon a purity condition (manifest in antimiscegenation laws and the color coding of class being) and a social paranoia as a response to the projected resistance of those it oppresses and subjugates. The concept of race emerged from this reconfiguration of allegiance and a concomitant shift from identification as English to identification as white. Out of a confluence of slavery, the purity concept, matrilinearity, paranoia, and organized political terror, the English settlers produced for themselves a sense of white nationality. Through it all, the process of racialization was never divorced from the operations of the state. The political inscription of paranoia marked the social space where juridical measures to engender prejudice had not worked. The political stratification constructed through the intermediary control stratum marked the cultural place where elite attempts at social stratification had been ineffective.

Historiographically, we must be careful not to confuse the statement of the purity condition with the existence of race itself. The purity condition could not have preceded colonialism as a condition for racialization, since it would not have preceded the existence of the colonial political dilemma that engendered it. As Europeans swaggered into other people's lands and took over, their interbreeding produced darker children. Politically, these children diminished the relative size of the European occupation group if they were not included in it, and they erased the hierarchical boundary between colonist and colonized if they were. But neither could the purity concept have followed from racialization, since it is the necessary conceptual condition for whiteness, and thus for an original ability to chromatically divide people. (Had the continuous human spectrum remained intact, color would not have been seen as a "characteristic.")

What the racialization of the Virginia colony implies is that the purity concept was already in place culturally, at least by 1682. But the need to pass antimiscegenation statutes implies that it was not in place during the entire century. From 1619 to 1680, there were probably those who abhorred English marriage with African people on some basis: that the Africans were bond-laborers, or that they were property, or that they were heathens, or that they were commodities, or that they were Africans. Nevertheless, intermarriage was plentiful enough to warrant antimiscegenation statutes. Those statutes prohibiting an extant practice become the stage on which the acceptance of the purity condition was demanded. Rather than protect whiteness and the purity condition, the enactments were essential to bringing them into existence.[45] The germination of a process of racialization in Virginia is the story of allegiance to a purity concept, across the religious and the sexual to the racial, as the form of organization of colonial society.

It should not be forgotten that while the purity condition led to enforced separation of African bond-laborers from the English, it was also manifest juridically in order to be able to impose it generally on English women. The purity condition established English women as the site where the purity condition for the English as white was to be represented and preserved, where the cultural supremacy of whiteness articulated itself, and where the cultural condemnation of Africans to slavery was signified. When black people were turned into ledger entries, white women were turned into icons or statuary.

In essence, white identity remained dependent on "the other"; its substance and center were external to it in the other. The other, the Africans, had to be maintained as internal to white society, and expelled from it as external, because they occupied the real center of white racialized identity. This internal contradiction in whiteness could resolve itself only by rendering the nonwhite other as nemesis. In other words, the relation of whiteness and domination is not one of historical precedence, of which came first, but rather of form and content. They relate not in temporality but rather as a common, discursively instituted space in which a purity concept, a paranoia, and an allegiance come together. Whiteness as an institutional notion, an institutionalization of comportment, is not simply an ideology or identity. Neither is it an ethnicity. As racializing, whiteness is a social relation, a social dependence on others. To become a race, whiteness must first produce a particular structure of gender domination that reifies a purity concept and an assumption of prohibited impurity in English women. To institute itself socially, it must renarrativize that gender relation, in order to disguise the history of racialization that produced it as instituted. It is, in effect, a circular lamination of fictions, each fiction being used to disguise another.[46]

It is worth noting that a different trajectory for whiteness manifest itself in the Caribbean islands. Eric Williams suggests that a racialized notion of whiteness developed earlier in the island sugar plantations. In the harsh conditions of "terminal slavery" practiced there, a stricter differentiation was required by the English masters between those laborers who could be worked to death and those who should not. In order that the English in the Caribbean not be considered laborers, they started looking at themselves as white in the 1670s, as opposed to the 1690s in Virginia (CS, 19). In the harshness and terror of the island plantations, the difference between whites and blacks was originarily a class distinction. As Paul Gilroy points out, terror always has a reason, a reasonableness, a rationale.[47] Ritual brutality is not an adjunct but a precursor to administrative sanctity, upon which the state builds itself. Power is the transformation of the ability to be brutal ritualistically into established administrative (or juridical) procedures.

For the Spanish colonies, organized on a military rather than a corporate model, the purity condition was not an issue. The Spanish intermarried and only guarded the purity of "blood" (ancestry) of the gentry, who controlled the military. While color difference eventually became a system of markers of class difference (between the expendable and the citizen), racial status was always grounded upon aristocratic inheritance, rather than on an identity/paranoia structure. While purity of blood gave the Spanish elite license and sway within the pragmatics of military administration, in the Virginia colony it became the indispensable ontological condition for the entire corporate form of colonial settlement. Ultimately, white supremacy and white racism cannot be thought without the confluence of paranoia, allegiance, and terror that form its fundamental elements.

Conclusion

Thus were slavery, whiteness, and race constructed on the Atlantic seaboard during the seventeenth century. Race theory and the various "scientific" treatises invented in Europe in the eighteenth century were efforts to explain slavery, to predicate slavery on inherency and essence rather than see slavery and racialization as mutually conditioning, as two sides of the same process. The biologization of race occurred in transoceanic terms, a discourse that crossed the Atlantic in the company of intercontinental trade. It was not simply the plantation form of production of the Atlantic colonies, nor the instituted structure of violence as a function of allegiance and paranoia, that produced a structure of racialization, and from that a notion of race that could be biologized. The theories of race that Europeans produced in the eighteenth century were their contribution to the century-long emergence of a system of social categorization that constituted the practice of racialization on the other side of the Atlantic. Finally, the three together—slavery, racialization, and biologization—constructed the concept of race and white supremacy that inserted itself as a whole into the subsequent expansions of European colonialism, its invasions of other lands, and its domestic thinking. The concept of race as theorized, the culture of white supremacy lived by Euro-Americans as a practical identity, the subjugating encounter with this by non–Euro-Americans as it washed over them, and the slave economy that powered the capitalist economy, which carried all this with it as it spread over the world, were all of a piece.

After the American Revolution, biologistic theorization became an urgent and prominent intellectual activity, aimed at preserving the slave system by resolving the contradiction between democratic ideals and the preservation of slavery on which the possibility of such ideals for whites as whites relied (RMD, 139). The discourses of "scientific" racism provided the legitimizations for continuing slavery by painting a picture of race that, for whites, rendered the possibility of freeing the slaves and socializing with free blacks "unthinkable."

The ultimate irony was the concept of social freedom born out of this structure of bondage, paranoia, and allegiance. Toni Morrison saliently points out that "The concept of freedom did not emerge in a vacuum. Nothing highlighted freedom—if it did not in fact create it—like slavery" (PD, 38). The slave system emerged in the Atlantic colonies as an entire social infrastructure composed of law, prejudice, solidarity, a sense of honor and entitlement, responsibility, a constitution of class relations, and an acceptance of certain modes of social brutality. Thus, at all levels of social discourse, a concept of freedom could be brought forth from the structures of slavery and racialization.

David Brion Davis describes how slavery was openly seen, and celebrated, as the source of freedom for whites.[48] Yet, Morrison suggests, it is a dehumanized freedom insofar as it loomed before the individual, white or black, as an ethos of social technology, of gratuitous violence and allegiance to the power of that violence. Violence created power (and the state) as its instrument, though it theorized itself as an instrument of state power, and thus constrained by a social will. Within that boundary, freedom as the instrument of violence renders violence the primary instrument of freedom. What Native Americans were never able to understand was why the white settlers felt so good when they were killing people. It is indeed significant that the idea of the penitentiary arose during the 1830s, during the Jacksonian era, just at the moment the nation was priding itself on its openness and freedom.[49] The prison represented a continuation of a social valorization of the technology of violence, obedience, and the discipline of allegiance. Like slavery, these are the "hallmarks of a captive society."

Morrison argues that a certain subhuman status marked what slavery reduced the slaveholder to, not in terms of misery or self-victimization, but in its valorization of cruelty, the enjoyment of brutality, the sense of ethical rectitude attendant upon absolute control, in violation yet in furtherance of all western humanist values. She tells the story (cited in Bailyn) of a man named William Dunbar, who exemplifies this dehumanization "in the act of becoming an American." Dunbar was a product of the Scottish enlightenment, an educated and cultured man of the 1770s, who went to Mississippi, staked a claim, and bought slaves to work his land. He became, in short order, a man who thrilled to his "absolute control over the lives of others" (PD, 44). For Dunbar, everything else, freedom, virility, individualism, and autonomy, were all made possible by that "absolute control." And that absolute control meant absolute brutality. He saw his slaves' every attempt at revolt or escape as "ingratitude" and punished them all the more savagely. The connection between slavery and the savagery of his punishments, which expressed his "puzzlement" at the depth of the "savagery" that would attempt to escape his "kindness and good usage," was quite beyond his understanding (which reveals the tenuousness of Enlightenment thinking). But that is only an extension of the sense of membership, of social solidarity that responds to the paranoia that resides at the core of white identity, and makes it a primary point of identification for most whites. Dunbar's brutality toward the slaves transformed him from a middle-class, cultured person into a slaveowner. For him, the slave's self-respect (attempted escape) was transfigured, to be interpreted as brutality itself, while his brutality in response would only be interpreted in turn as self-respect.

None dare call this psychosis; it was, after all, the glory of the British civilizing mission in practice, and the foundation of the American republic. It is psychosis not in the psychological sense but in the sense of obeying a socially given norm, a structure of belonging that inserts social rectitude into whatever the person does. One's social identity escapes, becomes other, and yet remains oneself insofar as it is in compliance with the given structure that one valorizes by making that structure one's own, and thus submitting to it. For Dunbar, the personal satisfaction he derived from his mastery over others transcended his economic gain and produced his willingness to kill or maim those he relied on, because he also relied on them as a place to exert that violence.

This "civilizing" mission devolved down to a structure of allegiance, paranoia, and terror. Insofar as allegiance names a structure of paranoia and inflicted terror, brutality references a structure that takes allegiance as its form and paranoia as its content, and paranoia names a structure for which allegiance is theory and terror is practice. As DuBois describes it, the psychological effect of having legal mastery over a human being was disastrous, inflating the ego "beyond all reason," transforming a person into an "arrogant, strutting, quarrelsome kinglet," whose "honor" required "insistent deference," rendering him easily "angered, jealous, and resentful" (BR, 53). The insistence of whiteness on domination is structural, not psychological. It is not that white supremacists insist on supremacy; they already have it, through the ethos of conquest and domination by which they live. If it appears psychotic in its practices and effects, that is because, as a social structure, it must ever reconstitute an independence out of its absolute dependence.

CHAPTER 2

Racialization and Class Structure

Racism and the Intermediary Control Stratum

It is not enough to recognize that race is a social construct. Refutations (again and again) of the idea that race is inherent in people neither pursue nor challenge racism's tenacity. If race is socially defined, and racism manifests a system of interrelated social categorizations, the social effects of that system—the feelings, opinions, or antipathies that it generates in people and leads them to impose on each other—only inform the existence of that system. Its content, what makes it tenacious, lies in the specific modes by which race and racism were on-going historical constructions.

We confront a structuring of society that categorizes people through the imposition of devalorizing and self-valorizing meanings attached artificially to physical differences. Physical characteristics are made to serve as signifiers by which people are then noticed and established as "known"—that is, socially determined. The act of noticing a physical difference, which is generated by the social meaning given to what is to be noticed, imparts a social importance and a valuation to the characteristic noticed. The entire process is circular. The establishment of a physical characteristic to be noticed gives that characteristic a social importance (through which the person noticed is disparaged), and the social importance given a physical characteristic determines that it must be noticed (and noticed as a devaluation). This circle transforms the imposed valuation into a mode of social categorizing. The fixing or instituting of this hierarchy of social categories in cultural thought as "natural" (its "naturalization") is accomplished through various biological theories, which impart to it a factual status that disguises its ideological nature. In short, the concept of race comes into existence only as a process of racialization.

Differentiation is not the driving force of racialization. What drives racialization on a daily basis is the system of social importances attached to the act of noticing, the self-superiorization that attaches to the inferiorization of the other. Racism is the name of this driving force, and racialization is its daily effect. Race does not stand in a cause-and-effect relation to racism (as prejudice). Instead, racism produces race (as social categorization) through a process of racialization. In other words, racism is not the expression of prejudice. Prejudice is an expression of racism, the insult heaped on those already injured by oppression, on those denigrated by having been forced into inferiorizing social categorizations; it is an expression of complex social operations which racialize. One does not ostracize a group because one is prejudiced; one becomes prejudiced against a group because they have been ostracized, excluded, and oppressed.[1]

In the brief history of the birth of racialization in the Virginia colony given in the previous chapter, one can discern the extent to which it involved every level of society. Emerging integrally with the evolution of a system of slavery, it was the means by which class relations were constructed in the colony. Alongside plantation slavery as a form of profit-oriented, mass-production capitalist agriculture that had reduced its labor costs to absolute barest subsistence, free white wage workers lived a double existence. As workers they were outside and ancillary to the main modes of commodity (plantation) production. As white, they formed the core of the intermediary control stratum, the policing apparatus upon which the plantation economy depended for its class stability (to keep its black working class in place).

As a policing "class," the intermediary control stratum formed the limit of the class structure internal to white society, the interface with the black working class upon which all white society depended and benefited. The control stratum was also a productive class. Its "means of production" were a variety of modes of violence, and its social product was the slave system itself and the maintenance of the social structure of whiteness. As a social class, the control stratum obtained semipolitical entitlement, while its cultural role was the concrete expression of allegiance to whiteness. Allegiance to whiteness through the terrorizing of black people was the political product of its operations.

This outlines the class legacy inherited by the United States at the time of the Revolution. The form this tradition took for white workers, which gave them their sense of belonging and of sociopolitical legitimacy, was their dual function of control stratum and maintenance mechanism for the sanctity of white society. While one effect was to submerge class relations in a framework of politically engendered social homogeneity, another established the intermediary control stratum function as entry into and identification with a middle class—a broadening and defining of middle-class identity itself. That is, the control stratum became a social domain of conjunction for white working people, an interface between classes with a middle-class sense of belonging. A class structure was put in place on the basis of a social ethos of whiteness that depended on this dual function. Herein one glimpses part of the hold that racism has always had on white workers in the United States. It has been at the center of a certain sense of productive participation in white society, albeit a structure of continual violence against others, as the continual reconstruction of the whiteness of white supremacy.

In this sense, racism has always been a central and almost insuperable problem for working-class organization. For those involved in union organizing, or the attempt to engender socialist class consciousness, the racism of white workers has been a continual obstacle to worker unity. Unionizing campaigns in the South and in California before World War II traditionally ran aground on the question of race, the issue of exclusion of black (or Mexican or Asian) workers in unions. Against the industrial union movement, a central motivation for a focus on craft unions for skilled workers was precisely to keep them white.

The violence enforcing this ethos of whiteness amounted to a system of terror. Black people and other people of color have had to think twice, and strategize carefully, before engaging in anything that would look like social or organizational autonomy. Whites have had to think twice before stepping across the line of allegiance to aid or act in solidarity with black or brown organizations—let alone suggest that black people join in white organizations. Nevertheless, workers of color, and especially black workers, have always organized, and sought to construct and express their class consciousness, for which they were most generally opposed, rejected, or abandoned by white workers. Where black workers were included in unionizing efforts, as in the meatpacking industry in Chicago during the late 1940s, the white workers had to be dragged kicking and screaming, one by one, into that unity. Yet despite that union victory in Chicago owing precisely to the transcendence of racism, antiracism did not spread to other major unions in the area.

The radicals and organizers who have traditionally explained racism as a tactic of the elite to divide and control the working class have thereby prevented themselves from explaining or understanding racism's power and tenacity. Few have dared to ask why it works so well—for to do so would be to admit that it touches something much deeper in the American cultural fabric than either ideology or material circumstances. But even the notion that racism is ideological points to part of its strength. Marxism addresses racism as ideological in order not to give it transhistorical or metaphysical status (RRR, 144). But the very notion of an ideology of race already assumes that race has real (natural) existence, that it does not originate in an historical system of social categorizations. Thus, Marxism falls into the double bind that constitutes the very matrix of racism's tenacity. To extricate itself, Marxism makes historical reference to notable exceptions in which multiracial class solidarity overcame racial antagonism, usually with spectacular results. But as arguments for racism's ideological character, these examples only end up highlighting themselves as exceptional.

The colonial history reveals that racism is more than an ideological tactic in a class struggle; it is a fundamental cultural structure in the United States, to the extent that racialization grounds the construction of class relations. But if racialization is the foundation for class structure (rather than the other way around), then traditional theorizations of working-class politics and social consciousness inherited from Europe (e.g., Marxism) cannot simply be transferred whole to the United States context. They would have to be modified to become relevant. A rearticulation of class relations based on racialization would have to be undertaken. This would not mean asking if the racism that kept workers disunited in the twentieth century is the same racism that produced race in the seventeenth century. They could not possibly be the same. It would mean asking what is weightier than class interest or class ideology if racism has persisted in the face of the multifarious ideological efforts to dispel it over two centuries of class struggle.

Ultimately, if race and racialization were a stage on which the founding of the United States and its invention of itself as a nation played themselves out, then it will not be sufficient to understand how race was produced by the colonization of "America." We must rather understand how "America" was something produced by race and racialization.

The Social System before the Revolution

Let us briefly recapitulate the social divisions that evolved in colonial Virginia. Three major strata emerged through the consolidation of the slave system: a working class of African and African American laborers held in permanent bondage; a class of plantation owners who formed the managerial stratum of the colony's corporate structure (and whose elite constituted the directorship, its governors and policymakers); and a middle class of white farmers, white tradesmen, and poor white laborers, who functioned as the intermediary control stratum—a police force ranging from patrols to sheriffs and bailiffs—between the white elite and the black bond-laborer class. (The use of slave patrols eventually spread to the North as well. Though slavery was not used for mass production there, it existed and was codified similarly.) As intermediary, this middle "class" might be more accurately considered a "stratum," since it included people from a wide variety of social sectors. It had no class disposition, income bracket, nor particular economic relation to plantation production to distinguish it. Indeed, one must be careful not to impose a nineteenth-century industrial conception of class on this eighteenth-century pre-Revolutionary structure. If it preserved the political relation of white owners to black bond-laborers, then it played the most essential class role in plantation society. It thus provides a lens through which to understand the class structure of the colony as it moved toward independence.

According to Stampp, the patrols were organized as a militia (PI, 214). Their members were appointed by the Colonial Council for a period of time, its operations and schedules were coordinated by the elite, and service was mandatory for all adult male whites. Thus, the patrols brought white people together organizationally from a variety of classes—laborers, farmers, artisans, tradesworkers, merchants, etc. Their main task was to guard against runaways and autonomous organization among the black working class (as slaves) (IWR, 251ff). Thus, they embodied both the violence on which plantation society was based and its allegiance to itself.

In both respects, the patrols were more than merely a mode of policing. On the one hand, their potential violence as a control mechanism engendered an ethos of impunity that expressed itself as terror in the face of their operations. On the other,

they appeared to the white population as the institution of peace and social tranquillity. Terror and impunity toward black people constituted the materialization of
white solidarity and tranquillity, and white consensus in solidarity constituted the
product of terror and impunity. The veneer of tranquillity produced by violence incar-
nated the allegiance that plantation society demanded for itself. In playing this double role, the patrols inhabited an unacknowledged political center in plantation society, the mortar that held together the entire culture of white supremacy. Its existence
symbolized and exacerbated the perceived threat (of slave rebellion) that the plantation elite used to cohere white society to itself (the threat of slave rebellion being
made more impending and dire by the very violence of the patrols). African American attempts at resistance were preordained by the oppressiveness of their conditions
of enslavement, but their options for actual resistance were severely limited. Though
the actuality or potential extent of African American social upheaval through organized means was for the most part preempted by the patrols, running away and disobedience were perceived as threats to tranquillity, as social upheaval. If subsequent
historians of the slave system have spoken of its harmonies and placidities, it is
because the underlying ethic of force and terror represented by the patrols had become
sufficiently ubiquitous to make that facade seem real.

Though the patrols were a political rather than economic element of the Virginia
colony, their task was a productive one. They produced a form of social stability out
of a complex class mixture. Plantation bond-labor produced the economic wealth of
the society, and the control stratum reproduced and maintained that system of production. That it did so was a cultural product of its own existence, functioning as the
axis of solidarity for white society by denying humanity to others. In effect, the patrols
constituted a productive-class apparatus whose product was the class system of labor
exploitation itself; that "product" (plantation exploitation) in turn constructed the
patrols as an incipient (middle) class constituted on a cultural basis. Stampp for
instance mentions that "the nonslaveholding whites, to whom most patrol service was
relegated, frequently disliked the masters almost as intensely as the Negroes, and as
patrollers they were in a position to vent their feelings toward both" (PI, 215). That
is, as a productive class, an additional part of the patrols' product was the attenua-
tion of class conflict between white groups by foregrounding solidarity and rechan-
neling intrawhite class antagonisms onto African American bond-laborers in the
process of policing.

Producing class society as its social product, and functioning as the political center
for the cultural cohesion of white society, the control stratum attained a certain political power through which to become conscious of itself as a class. It could call upon
its unique position to influence the course of social relations in the colony. On this basis,
a double and reciprocal political relation emerged between itself and the elite.

The patrols' common bond with the elite was their functional oppression of what
the elite had constructed as a common enemy both ideologically and by establishing
the patrols in the first place. Yet the patrols operated under elite direction. To influence the elite, they had to play a double game. Their leverage with the elite was their

prestige and political weight with the general white population as the kernel of white solidarity. The patrols could enhance this leverage through excessive activity, forms of hypersuppression whose effect would be an aura of heightened slave resistance, in the face of which the patrols' existence and operations would receive greater social recognition and approbation. "Slaveholders repeatedly went to the courts with charges that patrollers had invaded their premises and whipped their slaves excessively and illegally" (PI, 215). On the other hand, actual slave resistance had to be most often directed in retaliation against the patrols, and thus the patrols could plead that they were actually on the front lines.[2] If the first won concessions from the general populace, the second won them from the elite. It was a system rife with abuse. This double system transformed what would have been class interactions within white society into the dual practices of paternalism and patronage.

Paternalism in the context of the slave plantation amounted to granting or guaranteeing security to individual black people against arbitrary treatment by the patrols or vigilantes of the white control stratum. It emerged in large measure from the terrorism inherent in the patrol system. A black person spoken for by a member of the elite was to an extent protected against the inherent excesses of the security apparatus (RJR, 5, 135). Those not specially spoken for could be subject to continual unwarranted attack. It was a classical form of protection racket; the racketeer (whether the state, the police, or organized crime) sets up a form of terror against which it then sells safety and protection, either for money or some form of allegiance. The possibility of protection against the patrols presented itself as a form of humanitarianism,[3] and the exploitative plantation owner took on the mantle of peacekeeper between the black labor force and the white control stratum as guarantor of social stability. Thus, a dimension of the stability of the slave system and its legitimacy, its ability to rationalize itself in its own eyes, depended on the abusiveness of the patrols.

Alongside the paternalism, a system of patronage emerged between the elite and the patrols, that is, of rewards for their operations in the interests of white society. The poorer strata of whites, who stood in potential conflict with the elite, furnished the majority of the patrols. For those people, social advancement, or relief from economic duress, was to be had generally at the pleasure of the elite. The elite's dependency on the patrols gave poorer whites a claim for consideration. In their requests or demands for specific needs or favors, the poorer whites could play the ethos of white solidarity against the elite, or be lax in duty, again with respect to certain specific bond-laborers (ignoring runaways, leaving theft uninvestigated, etc.). In other words, the patrols could deploy a kind of solidarity with their victims as a weapon against the elite. This rarely if ever went to the point of actual unity between black and white laborers; it was a means of exerting pressure on individual landowners. Indeed, it reaffirmed the absolute class difference between black and white generated by racialization, to the extent that black people could be deployed as a political instrumentality for the white control stratum, for its own political purposes.

This form of patronage was necessitated by the slave system. The rewards extracted not only recognized the potential power of the patrols as a control stratum but were a means of controlling the patrols. Because performance in the patrols was mandatory, patronage was a tactic to divide the control stratum against itself, through the exclusion of some from bonuses and benefits. Thus, rewards could serve to divide the control stratum and constrain its political influence. While paternalism kept African American laborers at work against a background of terror, patronage kept the patrols at work against a background of poverty and ostracism. The two systems fed each other, each constituting the domain upon which the other became possible. The abusiveness fundamental to a protection racket lay the basis for the opportunism of favor seeking, and vice versa. In both, marginalized whites could embrace their appearance as protectors, maintainers, and indeed saviors of white society, gaining approbation and attention.[4]

Implicit in this system was a continual potential for and fear of betrayal. While some poor whites attained middle-class status through their bargain of white solidarity with the elite, that social pact always rested on the threshold of being discounted by the elite in the name of class interest. According to W. J. Cash in *The Mind of the South,* a southern form of individualism emerged around this fear of betrayal as a southern frontier mentality. In a situation where political cachet was rhetorically granted to people with little real economic weight, their desire to maintain social parity with those of great economic weight but a concomitant political dependency led to an overblown attitude of autonomy, which Cash identifies as a form of frontier ethic. The frontier individualism was an attitude of being able to take on the elite on whom they in turn depended. That is, as the police force of the slave system, the poorer whites sought to cash in on their inequality as equity itself, to logically compensate for their lower status. Though philosophers traditionally linked individualism to the Enlightenment thinking of philosophers such as Locke, this sense of American individualism was in reality a defensive posture adopted to forestall the social betrayal imminent in the political bargain. As such, it constituted a conformism to social whiteness expressed through an insistence on allegiance on the part of the elite in return for the allegiance the elite demanded as white solidarity.

This fear of betrayal further exemplifies the paradigm at the core of Bailyn's thesis, namely that subversion of social stasis is generally viewed in the United States as the greatest political threat. It constituted a force for conservatism insofar as certain exercises of power, whether from inside the government or from movements of reform, were subversive. The role of the populist movements was to unveil conspiracy and weaken power in the event of a breach of the bargain by capital.[5] Populism sought to defend itself above all against the violation of the solidarity agreement that power had made with the "producer," and to which it must be held accountable. When that condition is obeyed, no objection is given to the social structure of property and power. It is for the preservation of those structures that populism seeks to defeat the conspiracies of the powerful. In that sense, the American revolutionaries, fighting to defend the colonies against the subversive power of the English king, did not see themselves as subversive but as defending their liberties against abuse. For this reason, questioning slavery did not have weight in the revolutionary imagination of the time (Tise, 193).

Ultimately, the power of the control stratum to negotiate its own proper political and economic issues based on the essentiality of its social function was dissipated with the rise of an industrial economy. Industry requires a control stratum, but of a character more immediately integrated into productive enterprises. An environment of patrol terror is inappropriate to a system whose front line of discipline lies in the ability to fire people and render them unemployed. The active control stratum was shifted to anti-union legislation, labor spies, and in some cases labor contracts favorable to the enterprise. Though industry emerged in large part from the capital that the patrols as control stratum had made possible, it could dispense with the system of patronage at the core of that previous system. White workers realized that the industrial exploitation of white labor already constituted a betrayal of white solidarity, but white allegiance was still deployed as the ethos in which to grant white workers control over black.

The Free Labor Ideology

In the English colonies at the moment of revolution, slavery was well established everywhere; the major eighteenth-century theories of biological race, racial hierarchy, and the propriety of black servitude had gained social preponderance; and the Atlantic economy had developed the first stages of industrialization based on the wealth produced by the plantation and the slave trade.

Three sources of immense wealth had revealed themselves in the colonies, laying the foundation for a movement toward autonomous control: the vast land mass of the continent, the wealth in slave ownership as such (beyond its production as labor), and the beginning of industry in New England based on the profits of the slave trade—that is, wealth based on the seizure of land from its inhabitants, a system of forced labor, and an industrialization of kidnapping. It was to control the vastness of this economy that the colonists sought independence from England (PH, 58). The Revolution was not strictly speaking anticolonialist insofar as it did not seek or envision any change in property relations. Rather, it merely marked the separation of a subsidiary enterprise from its parent corporation in the name of autonomous control of social assets (real and projected). The question to address, then, is how the political economy of the post-Revolutionary autonomous (united) states conditioned the development of industrial class relations as industrial capital grew to dominance.

To understand the unfolding of a class structure in the industrializing economy, one must understand certain differences in the slave system between North and South. The term "slave" referred to property, an element of investment, and to a bond-laborer, a producer of wealth. In the South, bond-labor was employed in agricultural mass production; in the North, it was employed on small farms and as ancillary labor in various trades and industries. A large percentage of northern African American bond-laborers were artisans and highly skilled workers (BBN, 42; Z, 34ff).

Three major issues germane to working-class structure emerged in the wake of the Revolution. The first was the contradiction between the ideals of the Declaration of

Independence and the persistence of slavery. The second was the labor competition offered by slaves employed in trades and industry. The third was the obsessive fear of a black voting bloc on the part of whites, and their rejection of black political participation. While each of these issues will be dealt with more fully as we proceed, let me briefly outline the substance of each here.

The contradiction between the ideal of personal liberty and the existence of slavery presented itself as a problem of ethical and philosophical contradiction and consistency. It raised the issue (for some, the specter) of emancipation, of ending slavery altogether as an evil and a violation of democratic principles. The debates that ensued, however, generally reduced themselves to the question of compensation for the owners, the "problem" of accepting a population of free African Americans into society, and the possibility of sending them back to Africa in colonization campaigns. Emancipation proceeded slowly in the North through convoluted conditions of release as a way of "protecting" owner investments (to which we will return later in this chapter). Meanwhile, communities of free black people grew in northern cities. The political voices that African Americans organized for themselves (through churches, community organizations, participation in political parties, etc.) supported total emancipation, opposed colonization, and petitioned for full citizenship and franchise (NS, 80, 257).

Labor competition became an issue in industrializing regions to the extent that skilled African American bond-laborers, leased out by owners, cost less for their employers than did white skilled labor. While the black laborer worked alongside white, the conditions of labor were set by owners elsewhere and undercut the conditions white workers could demand. Hence, owing to the structure of slavery, white skilled laborers found themselves in a situation in which black bond-laborers appeared as "unfair competition."

Thirdly, in the 1830s the political voice of the African American communities was turned against itself. A vast movement of whites, generally in opposition to the abolition of slavery in the South, coalesced to bring about or continue the disfranchisement of African Americans, who were seen as a potential voting bloc that would disrupt the regulation of political affairs which whites had been evolving for themselves.

It is significant that not only did slavery survive the Revolution, but its practitioners were the ones who led the process of nation building, using slavery as the foundation for that leadership. The constitutional clause providing three-fifths of a vote for nonwhites was introduced by southern states to augment their representation in Congress based on their entire population (granting subcitizen status to bond-laborers) while maintaining their disfranchisement of those same bond-laborers (withholding full citizenship).[6] By the 1840s, proslavery had effectively become synonymous with nationalism.[7] U.S. politics had become an endless series of compromises between the cultural "norm" of bond-laborer "ownership," the production of a stable white political structure, and the instrumentation of democratic ideals (liberty and human equality) by which the society had been wrenched from the British and invented as a nation. These compromises represented vast undercurrents of convoluted and convulsive political thinking whose logical twists and tortuous turnings were founded on white supremacy and the structures of racialization.

A demonstration of this kind of thinking can be gleaned from a cursory examination of the "free labor" ideology that grew to prominence in the 1830s and 1840s. The free labor ideology was a political doctrine and ideal built upon the very sound idea that workers should be free and able to demand remuneration commensurate with their skill and tradition. It reflected a social approbation of labor as a social value for the whole of society. In its rhetorical form, as a social ideology, it acclaimed labor to be "the source of all our wealth, of all our progress, of all our dignity and value," and sought social recognition for this idea.[8] Lincoln himself would proclaim that labor was "independent of capital," and that capital was itself "the fruit of labor." In effect (still in its ideal form), it sought to position labor on a par with capital, and to affirm social development to be a result of the conjunction and partnership of the two. It held that unfree or enslaved labor not only was anathema to a free society, but that it tainted and dishonored free labor by its presence.

In great part, the free labor ideology derived from the Jacksonian valorization of the "producing class" of the 1820s. For Jackson, this "class" included farmers, planters, laborers and skilled tradesmen, and small businessmen, all those who in some sense participated in adding to the aggregate social product and to social wealth. For Jackson, the "producer ethic" was a call to populist solidarity against the banks and large financial establishments from whom he sought to wrest de facto political control of the government. It signified what could in general be considered the "middle class." For white workers, the producer ethic responded to the serious question of slavery as deleterious to their working conditions, to the extent it depressed wages and created competition for jobs.

Ironically, the Jacksonian producer ethic was also a response to the nearness of the frontier and what that meant for a society embarked on industrial development. Jackson recognized that, with open land available, it would be unattractive to sell one's labor to an employer in hard or unhealthy conditions, especially for that employer's corpulent enrichment. Economic development required a labor force that would not endlessly dissolve into newly opened territories. His appeal to the "producer," and to labor in general as a source of value deserving of respect, was an unspoken continuation and reflection of the earlier bargain of white solidarity at the core of the colonial structure of racialization. The other side of the bargain, the producer's side, was that the white worker would remain in place; in exchange for valorization, the white worker would not go elsewhere and would not break economic ties, however tenuous, with the others of his or her community. Granting a role instead of rule, the producer ethic was designed to keep white laborers at home and hard at work. In effect, Jackson rearticulated the populist deal: respect and recognition for stability and production.

Behind its social recognition of the role of labor, it also recognized that all labor, in all forms of production for commodity markets, operates under the shadow of some form of coercion. The social prestige promised by the producer ethic substituted social pressure for that coercion (the enforcement of indenture and slavery) through a condemnation of "abandoning one's post." It was not a form of democratization but an expansion on the capitalist process of establishing a working class for itself.

But while Jackson was valorizing labor in the eastern states, white workers were leaving and taking the free labor ideology with them to the new territories of the Midwest and California. There it was absorbed into what became the Republican Party platform in the 1850s, as a weapon against the Democratic Party of Jackson. Thus, in Ohio, Illinois, and Michigan, strong movements of white artisans and skilled trades people, eventually associated with the Republican Party, organized to bar slavery (FS, 40ff). The paradox in this was that on both sides of the political fence, the free labor ideology granted social recognition only to white producers. What characterized the free labor ideology was its program of monopolizing the labor field for whites and an exclusion of free black workers from skilled trades, from labor organizations, and from the new territories altogether. It saw no contradiction between its opposition to slavery in the name of labor dignity and its opposition to free black workers being considered part of labor.

The reasons given were legion: black people were naturally servile; or they constituted unfair competition because they would work for less; or they would bring slavery with them; or black people had been responsible for the existence of slavery in the first place; or black people simply had no place in a free society. The argument advanced was that black workers would work for lower wages than white, which would result in depressing working conditions, thereby giving slavery a foothold. The charge that black workers would work for less was made unblushingly, without even a wink toward acknowledging that white exclusion of black workers from various trades, from white labor organizations and unions, and from employment in the new territories would create the necessity for black workers to accept lesser working conditions. In the eastern states, the organizational ostracism of black workers by white is precisely what transformed black workers into erosive competition. Little thought was given to solidarity with black workers as workers. As their numbers increased (by the 1840s, the number of free black workers in the North had grown to sizable proportions, augmented by the constant stream of runaways brought north by the Underground Railroad), so too did the degree of segregation.

Even the antislavery middle class advanced the same idea. David Wilmot, in the halls of Congress, affirmed the "rights of white freemen" in 1847 in advocating the "free labor" standard for the territories taken from Mexico.[9] While the underlying program of the Wilmot Proviso was the idea of ending slavery by confining it to the South,[10] Wilmot concomitantly argued that white workers felt it to be degrading to be associated with black workers (NS, 47). In other words, exclusion of workers of color (African American in the Midwest, Asian in northern California, Mexican in southern California) became part of the bargain inherent in the valorization of "free labor."

The charge that black workers should be excluded from labor organizations because they offered unfair competition was a self-fulfilling proposition. By charging that they offered competition, and excluding them on that basis, white workers created black workers as competition. Had organizational inclusion been the choice, black workers would have offered no more competition than the immigrant workers from Europe, who were accepted and welcomed (except during times of depression). Had labor organizations adopted the policy of establishing worker cooperatives, they could have eliminated the issue of competition altogether by constructing their own job base. The desire to socially discriminate—which rendered the excluded more desperate for jobs—was instead advanced as a natural right of white hegemony. In effect, though the free labor ideology advanced the notion that slavery degraded all labor, the discrimination against free black workers meant that the free labor ideology was a disguise for the idea that black labor in any form degraded the honor of white labor. The implication is that the free labor ideology did not necessarily oppose slavery; it only sought to exclude black people from newly settled territories, or from growing industrial occupations, in the guise of excluding slavery.

But the free labor ideology was more complex than a slogan about labor dignity, class recognition, or a producer ethic. On the one hand, it was a political rhetoric specifically directed toward artisans and skilled laborers, adopted in large part by those opposed to the southern plantation aristocracy's hegemony in the federal government. Because it presented itself as an antislavery program for the new territories, it served to counter the movement for an extension of slavery and the growth of southern power that would represent. When the Republican Party was organized by bringing many antislavery forces together expressly in opposition to southern hegemony, it adopted the free labor platform toward that purpose. On the other hand, by functioning in the arena of national politics, the free labor program served to bridge certain class distinctions. As Foner points out, "free labor" also meant a condition of labor that had choices ahead of it (FS, 17). It assumed for itself a certain class mobility. The "freedom" of "free labor" was the ability to rise from common wage laborer to skilled laborer, to foreman, and eventually to forms of self-employment.[11] A laborer who worked hard, and made the right decisions and connections, should be able to escape the domain of wage labor altogether and go into business. In the Midwest, this meant homesteading and producing a cash crop; in the urban centers of California, it meant shop ownership (FS, 14).

In essence, the free labor ideology declined to admit that any irreconcilable contradiction existed between workers and capitalists (FS, 19ff). It promoted a sense of social homogeneity for which economic (class) stratification was implied to be of secondary importance. Though it recognized that capitalism produced its working class for itself in order to put it to work producing capital for capital, the free labor ideology infused this with a populist sense of common interest; labor depended on capital for employment and capital depended on labor to get the job done. The social parity implicit in mutual dependence translated into a promise of political inclusion and common economic participation in the growth of social wealth and well-being. That is, it was a bargain with capital in which labor got recognition for being essential; it was given a sense of partnership through class mobility and inclusion in the political processes behind the organization and development of society (FS, 15). This bargain was congruent with the other bargain contained in the subtle conflation of labor with white supremacy, the antecedent bargain of white solidarity that the plantation elite had long before made with the poorer farmers through the organization of the patrols. "Free labor" signified that the producer classes would be white, in conformity with the old forms of white solidarity. Labor solidarity existed, and European immigrant workers arrived bearing the ideas of class struggle as practiced in Europe. But the bargain superseded that class consciousness and affirmed the tacit agreement on a mutual recognition of interest, that neither class would abandon the concerns of the other. Indeed, in the 1850s in California, a populist movement erupted against the importation of Chinese labor, led by the Workingmen's Party, because white labor felt that capital had betrayed that bargain (IE, 78). After a number of pogroms against various Chinatowns, social stability was restored through occupational segregation and the passage of the Chinese Exclusion Act of 1882.

Thus, labor's exclusion of workers of color, free labor ideology, and the ideal of class mobility were tied together as a mutually conditioning confluence of processes. Some historians have seen this as a coalition of classes rather than a class collaboration;[12] for them, this coalescence was a temporary tactic advanced for specific social purposes rather than a political process in obedience to tradition and expressing something deeply cultural in U.S. thinking. But the fact that a coalescence of classes occurred through a common mode of domination and exclusion of black (or brown or Asian) people, toward which each established a form of property relation (as white), suggests the latter is more probably the case.[13]

There were serious contradictions in labor's bargain with capital and in the assumption of class mobility. From labor's point of view, capital had to go beyond mere recognition of labor as part of its society and give that recognition material weight by paying wages that would permit social advancement. From the perspective of capital, workers needed to recognize the indispensability of profit maximization demanded by intercapitalist competition. Competition made the need for growth and increased profitability primary over social recognition of the interests of labor, and it implied, under all conditions, the minimization of labor and production costs. To mask this contradiction, labor competition was given social valorization over labor as such. This tied a worker's possibility of social advancement through self-employment in business to industrial profits rather than to the worker's savings. Further, it legitimized the prioritizing of capitalist competition over common interest by rhetorically equating it to labor competition.

At the same time, the growth of large-scale mass-production industry made on-the-job competition between workers untenable as a mode of common advancement, and raised to new heights the level of capital needed to start a small business. In all, through growth, the narrowing of the competitive field, and the power of profit maximization, capital became more exploitative and placed severe practical limits on class mobility. This engendered the general feeling that industry had betrayed its social bargain, and it motivated the early labor movement to adopt a populist form. Labor engaged in electoral politics rather than focus on union organization, and acted against nonwhite competition. At the same time (at least until the 1890s), white industrial workers tended to reject industrial unionism as a violation of the bargain between labor and capital (we shall return to this question below). In its demands on capital, free labor populism came to consider the size of capitalist enterprise to be what rendered it oppressive and exploitative of labor, rather than its internal dynamic. Because size hindered worker mobility (RFL, 33–34) size and opposition to oligopolistic capital became the focus of an anti-exploitation stance. Thus, even the later movements of the 1890s against large-scale industry, railroads, and Wall Street banking were not anticapitalist as such; for them, it was not the system itself that was at fault but its having violated the bargain of class parity through trustification.[14] It was in part in response to the vast populist upsurge at the turn of the twentieth century that the antitrust legislation of that time was passed.

Clearly, the contradictions in the free labor ideology were astounding. White workers opposed black people to exclude slavery, and opposed slavery to exclude black people. Calling itself "free labor," it excluded free black workers as unfree. Calling itself a "labor ideology," it excluded a section of labor from solidarity with itself. Relying on numbers to build strength, the labor movement weakened itself by diminishing its own ranks to the extent of its exclusions. Tacitly white supremacist, it took hold most strongly in the new territories where the traditional white solidarity against an enslaved black working class did not exist, where white workers could have begun afresh with new forms of organization and new attitudes, and where their multiracial numbers would have given them greater political leverage. In effect, labor sought to solidify its political position by weakening itself as a class political force. That is, white workers sought to create a class political position for which labor unity was essential, but they succeeded only in establishing a white class position, a racialized position that would not involve class opposition to the white elite (capitalism).

But what concept of class is being revealed by the free labor ideology? Marxism, which defines class through relations to the means of production, is superseded by an historical social cohesion to whiteness in which a proprietary claim to social status by whites, exercised through exclusion, becomes itself a relation to property as well as a form of social property. The sociological approach to class which positions all in a middle class who can show citizenship and an ability to afford certain minimal material amenities is superseded by the even broader social homogeneity and inner consensuality of white solidarity that was earlier engendered as a political culture in the colonies through the operations of the patrols. The depth of affect of the free labor ideology seems to extend even up to the present. David Roediger raises this as an issue in *The Wages of Whiteness*.[15] He discusses the class language of white workers and critically elucidates the way white workers speak about their class situation. He shows how class is subtly and tacitly (as well as openly) linked to race (through rhetorical references to "slave labor," for instance) and thus to white supremacy. Late in the twentieth century, racial terms function as a cultural language, gaining class force through the rhetoric of their racialized origin, which Roediger's demonstrations implicitly link to carryovers from the free labor ideology. In short, white supremacist thinking still constitutes an important element of white working-class identity. Its contradictions with traditional class analyses suggest that what constitutes working-class consciousness in the United States is somewhat more complex than the accounts given by either sociology or Marxism. Clearly, an alternative view of class relations is needed.

Labor Competition and White Worker Identity

The issue of the labor competition offered by slavery in the North was the first issue raised politically by white workers as workers in the new nation. White labor opposed the existence of slavery not because slavery was unjust but because the competition was unfair. Worker organizations sporadically petitioned local and state legislatures from the 1790s on to bar slave employment in various industries or economic sectors on which they depended (NS, 161ff).

Labor competition is a significant issue. When a job is the only way to survive, the question of jobs becomes central to all other considerations. In communal situations, where work is socialized in the sense of being divided democratically among those available to do it, and the proceeds divided equitably among those who worked, competition is not an issue. Yet only in short-lived instances have communities sought to create such conditions, to obviate or transcend labor competition through communal means. Furthermore, during the entire history of the United States, immigration has been an issue associated with labor competition. Immigration and labor competition have been inseparable at the core of working-class politics, as sources of class division.

During the first half of the nineteenth century, labor competition was an issue peculiar to the North. There, the politics of employment were different from the South. Throughout the eighteenth century, in the South, the slave labor force was the working class, mass producing the wealth of that society. White workers, who worked mainly as artisans in small enterprises, or in transportation and commerce, were ancillary to plantation production. Industries, such as coke or hemp, that developed alongside the plantation economy, as part of its technological base, were often operated with slave labor. According to Starobin, in mining, iron foundries, tobacco, sugar, and brick production, to mention a few, slave labor was employed almost exclusively.[16] During times of economic crises or recession, white workers attempted to take over various job categories in those industries and exclude slave employment from them (not generally those jobs characterized as hard, menial, or dangerous). But southern capital had a motive for excluding white workers. What contributed to the use of slaves in industry was that white workers could organize and form associations, while black enslaved laborers could not. The state suppressed slave organization with violent means that it was reticent to use against whites, means that white labor was willing to support on the understanding that those means would not be used against itself. Union organization and overt strikes among black bond-laborers was considered insurrection and dealt with harshly. Resistance existed among African American laborers, but it expressed itself most often through slowdowns, stealing, sabotage, and feigned illness. While they constituted the working class, their means of "class" struggle were more closely curtailed than those of any others. White workers were thus a potential political threat to capitalist hegemony that black workers were not. Though perhaps not as profitable as wage labor, slavery was the most efficient means of insuring labor's availability, of binding laborers to enterprise and making them work (ISS, 117).

In the northern states, after the Revolution, a different politics of employment unfolded. There were fewer black bond-laborers, and they were not employed in the primary wealth-producing sectors. Northern economics revolved around commerce, manufacturing, and small-scale agriculture (NS, 4). The slave trade, with its mammoth profitability, had been the foundation of most industrial investment in New England during the eighteenth century. But slave laborers were only employed in small numbers, many working as domestics rather than production workers. A larger percentage of black bond-laborers were skilled artisans and tradesmen than in the South, however, of a competence equaling or exceeding that of white skilled workers. The labor costs they represented were less than for white wage labor, since they worked under absolute constraint.

DuBois quotes what was, in the pre–Civil War years, a fairly common sentiment: "I've seen white mechanics unemployed ... while black slave mechanics could get plenty of work" (BR, 28). But one would have to look carefully at this. The verb "could get" attributes agency to the black worker that, as a slave, he could not fully have. The speaker is attributing to the black worker, as slave to an owner, the same ability to negotiate and maneuver that a white worker as slave to wages has. The verb form signifies a desire to ignore the black bond-laborer's condition of servitude and see him as competition. It attributes a motivation the black worker would not have in order to hold it against him. Work may be imperative for both; the wages system makes work imperative for the laborer. But the coercion of slavery sets that imperative elsewhere for a bond-laborer, out of the laborer's control. In effect, the statement transforms the black worker's situation in order to discover competition with the white. The attribution of agency in the verb creates the black worker as a competitor in order to then see him as such.

There is a deeper structure to "slave mechanics could get plenty of work." In this expression, the black mechanics are first of all mechanics, since that line of work is the content of the observation; the fact that they are enslaved is subsidiary to that. As mechanics, they are also given agency as having learned the trade. In other words, the black worker is first recognized as a person (mechanic), while his personhood is taken away by the second act of recognition (as slave). In a third step, on the basis of this reduction of status, the nonperson (slave mechanic) is given back his humanity as an agent who goes out to "get" work, now as a malign being who takes a job from a white worker in need. The overall structure is one of granting personhood in order to take it away, canceling personhood in order to reduce status, and reducing status in order to return personhood as reduced. This form of triple thinking is a logic that is characteristic of racism. It mediates the imposition of a negative valuation on all that the subjugated person does. The issue of competition simply exhibits this logic with particular clarity.

But the reality of slave competition lies elsewhere as well, in the political economy of slavery. That political economy must be included if what the white worker is really doing in charging competition is to be understood.

In the North, with its small-scale agriculture, a diversified commerce, a burgeoning manufacturing sector, and primarily wage labor economy, the hiring of slaves became a widespread practice in the years after the Revolution. This meant that the bond-laborer would work for someone not the "owner," and the owner would get paid for the "use" of the bond-laborer. African American bond-laborers, though generally of equal skill with the white laborers, were paid less, having little choice in the matter.[17] For the employer, the bond-laborer's "owner" was providing a service through the use of his or her "capital goods." For the other workers, these laborers who appeared on job sites working at lower wages served primarily to depress wage levels. Both white "owners" thus reaped the benefits, and white-worker bargaining power was diminished.

Thus, black bond-laborers again mediated the relations among the white elite, capitalists and employers. The white owner of a black worker functioned as a kind of service-sector capitalist. The worker whose labor he leased to others (whether directly or by the black worker finding his or her own job) provided a service to other (white) employers in the form of cheaper labor. If their "service" was in demand, it was because the black bond-laborer's work was as good as anyone else's, while being cheaper. But that was incidental to the relation of service provided by one white owner to another. The black worker constituted, and mediated, a relation between white employers, rather than a relation between labor and capital. As industry developed, slave labor was at times employed to replace wage workers who had organized and struck an enterprise. This again was a "service" provided by the elite to itself. If the effect was to direct the attention of white labor organizations against the bond-laborers rather than the employers, it was because white labor was too deeply implicated in the structure of white society.

Against the competition of black bond-laborers, the white wage workers in fact had little recourse. While the competition came in the form of a slave, and took the guise of an African American bond-laborer, it was actually the white owner who constituted it and imposed it. The African American worker who filled the employment position only constituted the competition by proxy. Yet there was no common arena on which the white worker and the white slaveowner actually confronted each other. The slaveowner merely stayed in the background, exercising his or her "property rights." When white craftsmen and laborers petitioned various state governments (or colonial governments before the Revolution) to prohibit the use of slaves in various trades, it was generally to no avail. No prohibitions were imposed on the prerogatives of property, which took precedence over any complaint. Yet the rancor against the African American bond-laborers increased because the terms of the complaint focused on them (BBN, 44ff).

The social dynamic of slavery thus forced the majority of white laborers and skilled workers in two directions: down into the most exploited of conditions, begging for work as artisans, or out to the periphery of the economy in the new territories. That is, slavery pushed white workers toward two forms of marginalization through this structure of proxy competition. At the same time, black workers were forced to bear the brunt of class and personal antagonisms and conflicts among whites. Used by capital against white labor, and despised by white labor in its conflicts with white capital, the black worker was both the arena on which whites fought their class skirmishes with each other and the buffer that kept those disputes from ever really erupting into class warfare (NS, 160).

No recourse was open to black workers either. Against whom were they to rebel? Controlled by their owners, exploited by the employers to whom they were hired, and assaulted by the animosity of white workers who chose to see them as an enemy, they had nowhere to turn for solidarity but themselves, and had the entire white society to target even in their most minimal resistance. In effect, only the most extreme political positions and ideas (of either acquiescence or rebellion) offered themselves as realistic. White workers had the luxury of class collaboration bequeathed to them by the existence of the slave system, and by the structure of suppression of black bond-laborers (the intermediary control stratum). But black workers had only the daily desperation of their situation.[18]

In the face of this desperation, for which white workers were partially responsible, white workers were in a double bind. To rebel against the true nature of the competition they faced from the slave system would have meant discarding the structure of white solidarity that sustained them. Refusing to confront it by blaming the black workers for the competition meant accepting depressed economic conditions in the name of whiteness. To make common cause with black bond-laborers in the name of labor solidarity meant to break with white solidarity, and to break with whiteness in the name of solidarity with bond-laborers meant to betray labor solidarity by making a juridically impossible common cause with unfree labor. Either way, one subordinated oneself to the elite owners through an unacceptable form of class collaboration. Between labor solidarity and white solidarity there lay only betrayal and collaboration with the owners.

Thus, the entire tradition of the control stratum, the job of policing the mass of bond-laborers and the bargain of white solidarity, now a century old, operated against class consciousness. A class-conscious worker was caught between an impossible class solidarity (with black workers) that would appear to other white workers as unacceptable collaboration (with the white elite), and a class-collaborationist solidarity (with the white elite) that rendered real working-class solidarity (with black workers) impossible. To seek either one meant breaking white working-class ranks—both a source of disunity and a threat to identity. The result would have been any of a number of possible social ostracisms. The effect was to conjoin one's identity as white and as a worker into one. Class solidarity was equated with white solidarity; white solidarity implied class collaboration; and thus class solidarity implied class collaboration. It is from the circle of this paradox that a sense of white working-class identity began to emerge in the United States. Black workers were thus thrust into the role of mediating the relationship between white workers in a more determinate way than did white capital, precisely because white workers saw themselves as white.

As an early (and ironic) expression of their situation, and in the face of the unconfrontability of slave competition under the slave system, white workers in the North became active in calling for the abolition of slavery. Petition was made to local and state governments to bar slaves from various industries and trades, and proposals to abolish slavery altogether were supported by trade organizations and craft guilds. But abolishing slavery in the North turned out to be a slow process. In public debates, though the issue was driven by greater or lesser belief in the ideals of the Revolution, and by the deleterious effects slavery had on labor conditions, the central issue became the practical question of compensation to the owners to be deprived of their "property" by such measures. The abolition laws that were passed required slaves to work for years, sometimes decades, or up to a certain age, to compensate their owners for their "loss." For instance, children born of slaves in Pennsylvania were required to remain as "servants" until twenty-eight years of age.

The result was a gradualism that reflected the perspective and predominance of capital values, rather than democratic principles or the perspective of the person doing forced labor in thrall. Omitted was any mention that slavery was kidnapping and the owners were accessories, both being crimes under British law. Even the Quakers, whose earliest opposition (1688) to slavery recognized that "negroes were men," only projected gradual freedom "after some reasonable time" (NP, 66). Life and liberty remained secondary considerations to the right to own property. Though Pennsylvania prided itself on a long history of opposition to slavery, principally among the Quakers, it was unable to accomplish abolition in any but a slow and convoluted manner that allowed owners to squeeze out the last bit of compensation before relinquishing their property (NP, 82).

Massachusetts was an exception, but there the question was avoided altogether in light of a chance court decision, amid a lot of footdragging by antislavery advocates. In 1781, an African American bond-laborer sued for freedom on the basis of a promise of manumission by his owner, claiming as well that slavery had never been legal in Massachusetts anyway.[19] He won, and the case led quietly to the collapse of the slave system in that state; the census of 1790 reported that there were no slaves in Massachusetts (Z, 115). But in general, the abolition of slavery proceeded only gradually. Though slavery had become an embarrassment to legislatures in its contradiction to democratic principles, it was resolved on the plane of economics without having to grant the freed slave humanity. The freeing of slaves was seen as a moral act by the abolitionist movement, but it was considered by most white people an expropriation of a person's assets by government whose compensation would place an undue burden on the taxpayer. That is, within the corporate state, neither the owner nor the state was to incur expense in the process. Nothing was written into the law to grant black people humanity or political rights.

What lurks under the surface of this dispute is the awareness that slavery, the complex mediation of social relations between whites, between members of the elite, between classes in the economy, by African American bond-laborers, was essentially responsible for social stability. Emancipation was reduced to the issue of compensation, rather than ethics or rights, signaling that U.S. society was willing to compromise principle in the name of property and profitability as the dimensions of stability.

What is significant about white workers' support for the abolition of slavery was that, after slavery was abolished, they turned against the freed slaves and ostracized them. Black workers were barred from white labor organizations, and white workers, individually or as a group, refused to work with black workers. In many cases, this became guild policy. Increasingly, throughout the North, from 1790 to the 1840s, white workers opposed black employment in most crafts, and at times boycotted establishments that hired black workers (BBN, 183). They initiated or supported programs for legislated segregation of housing and the disfranchisement of all black people. In state after state, the right to vote and to participate in the judicial process (to serve on juries, to bring suit in court, to bear witness) was curtailed or left unenacted. In short, in the first few decades of the nineteenth century, the prototypes of later Jim Crow structures were instituted in the northern states.

The major charges levied against black workers to ground the rhetoric of exclusion were that free black laborers constituted unfair competition and that their work was inferior, that as laborers they were incapable of good work. Ironically, the latter charge was levied at precisely the time when the skills of black workers were at their height, equal to or better than the skills of white workers. Of course, the charge of inferior work contradicted the former charge, that (now free) black workers constituted competition. In the 1830s (in Connecticut and Pennsylvania in particular), white workers petitioned state legislatures to exclude black workers from certain jobs and professions, ironically complaining that whenever black people got employment, the white workers would be outcompeted and have to leave the area to find work (Z, 223–225). It was a tacit admission that the work was not inferior, at least from the employer's standpoint, and for that reason in demand. In effect, the white charge of black inferiority was a rhetorical demand for a monopoly over jobs, and it involved conscious and organized falsification. Of course, the confinement of black workers to certain menial jobs also served a familiar psychological function to which many whites admitted:[20] "If they did not do it, we would have to" (NS, 156).

By excluding black workers from their organizations in the name of combating labor competition, the white workers thereby created the competition they decried. In their rhetoric of black labor competition, which remained the same after abolition as before (though the black worker was more of an autonomous person), they were implying that they actually believed the black worker had been the cause of slavery and the real source of competition even as a slave, that black people created all those conditions (slavery, cheap labor, chattel status) for themselves. The desire to then exclude black labor from employment continued in programmatic form the paranoia through which black people were seen as social nemesis. That it is expressed at the very moment of emancipation implies that it antedated that moment. It is as if white workers had agitated to free the slaves in order to free themselves to be able to express a prejudice and hostility to which the institution of slavery had actually been an obstacle.

There were clear alternatives to the stance taken on competition. Ideas about worker cooperatives were extant, both in New England and Europe. At a time of economic upswing, worker cooperatives could have absorbed all additional laborers, both freed slaves and newly arrived immigrants, by creating their own job base. Instead of founding cooperative organizations, white workers supported abolition to free themselves for unhampered hegemony in the labor field (that is, unhampered by what they considered the "blight" of black employment). In effect, they chose prejudice over autonomy and unity.

The irony is that it occurs at the moment when white workers in the northern states had the greatest stake in swelling their ranks, to create a place for themselves as an important political force in the newly founded states. Without extensive property or economic resources, organizational size and solidarity constitute a worker's source of strength. For this reason, newly arrived immigrants were welcomed into their communities and associations—but not black workers. Litwack mentions that "White labor feared not only the competition of Negroes in the skilled trades, but also the loss of social status which resulted from associating with them" (NS, 158). In other words, at a time of new beginning, white workers traded away their potential strength for an old form of social status (through exclusion) they saw as more necessary to their identity. It is not enough to say this represents what Marxists call "false consciousness" on the part of white workers, as socialists have been saying for over a century. Race itself (not to mention racism) is already false consciousness. The very concepts of white and black, of race, of white solidarity and white racialized identity, even to the extent they constitute the basis of sociopolitical structures in the United States, are all forms of false consciousness. For the working class, white solidarity took precedence over class political influence; it was chosen over class autonomy as a preferred channel of political influence. It represented the class consciousness that white workers organizationally had chosen to accept for themselves.

Few statistics are available on the unfolding of the many forms of extrajuridical segregation that occurred. Frederick Douglass bemoans the fact, at the very time he was writing (1830s), that "every hour sees the black man elbowed out of employment" (BBN, 184; NP, 148ff). The Abolition Convention, in 1827, deplored the exclusion of black people from the skilled trades (NS, 171). In Philadelphia, a riot occurred in 1834 in which whites attacked the black community, destroying homes and buildings and beating people indiscriminately because blacks were being hired instead of whites. In other parts of Pennsylvania, meetings of "working men and others" sought to organize boycotts of employers who hired black people to do work that white workers reserved for themselves ("had been accustomed to perform") (NS, 101). Turner reports that, from 1800 to 1850, black people were beaten on the street throughout Pennsylvania, churches were burned, mobs attacked black communities at will, and in some cases rendered whole communities refugees in their own country. In Columbia, Pennsylvania, in 1834, under the threat of rioting, whites forced black homeowners and business owners to sell their property and leave town. Turner affirms that the feeling against blacks was strongest among working-class whites (NP, 146).

As violence became the prevalent mode of preventing black employment in work that white workers had reserved for themselves (NS, 159), disfranchisement accompanied the process. Whether black people were constitutionally barred from voting or not (they could vote in Massachusetts; they lost the right to vote in Pennsylvania after 1838), they were prevented from voting by whites (mostly working class) as an appropriation of voting itself as white. Riots occurred when blacks attempted to vote in Philadelphia. The threats made against those who tried were made openly, often in the press. Thus, the poorer whites continued their labor as patrols.

In effect, the white workers were accomplishing two things. First, they were maintaining their earlier role as intermediary control stratum, substituting exclusion and ostracism for their earlier policing. As the patrols of earlier times, white workers had essentially produced and consolidated the class structure of white owners and black workers, for which they themselves as workers were marginal; in the nineteenth century, they constructed a more complex class relation between white capital and themselves through the marginalization of the freed black workers. Thus, the second thing they accomplished was to overcome their former marginalization as white labor by excluding those who had previously constituted the working class under the plantation system, thereby establishing themselves as the working class. In exchanging margin for center, they assumed the identity of working class in place of being the police force of other class relations. In that sense, segregation and racism constituted essential elements of class self-definition. And in analogy with the former patrols, they again acted to produce a class structure. When white workers adopted the free labor ideology in the 1840s, they had already defined themselves as a class through the exclusionism it contained.

In sum, by establishing their hegemony through segregation, the white workers were seizing the identity of the working class itself from those others who had been that class previously (and still were in the South). This perhaps explains why white workers in the North made so little common cause with the slaves of the South; it would have put an end to their hegemony in the working class as a whole. They may not have articulated it to themselves in these terms, but their conscious exclusion and nonsolidarity with black workers, free or bound, testifies to it. The process of self-definition as a class, and self-valorization as white, occurred through the political process of initiating class segregation made possible by abolition in the North.

The major role of racism was not to divide the working class but to define the working class and what class solidarity was to include. If its other role was to divide people, that was a secondary function, since it depended on the primary role of creating the conditions in which to operate in that way. Racism is now a division in the working class and stands in the way of class organization and unity. But the unity it stands in the way of is between people who, because they have been previously racialized, confront each other across a class difference. If it is true that racism is a source of division in the working class, the reason is that it is the chief source of unity for part of that class.

This points out a central effect of early-nineteenth-century segregation; black workers were swiftly relegated to unskilled labor. "Northern emancipation took the form of economic displacement" (BBN, 197). Over time, through nonemployment and marginalization, they lost their skills and crafts. Starting with little or nothing beyond their skills, they were then deprived of a means of living beyond brute or menial labor. That is, they were relegated to proletarianized social status, which accompanied the politicization of their blackness through disfranchisement. In seizing working-class identity, white workers participated in consigning nonwhite labor, through exclusion, to a class status wholly different from theirs—that is, their relationship to black people had all the earmarks of a class relation.[21] In contradistinction to the propertylessness and disappropriation of black proletarianization, white workers aggrandized themselves by establishing entitlement in whiteness. They always had something more than their labor power to sell, something else to trade on. As Herbert Blumer argues (RFL, 18), this "sense of proprietary claim" to a certain social position, that is, an entitlement to certain jobs and job categories, became the content of the class distinction whose form was segregation,. For white workers, their whiteness signified nonproletarianization, a sense of propriety and social property as part of their claim for social recognition. Ultimately it is this class difference that the free labor idea expressed.

In short, white workers deployed black workers (through exclusion) to create whiteness for themselves as a social value, a social property, a form of social capital. Whiteness became a form of property right, valorizing all associated with it in relation to blacks, who were left in all senses propertyless. As social capital, whiteness inverted the sense in which African bond-laborers were capital values on the plantations. But the reservation of menial labor for black people by racial discrimination was only half the story; the restriction of black people to certain racialized job categories produced a class cohesiveness that amalgamated white workers as white (NS, 156). The proletarianization of black people served to produce a working-class identity as white, and to restructure society around whiteness as its cultural coherence. In other words, the concept of race marks a social structure rather than a biological characteristic. It is in fact a property relation, a mark of social status that differentiates those with (the) property from those without it.

As Allen suggests, there is a circularity to racism, a sense of mutual conditioning of its aspects. Where racialization established certain white privileges, it did so through a prior generalization or social dedifferentiation of black people. What racialization produced, as the setting aside and proletarianization of black people, was segregation. But black people had already been set aside as generalized, as a homogeneous group through the efforts of prior segregation. Thus, dedifferentiation (or generalization), racialization, and segregation were all productive of each other. Generalization produces racialization, racialization produces segregation, and segregation produces and intensifies generalization.

This cycle engages white people under different auspices at different times in the construction of white identity through the reduction of black people. In the 1690s, there was the role of colonial administration as enforcer. In the 1800s, there was the seizure of working-class identity as white. In the post-Reconstruction period, the rise of an industrial working class occurred through the increasing criminalization of black people as the motivation for increasingly harsh Jim Crow laws. Each epoch produced a new mode of oppression and segregation. The first was the production of the black laborers as the plantation working class (unpaid). The second was a reduction of black workers to unskilled (proletarianized) status in order that white workers become the working class. The third was white workers' universalization of white entitlement by absorbing the unskilled positions of new industry. In the first mode, generalization came first and produced racialization as new. In the second mode, reracialization occurred, leading to segregation and a new generalization. In the third mode, segregation was instituted that led to generalization and a new form of racialization.

Black people of course understood the import of the racial proletarianization being constructed for them at the hands of whites. It would mean the corruption of democracy, social stability, and morality for an entire nation. Argue as they would with white workers for class solidarity, and with whites in general for humanity and inclusion, for democracy and citizenship, it fell on deaf ears. David Walker's *Appeal* made such an argument in 1829. He was called a dangerous man and his pamphlet labeled sedition. DuBois put forth the argument in *The Souls of Black Folk* in 1900. It was ignored. When Malcolm X called the question on black proletarianization in 1963, he was assassinated. What made each of these black voices dangerous to white society was their assumption of black humanity, autonomy, and inclusion, and their call to black people to act on those self-evident attributes. Though whites have spoken of class solidarity among themselves throughout U.S. history, their refusal to hear about it from black voices signified that they actually understood racial segregation as a class difference, beyond the purview of class solidarity. In conflating white working-class consciousness with an allegiance to whiteness, nineteenth-century white workers submerged themselves not only in a self-serving deafness to the meaning of their proletarianization of the free black workers for black people, but in a similar blindness to what solidarity with the freed slaves would imply for class political influence, as well as to the class collaboration contained in their refusal.

In the United States, racism has always been a more powerful force in a worker's consciousness than class precisely because class relations are grounded in it. More than a mere division between people, racism is something white workers (along with all whites) have refused to relinquish because it is the foundation of their (working class) identity. The unions that grew along with evolving industrialization during the nineteenth century, rather than contest capitalism for hegemony, sought mainly to gain recognition from capital as white, and to secure certain jobs for whites. To embrace a politics of inclusive class solidarity would have meant giving up the foundation of their political participation in capitalist society. When the free labor ideology proclaimed the black worker inherently a slave, it was not out of habit, nor prejudice, nor simply because slave status had been central to inventing the racialized concepts of "black" and "white" in the first place. For white workers, it was an essential element of their own demarginalization, for their recognition by the elite—for which segregation was exchanged as the ordained task.

When twentieth-century industrial unionism brought black and white workers together in the same movements and organizations for the first time, the result was still an aberration, a freak union when seen through the eyes of European class struggle; an apolitical industrial union was something unheard of. The refusal of the industrial union movement to contest the prerogatives of capitalist property, its willingness to restrict itself to "bread and butter" issues, its acceptance (albeit bitterly) of runaway shops and the erosion of its own job base have all been reflections of the same cultural motif, the class collaborationism implicit in the fact that U.S. working-class consciousness is white. Those voices that do contest the prerogatives of capitalist property have always spoken of necessity from outside the union movements, because their call has been wholly abjured from within them. (The exception is the Western Federation of Miners, whose socialist position in the 1890s spearheaded the foundation of the Industrial Workers of the World, an event which so dazzled that union that it fled the IWW shortly thereafter, stripping the socialist banner from its constitution and changing its name.)

In sum, the segregation that followed northern abolition marks the moment of inception of the white working class as a class. It is an ambiguous class because it is not simply the product of capital. The white working class was a product of economic (capitalist) property, yet defined by a social property (whiteness) through which it became the producer of the society of (that) property.

Prior to emancipation, the African American bond-laborers on the plantation, and therefore elsewhere as well, constituted the working class, to which white workers were generally ancillary; after abolition, the role of marginalized worker was transferred from white to black. Two different forms of marginalization changed places. By marginalizing black workers, white workers asserted and seized a different place for themselves, a place they refused to black workers. If they supported abolition in pursuit of class interests, their involvement in the disfranchisement and segregation, as a reflection of a class consciousness, revealed what those class interests were, a claim on class being within a structure of racialization.

The Politics of Class Definition

The seizure of working-class identity by white workers, and their production of a class/property distinction between themselves and black workers, did not happen in a vacuum. From its inception, the new nation's political development provided a context that fostered it. Part of that context was the question of North and South hegemony in the federal government. Another was the evolution of the political party system. Social class consciousness is always a matter of political process. In this case, white working-class self-definition was abetted and co-opted by the developing party system, and used for the purpose of that system's self-definition.

After the Revolution, the plantation states, being the most populous, controlled Congress and the executive. The party of the southern landholders—whose name went through a number of changes: Republican under Jefferson, Democratic-Republican during the Andrew Jackson campaign, splitting off a National-Republican Party after that, and becoming the Democratic Party in 1829—was the dominant party until the 1850s. During that period, in all its guises, the Democratic Party was essentially the party of the ruling class. The northern state Democratic Party organizations, under both the wing and the shadow of southern Democratic hegemony, found themselves caught between northern movements to abolish slavery and southern Democratic demands that they advocate the continuation of slavery. The northern Democrats had in some manner to accede to those southern demands if they were to have any influence or get concessions from the controlling southern Democrats in the federal government (BBN, 186). Their proslavery position did not necessarily entail preserving slavery in the North, but it did advocate nonopposition to southern slavery or the extension of slavery to new western territories. The Democratic Party was, however, instrumental in slowing down the process of abolition in the northern states.

While the preservation of slavery was not feasible in the North, of major interest for the southern elite was a reduction of the living conditions for northern free black people to a level of destitution that would dissuade slaves in the South from running away. This was accompanied by demands that the northern states return runaways and fugitives.

The establishment of these conditions formed the basis of an alliance between white workers in the North and the Democratic Party. While white workers imposed employment segregation where they could, as a springboard for their own self-definition, the Democratic Party assisted by publicizing and propagandizing the issue of competition, and it introduced legislation to codify segregation and disfranchisement. While legislative prohibitions on employment rarely succeeded, the Democratic Party did get certain restrictions on the use of black labor passed. In exchange, having supported abolition in the North, northern white workers opposed abolition in the South through the Democratic Party. Their rationale was a version of the anticompetition argument: that abolition would free millions of workers who would come north and take their jobs. By the 1850s, as Eric Foner points out, when the Republican Party was building its constituency primarily among the middle classes and the self-employed, the Democratic Party was already the party of what one editorial termed the "aristocratically associated and affiliated . . . and the lowest class" (FS, 34). As the agents of the southern elite, the Democratic Party thus functioned to maintain a form of worker allegiance to the white elite in common cause against the freed slaves as workers. In short, while white workers were using segregation for class identity, the Democratic Party was assuming the political role traditionally played by the intermediary control stratum of maintaining white solidarity and white consensus.

Ultimately, the spread of segregation in the North enabled the southern plantation class to maintain its hold on the federal government. But the process of working-class self-definition provided, in complementary ways, a means for the Republican Party to contest the Democrats for control. When the Republican Party was organized in 1854, it brought together many political movements that had sought to keep slavery out of the new territories, as a way of undermining the proslavery majority in Congress. In the Midwest and in California, this movement foregrounded the slogan of "free labor," to steal a march on Democratic monopoly of the segregation issue in state legislatures. In other words, it used the same working-class desire for segregation co-opted by the Democrats in the East against the hegemony of the Democrats in the West.[22]

In effect, both parties functioned to valorize the political process by which the white workers of the North and West seized their identity as the working class. It was not the programmatics of either party (which were significantly different, and in ways antithetical) that led white workers to become racist and to invent the prototype structures of Jim Crow with respect to black workers. Rather, the white workers' traditional role, the vestiges of their social positionality within colonial society as the intermediary control stratum that structured slavery, already directed them down a road on which class consciousness and class collaboration, white supremacy and white solidarity, and the ethos of segregation were conflated and conjoined.

By the 1830s, as Larry Tise points out, the proslavery position was ubiquitous. It was not restricted to a certain economic interest or region, and was propounded by people within every stratum, state, class, and profession of the country. But opposition to slavery was just as ubiquitous, and the South was fighting a losing battle, trying hard to maintain an eroding hegemony. Antislavery founded itself on the ideals of the Declaration of Independence and the contradiction between slavery and those ideals. Yet this was a weak position to take. That same Declaration was used to defend the right to property, which included the right to own slaves, and the right to white entitlement. It could therefore be interpreted as applying only to white people. Just as the self-definition of the white working class could be used by both sides in the dispute over slavery, so could the Declaration of Independence. If what have been called the "American ideals" got lost in the political shuffle through overdetermined use, the concept of working-class interests got similarly lost between the co-optations of working-class identity and working-class consciousness.

White Supremacy and Class Consciousness

After emancipation, the white workers got the chance to be white workers, rather than split themselves between whiteness in one social situation (control stratum over black people) and class in another (capitalist enterprise). And they took it. Abolition gave them the ability to integrate economic class being and the cultural production of whiteness—a confluence of livelihood, social solidarity, and identity. No longer simply an intermediary control stratum caught between paternalism and patronage, they could now participate in policy through their activity—in this case, the segregation of black workers. White supremacy facilitated this by making a fictitious relation (competition by slave labor) seem real, and a real relation (reduction in social status by white slaveholders) seem fictitious. When the slaves were freed, the real economic relation of labor exploitation remained ghostly behind the disguise of white solidarity. In living the disguise, white workers enmeshed themselves in two class relations, each of which became the disguise for the other, rendering the disguise itself two-faced and impenetrable. The first was as the "producer class" in the "white nation," economically exploited though politically at the center; the second was as holders of "white property" through their proletarianizing of black workers, politically exploiting though economically at the margins.

One could not say that the white workers, after having seized their working-class identity, were wholly without consciousness of themselves as a class. DuBois quotes the iron molders in 1859 who referred to themselves as the "mechanics of America." It signified their ongoing concern with establishing a political position and presence for themselves in U.S. society (BR, 25). When they struck, they called for "labor solidarity" (then as now). But it did not include black workers, only white. Whiteness took precedence over full labor conjunction. It was black workers who would put forth the call for working-class solidarity, but that call was refused by whites on the unstated (and perhaps unthought) basis that there existed a property differential between themselves and those black workers.

This feeling became evident in the wake of the Civil War, when the first attempts to unionize U.S. industry on a national basis were launched. Though the inner structure of white working-class consciousness had its cultural origins in prewar segregation, it discernibly broke the surface afterwards. The National Labor Union (NLU) was one of the first such efforts. It dedicated itself to seeking the "success of republican institutions," and proclaimed the independence and honor of the "producing classes" as its goal.[23] By the "producing classes," the NLU meant wage workers, laborers, and artisans, and in its reference to "republican institutions" it affirmed its faith that class disputes could be handled through political structures and processes rather than social upheavals. In the NLU's ideology, unions were organized to give labor an equal voice, to adjudicate differences, and gain labor its rightful share of what it produced (CA, IX: 153). That is, its axiom was a shared interest between labor and capital, and against the excesses of the latter it sought recognition of labor's rightful place in the social scheme (CA, IX: 151).

Though the NLU recognized black workers as workers, it refused to include them organizationally. In spite of advocating overall worker unity, it called for black workers to form their own unions and their own locals. Common cause was proposed only grudgingly, as a pragmatic concern rather than a sense of class commonality: "if we don't make friends with them, capital will use them against us" (CA, IX: 159). Just as the craft workers of New England had done in 1800, they proclaimed black workers to be competition (automatically vilified as an implicit class enemy), and addressed them as an issue rather than as people in order to neutralize that competition. That is, black workers were considered outsiders, and talk of cooperation occurred only in the context of separation. In effect, the NLU looked at black workers through a sense of contradiction first, not of common class interest.

This is confirmed by the words of white observers to the 1869 National Colored Labor Convention in Washington, D.C. Black delegates to that convention who affirmed the white attitude toward labor organization, and the necessity to collaborate in "shared interest" with capital, were praised as intelligent. But when some delegates suggested that trade unions which excluded black workers were committing an injury to the class, they were declared to be unintelligible (CA, IX: 243ff). In effect, they had questioned the white solidarity upon which white working-class existence depended. The observers remarked, with temerity, that black workers "do not see as we do in this labor movement" (leaving unsaid what is not seen). They then reproached the black workers for not "joining us" in that movement—"joining" by building separate unions (CA, IX: 246). In other words, their tacit response was that solidarity with black workers would call in question the basis for white workers' identity as workers. The position that black workers found themselves in was a total anomaly. They existed in real class contradictions that they could speak about, but not be heard; and they could speak about white class relations that for them were not real, and be heard.

The contradiction with black workers that white workers prioritized over common cause extends into the present. It did not just represent a hegemonic stance toward black workers that said "It is up to you to do what we say." Support for segregation was part of a tacit alliance with capital as white. By and large, unions remained segregated until the civil rights movements tore down Jim Crow. Throughout the twentieth century, though class antagonisms have repeatedly shaken industrial capital, unions rarely allowed themselves to think of contesting profitability or questioning its propriety. Even the national labor upheavals (or "labor populism") of 1877 and 1894, with railroad unionization at their core and socialists in their leadership, did not as class movements contest the prerogatives of capital.[24] The Knights of Labor, which came the closest to constituting an alternative class-oriented political structure, plummeted and disappeared almost overnight as soon as it attempted to effect that alternate structure through actual strike activity (which quickly foregrounded the issue of including black workers or not). In 1907, J. P. Morgan proposed that large-scale industry recognize unions and unionism. The purpose, as he saw it, was that as industries got bigger and bigger, the job of labor discipline would get greater and more expensive. Labor unions and labor contracts would become a means of policing internal worker discipline, as a control stratum for the corporate structure of huge factories, without costing as much. Not only was he following directly in the footsteps of the Virginia colonial administration of the early 1700s, but he was reading the class consciousness of the unions as still bound to their historical bargain.

On the other hand, before unions were legalized by the New Deal, industrial unionism was often labeled treasonous, not because it betrayed the nation, or opposed profitability, but because, in its militancy, it organized all the workers in an industry. Those unions were betraying the original bargain of white solidarity made and assumed by the corporate state, in which one class guarantees the sanctity of whiteness, and the other class recognizes the first as essential to the production of white society. When the New Deal recognized the unions and the right to collective bargaining, it was returning to the "producer ethic" in a modern form, reestablishing the exchange of solidarity for recognition. In the mid-1990s, during the debates on NAFTA, the labor movement did not advocate labor solidarity across the border with Mexican workers; it took a protectionist stance instead, in solidarity with American business. It is a cultural and ideological thread woven through the fabric of white working-class consciousness that spans two entire centuries.

Protectionism, as a disguised form of white solidarity, and a rehash of earlier patronage structures, is perhaps the only stance that has ever made any sense to the white labor movement in the United States. It has always seen immigration as competition and called for its curtailment. Looking backward, one can see it expressed before the Civil War in various antiblack campaigns; in Pennsylvania, immigration was a predominant issue for which whites turned to protectionism, not against foreign immigrants, but against the arrival of runaway slaves, refugees escaping the extreme bondage and repression of neighboring southern states (NP, 150).

After the Revolution, repression and duress increased in the South, and more stringent laws were passed against free African Americans in those states. Looking for freedom, they came north with very little, and sought only to live a useful but autonomous life. Many settled in Pennsylvania, and it was in that state that the Underground Railroad was first organized. In 1847, Pennsylvania even passed a law barring compliance with the federal fugitive slave act. Yet, at the same time, increased immigration from the South intensified the processes of discrimination already in place in that state. Its rationales were powered by the familiar circle of prejudice. When newly arrived refugees from slavery sought to vote, they were denied on the basis that, as former or runaway slaves, they were unfit for the franchise. If they did not seek the vote, in order to live unnoticed as far as possible, they were deemed unfit for not having participated in the democratic process.[25] If nothing else, that circle was used to ground eventual disfranchisement. Disfranchisement, and the failure to vote in the face of white hostility and open violence, Turner reports, then became a cause of contempt toward black people. Thus, Pennsylvania revealed at the level of state policy that old familiar stance of being antislavery and antiblack at the same time.

Of course, an immediate effect of white anti-immigrant discrimination was pauperism. While more refugees from slavery managed to arrive in Pennsylvania, their numbers amounted to diminished employment opportunity and more restricted living space in the face of increased hostility. More people crowded into smaller neighborhoods, producing destitution and a further depression in wages. In 1815, a commission was empanelled to derive methods of preventing the immigration of black people from the South. Even the Quakers lamented the "deterioration in character" of African Americans in Philadelphia. They evidently were not living up to the "civilizing" efforts of the "good white folks." Housing segregation grew under the fear of depreciating real estate values (NS, 169). Again there was the familiar circle: "We would not rent anything but a cellar to black people, but we don't want people in this neighborhood who would be willing to live in a cellar" (NS, 170). That is, the effects of segregation are used as the reason to segregate.[26]

The white demand within this structure of prejudice was always that black people come up to white standards of sociality (a nondescript and undefinable quality often called "civilization"); yet the very establishing of such a standard already implies that no black person would ever succeed. That failure was built into the very concept of creating a standard in the first place in such a domain. If the ability to come up to any standard is not a question, then it does not become an issue. When it is promulgated as an issue, the resulting standard may govern inclusion in form, but in content it constitutes exclusion itself. It is not a standard the standard makers have to meet. Rather, the standard makers are the standard, and the fact that they make one (on being "civilized," for instance) serves only to lock their prior judgment into place socially. In other words, to have met the standard means that none existed for one. To try to meet the standard means a priori not to have met it. The fact that this is decided a priori for those outside means it attaches to their very being; that is why it implies they will never meet the standard. The impossibility (and indignity) contained in the imposition of a white standard was evident to most black people; for not bowing to such indignity, and not making the attempt to meet it, they were in general punished. For whites, such standards have always been a huge game, one of their many acts of hegemony, in deciding what would constitute "progress" toward being "civilized."

After all, to proclaim that black people must make or "had made" progress only revalorizes the notion of inferiority attached to the concept of progress in the first place. It implies that progress must be made toward being equal to whites. But in practice, would this mean being equal in racism? In the ability to discriminate against black people? Would it mean equal support for white segregationist policies? It was not up to African Americans to become equal with whites in being free from attacks by whites. Black people had lived in white society all their lives, and navigated and fended off its constant attacks on them successfully. That was something no whites had ever had to do; on that score, it was whites who were essentially unequal, being inferior in that capability.

But the parallels between the 1800s and today go beyond the issue of immigration. Whites complained that black people would become wards of the state, ignoring the fact that many had nowhere else to turn under white segregationist policies and hostilities. A tax was proposed in 1804 on free black Pennsylvanians specifically to be used to support indigent black people, should that become necessary. Again, it was the familiar circle of barring people from supporting themselves and then judging them unworthy because indigent, and thus to be taxed. In 1834, white workers demanded that the state assembly set even more job categories aside as off limits for black workers (NP, 159). If anything, such segregation only marks the competence with which black workers did compare with white workers on the job. The black community fought back against discrimination and disfranchisement through the courts, with petitions to Congress and state legislatures, and the formation of organizations, in order to open for themselves the possibility of living autonomous lives, but to no avail (NS, 73, 74, 87). By 1850, except for the few who had some property, the black population was essentially relegated to shantytowns on the margins of the state's major cities.

Another issue of those early decades that similarly mirrors the present was crime. No one can deny that poverty breeds unlawful means of surviving; to remedy that, one must alleviate the causes of poverty. As Ruth Gilmore has said, crime is not a realm into which one simply wanders; it is produced in certain people by social processes of criminalization, which are used to reinforce the state and reestablish its legitimacy. But in 1820 (as in 1990), black crime was not seen as a result of discrimination or impoverishment, but of racial malignancy. That is, it had an absoluteness and generality that only emerges from the prior and general criminalization of a group. The prisons were filled with black people at four times their proportion of the population. Moreover, certain black neighborhoods were reported to be unsafe for white people to walk in. The reported behaviors that made the black quarters dangerous were mostly style of life items, social comportment on the street or rowdy working-class behavior in taverns. Nevertheless, they took on the aura of criminality for those reporting because they pertained to a black community.

If the issues that whites were using to construct themselves as white in the early nineteenth century are the same as those at the beginning of the twenty-first, then the United States as a nation has made no progress over two hundred years of its existence. It still has to use the same old modes of denigration and criminalization, of repression and disfranchisement, to sanctify itself as a free and democratic nation.

What would have shown progress and promise would have been, for instance, international solidarity with Mexican unions and peasant organizations against NAFTA, or the development of worker cooperatives that would reconstitute an autonomous and growing job base. The alternative of using the organizational strength of unions to underwrite the formation of cooperatives, into which as many workers as possible could be welcomed, has never had currency. It was up to the Black Labor convention of 1869 to make the call for cooperative workshops and building and loan associations (BR, 364). For black workers, such remedies were repeatedly necessary in the face of racial segregation and exclusionism; for white unions to have been open to such remedies would imply that they saw themselves as autonomous political forces, outside the rules of the white bargain. This issue recalls again the primacy of the Racial Contract, as Charles Mills describes it.

DuBois points out an interesting inversion of the idea of class collaboration under which white workers labored (BR, 209). After 1865, southern poor and middle-class whites generally felt that black people should not have the vote, since they would be controlled by the landowners, giving the landholding class an unfair advantage; that is, it would unbalance white interclass relations. It was an alienation of black people by poor whites that recalls the charge of "unfair competition" levied by white workers in the North. This argument (which was opposed to free labor but in harmony with the "free labor ideology") was an extension of the prejudice that black people were naturally servile, that black workers were thus wholly factotums of the rich and would vote as the rich dictated. It echoes the act of holding the slave responsible for his or her competition under slavery, and ultimately for slavery itself.

What it does not assume is that solidarity between white and black workers is possible. Indeed, it assumes that such a possibility has already been obviated before the fact. Yet again, the discrimination and exclusion to which black workers had already been subjected would have left them nowhere to turn but the paternalism of the elite. It is another example of the self-fulfilling proposition. It is the conceptual circle known as "blaming the victim"—whites holding against blacks what whites have done to them. The cycle of violence by poor whites against black people, and the subsequent ability to use black workers to undermine poor white conditions of life, becomes unending. What makes the "logic" of that circle work, or rather what makes that circle look like logic, DuBois suggests, is that any attempt at autonomy by black people, to extricate themselves from their instrumental deployment between poor and rich whites, leads immediately to aggression and violence against them from both sides (BR, 489). If black autonomy threatens rich and poor whites alike, even in their conflicts with each other, it simply demonstrates that not only is the rich-poor conflict predicated on a prior commonality, but that commonality is grounded precisely on the nonautonomy of black people, an enforced nonautonomy with respect to which whites look autonomous, especially in relation to each other.

This cycle not only has a long tradition but has always been predicated on violence. For instance, while arguing against abolition in 1836, Senator Leigh of Virginia pointed to the several white mob riots that had occurred in Cincinnati, Philadelphia, and New York against the few free black people living there and asked what those riots might have been had there been general emancipation. No question was raised about possibly charging the white mobs with criminal behavior or bringing their instigators to justice. Rather than be marked as illegal, the white mobs were understood by Leigh to be simply demonstrating the Anglo-Saxon propensity to dominate and "enslave other races" (RMD, 209). It was a covert way of claiming that black people should be enslaved for their own good, so that good civilized whites would be spared the necessity and indelicacy of mob barbarity. On the other hand, during the same period, the abolitionist whites who were arguing for emancipation were the ones criminalized and attacked for inciting the violence and for potentiating even greater mob violence.[27]

Whites, in perpetrating violence, were generally seen as entitled to their antiblack prejudice. As early as 1795, a Virginia judge (St. George Tucker) wrote that deeply rooted white prejudice created "the impossibility of assimilating [black people] into white society" and that "every white man felt himself born to tyrannize [blacks]." This is a form of the "democratic" excuse, that if a majority of the people think and act this way, then it has to be accepted as their democratic will. That is, a democratic rhetoric is used to defend an antidemocratic order under the aegis of which democracy is structured as a purely white prerogative. It signifies in practice that the democracy envisioned by white people was only white democracy (NS, 14–15). In Pennsylvania, during the first half of the nineteenth century, black people were shot, jailed, and tortured, almost as a daily occurrence, for the crime of existing. The gradual accretion of such daily incidents would erupt into general social paroxysms as whites rioted against the people they had already tormented with guns, murder, and beatings in order to maintain white corporate society's class domination over them (e.g., in the antidraft riots of 1863 and the Memphis riots of 1868). Because these upheavals were treated relatively benignly by the government in many cases and allowed to work themselves out (in Memphis, the police were more concerned with disarming the black community than in stopping the white attackers), they received a certain sanction by the state. The violence of white people against black was not about defending white identity against an assault upon it, but rather constructing that white identity through violence, and in the same act defending it by reinstating the violence with which white identity cannot dispense for its very existence.[28]

DuBois points out that socialist thinkers were not averse to getting into bed with white supremacy, excusing themselves by saying that abolition was capitalist and sentimental (BR, 24–25). This points to a very important aspect of the whole situation; the nineteenth-century abolitionist movements contained many contesting positions, and many points of view were expressed. They were divided between moral and class positions, and many argued for real class unity (against the stance taken by the labor movement). Thus, there was a division between the abolitionists and the socialists over the meaning of class unity, what it was for, and its strategy and tactics. Intersecting this division of movements was the split within abolitionism along racialized lines; there were those who only sought the elimination of slavery and those who also opposed segregation (some of whom also opposed disfranchisement). This paralleled a division in socialist thinking between those who acceded to white supremacy and those who called for full class unity. Socialist politics, tied to one form of class relations, divided along racialized lines, and antislavery politics not tied to the same conception of class expressed a similar division. In other words, politics divided along racialized lines more fundamentally than along class lines.

In effect, the divisions in U.S. society, from its foundation, are more intelligible in terms of racialization than in terms of class interest. It would be beyond the scope of this book to investigate the inner dynamics of the socialist and abolitionist movements in this respect. Suffice it to say that, at the time, people were not "flying blind"; alternatives were presented from many quarters in articulate form, and the course people chose expressed a consciousness of their situation.

A Reconfiguration of Class Analysis

Let us recapitulate. The central socioeconomic dimensions of the continental plantation colonies in the seventeenth century were (1) allegiance to the colony, (2) a corporate mode of social organization,[29] and (3) the evolution of a system of slavery. All three became integrated and coherent with each other through the formation of an intermediary control stratum that served to unify and restructure colonial society's diverse economic positions through a strict differentiation between the colony and its labor force, based on violence and internal solidarity.

The intermediary control stratum represented the social consolidation of the institution of slavery. It focused the integration of all white people into an inclusive and stratified administrative apparatus, that is, into a corporate state, and it concretized a functional form of white supremacy that could counterpose itself to allegiance to

England. As such, it attenuated class conflict among whites by positioning all in an administrative structure, so that differences in class interests devolved to levels of power within a common allegiance to whiteness. At the same time, it reified the paranoia upon which whiteness was constructed as one of the intangible social functions of its violence. Its overall effect was to array against the African and African American bond-labor class the entirety of white society in a stratified but integral form.

The primary formal characteristics of a corporate administrative entity are its hierarchical structure and its internal allocation of control responsibilities, for which it establishes organizational coherence through centralized direction. The primary political interrelation between people becomes administrative; that is, within the hierarchy, individuals participate differentially along a scale of graded power. With respect to production, one's position in the structure of administration becomes primary over juridical relations to the means of production. Thus, supervisors are deemed to be of a different class than production workers, though they work for the same enterprise and hold no ownership in it. Administrative positioning thus constructs one's economic and social identity, including how one makes a living, income level, and political party connections. In the United States, occupation is part of who one is: a machinist, a writer, a teacher, etc. These name administrative positions because they answer the question of what one administers, rather than whether one works for a wage, a salary, or freelance. This differs from the preindustrial notion of trades, such as cobbler, tailor, blacksmith, which named skills and knowledges. Though machinist and teacher name skills, they refer more generally to the social substructures to which one belongs, organized as factories, schools, professions, and bureaucracies.[30] The alternative question of what one thinks, which requires dialogue, is left aside as secondary. Those who actually do the physical labor of production find themselves in a fluctuating hierarchy, between foremen and lower job or skill classifications (pay and responsibility scales as concretized by their definition in union contracts, for instance), and often see themselves as administrative as well, if only over the job they are performing. Only those who are proletarianized are denied a role in that administrative structure, as their political relation to it.

The main thing a corporate structure provides, and prioritizes, is nonresponsibility. Within the corporate structure, each individual is responsible to those above, in diverse ways, but one has reduced or voided responsibility for what one does to those below, unless it threatens to disrupt the system's function. This principle of insulation from responsibility contributed to the focus on compensation during the entire abolition debate in the North, on the grounds that neither "owners" nor the state should bear the responsibility for the situation they confronted, that is, the condition of those below them. Welfare reform, downsizing and lay-offs, redlining, the use of stun-belts, and many forms of social victimization or assault (racial mob action, police brutality, and racial profiling) are honored, sometimes directly by exonerating the perpetrator, sometimes indirectly by blaming the victim. Only unauthorized autonomy or independence is impermissible. Should a local entity get too independent, democratic, or resistant, it will be suppressed or put into receivership—as was done in 2000 with the Teamsters Union, after a reform leadership had been elected.

Overall coherence is maintained by the top level (the "directors") in taking responsibility for social operations (law, control of labor and labor supply, marketing, resource allocation, and economic development). Coherence within the body of corporate society is maintained through allegiance to its unifying membership principle (in the case of the United States, whiteness; in the case of production corporations, prestige, power, or simply employment). What unified and integrated these two modes of coherence for the Virginia colony was the intermediary control stratum, which made directorial responsibilities functional through the preservation of order, the enforcement of "proletarian" production (keeping the bond-labor force at work), and the stratification of society around white solidarity rather than across class interests.

Because the major form of social differentiation was one of position in an administrative framework rather than economic relation—that is, an administration's relation to its many social functions: foremen, supervisors, managers, police, bureaucrats, or strawbosses—the corporate structure provided unspoken control over individuality, personal life, thought, and personal relationships. It constituted, through its control stratum, a social machine that brought all whites together in a class relation to the labor force, which was black. It transformed social identity and membership in whiteness into a social ethos, the enforceable cement that held the corporate administrative structure together. In urban settings, even neighborhoods participate in the corporate or administrative framework of whiteness. Structural positions and social stratifications of whites are established as levels of membership, and those who refuse to be sufficiently white within that framework (administrative structure) are questioned or ostracized. If there is still housing segregation—and whites still insure that there is, at many levels—it represents a way for those in white neighborhoods to collect their dues from each other.

When, with the rise of industry, different forms of labor relations emerged (e.g., wage labor, subcontracting, prison labor), they were integrated into this overarching social machine according to their level of development. Neither early industrialization nor the Revolution did much to distort or transform the primary class relation in plantation society between the planters and African American labor living in total bondage. Indeed, early industrialization depended on the latter's profitability, and that of the slave trade, for its initial capitalization. If the Revolution raised the issue of emancipation, it closed it by prioritizing property rights of ownership, and that opened the space for white workers to seize the role and identity of working class without putting in question their whiteness as a form of property nor therefore their membership in the corporate state. This actually made it more natural for the nineteenth-century union movement to focus on organizing skilled workers who had administrative control over unskilled labor.

But between the white working class and those it proletarianized, there was a different relation. That relation, between the racializing and the racialized, inherited from an antecedent colonial class structure, was a real social relation that reduced the racialized to proletarianized status after the Revolution. Rather than divide a previously united working class, racism and white supremacy were the means of uniting white society in a class opposition to people of color. White workers were given the space to define themselves as the working class for both the racializing and the racialized, as well as become the interface between the two. The fact that white workers were productive workers in two incommensurable domains (producing wealth and white consensus) meant that there were essentially two systems of economic relations, overlapping at one point. Colonial society had evolved two disparate economic spaces, with distinct modes of relations within them, as a kind of double class structure. The first was a relation between white (English colonial) society and the mass of African American bond-laborers it held in thrall. The second was a system of emerging class distinctions internal to a society congealed around the white identity it had engendered for itself—between large and small farmers, tradesmen and artisans, capitalist enterprises and white wage workers. Their potential for becoming antagonists in the struggle for power was attenuated by their respective participations in white unity and the corporate-state administrative structure. These two systems of relations overlapped in the domain of the white worker, who was a worker in the latter system and a producer of whiteness through the machinery of a control stratum in the former. The first structure could be considered a class structure produced by the production of whiteness; the second could be understood as a more or less classical capitalist system, but embedded and contextualized in the first, and collocated around allegiance to whiteness.

This double structure was preserved with some variation after the Revolution when white laborers seized working-class identity for themselves, instead of working-class unity. When colonial society nationalized itself through the Constitution, white workers transferred their control function to a political relation to black workers, and their allegiance to a white corporate state that class recognition as such gave them. The seizure of working-class identity through segregation seemed wholly logical because it followed from their political position within the white bargain of solidarity.

Three distinct class relations had thus consolidated themselves: the relations of white society as a whole to black labor; the relation of white elite (capitalist) to white working class; the relation of white workers to black workers. The proletarianization of black workers (at the hands of social segregation and political exclusion) extended the first into the postslavery economy; the double role of white workers in the second and third (as workers and as white) marked the boundary between the two economic systems (the first and second). Both white working-class roles were productive—of social wealth on the one hand and of the whiteness of corporate society on the other.

Parenthetically, what the Jacksonian "producer ethic" represented was the elite's post-Revolutionary fulfillment of its original bargain with the control stratum. Though the bargain stemmed from before the Revolution, the social (policy) valorizations of "producer" and working-class identity as white were threads in the same cloth. There is a transhistoricality to it in that the nation reached back into a society it had overthrown and retrieved former structures to again place at the center of its endeavors. We shall see how this collapse of history back into itself conditioned many court decisions of the mid-nineteenth century. The Jacksonian ideology was also transregional.

Though Jackson was from the South, and the seizure of working-class identity occurred in the North, the two regions were in alliance through the Democratic Party—for the preservation of slavery in the South. Though northern white workers brought about a new labor configuration, it too preserved the form of the old structure. Finally, Jackson's original notion of the "producer" transcended class lines as a reflection of a corporate social and administrative apparatus preserved from the past; though the new society proclaimed itself democratic, it infused its transsociality with the ethos of allegiance to whiteness that had been the matrix of the pre-Revolutionary corporate state.

Traditional class analyses will not work for this situation of a double class system. This is not simply a two-tiered structure of working-class exploitation, in which there is an exploited section and a super-exploited section of the working class, divided against themselves by racism, but situated in parity with respect to capitalism. The administrative system built on white solidarity and white class collaboration is a different class structure from the control paradigm built on exclusion and proletarianization of people of color by white society. In the first, class exists as a class collaboration immured in allegiance to a social corporatism which substitutes administrative hierarchy for class difference. In the second, class antagonism (proletarianization) flows out of historical social categorizations and colonialist control mechanisms and succeeds in generating class difference outside administrative hierarchy. The divided identity of white workers, in their two irreconcilable and inseparable roles (as white workers), is the dividing line between them.

White class conflicts become other than simply class conflicts within the corporate social body because they are secondary to racialization, not only because of the violence or invasiveness of white supremacy, but because the processes of racialization have been the basis on which class relations within white corporate society have been integrated into the corporate structure. There is very little room for autonomous working-class interest between these systems. Because allegiance and social profitability are central to white membership in the corporate state, even massive class struggles fought by the working class within the white class system of corporate society have rarely been able to see beyond the consensus on profitability and allegiance that constitutes white corporate society's cultural foundation. A different way of understanding class beyond the European model must be articulated for the United States.

Models of a Double Class Structure

A fairly unusual picture has been drawn here: a double economy with two incommensurable structures of class relations, one somewhat congruent to the industrial class relations of classical capitalism, but embedded in a matrix of class collaboration derived from and essential to the second overarching structure of racialized class relations. The same class of people, white workers, plays incommensurable roles in each area of the double ecomony, forming a boundary between them. Are there any models of such a structure that can be used to help understand it?

One model might be colonialism itself. Colonialism is an imposition of control over peoples external to the colonial power through a governing administrative apparatus that relies on violence, and whose role is to preserve the integrity and domination of the colonizing social community over the colonized people and territory. It establishes an overarching structure that unites the colonizing community and excludes the colonized. One of the tasks of the administrative structure is to keep the colonizer's class structure intact in the colonizing community, preserving the class relations reflective of the nation from which it comes, yet in national unity against the colonized. In the case of the United States, the colonizer sought to "terminate" the indigenous cultures and brought a substitute colonized people to itself (from Africa), interrupting cultural traditions for all three and building an administrative and class structure upon those very interruptions. To structure its colonial relation to the imported colonized people, the colonizer invented racialization and whiteness, race and white supremacy; these then produced the axis of cultural unity, integrity, and administrative coherence on the social plane for which later European colonialism would use the concept of nationality.

For traditional colonialism, national identity has always had priority over unity between the colonized workers and those of the colonial power. The colonized workers will not trust the colonialist worker because the latter arrives as part of a colonialist community and apparatus that is imposed violently against the will of the colonized. The colonialist workers will not trust the colonized worker because they know they have arrived in the colony as part of an oppressive apparatus and fear the retaliation of the colonized if they get too close. Though both are workers, they have no common interest; they stand on opposite sides of the issue of the national liberation of the colony. For the United States, national liberation is not the issue. Instead, the issue would be a de-racializing liberation, a liberation from white supremacy and its structures of racialization. This would not only entail a necessary de-racialization of whiteness, but a recognition of the community autonomy and self-determination of those previously racialized by white supremacy. It would be a de-racialization conditioned by a respect for the identities that racialized communities had constructed for themselves against white supremacy, and as a means of surviving the oppressiveness of their racialization. If it seems paradoxical that nonwhite racialized communities preserve community autonomy as a source of their own cultural identity while the society at large (overarching) deracializes, it is only a necessary inverse reflection of the double bind within which all people find themselves in a racialized society. The process of deracialization would have to respect the autonomy of nonwhite racialized communities as represented by the identity and mode of community by which they survived racialization and colonization in the first place.

A starker model of the double class structure presents itself in the prison system. In a prison, the administration governs both inmates and guards, and treats each oppressively in a different manner, as part of its modus operandi. Whereas the inmates are the source of the prison's existence, and of its political constitution by a state, the guards are the instrumentality through which it works. The juridical status of guards and inmates is incommensurable; the first have legitimacy as workers, though their role is one of violence against the inmates, while the inmates have no legitimacy, yet are the reason for the prison's existence. (Leaving aside the issue of violent crime, which in a society based on administrative state violence is undiscussable in any but dogmatic or ideologically rhetorical terms, the hundreds and thousands of people incarcerated for victimless crimes, crimes of personal behavior, can be seen as a direct reflection of those Africans caught by slave traders by being in the wrong place at the wrong time.) An analogy can be drawn between the prison administration and the plantation class in the eighteenth-century colony, in which the juridical difference between guards and inmates stands in isomorphic relation to the juridical distinction between the patrols and the African bond-laborers of the colony. Though the guard/inmate relation is not racial, it functions in a manner analogous to the racial (and is, in fact, becoming racialized under current criminalization campaigns that have produced a prison population that is 75 percent of color).

The guards, when they form organizations, or unionize, do so not to free themselves from the administration, or to transform the prison, but to enhance their standing in prison operations, to acquire modes of participation in policy making whose aims are a better life for themselves and more efficient control of the inmates. Though they organize against the administration, it is in the context of a concrete solidarity with the administration over the inmates. The guards will not cross the juridical boundary to make common cause with the inmates, and the inmates will not make common cause with the guards as workers because they are guards and civilians.

One could say (and classical Marxism would agree) that the "real" class relation, across the "means of production" of the prison, is between the administration and the guards. In such a view, the relation between the prison and the inmates is secondary; the inmate is the "product" that the prison is built to produce. The conjunction of administration and guards is coherent because of the existence of the prisoners, and any class conflict within that conjunction is beyond the purview of the prisoners; it is an administrative dispute over conditions of internal stratification that does not involve them. Against them, the administration and the guards are in solidarity. That solidarity gets its force, however, from the fact that the relation between the inmates and the prison is primary, the reason there are guards in the first place. Ultimately, of course, the inmate/prison relation is considerably more than merely a class relation. The prisoner is the means by which the state produces its overarching power, which it superimposes on class and cultural structures; the prisoner is the sign of the state's assumed political legitimacy. State power, law, police presence, and labor discipline all get their force under state regulation through the structure of the prison. In that sense, the relation between the administration and the guards, though a class relation, is wholly secondary.

While the first (essential) class relation (administration/prisoners) is one of juridical incommensurability, the second (administration/guards) is a relation of "political economy," a realm of class difference reduced to minor conflicts within the arena of administrative hegemony and incommensurate with the first. But the tertiary relation that exists between the guards and the prisoners nevertheless remains unintelligible. From the perspective of political economy (the guards), it would be a production relation, producing the prison in one case, and reproducing civil society on the other. From the perspective of the juridical (the prisoners), it would constitute a system of social categorization that transforms humans into prisoners, a production of social and state power using humans as raw material.[31] For white corporate society (on this analogy), the proletarianization of black workers at the hands of racism and segregation is analogous to the juridical nonstatus of inmates in the prison system. Between white workers (guards) and people of color (inmates), there is no common interest. For black or brown people, any attempt at common cause between white and black workers, as long as the dual class structure (and the structures of racialization that produce it) exists, will be seen as a form of opportunism on the part of whites—that will probably dissolve into separation sooner or later.

Labor History and Populism

Colonialism and the prison system are fairly stark models. But the dual class structure they symbolize perhaps explains a strange paradox of United States history: why, of all industrial countries, its labor history has been the most violent, while never giving birth to a broad working-class revolutionary movement. Against mere unionization, the United States has deployed martial law, concentration camps, mass jailings, and torture on a scale seen in Europe only during revolutionary insurgency.[32] There have been massive campaigns of violent suppression (for instance, against the western miners at the turn of the twentieth century, steel workers in the 1890s, Kentucky miners in the 1930s, textile workers in the Northeast and South, and railroad workers in 1894), in which hundreds of workers were shot, jailed, and tortured. Socialist leaders and thinkers have been assassinated on the streets or in law courts, without there being any extant threat of a revolutionary upheaval. In a traditional Marxist framework, while the intensity of ruling-class reaction is explainable, the absence of a revolutionary movement is not.[33]

   In the context of the white corporate state and a racialized society, however, a certain intelligibility can be given to this disparity. For the corporate state, industrial union organization represented a breach and betrayal of allegiance to white corporate society. Industrial unions organized those charged with maintaining the boundaries of racialization, and then turned the force of their attention the wrong way. In seeking to organize an entire industry, potentially across racial lines (which did not happen in all industrial union efforts), the entity and the hegemony with which industrial unionism broke faith was the white nation. This constituted treason, not to the state but to the white bargain, since white corporate society (in its paranoia) then felt unguarded within. For industrial white workers to strike against corporate society was to step outside it, to place themselves objectively therefore among the colonized, the proletarianized, the nonwhite; the ruling class therefore treated them as such. Yet, while ruling-class violence was in part to punish white workers for leaving their racial post, it did not produce a revolutionary sentiment against abusive state power because the underlying assumption on both sides was still that of the bargain of mutual recognition within a matrix of white solidarity. From the elite's perspective, the industrial union demand for recognition overstepped its bounds; in the white worker's eyes, state violence, while excessive, did not contradict membership in whiteness and corporate society.

Until the 1960s and the civil rights movement, industrial unions were essentially considered alien entities, even under the New Deal. They sit on the boundary between the administrative structure and a nonwhite working class they have tended to ignore—even when non-white workers were integrated into industrial organizing campaigns. It was against this subtle exclusion that the League of Revolutionary Black Workers and the various black caucuses in the auto industry arose in Detroit in the late 1960s.[34] Even when organized, white workers enjoy their white solidarity as primary. The emergence of a radical black union movement in the 1960s, the nationalist protectionism of the "official" unions in the face of NAFTA, and the success of anti-immigrant and anti–affirmative action campaigns, which reach far into the working class, testify to the unity that racism gives the white working class.

The dual class structure also presents a context in which to understand the forms that populism has taken. In the United States, populism has been a major mode of oppositional movement and organization, attacking oligopoly in the name of social recognition. Its major focus has generally been on rectifying the effects of impoverishment at the hands of economic enterprises and influences that had gotten too big and thereby broken the bargain contained in the producer ethic. The major components of populist thinking that first emerged in Bacon's Rebellion have reappeared continually throughout U.S. history. Bacon's campaign, as we have seen, consisted of a rhetorical struggle against the rich on the part of the marginalized, a demand for greater political representation, and an opportunistically machinated campaign against the indigenous as the "real enemy." In California in the 1850s and 1860s, as Saxton has shown, a working-class movement defined itself through its exclusion of and attacks on nonwhite labor (mainly Chinese at the time, but black as well) (IE, 92ff) and compromised with white capital as soon as forms of labor segregation and immigration restrictions could be agreed on. The Workingman's Party won its fight for the Immigration Acts through a xenophobic campaign and the use of the "free labor" ideology, which the political structure of California supported through social recognition. That recognition together with the Workingman's Party's racist stance against nonwhites constituted the essential coordinates of their class self-awareness.

In the case of Watson's People's Party, the enemy was Wall Street and the Democratic Party. What the People's Party fundamentally fought for was recognition of the farmers as the producers of the agrarian product.[35] While Watson himself advocated bringing black people into the movement, it was not in alliance, but as a strategy to keep them from voting with the Democratic Party, the party of large landowners. It paralleled the thinking of the NLU leadership that saw the black population as a pawn in political maneuvers between whites. What Watson did not take into account was that his party's members were by and large the same people who had formed the patrols and the mobs, who had murdered and tortured black people ever since the Civil War, and whom black people therefore refused to trust. When, for these reasons, they did not support the People's Party, Watson switched to advocating segregation and disfranchisement, the other way to neutralize the black vote. Thus, he ended as a rabid supporter of the Jim Crow laws that swept the South in the 1890s.

The agrarian granger movement was similar. The granges were associations designed to establish parity with the banks that had gained mortgage domination over those who worked the land, creating a form of debt servitude. The idea of the grange was to form an organization large enough to neutralize this hold over the "producer." They organized loan, seed, and marketing cooperatives, but not to the point of questioning the property system in which they sought the parity that necessitated those cooperatives in the first place. It was a movement to establish the organizational basis on which to be recognized, rather than change the terms under which the labor of its members was to be performed. The source of legitimacy it claimed for itself was the "producer ethic" whose precursor had been the bargain of white solidarity.

The populist right-wing movements that have emerged in the United States during the Reagan era follow suit. They attack multinational capital as superseding, in its power, the rights of U.S. citizens, but they claim that this has come about because liberalism has become predominant in governance, interrupting the recognition due those whites who do the work in the nation in favor of nonwhites. Through issues such as welfare fraud, reverse discrimination, and immigration, they use black and brown communities as scapegoats in whose name they claim the government has forgotten about "white people."

Most populism has been openly racist, in contradiction to its inherent needs as a popular movement for the greatest numbers. But its racism was not simply an effect of social prejudice. Racism provided populism with the ability to do two things: (1) redefine the identity of the impoverished white people who joined it as white and therefore entitled to social recognition, and (2) allow the oligarchy it opposed to grant that recognition without having to change the terrain of economic and class relations on which populism fought it. That people of color might have identical economic interests did not matter; their exclusion was the core of the white solidarity bargain that populism sought by political means to renew.

In these terms, above and beyond economic issues, the centrality of union recognition to twentieth-century union movements can be seen as a form of populism. The unions became primarily a countervailing force, a means by which white workers could hold the elite to its bargain of recognition, with respect to which workers agreed in turn not to question the legitimacy of the property concept on which capitalism was based. One sees the primacy of this bargain well into the twentieth century in literature about the working class. In *The Iron Heel* by Jack London, the central charge that London's hero levies against the capitalist class, against which he organizes a vast populist campaign, is that "they mismanaged"; that is, they did not do their job.

But What about Marxism?

What happens to working-class ideology such as Marxism or socialism in the context of a double class structure if that structure and the history of working-class transformation after abolition imply that a different account of class relations is needed?

Marxists understand themselves as a community struggling for a liberation of all toilers; they are generally the first to join any antiracist struggle. But they have not been able to establish a stable labor party in the United States that would focus political organization of the working class (as in Europe). Nor have they been able to break the hold of racism in the white working class. Nevertheless, radicals who see this society as oppressive and who need a theoretical means of opposing it, to replace the hype of two-party representation with something more democratic, find no ready alternative to Marxism's offer of an answer. Marxism provides an ideal vision, a mechanism of oppositional power, and it seems to explain why white workers are racist, why they have been turned against themselves, and why they put up with evil, injustice, governmental crime, colonialism, and their own exploitation.

In focusing on class relations as foundational, however, Marxism marginalizes the cultural structures by which all this has been accomplished. Many still see racism as a capitalist instrumentality, a thing designed to maintain class rule, an adjunct to class oppression, to be used to further capitalist profitability, leaving aside what makes that particular tactic work so well.[36] For them, a general opposition to capitalism resides in making its oppressive nature unprofitable. But this tactic works only if the work force is not expendable. In Europe, Marx argued, the work force could not be simply swept aside without capitalism throwing itself into crisis. Capitalism had brought the working class into existence for itself as its sole source of profit, and was thus wholly dependent on it. The working class was indispensible; that was the source of its class power. In the traditional Marxist theory of class struggle, the political destiny of a class hinges on both its awareness of its historical position in the relations of production, and the programmatic ideals it can adopt for itself out of its own experience. Marx proclaimed the ultimate task of the working class to be to end all systems of exploitation altogether by seizing the means of production and democratizing them. Since capitalism had rendered production social, the elimination of private appropriation of the social product was at issue.

In the United States, however, the expendability of the working class is separate from the ultimate destiny that proletarianization makes exigent. For capitalism in the United States, part of the role of the proletarianized working class of color is precisely to be expendable. Its expendability was indispensable in providing the target for the intermediary control stratum to foster white solidarity, and as a means of rendering class struggle populist. That is, a form of genocide—the potential or actual elimination of a culture, a people, or the actual lives of a community—is inherent in the specific proletarianization of people of color. If racialization deploys a logic of genocide, then the racialized class structure cannot be made unprofitable. The dispensability of the people on which the system feeds to support its white corporate class structure becomes part of its accumulated (social) capital. Within the dual class structure, the act of genocide contained in the structure of proletarianization is an "economic" factor, and "profitable" in a sense related to whiteness being a "property."

In Marx's analysis of the social domain, capitalism requires free laborers who can sell their labor power. It is not just that wage labor is the particular form of exploitation for the capitalist production of surplus value. The formation of a local market in which wage laborers can function as consumers, and thus provide for the growth of local circulation, is also essential. Translated to the plantation economy, this meant that the white workers, even those participating in the slave patrols, constituted the productive element of a capitalist economy. Indeed, Marxists of the mid-nineteenth century argued that the slave was an "economic category," rather than a worker conscripted into the utmost mode of exploitation. While this historicizes the economic category of the slave, it dehistoricizes the category of race as a raw substrate to economic function, a question of human essence. Thus it participates in the dispensability of the slave as a person, withholding from him or her the honor of being value producing on a par with the white working class. In short, Marxism's acceptance of a white understanding of race results in a dehistoricization of race, in the name of a white historicization of racism.

Though Marxists in the United States spoke against exclusion of free black workers from unions, they acceded to the segregation insisted on by whites, considering it a temporary aberration of consciousness in a working class trying to mature and find its way.[37] Thus, they ended by advocating the organization of white workers, but not black, within the white supremacist perspective that black workers would make it more difficult to organize the white. In their "objectivity," the Marxists acceded to and valorized the class identity seized by white workers, even in the context of its class collaboration. But in doing so, the more general Marxian concept of class consciousness, reflecting the experience of European working classes, was obviated (CR, 323). In this sense, Marxism racialized itself in its class stances with respect to slavery, and abandoned the African American bond-laborers, though they constituted the working class of the plantation economy. As Cedric Robinson argues, Marxism was already racialized as a nineteenth-century European thought system, seeing U.S. slavery through white eyes, and analyzing the situation of the black worker and the black community from the perspective of white workers.[38]

In general, the Marxian conceptualization of racism as a tactic to divide the working class may intend to oppose working-class white supremacy, but it does so only from a white point of view. For instance, it must assume the existence of a hierarchy of superior and inferior races to which the racist ideology makes reference, in order to oppose that ideology in its own racialized terms. In decrying the effect of racism (division), the critique must assume the existence of its foundations (race hierarchy) and, in doing so, assume the objective existence of race rather than see race as a social relation of groups racialized by one of them (whites as metaracial) hierarchically. It ignores the fact that racial hierarchy is the result of a process in which one group (which includes the white working class) actively inferiorizes the other.

The "divide and rule" analysis of racism also assumes that a (theoretically) unified working class capable of inclusive solidarity actually existed, or was a natural tendency, one which became divided and disrupted at one point by racism at capital's hands. Yet even the nineteenth-century Marxists knew that to admit black workers into white worker organizations would have split white workers against themselves, between those opposing segregation and those promoting it; that is, the split to which they referred was a split among white workers, in effect again considering that working class to be in fact white (YI, 151). Both assumptions contained in the "divide and rule" analysis are consistent with the white working class's view of itself as "the" working class; they are consistent also with white supremacy.

What the history of racism and white supremacy suggests is that both were socially invented to construct a system of capitalist class relations in the specific context of the plantation economy, and that rather than one working class, there have always been two, in contradictory relations with white capital but incommensurable with each other. Thus, the idea that racism divided the working class is part of the double bind of white supremacy.

Barbara Fields, in attempting to pinpoint a moment when slavery produced race as its ideological effect, illustrates the logic of the double bind herself. She argues that, in opposition to the plantation economy, an economy of independent farmers not conscripted into bond-labor or wage labor for capital enterprises (whether agricultural or industrial) would have suited both the poor whites and freedmen. But only their prior unity would have brought it about. Moreover, there would have to have been such an economy already, in order to provide the possibility of such unity. "That sort of unity would have required as a minimum precondition the very material circumstances to which it was prerequisite" (RRR, 166). Conversely, one could add that the necessity to have a dominated group to exploit does not explain the maintenance of black people as that bottom rung. One has to examine the function the lower classes fulfilled in maintaining the bottom rung as such, as a social or cultural project that was meaningful to them, and what else was maintained as the upper rungs in the process of doing so. Those cultural meanings establish the function, and the function establishes those cultural meanings. What both of these arguments imply is that the cultural conditions for social unity are always the conditions that depend on that social unity to bring them about. If white supremacy is the principle of unity of white corporate society, then it is a form of unity that will condition all cultural situations in which other forms of unity are sought. Division is not the question here, but a social unity that provides the foundation for all other forms of unity.

Roediger advances his analysis of how whiteness functions in contemporary working-class consciousness in part to counter the problem into which formulaic approaches such as the Marxist fall. The Marxist view, that the patrols functioned as a productive force in society because they represented a stage of working-class organization, ignores the fact that the patrols' direct product was the subservience of African American bond-laborers. The patrols explicitly established a social difference between themselves and those bond-laborers as an essential element of primary class organization. Roediger's description of how late-twentieth-century white workers think of themselves as white, honoring certain modes of labor and derogating others as "slavery," points to an historical reflection of the patrols as producers of white society, and slavery as their other product.

While plantation production and industrial capitalism are both forms of capitalism (exploitation), they constitute different forms of oppression. Because white society, as a corporate class system, defined itself as a whole through its domination of black people, it set every white class, beyond their mutual class relations and contradictions, in an essential relation to black labor as their primary reference point as white. White workers had no way of thinking about this on a working-class basis, once they accepted the idea of being white. No solidarity with black workers is possible without a transformation of identity that breaks the solidarity with white society that takes black people as that reference point. (Historically, for working-class organizers, it was black workers who had to establish solidarity with white, and white who had but to "accept" that solidarity, as in the packinghouse struggle.) The free labor ideology was the first well-defined expression of that common reference point for the nineteenth century. It established, through that reference point, that for white workers, even free black workers were not free. Freedom itself was racialized as white. The wage laborer, free to sell his labor power where he could, was by definition white, and those who were not white could not be left free to work in the same way. To have allowed that would have been to establish a form of worker solidarity that would have violated and betrayed white worker solidarity, as well as (white) worker identity. For collective strength, the only permissible solidarity the white worker as white could call upon was a white solidarity.

Marxism vs. the Double Class Structure

Ultimately, it is the double solidarity of membership in white corporate society and (white) worker identity that has rendered the essence of the Marxist position unintelligible to white workers in the United States. The great historical task of the working class, for Marxism, is putting a final end to all class systems and opening an era of history in which people live free of class exploitation. Without a sense of an historical destiny or role for itself, such as ending class society, class consciousness would never extend itself beyond reformist and trade union consciousness. Those who imported theories of class consciousness from Europe understood this and attempted to articulate those ideas of historical task. They were never able to fathom the structure of racialization and white solidarity by which the white working class was constructed, because they could never understand the submergence of class consciousness in a social solidarity always on the watch for betrayal. For white workers, there was no historical role to grasp beyond what they were already in the process of fulfilling, namely, enforcing whiteness (as both their "property" and their identity). Even at the height of industrial union organization in the 1930s, the centrality of union recognition and labor segregation to all other positions or activities reaffirmed the white workers' sense of historical role, of standing within the white corporate state. The exceptions, and there have been exceptions, have succeeded in gaining "recognition" for black workers—but mainly as black adjuncts to white hegemony and not as workers. That is, the black workers have had little role to play other than solidarity with the white struggle for recognition. White workers had already fulfilled their historical destiny by being a controlling administrative stratum over those they displaced in order to become the working class. A further historical destiny to fulfill would require a consciousness that would directly contradict the consciousness of their prior "historical task." It is this contradiction that in part gives their identity as white its power for them. The civil rights movement changed this, but only to the extent of mapping out a "domain" to be known as belonging to black political activity. As yet, no domain in which to break the power of white identity has been mapped out (against either white solidarity or its class collaboration) that would liberate the white worker in and with a "black political domain" (the domain of the proletarianized).

Because white workers combine in themselves the dual roles of producing capital as exploited workers and producing white society as control stratum members (as white), they put themselves in a position that is more analogous to what Marx describes for the petty bourgeoisie than for the working class in Europe; and DuBois makes this case (BR, 30). Marx argues that, as a class, the petty bourgeoisie can be pushed both ways—toward working-class alliance when their social conditions become oppressive, and toward alliance with the capitalist class against the working class when business is good or they fear the socializing power of the working-class movements. But the European petty bourgeoisie has no consciousness of having an historical task. Similarly, white workers will swing toward multiracial alliances when desperate enough politically (for which impoverishment is a secondary consideration), and return to segregationist policies when the economic opportunity permits, or their bargain with white capital and white society has been renewed. They reject a lasting multiracial alliance not because they fear true social integration with black or brown people; they refuse because it would endanger the bargain from which they receive their social identity.

What socialists or Marxists present as a working-class politics is thus in essential conflict with what white workers interpret as their own "interests." Interests, of course, cannot be assumed to be self-evident; nor are ideologies always consciously fashioned to reflect them (FS, 5). What appears as a contradiction in interests is often in reality a contradiction between ideological interpretations. The actions of a group will be governed by the interests it perceives for itself. The interests that another ideology might delineate for it and its actions would be in conflict, and even represent an alien social perspective to the extent it was other than how the group experienced itself. The idea that racism contradicts working-class interests assumes that those working-class interests are objectively evident, rather than resident in modes of solidarity through which white workers already defined themselves and their experience. When Marxism points out a contradiction between racism and working-class interests, it is actually pointing out that racism contradicts the interests of the Marxist movement, which it substitutes for the racialized interests of the (white) working class as white.

The Marxist position is, of course, that it bases itself on objective criteria and descriptions. But it refuses to recognize that objectivity is itself an ideological stance which generates what counts as a social object to be looked at objectively, and what does not. The ideological notion that white solidarity is a concrete social object in U.S. society (that even outweighs impoverishment) appears to the Marxist prioritization of impoverishment as a conflict of (political) interest. The issues that Marxism claims to raise as objective are ultimately settled ideologically.

If the white workers of the early nineteenth century saw segregation as the necessary road to their own working-class identity, as an element of working-class consciousness, then it is not, for them, in contradiction with anything. It does not matter that segregation was a source of weakness for them in class terms; in cultural and identity terms, their proletarianizing of others, and their nonproletarianized status, was their source of greatest strength.

To understand this means that a different ethicopolitical argument or discussion must begin. It is to ground such a discussion that the idea of a dual class structure is important. On the basis of class theoretics, and a strict distinction between class and race issues, white solidarity is a class question between whites, and racism is a relation between whites and blacks. But on the basis of the dual class structure, white solidarity is a central aspect of a racialized class relation (whose language is violence) between whites and blacks, and racism is a relation between whites in which the racist violence that expresses it is always gratuitous for its victims.

The Marxist insistence that Marxism is objective has hindered it from deriving means of confronting and combating the white supremacy that has given white workers their working-class identity and made white solidarity primary for them as a racialized class. This is not to disparage the Marxian notion that labor and capital have irreconcilable interests. But it is a blindness to see racism as merely an ideology and class as something transcendent. One renders U.S. white working-class identity and consciousness unintelligible if one thinks that the ideological position of unity of the entire working class is objective and has equal class weight with white solidarity. If the criminality, violence, and oppressiveness of white supremacy is to be overthrown, white workers' class consciousness as white has to be understood better than that.

Indeed, it is precisely on the issue of the objectivity of class consciousness that Marxism as a theoretic critique falls apart. The Marxist critique of capitalism is centered in an analysis of exploitation (the production, appropriation, and realization of surplus value). For Marx, a revolutionary upheaval would be forced upon the working class by the accelerated impoverishment and dehumanization required by capital accumulation. The capitalist wealth that shackled workers to their proletarian condition would leave them no other way out. Lenin, of course, argued that spontaneous class resistance to exploitation would only generate an economically focused trade-union consciousness (for a bigger piece of the pie) and fall short of generating a revolutionary perspective. Moreover, trade unionism was just a treadmill, endlessly reproducing the need to combat impoverishment at the hands of capital accumulation. Only a transformation eliminating the structure of exploitation would end the treadmill. The many socialist thinkers who sought ways of linking spontaneous resistance to a revolutionary social transformation and democratization of production (Lenin, Luxemburg, Plekhanov, Kautsky, to name a few) only testified, in their plurality, to the contingency of the link.

Marx deconstructed capital's pretensions to being natural, rational, and eternal by showing that property was not natural but a political enactment, that profit represented forced labor, and if capital had a beginning in spite of its self-mythification, it had a conceivable end. Lenin deconstructed Marx by showing that the historical task that Marx had derived for the working class and equated with class consciousness was on Marx's own account limited to the historical terms given by capitalism and could not transcend the capitalist paradigm from within them. For Lenin, a revolutionary party was necessary to carry consciousness beyond that. Lenin's theory deconstructs in turn on the question of what produces class consciousness: capitalist exploitation itself (which a revolutionary party simply organizes) or the party (meaning exploitation is not sufficient to produce it). Such a deconstruction may imply that the answer is both, mutually conditioning each other, but the priority given the "material base" by both Marx and Lenin, as well as the historical movement projected by their dialectics into an envisionable future, would give primacy to one or the other.

The historical evidence has been that no revolutionary party in industrial Europe was ever able to decide when the working class was ready to revolt; all have vacillated, all have been defeated (except Lenin's). It remains undecidable whether capitalism inherently fosters the need to demolish it, or the need to demolish capitalism is a political product of critique and not of its inherent character. This question cannot be resolved dialectically because its terms are not a contradiction. They exist at different levels of discourse. Though they use the same terms, they speak in different languages; they are thus untranslatable into one another, since the terms used are the same. Though Marxists consider this the situation of ideological struggle, Marxism in general deconstructs on this incommensurability. The undecidability between the programmatic and the automatic has left Marxism at sea, blind to its incapabilities and still pretending to be scientific.

Indeed, its scientificity blinds it to the real class collaboration upon which white working-class consciousness is built in the United States. This has rendered unintelligible the fact that white workers (principally in the South) have been willing to forego trade unionism in the name of white solidarity, even at the height of the Depression. The double class structure that produced this class collaboration can only be grasped as a social force in terms of the structures of racialization, not those of economic structure. It escapes Marxist analysis because it has no commodifiable dimension. The white worker's perceived ability to "capitalize" on whiteness transforms the "labor market" by deproletarianizing white workers, but for those reasons it escapes the value terms of the Marxian analytic. Whiteness may provide for higher wages, but it is not a market transaction, such as occurs when getting hired. Instead, the recognition of a property ownership socially bestowed upon an individual is the condition for getting hired in the first place.

Racialization is not a metaphoric description of U.S. society, and neither is the non-proletarianization of the white working class; both are strictly referential. But they exist at different discursive levels—like the discursive disparity between the originary (critical) and the strategic (automatic) functions of the revolutionary party. White-worker resistance to affirmative action represented a continued insistence on the social value of whiteness. Even when whites oppose affirmative action by saying that "all discrimination is wrong," despite the irrelevance of that idea to affirmative action (correcting the crimes of past segregation and proletarianization), they show themselves caught in an identity crisis between democratic ideals and solidarity with white corporate society. The identity crisis of whiteness unfolds as an interface between social identity and political economy, and mediates class solidarity and class collaboration as white solidarity.

That interface transforms Marxism's deconstructive dilemma. Capitalist exploitation does not spur spontaneous anticapitalism in white workers in the United States because it becomes acceptable with respect to their relation to black and brown workers. No historic role as vanguard can be theorized for them by a party, since their function as intermediary control stratum already embodies an historical role beyond proletarianization, a "vanguard" in white social construction, and a modicum of participation in being a part of a ruling class. Their inclusion renders socialism socially unnecessary. Standing outside this conflation of conservative conditions, Marxists continue to think of working classes in classical theoretical terms. For instance, the fact that unionism in the United States has always seen revolutionism as in contradiction with itself has always been a mystery for U.S. Marxists. They had to theorize that the unionized labor force was eternally misled by opportunist union bureaucrats. But that is as superficial and ahistorical a view as to say that racism is a capitalist tactic to divide and conquer the working class. The idea that the class unity of a labor movement (black and white, with its programmatic of democracy) was in contradiction with white class solidarity (and its class collaboration) did not compute. Ultimately, this only confirms Robinson's thesis that Marxist theory is itself racialized as white. In Europe, Marxism's deconstructive dilemma is ensconced in its own theorization of class consciousness; in the United States, the dilemma that fractures Marxism is its own racialization.

Black workers, who have been proletarianized by white, understand the Marxian programmatic of putting an end to class society in a way that white workers do not. But for black people to take such a proposition seriously as a community and a class, they would have to be convinced that some form of solidarity would be forthcoming from white workers. That is not something that many black people are going to be convinced of these days.

In sum, identity becomes an interest that is often culturally more profound and compelling than economic interest. This has been seen in Europe in a different form. When various socialist parties retreat into nationalism (as they have done in the past), they too are placing identity above even perceived economic interests. Marx's insistence on working-class internationalism was itself a recognition that internationalism did not spring naturally from objective working-class conditions (which does not make Marx wrong nor the nationalists right). But similarly, Marxism retreats into whiteness, in the United States, in considering working-class consciousness from a white perspective, placing that cultural identity above a critique of the structures of racialization to which Marxism accedes. That white workers are simply mistaken in not opting for unity is a meaningless statement. If class ideology is in part identity based, then one has to understand working-class consciousness from the point of view of the social (class) identity that constructed its ideology for it, and why it constructed it in a particular fashion. The social source of that identity must be understood, otherwise one falls into simply pitting one ideological perspective against another.

Conclusion

The factors that came together in the construction and generation of a working-class consciousness during the first half of the nineteenth century were the participation of white workers in the mediating control stratum of the slave system, a culture of white solidarity, the implicit need to abolish slavery in the United States without contradicting the guarantee of the right to own property, the Jacksonian producer ethic, the ubiquity of a structure of white supremacy, and a tradition of populism which deployed a nonwhite other as both nemesis and the necessary domain of connection with the elite on which to organize a struggle against it. This confluence produced a sense of working-class solidarity within a matrix of class collaboration within an integument of white solidarity. The process of becoming the working class in the North became the defining paradigm for white workers in the United States from then on (though it took different forms after the civil rights movement of the 1960s).

By tracing the central aspects of how the working class has defined itself in the United States, we are also tracing the central motifs by which the United States as a social structuring of a capitalist economy has also defined and constructed itself. The fact that the inclusion of excluded people seen as nonwhite is an issue, and has been for the entire history of working-class organization in the United States, from the time the first black laborers were manumitted in the North until the present, in which Proposition 187 (which curtailed health, education, and social services for immigrants) and Proposition 209 (eliminating affirmative action) in California got working class support, means that the context in which inclusion is raised is the social structure of whiteness. This includes the working class as itself white. Politically, the working class is white, even though in actual economic terms it is stratified across many racialized colors. This means, again, that racism is not a division in the working class but the way the social structure, including the working class, has defined itself. Racism is the very mode by which white workers have become a class in this capitalist society. It is not an ideology that can be defeated by argument or practice, but the cultural foundation on which capitalism has taken the particular (corporate) form it has in the United States. It is the substrate of daily violence upon which the peculiar confluence of violent class struggle and white class collaboration has grounded itself and its profound cultural obeisance to private property.

The racialization of the working class has not produced a two-tiered system of class exploitation; rather, racialization has produced a double economy comprising two qualitatively different systems of political economy, overlaid upon each other: a corporate state comprising a white class system, and an overarching racialized class system composed of white corporate society and people of color. While the corporate society is a class system in itself, it functions as the "ruling class" in the racialized class system. Ever shifting forms of the intermediary control stratum—from the patrols to the KKK to the prison-industrial complex and racial profiling—have maintained the duality of the system and conditioned the integrity of the white economy within it.

In the corporate state, white workers do not have a common interest with black workers, because they have a different relation to capital than black workers have (and that other workers of color have). White workers belong to the corporate state, from which black workers have been excluded (as have others of color, and the third-world countries in the U.S. political sphere). The primary relation between white workers and capital is not across the means of production, but rather through a stratified and flexible social administrative hierarchy. Their relation across the means of production remains secondary and collaborative, as long as the administrative stratification that conditions it remains functionally in place. Though unions have been integrated, and black workers participate as membership and leadership in various unions, all the way to the top, it is not in proportion to their numbers. It varies with respect to a tacit (and only somewhat less rigid) classification of jobs between white labor and black labor. The unions operate primarily as economic service organizations, continuing their bargain with capital, rather than as organizations of class unity and class interest, which would require them to take political stands. (The International Longshore and Warehouse Union [ILWU]) stands out in this regard as having gone on strike in opposition to the centralization of corporate hegemony in the World Trade Organization, in opposition to unloading cargo from South Africa during the divestment movement against apartheid, and in advocating a retrial for Mumia Abu-Jamal.)

Socialism calls for democracy in the workplace, and for assuming collective control and a nonhierarchical sharing of administration in one's daily life. For the white working class, which is the majority, this would mean countermanding the structure and standards necessary for maintaining their standing as white in the corporate structure, and their identity as "the" working class that whiteness has given them. When socialists call for working-class democracy, it implies the inclusion of black or brown workers, and violates the structure of white solidarity and identity within which white workers define and valorize themselves as a class and as workers. This does not prevent black workers from being active in a union, but it stands in the way of that union reorganizing itself as a truly democratic organization of its membership, and it blocks the union from ever questioning the prerogatives of corporate management or proposing that the economy be democratically reorganized. For whites to consider real democratic structures, even for a union, would mean stepping outside their positionality in corporate society, transforming the notion of social administration, and eliminating a hierarchy that has defined the very meaning of their existence. Because white solidarity is prior to class solidarity, white workers could conceptualize democratic control of jobs and industry only by abandoning their corporate positionality, abandoning their identity as white, and abandoning their role in producing whiteness. This would directly constitute a psychological as well as conceptual contradiction for them. At best, for white workers, socialism could be conceived only as white socialism, to which black workers might stand in solidarity. White socialism is, however, anathema to any notion of working-class democracy.

The class relations inside the corporate state are attenuated across the means of production, as classical class struggle, because white solidarity has shifted class politics to the domain of administrative stratification, class recognition, populism, and a role in the corporate social structure. Identification with whiteness makes culturally incomprehensible the Marxian concepts that workers are in ineluctable contradiction with capital across the means of production and that their role is to eliminate property and create social and economic democracy. If property remains uncontestable in the United States, it is because the class that might contest it has a stake in cultural possession of the property of whiteness. The notion of an historical working-class role to put an end to property, and socialize the means of production, crashes against this social stake and becomes unintelligible. In the United States, the historical working-class role has been to be white, and to maintain the social structure of whiteness.

Ultimately, the socialist call for class unity, which addresses itself to white workers as workers, has had no meaning for white workers as white. It has meaning for black workers as workers—but as black, they hear it as a call for unity with workers who have always refused unity with them, and is thus for them in general a false or futile call. Socialism has remained blind to the fact that race is the foundation for the unity of the white working class within a dual and heterogeneous economic structure—that is, that white working-class unity is also white unity, a structural form of class collaboration. Racism has been an obstacle to building (idealized) working-class organizations because racialization has been fundamental to how class relations and class identity have been constructed and organized.

It is necessary to understand this in order to understand why socialist ideas have generally not gotten a hearing in the United States. Those ideas did not address the basis on which the white working class had defined itself as a class. They have spoken to it as workers, while not seeing that what their ideas said to that class as workers did not compute for them as white. Socialism has not seen that, in the United States, the condition for working-class unity is the condition for its disunity.

CHAPTER 3

The Contemporary Control Stratum

The Culture of Racialization

A number of structures have been described in this book. One is the political structure of racialization by which Europeans became white. Based on a purity concept, whiteness marks the hegemonic moment in a system of social categorization called "race," for which racialization delineates the modes of social inclusion within an encompassing system of categorization and in which whites are hegemonic and exclusive. The structure of racialization constitutes the process by which the meaning and valuation of whiteness are derived from the demeaning and devaluation of others. Since whiteness defines itself through a purity condition, it does not define itself through chromatic difference (differences in bodily coloration between people). Instead, it defines all chromatic difference in terms of itself, as separated from the human color continuum and chromatic differences by its self-defined purity condition. Colors have parity; difference in color is simply difference, not hierarchy. Insofar as whiteness renders color a "characteristic" of people, a particularity to define and notice in general, it abrogates parity. It does this to insist on dominance, the power to define. Whiteness thus constitutes itself as different from mere chromatic difference, a difference in chromatic difference. In historically constructing a hierarchy based on color, a differential stratification of chromatically designated people, whiteness arrogated hegemony to itself by self-definition. Whites then legitimized the gratuitousness of this white supremacy by means of biological theories of race.

Another structure examined here is the dual class structure, a double class relation, that first appeared in colonial plantation society through racialization. Racialization imposed a system of social categorizations that were transformed and consolidated as a class structure through the organization of an intermediary control stratum (patrols). The control stratum consolidated the slave system and concretized a cultural ethos of white solidarity in white colonial society against black plantation workers. As slaves, these workers were seen to pose a threat of rebellion, though that threat was created by the oppressiveness of the slave system itself, the brutality of the control stratum, and the entire structure of racialization. For plantation society, the African American bond-labor force constituted the working class. The structure of white solidarity served to homogenize white society to an extent, blurring what would have been class oppositions within it, and stratifying it along lines of administrative control. It also produced a class distinction between white and black workers.

These structures produced a confluence of cultural phenomena peculiar to the continental colonies: an obsessive insistence on social allegiance, the production of specifically racialized forms of violence through the intermediary control stratum (against both the African American bond-labor force and those whites who would question the ethics of slavery), and a paranoia with respect to the black population (both bond-labor and free). These coalesced in the sociocultural foundation for white colonial society, as a culture of white supremacy. The paranoia served to oblige allegiance and to rationalize the racialized violence. The organizational form was the corporate state, of governance through administrative hierarchy as an organizing principle.

The culture of white supremacy, with its purity condition and its concept of race—its categorization of all other chromatic differences according to white-invented valuations, all of which were arbitrary because self-defined—was subsequently spread to other societies around the world through Europe's eighteenth- and nineteenth-century colonialist endeavors. People nowadays regard themselves as belonging to a race as part of their biological condition. But race remains what its origins established, a complex sociocultural structure composed of the concept of whiteness (based on the purity condition) and whites' racialization of others through that concept. Thus, race is a social structure, a system of social categorizations and exclusions, a system of identities responding to those imposed categorizations, and a structure of social administration. As a social structure, race depends on whiteness defining others chromatically in order to bring itself into existence as white, and it depends on its self-referential definitions of social categorizations and exclusions in order to constitute itself as normative. Though race can be defined through the physical or cultural characteristics of a group, the complexes of such characteristics will eventually be iconized by a color designation, in order to be made to belong to what can be categorized as "nonwhite."[1]

The process of racialization and the social structures through which it realizes itself are alien to biology. Thus, the process of racialization is "metaracial" in constituting races and in instituting how race is socially constituted. This means that these processes are not themselves racial, but that race is what they are about, what they bring into existence as their effect or content. In effect, whiteness and white supremacy are quintessentially metaracial, and racism can be understood as the social ethos by which whites continually, by overt and covert violence, by oppression and social constraint, reinvent and reconstruct race metaracially (as a system of social categorizations). It is not that whites set themselves outside and above a domain of races in which they discovered themselves, as one racial category among many. The domain of races was defined metaracially by whites for themselves as the domain they were by definition already outside and above. In other words, whites did not win a position of superiority within a spectrum of chromatic differences they then hierarchized; their assumption of the power to define, to characterize, to dictate the nature of all those they characterized metaracially and chromatically was already totalitarian, already a position of superiority.[2] The notion that race is a biological aspect of being rather than an imposed social concept and value simply disguises that racialization brings into existence what it is metaracially about.

Because of this, racialization is gratuitous. There is no extant reason for it, even after the fact. It is explained by neither a white obsession with power over others, nor a white obsession with the profitability made possible by the cheap labor that racialization provides, since nothing necessarily ties either obsession to the need to invent race or racial categorizations. Both obsessions may exist, but it is contingent that they take the form of racialization. Nevertheless, in the United States and its antecedent colonial society, they did take that form. This is important because it is the gratuitousness of race and racialization that makes racism and white supremacy so impervious to reason, argument, or ethics.[3] For the white supremacist, the existence of white supremacy is its reason for being. No refutation will touch the fundamental rationalization for its existence, that is, its existence itself. Any and all argument will serve only to fill the conceptual vacuum of its gratuitousness—and in fact serve its purposes by granting it an existence it would not otherwise have.

But gratuitousness reveals a further insularity in being circular and self-reinforcing in structure. Insofar as it has only its own existence as its reason for being, its violence, its paranoia, and its demand for allegiance to whiteness, all condition and generate each other. The violence against the class of black bond-laborers by the patrols engendered a paranoia; the paranoia toward the black bond-laborers engendered a call for solidarity and allegiance; and the requirements of allegiance demanded violence against the black bond-laborers. Or, to put this another way, the enforcement of (white) allegiance to whiteness took the form of organized and systematic (real and potential) violence against the class of black bond-laborers in order to express the social paranoia behind it. The paranoia took the form of a call to solidarity and allegiance to whiteness in order to rhetorically rationalize the deployment of aggressive violence behind it. And the violence against the class of black bond-laborers took the form of a paranoia toward them in order to cement the demand for allegiance that violence depended on. In short, they are intimately interlinked and inseparable within the white supremacist framework; racial violence is the expression of allegiance, allegiance to whiteness is the expression of a paranoia, and paranoia is the expression of a gratuitous violence. One could not break into this circle at any one point to contest its rationale or validity without facing a prior factor whose dependence on the element under contestation was hidden by the third factor. With the purity concept at its center, the circularity of allegiance, violence, and paranoia renders whiteness and its structures of racialization insular with respect to argument or experience.

None of this has ever occurred without the participation of the state. If the cultural operations of allegiance, violence, and paranoia are the ground upon which the structures of racialization in the United States are based, none emerged in the colonies without state enactments as a mode of "concrete substrate" for their existence, and as the foundation of the political discourse that rationalized them. As cultural dimensions of the colony, they represent inherent aspects of stratified administration, and thus reflect the form of corporate state that brought them about.

If the structure of racialization, constituted as a self-generating machine of allegiance, violence, and paranoia, lies thereby at the cultural core of this nation, one can ask what forms it takes today. The question does not assume that the process of racialization persists; the answer could be none. But it is a question immanent in the history we have been examining. If racialization persists, what forms does it take? Are the axes of an insistence on allegiance, the enactment of gratuitous violence, and an obsessive white paranoia still predominant elements at the cultural core of the United States?

The Corporate State

Since the cultural elements of whiteness have relied on their being embedded in a corporate social structure, an approach to this question could logically begin with the issue of the corporate state and corporate society as its integument, its supervening matrix. Such a theorization of corporate structure is not a new endeavor, but the corporate state has been theorized from a somewhat different perspective than that of racialization.[4] Such theorization is nevertheless important and will be useful here, since it provides a kind of unification of conception applicable to the two incommensurable forms of class organization that we have been examining. Such theorizations have generally not addressed the United States on the assumption that the concept of a "corporate state" was wholly foreign to it and did not apply. The concept may be foreign to the ideals of democracy that the United States espouses, but it is not foreign to U.S. history or administrative practices. Thus a few of the predominant themes of this field will be worth outlining in order to translate them (belatedly) to the United States.

The basic project of the corporate state is governance over the functional organization of society. Andrew Shonfield describes modern corporatism as the state oversight and coordination of interest-group activity (corporations, unions, cities, parties, etc.), that is, the regulation of group development and behavior along a projected path toward a general goal of economic welfare and stability (CCW, 51). Corporatism does not inherently require a single-party state; it can proceed in a pluralist society and a multiparty political system. While most corporatist theorists assume a plurality of intermediary state-regulated interest groups in any category, they also tend to assume a noncompetitive field among those groups (owing to the fascist applications of the corporate state in Europe before the second world war). Then they will generally make apologies for the totalitarian tinge that is associated with the notion of corporatism. In other words, they get stuck between competition and regulation, theoretical democratic possibility and historical totalitarian practice. Nevertheless, for most theorists, the hallmark of the corporate state is a strong executive, which only in a very limited sense would be responsible to the social strata below it (CCW, 70). Yet no general criteriology of executive function has emerged from the many different theoretic descriptions of the corporate state. Peter Williamson argues in *Varieties of Corporatism,* for instance, that the existence of a "common ground between corporatist ideology and authoritarian practice" (VC, 8) means that one's understanding of corporatism must at all times include the space between its past sociopolitical practice and a criteriological description. But this blurs the distinction between theory and description, and promotes empirical description of corporate state operations to the position of theory itself.

A distinction should be made between a corporate structure and corporatism. The former marks a mode of corporate governance that may admit of such notions as freedom, Lockean individualism, democratic procedure, and the property rights of the individual, while the latter theorizes the conditions and assumptions of partial totalitarian control.[5] The former emerges out of its own historical practice, whereas the latter serves to organize state practices with respect to a social program. The actual operations of governance may be the same but would have different meanings in the two cases. At its most abstract level, one could say that corporate governance focuses on centrally guided economic development, regulated labor supply, and the maintenance of markets. It is not necessarily authoritarian; what is central is the symbiosis of social consensus and the administrative delegation of power to intermediary levels.

Norman Birnbaum describes consensus as "the result of a more or less conscious adherence to certain beliefs about the political community" (CIS, 71). If people consensually identify their communities as "repositories of objectively valid ideas of political order," that permits them in good conscience to "perform their assigned social tasks" and "accept the authorities set above them." In effect, consensus actually signifies the extent to which there is a hiatus between administrative function and popular participation in governance. That is, it marks the ways in which people "know what to do (or support) without being told," while those tacit "directives" represent higher social decisions in which they played no role and did not participate. (U.S. foreign policy is an example.) Consensus marks a central aspect of ordinary corporate organization. In ordinary corporations, there is a structural gap between ownership and control, between shareholders and directors. Control over intermediary operations assumes acceptance by both shareholders and employees of the hierarchy of control exercised by the directors. Within such a consensus, Birnbaum continues, people think "thoughts other than their own" (CIS, 72). They then live those thoughts and defend them as their participation in them.

In those corporate societies that pretend to representational structures, a hiatus potentially exists between the citizen and political representation.[6] The corporate state prioritizes administrative function and an acceptance of stratification over channels of popular political participation, which are shunted into the machinery of representational operations. What disguises the ensuing separation between the people and the government, or between the represented and their representatives (analogous to that between shareholders and directors), is the assumption or enforcement of consensus with respect to a pretended maintenance of connection (between the people and the government). Because consensus and representation operate in incommensurable dimensions of social space, when one attempts to step in for the other, it produces a political crisis between citizenship and corporate regulation. A corporate state becomes unstable to the extent it cannot find a means of resolving that crisis. For the European nations, nationalism fulfilled that function. In the United States, that has been the role of race and racialization (white solidarity and white supremacy).[7] Indeed, in the history we have been examining, nothing has demonstrated the importance of white supremacy to the stability of the corporate state better than the fact that the courts of the nineteenth century reached back to the previous and superseded colonial structure for precedents by which to define slavery and the racialization of citizenship.

Structurally, one can identify two fundamental levels to the corporate state: the state organization itself, and the subsidiary organizations at the social level that it licenses and permits a regulated autonomy. Society gets divided into three strata: (1) the elite, namely the directorship of the state, (2) the intermediary corporate organizations to which the state gives recognition and certain privileges (social organizations, interest organizations, unions, occupational groups, etc.), and (3) the people (or perhaps one should say "persons"). The third level serves as the predominant labor force or "resource" to be kept at work; for such "persons" there is always a distinction of status between being a citizen and having citizenship (between participating in social decision and being able to defend oneself against abuse as a social "resource"). The second level is the realm from which intermediary control strata between the elite and the work force are constructed. Intermediary levels of organization can be semiautonomous, while administratively restricted to certain jurisdictions and functionalities by the state. This is not a question of political parties or unions having their own constitutions and by-laws, but of being constrained by an accepted social logic to only certain realms of endeavor; foreign policy, for instance, is not in the purview of unions—or of movements that seek to influence foreign policy, such as an antiwar movement (which is the reason it exists essentially as a protest movement). Political debate and political representation or influence (that is, politics as such) occur within the administrative ranks of the intermediary organizations. The average person, then, is able to function and have social influence only through intermediary organizations. This was the nature of the influence (through a patronage system) that coalesced around the slave patrols and made them a political force for disfranchised whites during the eighteenth century.

A focus on administrative stratification both resulted from and produced a solidarist sense of belonging. On the one hand, it subordinated consciousness of being exploited to structural locatedness; one the other, it subjected democratic participation to control structures. Administrative structure, as distinguished from bureaucratic position, has become the context of social situatedness. In the United States, it appears as white society itself. Class contradictions appear embedded in it. For whites, the ethos of an intermediary control stratum, the vision white people have of themselves as middle class, the priority of white solidarity as white nonproletarianization (with its class collaborationism) over class or political solidarity, and finally capitalist exploitation itself, all center administrative structure over articulations of social contradiction or political oppositionality.

Because its role is the structural substitution of administrative hierarchy and control chains for class relations and contradictions, the corporate state can deploy any number of forms to establish economic or social order, and operate at many levels of governance. The colonial form of corporate organization was a centralized, hegemonic body. Towns, counties, and state agencies are organized on a corporate model, for which a governing body (of supervisors or county commissioners, for instance) is elected. Carrying this principle to its logical conclusion, U.S. courts recognized the economic and political significance of the corporate form most profoundly in decreeing personhood for such entities (*Santa Clara County vs. Southern Pacific Railroad*, 1886).

This principle was extended to labor unions as well. The state gives labor unions "juridical personality" by licensing them (through recognition by the National Labor Relations Board), in order for them to have political legitimacy and legal rights (CCW, 104). It is not that unions could not function without those rights; if unions get strong enough, they force recognition without the juridical licensing. What the state provides is status within the corporate society, bestowing respectability, social authenticity, and structural legitimacy—in other words, a niche in the administrative network of command and control. In regulating the unions, the state not only sanctions their existence and provides limits to their operation, but fulfills its role of regulating industrial relations for socioeconomic stability by delegating the unions the job of subgoverning (policing) their members (VC, 10). In that sense, the slave patrols stand as the first form of state regulation of industrial relations in practice.

Conversely, for the corporate state, ad hoc movements and groups are not legitimate, have no juridical standing, and are thus subject to executive discretion. The primary problem for the government with respect to the civil rights, environmental, women's, and antiwar movements, all of whose aims called for political participation where that had been obstructed, was control. Legitimization of popular or populist movements is not an option without critically contradicting the corporatist structural ethos. The failure of the populist (and other third) parties lay not in falling short of recognition for their members (whether as "producers" or as "citizens"), but in being unable to surpass the structural barriers to organizational legitimacy.[8]

Other examples of corporate forms include the two-party system, governmental regulatory agencies, and the World Trade Organization. A two-party political system within a representational government, with winner-take-all, single-delegate districts, is a form of corporate organization insofar as it requires each district's array of class interests, cultural identities, and social-group needs to connect to governance through the same single entity, the person of the representative, who can act only administratively rather than in terms of the various ideological positions of different classes, cultures, or identities in the district. While the liberal corporate state has established certain regulatory agencies, which are given economic oversight, control over those agencies is in turn given to the corporate interests involved in that regulatory action or procedure (VC, 39). Finally, the establishment of the World Trade Organization in 1995 constitutes a global corporate state that makes its own rules, which then hold administratively for all nations that are treaty signatories to it.[9] In other words, today, the corporate form of organization perfuses U.S. society from top to bottom.

The ethical problem that continually re-emerges for corporatist theory with respect to industrial relations (from liberalism to Mussolini's fascism) is the question of social justice as a function of social peace and social stability rather than as a domain of independent social concern (VC, 58). The English colonists in the eighteenth century confronted the atrocious evil of the enslavement of thousands of humans, yet rationalized it through principles of social rectitude and a rhetoric of civilization. This only made the need for a theory of the African's innate inferiority more imperative and more obsessive. The subsequent theorization of biological race was designed to transform patent injustice into a sense of justice around which white society could establish social peace with itself, and for itself with respect to agricultural production.

To the extent that whiteness and white supremacy are the matrix that bestows coherence upon the United States as a corporate society, they become the defining characteristics of this society's cultural structures. This does not mean that white people are by nature evil. No innate "racial nature" exists to be judged in that manner. It is the structure of white supremacy that sets white people into an administrative structure that valorizes violence, aggression, hostility, and irrational dehumanized behavior. If white people do these things, it is because they accept the white identity imposed upon them, as well as the thought that white identity bestows on them something other than the criminality or obsessive hatred its violence demands of them and produces in them.[10] What is truly evil about one's identification with whiteness is the extent to which it leads people into thinking that the violence and criminality upon which whiteness is based, and through which it constitutes itself, are really good. The social psychosis or paranoia inherent in such identification manifests an ethical reversal in which criminality and violence are seen as moral. Not all whites fall into that mode of ethically dysfunctional or dysethical thinking, but very few see the social structure through which they are constructed as persons, and which enmeshes them in that dysethics. It is the social structure of whiteness that we are attempting to understand here.

As we have seen, in the United States, white corporate society is both a class society and a class entity. Though within corporate society there is a characteristic capitalist class structure, it is morphologically transfigured by the structure of white solidarity necessitated by the overarching racialized class structure, and in which it functions as a ruling "class," with white workers constituting the interface. Both class systems produce social value, though in incommensurate domains. Each working class (the black and the white) produces wealth for the white capitalist class of white corporate society. The white working class produces white corporate society as white through its various proletarianizations of workers of color, amounting to different class segregations, and it produces itself as "the" working class by producing the black and brown working class as proletarianized. Workers of color (categorized as "minorities" or "ethnicities") live in continuing class contradiction with respect to white workers. If white workers accept this, because the notions of ethnicity and minority make sense to them as white, it is an inherent part of their inclusion in the white consensus that constitutes the "majority."

This now gives us a foothold from which to address the question of contemporary racialization and the corporate state. If the terms "minority" and "ethnicity" are used in the rhetorical place once filled by the word "race," it represents a transformation in the structure of white corporate society. What that transformation has been will allow us to see how the corporate society of the present has been reconfigured, and how it now operates.

Affirmative Action and the Dual Class Structure

There have been three moments in U.S. history when the dual class structure produced by white supremacy and its structures of racialization faced the possibility of being broken down. The first was at the time of the Revolution, when a new possibility of simply declaring all people citizens, free and equal, presented itself. Having liberated themselves from the British, the revolutionaries could have truly implemented the ideals they expressed and transformed the social structure inherited from the colonial period. Slavery could have been replaced by a society responsible to the will of all the people. But while the Revolution broke with previous colonial forms of political organization and governmental dependence, it did not qualitatively transform property or jurisprudence. Instead, it proclaimed the founding of a white nation. In other words, the Revolution was not really a moment of lost opportunity; the "opportunity" was not seriously envisioned. Instead, the Revolution sought independent control of the wealth embodied in the black bond-laborer and wrested that wealth from England's distant grasp (VC, 59).

The second moment when the dual class structure might have broken down was the Reconstruction period after the Civil War; the third was the civil rights movement. Though Reconstruction officially ended with the withdrawal of federal troops from the South in 1877, it was in large part overturned or stillborn even before that date. Economically, a form of debt-slavery replaced the former chattel form of labor;[11] politically, paramilitary groups (the KKK and many others) emerged that used terrorism to put the Democratic Party and the plantation owners back in political power.[12] Subsequently, the system of segregation and disfranchisement known as Jim Crow was installed through a vast campaign generating paranoia around an invented threat (sexual and otherwise) personified in every black man.

The civil rights movements brought about the juridical dismantling of Jim Crow structures and opened up avenues of participation in the political process for all people. Following the African Americans' lead, Native Americans and Mexican Americans organized against their own particular forms of racialized oppression within the dual class structure, and a powerful women's movement fought against the many dimensions of gender exclusion and oppression known collectively as patriarchy. While these movements accomplished the dissolution of an ethos of discrimination and the creation of antidiscrimination machinery to handle future cases of racialized and gender-based exclusion, they did not end all covert exclusionism. For African Americans in particular, redlining, profiling, neighborhood segregation, and housing discrimination, as well as open racial hostility on the part of most whites (many of whom were not even aware of it), persisted. One of the most important successes of these movements was the affirmative action process, designed to correct the inherited disparities and inequalities engendered by centuries of discrimination and racialization.

Affirmative action, because it addressed itself primarily to employment, began to blur the boundary between the two class structures. Unions were integrated; people of color and white women were elected to office in government, institutions, and organizations; schools were integrated. People of color attained positions in the administrative and economic structure of this society.

There are no generalizations to make about this. Some people of color have moved into the middle class; others have high positions of social responsibility in government and corporate bureaucracies. They are still grossly underrepresented in all areas except those traditionally set aside for people of color. For many, it has not been easy to move into sectors of social participation that had been wholly segregated fifty years ago, and different people have related to this mobility in different ways. Some have come to see themselves as "white"; others feel they have betrayed the particular group from which they came by accepting a career. Surrounded by a society that still characterizes them chromatically, yet which adopts an official pretense of color-blindness, many feel they are participating in a social environment of imposture. Most people of color still have been left out of the social process, outside political participation, marginalized in universities and professions, considered expendable in industry, working the same menial jobs as before, and facing derogation and criminalization at the hands of the surrounding white society.[13] In most black, Latino, Native American, and Asian communities, a sort of internal (alternative) economy has evolved to provide a means of survival. In some cases, it is a drug economy.

Whites' attitudes toward the civil rights movement have generally varied from acceptance of integration to daily harassment, from friendship to attempts to ostracize and exclude people designated chromatically. Some whites feel secure only when the purity condition on which they depend is reaffirmed; they often think the purity concept is threatened by each step toward integration, as if questioning it amounted to a violation of sacred principle that would put an end to them as persons. In particular, the rejection of (and even panic over) miscegenation, the idea that mixed-race couples symbolize the end of the "white race," represents the depth of this obsession—as does the unthinking suppression of any sign of social or political autonomy on the part of a racialized group. The more or less successful effort to repeal all affirmative action legislation has been one effect of these feelings.

On the other hand, reaffirmation of affirmative action is not a call for integration. Integration is an empty concept, precisely because black people have always been integrated in U.S. society; they have always been at the center of how white society has defined itself as white. Part of the paradox or double bind of white supremacist society for black people is that they confront two contradictory forms of integration: equality and parity, or inequality and segregation. The first, which the integration movement struggled for, means integration into a white society that has excluded them, a form of struggle for acquiescence to what had been exclusionary. The second, which the civil rights movement struggled against, is integration as an indispensable target of violence essential to white supremacy's constitution of itself. Both forms have the same content, the same denial of humanity, the same origin at the core of white society as such. Antiracist integration would not change that denial for black people because they would be integrated as black and not as people, their humanity admitted by white society only as a further exercise of hegemony. It would be an equality established as an inequality, a parity that was still a form of disparity, a redefinition of white society as white, again through black people.

In that sense, equal opportunity is a misnomer. Race, ethnic or minority status, and gender hierarchy all name something that someone does to someone else. A call for parity assumes an innate source of disparity in people, rather than one concocted hegemonically. To call on whites and men to stop doing what they are doing that engenders disparity is a different kind of call. The difference reflects the incommensurability between the act of defining and the state of being defined.

Many (perhaps most) whites consider the attempt to equalize representation in all employment sectors or in political participation (that is, to dismantle a systematic underrepresentation) a quota system. These whites do not consider segregation a quota system, however, even though (or perhaps, because) whites were guaranteed a quota of 100 percent. They cannot see that the notion of "*under*representation" of black people in a job category or academic field, for instance, implies that the only cause of exclusion from those fields was color—that color rather than capability (or something else innate) led to disproportionate representation in various job categories. They do not see that underrepresentation, if preserved through canceling affirmative action, implies a return to a former quota system. Those who think that overcoming underrepresentation is imposing a quota are tacitly claiming that something innate in black people beyond mere color had disqualified them. In other words, seeing affirmative action as a quota system means believing that race is a biological aspect of humans and not a social construct.

The history of the invention of whiteness and race suggests that there was nothing beside color for which black people were excluded from most social domains by whites. It does not answer the question of whether there may be something innate in whites that leads them to act in this dehumanized and dehumanizing manner. Furthermore, the history does not suggest why whites chose racialization to organize their domination of other people, or why they so consistently chose domination rather than dialogue and community. Be that as it may, the white critique of equal representation as a quota system signifies that those whites consider black people (or others, Native, Asian, white women, etc.) to be in some sense innately less qualified than whites (or white males).

The results of the civil rights movement were partial to the extent they did not change the fundamental social ethos that maintained racialization as the primary mode of social categorization disguised behind theories of biology and innateness. I will not call what the civil rights movement accomplished "gains," since those who had to fight for civil rights politically were due them all along, whether governments agreed or not. What appear as gains to whites are, for people of color, the begrudged release of what is due, or even of stolen goods. To consider social participation a gain assumes there was a certain propriety in the initial state of exclusion; but that exclusion was wholly improper. Equality and participation should have been assumable and extant; they were not. The establishment of full equality and participation should have been seen not as a gain, but as a return to a proper place—though perhaps a place where we as a society had never been. But the existence of an anti–affirmative action movement implies that even that return to a place in society would be taken away again.

As the anti–affirmative action movement grew, it became a process of reracialization and recategorization. It grew as the civil rights movements waned and dissolved. The implicit issues of contestation were the opening and closing of doors, while the place of contestation was the courts.

The movement to repeal affirmative action, which grew during the 1980s, began in the courts. Anti–affirmative action took many subtle forms, such as the Bakke case, nonprocessing of grievances by unions, and Propositions 209, 187, and 21 (the Juvenal Crime Law) in California. It also took openly aggressive forms, such as anti-immigrant lynchings on the Mexican border in Arizona and Texas, the organization of militias, and a new public appearance of the KKK. Its main arguments were that affirmative action was "discriminatory," a "reverse racism" (as if such an expression could have any meaning). These were developed through rhetorical dysinformation, such as the equation of affirmative action with quotas, and an invocation of a "merit" system that had never existed (especially across racial lines). It led to the passage of voter initiatives, and repeal by Congress. What astounds about the debate was not only that attacks existed and sought to undo affirmative action, but that the response in defense seemed only to have moral arguments to fall back on, and thus appeared weak.

The problem with affirmative action for white people was not that they were suddenly unable to get access to social and economic positions, but that they no longer had clear access as whites; they could no longer lay claim to prior entitlement. To the extent affirmative action was about jobs from which black people had previously been excluded by segregation, the anti–affirmative action movement was reasserting that those jobs belonged to whites. It was the idea of prior entitlement that was at issue, that evaluated nonwhite applicants as unworthy or without merit a priori, and that refused restitution against a discriminatory past on the grounds that such restitution was a quota system. The anti–affirmative action movement responded to the alleged loss of white proprietary position in a populist manner, attacking the government (in the guise of liberalism) for betraying the racial contract, and for withholding recognition from the "truly worthy" (the white "producers"). The white charge was that the government was selling out the nation by discriminating against white people. It was against the charged betrayal that the arguments about "merit" or "quota" took on political meaning.

For black people, the question was not whether they were qualified or not, but whether they were going to get a job this time or be discriminated against as usual. The white call to return to "merit" hiring simply reflected in modern terms the old charge of "unfair competition." For the black applicant, "merit" and "quota" were just more Jim Crow arguments against equality and participation because they simply continued prioritizing the noticing of color over the application for the job itself. But when the issue got to court, what black or brown people thought, or had experienced, no longer entered into the equation. The overall white response to black and brown attempts to reenter the discourse were: "We've eliminated Jim Crow; now get over it"—as if that act were simply a minor disruption of life, though the impatience in the attitude bespoke a secret and almost panicked defense of white identity.

The defense of affirmative-action marshaled what it could for its arguments. Statistics showed that the process of equalization was far from complete.[14] After three decades of civil rights struggle and active antiracism, along with government institutionalization of civil rights mechanisms, there was still a lot to do, a lot to make up for. The original arguments, which had initiated affirmative action programs in the first place, still seemed germane (understandably, given the irrationality of the reverse racism charge in a white dominated society). But these arguments were not an answer to the claims of white "victimology" or reverse discrimination, and the call for civil rights for whites. It is hard to know what to say to such notions in a white supremacist society, or how to pull them back to some semblance of reality. The anti–affirmative action process was turning the institutedness of civil rights against itself, by using its own goals against it; in the process, the very language of justice self-destructed. What the defenders of affirmative action did not take into account was that the institutedness of civil rights had totally changed the situation.

To see the depth of the changes, we have to look at the internal social and class structure of both affirmative action and its opposition. Affirmative action was on the surface about jobs, education, housing, and history (space and time). Jobs, education, and housing were issues because of a history of segregation, and history was an issue because of prior state codification of exclusion from jobs, education, and housing. When first instituted, various affirmative action programs began the long hard process of bringing black and brown men and women, and white women, into the economic process. Craft training programs were opened, college and university roles diversified. Hiring guidelines were instituted for insuring that previously unconsidered groups would get consideration. It started to work. Jobs, education, and housing became the concrete symbols through which social participation by people of color and white women was signified. Black and brown communities and women's organizations were suddenly spoken about as voting blocs in elections. These groups all worked through the two-party system, as though voting, employment, schools, and neighborhoods were simply political issues and not embedded in unspoken social and cultural structures for which a transformation of "political culture" was necessary.

But the civil rights movement was not just about jobs, education, and housing. In substance and intent, the civil rights movement (and affirmative action) was to change the priorities of this society from inferiorizing to anti-inferiorizing—not only for black people, but for Latinos, Native Americans, white women, and other "minority" groups. The purpose of attacking Jim Crow was not to invert the structures of racialization. Where Jim Crow, in the 1890s, had reracialized the original black-white binary of the colonial period that had been weakened by emancipation and Reconstruction, the dismantling of Jim Crow was an attempt to deracialize that black-white binary altogether by prioritizing mutual respect and the recognition of cultural dignity and sovereignty.

In that context, to speak about affirmative action is not just to speak about participation, history, and steps toward social inclusion; it is to enact nonexclusion, as the permissibility of cultural autonomy and difference. As a positive move against and beyond discrimination, it was to enact the cessation of something, to discontinue the structures of racialization. Affirmative action programs were designed both to include those previously excluded, and to deuniversalize the white proprietary claim on social entitlement and hegemony. But it could not do both. For people to demand "inclusion" means an implicit acceptance of the hegemonic structure into which to be included, a white hegemony in which whites ultimately decide whom to include and whom not to. The enactment of nonexclusion, the demand to end or dispel that structure of domination, is to refuse to accept white hegemony or the society based upon it. This was another form of the double bind into which racism traps antiracism.

In the face of this dilemma, movements had to leave to the government the terms in which the history of segregation and racial exclusion were to be addressed. Inclusion meant that the prior structure of exclusion would open its doors—though that required federal troops in a number of significant instances. The enactment of nonexclusion, on the other hand, was reduced to simply enforcing antidiscrimination standards, for which a juridical procedure was invented, but nothing more. From Little Rock on, desegregation meant administratively opening doors and placing people together, with no responsibility for bringing their different narratives and cultural frameworks (by which they lived their experiences of each other) into contact or dialogue. The failure to address the hegemony of the white narratives by bringing about a dialogue early on was later transformed into "sensitivity training," another form of paternalistic white hegemony. The process of integration was administered simply as a mechanical idea and never became an enactment of nonexclusion. As instituted, it left the proprietary and hegemonic claims of whiteness intact, precisely through its administrated institutionality. This transformation of civil rights into a structure of political institutions opened the possibility of a rhetoric through which whites could pretend to be the victims of discrimination, since the government was doing it (by "including" civil rights into itself).

After the courts valorized the reverse discrimination idea (and with it the rhetoric of quotas) in a series of decisions beginning with the Bakke case, the government proclaimed the situation of racial discrimination resolved. If both sides could discriminate against each other, it meant that all were equal, with no need for special attention to prior historical aftereffects. Antidiscrimination, which targeted white hegemonic exclusion, was transformed into nondiscrimination, thus hiding the ongoing realities of racialization behind a rhetoric of democracy. The original affirmative action programs were dissolved slowly and absorbed into the legalist approaches to continuing discrimination that marked the extent to which instituted structures of civil rights, as agencies and offices, would go. Ultimately, all was papered over by a government proclamation of colorblindness, pretending that color was no longer a factor because the government, at the behest of anti–affirmative action decisions, decided to ignore it.

The problem with the "colorblind" idea is that it falls prey to the same double bind as the idea of parity or equality (in the sense, for instance, that inequality is not a state but something people with power do to others). Black or white people, for instance, are not born black or white; they are given this as a social categorization by a society that racializes. If you claim to be colorblind (as does the law nowadays), you consider "color" real, pertaining to skin or bodies rather than functioning as a reference to social categories that "blindness" is not a relevant mode of "ignoring." To claim to be colorblind is to see color from a white point of view. In confusing the two, the law reifies race while claiming not to recognize it any longer. In adopting the white point of view, it establishes white as the one color it sees in its colorblindness. In other words, the corollary to colorblindness is that black people are supposed to stop seeing themselves as black, while whites do not have to do stop seeing themselves as white, which in turn relies on seeing black people as black.

The proclamation of colorblindness has set the stage for the recriminalizaton of race. Although campaigns to "stop crime" adopted the colorblind label, their targets were overwhelmingly people of color. Racial profiling became generalized throughout society (in police stops, neighborhood police patrols, employment, department stores, real estate, finance), and amounted to a criminalization of color.[15] A prison population has been generated that is the largest in the world, both in absolute terms and per capita. Not only are these prison figures absurd for an allegedly democratic country, but 75 percent of the prisoners are black or brown and two-thirds have been convicted of victimless, nonviolent crimes. Victimless crime laws have generated a mass of victims, most of whom are people of color. Their incarceration constitutes a legalist process of reghettoization (in the literal sense in which "ghetto" means "wall" in Yiddish). The process also has effected a massive disfranchisement insofar as black arrestees are charged with felonies where whites would be charged with misdemeanors, and in most states felony convictions result in a loss of the right to vote. Politicians have persisted in being "hard on crime" in the midst of a declining crime situation, not because crime remains a problem, but because it became a hidden way of declaring white solidarity. We can see here the paradigms of new structures of racialization.

The government institutionalization of civil rights, in appearing to betray the white solidarity bargain, opened space for white adoption of a victimology. In so doing, it steered the civil rights movement's attack on white supremacy into the blind alley of colorblindness and criminalization. How did this happen? What was the nature of the social context in which a movement for deracialization and democratization could be turned into its opposite? Why would an institutionalization of civil rights permit the rhetoric of those fighting for civil rights to be shifted to a white opposition?

Civil Rights Institutionalized: Minoritization

The civil rights movement began as a movement of African Americans against antiblack racism and segregation. Through court decisions and various federal civil rights acts, Jim Crow was replaced by a different legal paradigm. The government did not establish proactive antidiscrimination procedures. It only instituted passive machinery to which charges of continuing discrimination could be brought through antidiscrimination suits. Racial discrimination was not criminalized; it was denominated a civil dispute, one that the government would arbitrate. But juridicality is a domain in which dispute can be engaged only in form, not in content, while the proactive nonexclusion dimension of civil rights required confronting the issues of racialization and white supremacy as social meanings. That is, the government not only established itself as the arena of civil rights struggle (as opposed to the society at large) but, in doing so, restricted civil rights to political procedures that obstructed or delegitimized its political critique and principles.

One effect of moving civil rights from the realm of collective community action to governmental procedures was to fragment or atomize the civil rights movements. The massive confluence of black and brown people, acting autonomously and in concert, which had begun to dispel white racism, was thus dissipated. The overtness of the mass movement had been central to presenting white identity and white consensus with a phenomenon it was not equipped to recognize or interpret through its old paradigms or narratives. While many whites were courageously facing the necessity to reconstitute themselves with respect to this new reality, to recognize that the old allegiance and the old violence were obsolete and undemocratic, and that the narratives of white supremacy were anachronistic, the government, through its institutionalization of civil rights protagonism, was preparing the means to roll it all back.

A second effect of this institutionalization was to create a new cultural disparity between whites and blacks. Civil rights is not the same issue for those who have faced discrimination or minoritization and those who have not. For whites, civil rights are a cultural given; they were assumed as part of the social air one breathed. For those who have faced discrimination, civil rights is a political question. Thus, whites and people of color had to approach civil rights on wholly disparate grounds. Cultural givens and political issues of contestation are incommensurable. Through government establishment of judicial machinery, civil rights was relegated to an arena of continual political struggle, rather than cultural assumption (as it was for whites), and at the same time constrained to formalities rather than social transformations. Whites, for whom civil rights could be assumed, looked at the ongoing black struggle and asked, "What's the problem?" Blacks, based on their ongoing necessity, looked at white complacency and rhetorical support and asked, "Why aren't you acting to get rid of racism among yourselves?" The institutedness of civil rights set those against each other.

A third effect of institutionalization was to insinuate the government into the midst of the civil rights communities, both as the source of civil rights themselves and as a source of funds for community organizing projects. Rather than criminalize racism and discrimination, the government provided funds for "uplift," as if insufficient resources had been the problem for black communities all along. Institutionalization hindered the development of black economic and social autonomy by giving the government strings to pull, and shifted the focus of community development from social cohesion and awareness to institutionalized government money. The War on Poverty, in making money available, created another political disparity between black and white communities, a dependency on the part of the black communities, and a feeling of having been left out on the part of the white. The immediate effect of that money was a lot of good organizing, and many people were assisted, rescued, and brought to modes of participation through it, but structurally it had a different long-range effect.

A fourth effect of institutionalization follows directly from the preceding. A sense of competition developed for the governmental civil rights "pie." Women's organizations, Latino and Native American groups, and others who struggled against discrimination entered the government arena, filing suits, applying for government funds, and seeking thereby a certain recognition and placement on the political map. Community organizing for social, artistic, and career opportunities, legal resources, and the opening of job categories were priorities that had to go through the government. Since funds were made available on the basis of degrees of discrimination, impoverishment, or exclusion from economic participation, different groups had to vie for institutional attention on the basis of a victimology. Competition broke the solidarity which had been the force that won civil rights institutionalization in the first place. Each group had begun to establish a new identity and self-awareness through its collective action and social organizing. While these newly apprised identities brought about greater internal cohesion in the groups' resistance, they created separations and named differences that needed to be recognized, but not reified as categorical distinctions. To the extent that each group had to fulfill its needs through a centralized institutionality rather than in solidarity with each other against a common condition, the process of identity separation took priority and transformed "identity" into an ideologized "identity politics." Identity politics flowered from the dialectic between movement resistance and government institutionality toward movement demands.

Within this process, antiracist white radicals played an ironic role. Affirmative action was seen as a way in which antiracism could be mainstreamed. In general, white antiracists agreed among themselves that racism was a divide-and-conquer strategy to prevent popular unity in dealing with pressing political issues, such as the war in Vietnam, runaway shops, unemployment, or tenant's rights. But they missed the fact that antiracism had become effective in dividing minority groups from each other at the institutional trough. Their mainstream white antiracism became an antiracism within a white governmental context which, as white antiracism, understood those designated as nonwhite as "other." Though they called for overcoming the civil rights competitions, they could not see that, as white, their calls for unity meant unity under white hegemony, however antiracist it might appear to them.

Finally, there was an all-important transformation of language. The relegation of civil rights to an institutional arena changed the social categories by which discriminated groups found themselves designated. Though the civil rights pie put different groups in competition with each other, its institutedness opened the possibility of gaining influence over it through the political process. That is, the outcome of the competition could be affected by political action and electoral politics. Within the framework of electoral participation (re-enfranchisement), the identifications of discriminated groups shifted from race to the notion of minority, and minority interest.

Strictly speaking, the term "minority" applies to bloc voting strength; it is a term that belongs to the discourse of democratic procedure. The notion of minority became relevant when racialized (or ethnic) groups moved into the electoral arena. What it meant was, first, that the group was of lesser electoral weight then the majority, but second, that its members, as a group, were not going to be integrated into the (white) majority simply as additional participants. The language changed from a discourse of race to a discourse of minority, in order to reflect the fact that the discriminated groups were of lesser voting strength, and would be treated as such.

A minority is a group that gets outvoted in the electoral or legislative arena. To categorize a group as minority, to give it that character, means to relegate it within electoral discourse to being outvoted (however just or urgent its issues may be). But it means being outvoted as a question of status; to be given the "status" of a minority means to be outvoted before the voting takes place, and not when it does. It implies being nonmainstream, a group that always loses, which takes on the aura of being socially or politically in the wrong. Because a group is relegated to seeking representation as a minority group, it is proclaimed to have "special interests." The shift from racialized to minority status essentially amounts to a substitute marginalization. This political reorientation of the antidiscrimination struggles did not open space for a group's simple participation even as an autonomous self-constructing community with interests of its own. Instead, it engendered a category of "special interest" groups to be dealt with politically as "other." In terms of democratic principles, there should be no such thing as a minority group. Minorities exist on specific issues, since all votes include those who are outvoted. But to declare a group a minority in advance, to proclaim special interests for it as a minority, goes beyond this. It signifies that the group is not, and therefore cannot be in some ontological sense, a part of the political processes that engage the majority, except as some kind of adjunct.

In other words, it is a different process of exclusion, an act of exclusion by a majority from participation in its own internal social and political processes of decision. A group is made a minority by others who reaffirm themselves as the majority in so doing, and in the process reaffirm for themselves the power to exclude. Minority groups come into existence through a process of "minoritization" at the hand of a self-referential majority; they do not exist in and of themselves as such. That is, a minority is the effect of a process of minoritization by a majoritarian group that reconstitutes itself as the majority through its act of exclusion and minoritization. Within the institutionalization of civil rights, the process of minoritization became a substitute for the process of racialization.

The immediate effect of this is that a primary special interest of a minority group is overcoming the social dynamic that renders it a minority in the first place. The special interests defined for each minority group by the majority—though supposedly something the group produces for itself—get shunted into its identity politics as participation and become attempts to overcome the very minority status that was produced by its exclusion. Yet undoing the process of minoritization remains out of reach for the minority group since, by definition, it will be outvoted on the issue and left either unrepresented or represented only by proxy. The promised inclusion of formerly disfranchised people as minorities preserves their disfranchisement to the extent that their only choice is proxy representation through the majority parties that minoritized them.

Through this form of nonrepresentation, the minority voter is constructed as a minority bloc. Any elected member of the group comes to be seen as bestowing representation upon it, as if to elect a woman is to represent women in government, or to elect an African American is to represent African Americans. This only transports the old forms of generalization into the new civil rights categorizations; as generalized, people remain concepts rather than participants. The election of black candidates (for instance) to office in legislatures or administrations does not represent the class interests of racialized people or of the racialized class structure within the governance of white corporate society. These representatives may present a black voice and consciousness in the halls of white government. They may signify that a degree of social organization is going on among black people. But they do not represent "black people" as such. Similarly, a woman elected to office does not represent women; she simply presents a woman's voice in the halls of patriarchal governance. (The appearance of white women and people of color in elected or administrative positions does not change the nature of minoritization; it holds minority representatives up for notice, thereby reifying the difference that their presence is designed to attenuate.) Ultimately, to render a group a minority by exclusion from any but proxy representation means to submerge its members in the special issues proclaimed for it. This reinforces the assumption that the group will have homogeneous interests and points of view. Thus, another self-fulfilling circle of generalization is created.

Minoritization does not overcome racialization; it simply changes its name (while highlighting the fact that it is a social structure). The central racializing binary (white and black) gets rearticulated as white and minority, while the minoritized group remains inferiorized and marginalized. It remains excluded from power as a minority, just as it had been when segregated as a racialized group. Minoritization becomes the form that racialization takes within the institutedness of civil rights. Institutionalized civil rights only continues the racialization of communities of color by other means.[16] The corporate state thus absorbs the movement that had disrupted its structures of racialization and, in the name of guaranteeing civil rights, reproduces a marginalization of struggles against discrimination and marginalization.

In this context, the insufficiency of passive civil rights institutions becomes clear. No effects of segregation were going to be overcome by such passive means. Positive efforts to reinclude those structurally excluded had to be made; nonexclusion had to be positively enacted in all areas. Affirmative action was proposed to meet this need, though not simply to end discrimination by atomizing social discrimination into individual acts and individual complaints against those acts. It really meant structurally dismantling the class difference between white and black/brown and the proletarianization of people of color by whites; the primary implication of affirmative action was in fact a deproletarianization of people of color. It thus threatened a central social factor in a white worker's life, what s/he had used against being proletarianized in turn: white entitlement. White entitlement is the aspect of white solidarity for which white workers have exchanged thinking about real class interests or consciousness. It is the subtext of the white bargain.[17] It is the issue that rendered affirmative action a class struggle within the racialized class structure.

It was as a manifestation of white entitlement that affirmative action got recast as a quota system. A familiar sense of paranoia accompanies the concept of quotas, not because of a desire to return to the 100 percent white quotas of segregation, but because transcendence of the 0 percent black quotas meant a loss of something. The institution of that transcendence meant, to the paranoid mind, that all control would shift to other (black) hands. In the Manichean logic of white supremacy, either "we" control or "they" do. Within this logic, it made perfect sense to proclaim that job quotas (however small a percentage that entailed) meant that African Americans were "taking over everything." For whites unable to see beyond the notion of "unfair competition," the rhetoric of quotas became irrefutable, though it made no sense with respect to democracy or fairness. But within the dual class structure, the class struggle invoked by affirmative action around the property of white entitlement rendered moral arguments of fairness and history of little meaning. The paranoia that had originally been used to construct the system of racialization took on the aura of immanent truth.

Nevertheless, for black and brown communities, quotas were not the issue. Overcoming the proletarianization euphemized as "poverty" was the central issue, and that meant community development and autonomy through entry into commerce with the surrounding economy. The defenders of affirmative action knew the issue was white entitlement, against which the moral arguments had become ineffective.

But to raise the issue of white entitlement meant to address a class relation where few were prepared to look for it. In effect, the domain of struggle had been shifted. Having brought affirmative action into existence, the civil rights movement had reconfigured the white corporate state, which could no longer be thought of or analyzed in the same way. Civil rights had transformed the situation in which civil rights still needed to be fought for. It revealed that anti-exclusion required struggle in a racialized class domain. Yet the recognition of the need to continue overshadowed that understanding. Thus, in returning to the original arguments about democracy, history, and jobs, the defenders of affirmative action fell prey to the trap that anti–affirmative action set in its rhetoric of reverse discrimination and quotas.

For white supremacy in its attack on affirmative action, the arguments did not matter as long as they established the issue on a racialized basis, rather than those of history or justice, for instance, or in affirming social participation. Racism holds against the other what it does to them; it dominates by forcing its victims to respond as defined, while defining them as unable to do so by nature. The victim is doubly put on the defensive, first as attacked by (the) definition, and second against the inverted onus of the attack. Argument will not defend affirmative action against this double inversion of language. The battle is won by white supremacy as soon as the discussion returns to the representation of race, rather than the social structures of racialization.

Affirmative action was not just a political attack on an ethos of entitlement, but a disclosure of false property, the property constituted by whiteness. Openly raising the question of whiteness as property, however, would have been to socially contest the whole notion of a mainstream. Mainstream society in the United States is white. Whiteness constitutes the central "imagined community" of the United States, and white solidarity amounts to its nationalism. What is not white is seen as in some essential sense alien, because constructed as such (even though, or rather because, that subsumes the majority of the world, and the indigenous inhabitants of this continent). The ideology of integration inherent in affirmative action sought to extend the notion of mainstream beyond the boundaries of whiteness. To end minority status (without losing cultural autonomy) within the logic of democracy, a minority has to become part of the mainstream. But to end minority status within the logic of a white mainstream (which thinks of itself as democratic), a minority has to abandon its cultural autonomy. Because the mainstream is white, the arguments for inclusion by those minoritized only reify the sense of alienness between whites and minorities. The demand by minority groups for cultural inclusion induced the white mainstream to take itself as cultural, and proclaim a white-defined multiculturalism. This only rearticulated the minority binary as white/multicultural, as a different version of minority status. In the United States, even the logic of democracy traps minorities in minoritization.

In threatening white entitlement, whiteness as property, and the proletarianization of those that whites had chromatically disentitled, the existence of an affirmative action movement polarized a class contradiction between white and black workers—even while bringing them together on the same factory floors. However much one might have expected desegregation and affirmative action to have evoked class solidarity, and union engagement in areas of organization previously foreclosed by Jim Crow norms, the influx of new workers into already unionized industries mainly raised the old cry of "unfair competition" (of course, there were a few exceptions). In general, it threw white workers into a populist mode. This was accompanied by a strange quiescence with respect to capitalism. In the face of runaway shops and automation, white workers went to the government to reconstruct the job market for them, but not to stop capital from eroding the job base by moving or computerizing. Though they often went on bended knee (or the embarrassingly bent knee of a labor leader) for what they thought was their due, it was in lieu of developing political resistance to economic displacement. As before, during the nineteenth century, no autonomous workers' co-ops were proposed by the unions. Indeed, the farthest the unions have gone toward preserving their job base has been the organization of union hiring halls. DuBois points out that it was black people in the South during Reconstruction who, when rejected by the new labor movement, had begun a process of organizing worker, finance, and farmer/tenant co-ops. In the 1970s, this process started again, also in the South. While the unions claim strength in numbers, they belie this by accepting capital's prerogative in deciding how many jobs there will be, or whether jobs will remain or run away.

For white workers to have continued in this stand during a wave of runaway economics that was totally transforming the employment landscape meant that something other than job preservation was on their minds. As the economy reconstructed itself, white entitlement would mean that white workers would get first pick of the new jobs (as a kind of inverse affirmative action), and the working class would become white again. The confluence of industrial contraction and the assumption that they would get first pick of new replacement jobs or programs, before black workers who were in the same situation, constituted the other side of the demand for affirmative action's repeal.

Ultimately, both affirmative action and anti–affirmative action functioned within congruent class contradictions in the dual class system of the United States. Those that whites in general had chromatically proletarianized threw themselves against the white elite in an effort to rid themselves of their racialized class contradiction with the white working class, and charged the elite on moral grounds with not living up to its own democratic ideals. The white working class charged the elite on political grounds with having violated its bargain of white solidarity, but then threw itself against those it excluded chromatically, seeking to preserve its white identity as the working class (nonproletarianized) by cashing in on the bargain of white solidarity. There was an absorption of affirmative action into the corporate state, and an assumption of a control stratum role (complete with patronage) by white workers. In other words, both affirmative action and anti–affirmative action were working-class campaigns, but in different class systems: racialized and white.

When the terms of affirmative action were transported into the white class system, they were transformed into sociological terms (made academic) that had nothing to do with the real issues. Black proletarianization became "poverty," equality became "quotas," and positive nonexclusion became "merit." In sociological language, poverty euphemized inferiority, quotas constituted hegemony, while merit already constituted equality—and the terms "participation," "fairness," and "equality" became all but unintelligible. In seeking to move the poverty issue back to participation, quotas back to fairness, and merit back to equality, affirmative action's defenders found themselves institutionally imprisoned within the language of white corporate society, with only moral grounds to deploy. Ultimately, the unintelligibility of the real issues when articulated in sociological language became part of a renewed criminalization of black and brown people, owing to the regeneralizations made possible by it, and to which the political discourses were reduced. This, in turn, decriminalized white violence in defense of entitlement. In effect, the constant shifts of discourse obviated discussion of the issues and opened the way for rationalizations of the violence of remarginalization upon which the dual class structure of racialization depended.

In sum, the proposal (or demand) for deproletarianization within the context of the dual class structure produced a double bind for the defenders of affirmative action. Pro–affirmative action and anti–affirmative action confronted each other across the same class contradiction that stood between racialized black and brown workers (proletarianized) and white workers as intermediary control stratum, but from within incommensurable class structures. Both confronted the same white elite of corporate society, but on different fronts of political struggle. Pro was never able to conceptually debate contra. The institutionality that government imposed on civil rights separated pro–affirmative action and anti–affirmative action onto different social planes, without a common language with which to confront each other.

The Two-Party System

The necessity of winning the goals that affirmative action had set for itself remain, while the problems have become more complex and intractable. The success of the anti–affirmative action movement implies that former approaches will not work, not because anti–affirmative action won, but because the former approaches have been rendered irrelevant structurally and obsolete conceptually. Against the institutionality of civil rights a counter-institutionality is in progress with respect to minoritization, involving a general recognition of white entitlement and a disrecognition of race. The rhetoric of social colorblindness, the development of the prison-industrial complex, the repeal of civil rights legislation, the political harassment of people of color, and the anti-immigrant movements all serve to reconstruct the ability of whites to redefine themselves as white, rather than simply as a majority with respect to minorities. That is, undoing the pseudodemocratic ideology of "minority status" will only lead back to a reracialization of those minorities. Minority status may then get abstracted back into a literal black/white binary, an eventual reamalgamation of the minoritized into a single racialized other. The de facto disfranchisement that minorities faced in being cast as voting blocs without autonomous parties to represent them (thus misrepresentable within the two-party system) provides a ready basis for this process. What was seen in Florida in the election of 2000 may be a harbinger of the near future with respect to disfranchisement.[18] The reracialization of minorities would then suggest that minoritization had only been a temporary substitute, a trap for civil rights by which white supremacy could buy time.

If this is the case, the problem of civil rights and affirmative action shifts away from how to reconstitute a movement to restore the principles of affirmative action, to how to operate now within the new structures of racialization that are emerging in their wake. It is not Jim Crow we confront, but the forms of racialization produced by the institutionalization of civil rights. The real problem to which the defense of affirmative action was responding, whether it understood this or not, was the racializing character of minoritization. Where the deracialization implicit in the original move for civil rights could define itself through its attacks on Jim Crow, deminoritization (with accompanying reracialization) presents a different problem. The structure of minoritization is given by the two-party system; therefore, the two-party system is already the arena in which white supremacy can engineer a return to a new form of racialization. For the next steps against white supremacy, the role of the two-party system and the possibility for political alternatives to it become part of the problem. The institutionality of civil rights and the decentering and dependency effects of government grants (to the extent they are still forthcoming) hinder movement toward autonomy of economy and culture on the part of minoritized communities and minoritized people. But central to a political vision of autonomy is the electoral system itself and its ability to marginalize the minoritized within a structure of nonrepresentation. One problematic to be addressed would be in what form real representation becomes possible.

Because the electoral machinery is implicated, one alternate possibility is that of proportional representation, a systemic change that would provide the possibility of greater participation and better representation. By proportional representation I mean a system of multiple-delegate districts in which different interest groups, classes, cultural identity groups, and communities could field political parties to be their voice, and gain representation in the delegate assemblies in proportion to the vote they received. Proportional representation would create a political respect for all voices, because it would not exclude from legislative councils those who received more than a small minimum. It would permit the debates on issues and conflicts in society to proceed in the halls of government, rather than simply in society at large with each group then seeking to garner influence with the representative from their district.

In the current two-party system, real representation is impossible, since each district elects a single representative on a winner-take-all basis.[19] Not only does this mean no group gets representation, since there is only one delegate to represent the multifarious interests, identities, and communities in the district, but 51 percent of the vote gets 100 percent of the representation. Winner-take-all guarantees that a mainstream will always be given not only precedence over minority interests, but also the determining voice over what those interests are when considered by governing bodies. It even insures that what is mainstream gets defined by the two major parties themselves.

In providing minorities with the ability to elect direct representatives to legislatures to represent their particular communities, proportional representation would finally accomplish the task of enfranchisement that was the goal of civil rights before it got institutionalized. Civil rights brought about an end to segregation, but a structural change is needed in the United States to bring an end to minority status (as a social category), not in reracialization but in participation (without abandoning what had already been established, however tenuous it may be). Proportional representation would thus be one mode of furthering the goals of affirmative action (of equality, participation, and justice), rather than simply defending them. Establishing a system in which the notion of a "minority" authentically means participation rather than special interest would be one way of transcending an endless interchange of minoritization and racialization.

Yet it is necessary to be clear about the meaning of this proposal. It is not a mere reform, any more than the dismantling of Jim Crow was a mere reform. The issue is a lot more complicated than reform, especially in the context of the dual class structure of the United States.

The common assumption about the two-party system and its political procedures is that a third party could form around a program or idea and run in elections. A black community, for instance, in order to promote its particular interests as a community, could theoretically organize a party and gain representation for itself by electing candidates from among its own people. Similarly, the project of instituting proportional representation would require a party that promoted the idea and tried to institute it as a third-party effort. But third-party campaigns, while capable of small temporary successes through tremendous efforts by large numbers of organizers, have been structurally impotent and vacuous as a way of expressing a people's or a group's interests. The major reasons for this futility need to be examined.

The winner-take-all basis of district representation means that a third party would have to gain a majority in order to have a voice in government. A tremendous effort must be expended just to get on the ballot in state and local elections, and this effort produces neither results nor representation as long as the third party gains only a minority of the votes. Third-party efforts form because a constituency thinks neither major party sufficiently represents its issues or interests as a community, class, or culture. The need for third parties is real, since the two major parties are structurally unable to represent such class, community, or cultural needs, owing to the winner-take-all structure; it is not a question of failure or refusal to represent, but a real inability. The third party enters the electoral arena to pressure one of the major parties but is immediately counterproductive by giving aid and comfort to the other major party. The more evenly matched the two parties are in any election, the greater the defections from the third party's ranks will be in order to avoid that inadvertent support. While the third party is working to gain a majority, its efforts essentially serve counterproductively to preserve its marginality and minority status.

This is part of the self-perpetuating machinery of the two-party system. In the 2000 presidential election, the Green Party ran Ralph Nader with national presence, yet even organizers and leaders of the Green Party finally voted Democratic rather than have the Republican elected. In that election, people voted for the lesser of two evils, not out of support for one major party, but out of abhorrence for the other one. Voting for the lesser of two evils is not an affirmative vote but a privitive, a vote of derogation. Nevertheless, a lesser-of-two-evils vote is inherent in the mechanism whereby a third-party effort enhances rather than reforms the two-party system (Tise, 248ff, 347ff). The third party serves only to make things worse for itself, rather than better.

The ultimate effect is fatigue. The third party does not get enough votes to stay on the ballot, so it has to expend the same tremendous effort again in the next election. It experiences organizer burnout. Getting the signatures to put a new third-party candidate on the ballot takes an enormous amount of money and effort. The organizing energy required to set up a campaign itinerary and strategy, and get people going door to door to build a constituency, is prodigious. While opposition to the oligarchical hegemony of the two-party system will carry many people far along this road, few will persist after seeing their efforts thrown away at the polls a couple of times because people vote for the lesser of two evils. Third-party activists confront the factor of ultimate futility.

But suppose a third party acts in coalition to gain a political foothold. It then confronts the structural vacuousness of what is called representation. As mentioned above, each district is a diverse mixture of conflicting and competing interests and identities. No single representative can represent its diversity. Differences become amalgamated at the governmental level, and representatives become traders in governance rather than voices of representation. Getting elected is to be thrown into a position of dealing in influence and influencing deals rather than representing interests and political needs. The highest bidder, in most cases, wins the representative's attention. Every movement that has formed to contest the two-party hold on local government has realized that electing an independent candidate becomes the lesser half of the struggle; keeping the elected candidate accountable to the movement responsible for his or her election is the next task, and the harder one, since the elected representative has independence as well as power. It is indeed a thankless task, and rarely successful; U.S. history has shown that delegates go their own way once they enter the legislative arena, because all the other delegates or representatives are also maneuvering independently, with an eye toward reelection rather than representation. The real benefit from proportional representation would be that the elected would actually represent interests, ideologies, and identities rather than districts.

But finally, this amalgamation of governance and influence in place of representation creates a situation in the halls of government in which a third party poses a real threat, that of a tie-breaking vote in an evenly contested issue between the major parties. In such circumstances, the third party would have power out of proportion to its real strength. As the tie-breaker, a third party would actually control policy. This is not something the two major parties would allow. Whether through consolidated control of the media, or connections with major business interests, or the purchasing power of the party purse, they will prevent a third party from becoming such a presence in any legislative body. This is not a policy matter that a third party can argue or strategize around; it is a structural aspect of the two-party system that any third-party attempt touches directly.

These are the major structural reasons a third party is futile. Clearly, third parties would become viable only through a form of proportional representation. But proportional representation would require that single-delegate districts be changed, so that multiple-delegate representation would become possible. This would enhance the nature of representation immeasurably. Issues and interests could be confronted inside the legislature, where they could be resolved, rather than left outside or dissolved in the whims and horse-tradings of representatives not tied to the people behind the issues. It would also curtail the ability of corporations to hold districts hostage to their job-producing capacities, since it would change the political nature of the district.[20] But to transform single-delegate districts would, in most cases, require a constitutional amendment, which the two major parties will oppose. In other words, to pass an amendment instituting proportional representation, a third party would have to become a majority party; that is, it would have to become a majority party in order to make itself possible as a minority party.

An electoral system that makes third parties impossible or futile is a system that incorporates at its foundation an ethos of disfranchisement. One is disfranchised by having no way of making one's vote count, just as much as if one had no vote at all. In districts in which one party has such a strong hold on the electorate that the other major party has a negligible chance of winning, the members of that second party are essentially disfranchised because they are locked away from having representation of their own. Under normal operations, because the two parties are both autonomous and oligopolistic in determining their issues and candidates, they are essentially saying to the electorate, "Your vote will mean what we say it means." There is no substantial difference between taking the vote away and determining what it will be. In sum, disfranchisement and an absence of proportional representation are two dimensions of the same phenomenon. The two-party system and its self-defined white mainstream constitute a tacit disfranchisement of third-party or minority interests. Racial hierarchy is thus maintained by the very logic of two-party democracy.

What all this suggests is that proportional representation will not be won through electoral politics—any more than Jim Crow could be overthrown by electoral politics. Proportional representation can become a feasible goal only through a movement that demands real rather than rhetorical democracy. A campaign for proportional representation to rescue civil rights from its current situation of institutionality and reracialization will be nothing less than a continuation of the longest issue in the history of the United States: the disfranchisement of people of color. If the two-party system is in reality a veiled form of disfranchisement, then it is the center of the issue of civil rights today.

The disfranchisement of black voters has been a major issue throughout U.S. history. Following the Civil War, the issue was hotly debated; it led to the impeachment of President Andrew Johnson, not because of his opposition to it, but because he flaunted his executive responsibility in opposing it. After Reconstruction was overthrown, the political thrust of Jim Crow legislation was the total disfranchisement of the black voter. Native Americans were not even citizens until 1924, so their enfranchisement was not an issue until then. Today, the massive felony incarceration of black and brown people for minor and victimless crimes, as part of a general rise in racial profiling and the prison industry, constitutes a subtle but no less insidious process of disfranchisement. In most states, felony conviction results in loss of suffrage, placing the voting rolls in the hands of the state's prosecuting attorneys. In 2001, it was estimated that fully 10 percent of black voters had been disfranchised by this process.

Franchisement was very openly debated during the first decades of the nineteenth century, right after the Revolution. The following vignette will perhaps give a flavor of those discussions. In 1800, a group of free African Americans from Pennsylvania petitioned Congress to end the slave trade and begin the abolition of slavery altogether. A mere twenty-four years had passed since the Declaration of Independence had proclaimed all to have the right to liberty. Though the petition was mild in its terms, it was rejected outright by Congress and resulted in a debate on the denial of right to petition for African Americans (NS, 34). The general experience of African Americans (until the massive—and costly in terms of human life—voter registration drives in the 1960s) was that any attempt to exercise citizenship would result in an attempt to suppress that right. There were areas of the country where black suffrage had not been banned. In Massachusetts, for instance, the right to vote had not been denied to black people; but in 1850, white voters in Massachusetts drove those black people who attempted to vote from the polls (NS, 91). Violence was often a substitute for the banning of black suffrage. The attempt by African Americans to vote was the cause of massive white riots in the 1830s in Philadelphia, Cincinnati, and Boston.

In generally maintaining its disfranchisement of the African American vote, the white electoral system (whether official or ex officio) reenacts in content, though in different form, the tradition of the intermediary control stratum by which white society has consolidated itself as white. There is an element of extreme paranoia in the continual obsession with the black vote that stretches from the time of the Revolution until the civil rights movement, reminiscent of the social paranoia that drove and was driven by the slave patrols. It is part of the (racialized/class) interface between white corporate society and the black working class. But what the history reveals is not that the two-party system, as the structure of the electoral process, conspired to disfranchise black people; rather the desire to disfranchise black people was instrumental in the evolution of the two-party system.

The two-party system evolved over the course of time and went through a number of stages. Immediately after the Revolution, many were suspicious of organized political parties, fearful that they would constitute "artificial aristocracies," as Jefferson put it (RR, 12). Jefferson reasoned that political associations or combinations would be prone to corrupting the republican political process. Against what he called "legislative tyranny," or "elective despotism," only the independent involvement of the citizen (small landholder) was guard and guarantee (RR, 11ff). Washington too warned against "party competition" (RR, 17). But such views do not correspond with how people do politics, as Adams and Van Buren pointed out. The electoral structure requires organizations that can compete with each other in campaigns. By the 1820s, political thought evolved to the point of recognizing that parties were the agents of the independent citizen, and thus guards against both the autocratic abuse of power and anarchy. A multiplicity of parties had formed by the 1830s: the Democratic, Whig, Liberty, Know-nothing, Free Soil, and Workingman's parties. Within the dominant parties (Democratic and Whig) there were regional factions that grew to have independent influence, such as the Radical Democrats and the Conscience Whigs (Barnburners).

While the Democrats represented the ruling interests of the plantation South, other parties formed and dissolved around two major issues of opposition: slavery and states rights. Opposition to slavery expressed itself in various strategies: abolition, nonextension to the new territories, gradual elimination, establishment of a colony in Africa for African Americans. In opposition to abolitionist ideas, support for slavery manifested itself as increased repression of free African Americans everywhere—especially in the North and West, in order to dissuade slaves from running away. Indeed, many free African Americans moved to Canada as segregationist pressure increased. Others toured Europe, speaking about the conditions of black people in the United States (NS, 232). Yearly conventions of African Americans were held from 1830 on, to develop strategies for changing the law if not the mind and attitude of white society. Ultimately, two predominant political phenomena emerged: the first was a devolution of the electoral spectrum toward two parties; the second was an anxious attention paid to whether the black vote would wield the balance of political power between them.

As antislavery sentiment coalesced in the Republican Party, a strange checkerboard effect emerged in political alignments. Though the Democrats generally defended slavery, their radical wing saw it as evil and afoul of American ideals. Though the Republicans attacked slavery as evil, their conservative wing supported segregation. In effect, the issue of abolition threw the two parties against each other, and at the same time divided each down the middle (Z, 183). But a more insidious force lay under the surface: the question of a party's national existence. If a party desired to have national presence, it had to adopt ideological stances that would be acceptable in all sections of the country, and reduce its program to what was arguable in all areas. This was especially critical with respect to slavery and emancipation. A strict anti-slavery stance would receive no hearing in certain parts of the country; it had to be rendered equivocal if an anti-slavery party wished to function nationally. Thus, politics around the question of slavery was reduced to instrumental attempts to navigate lowest common denominators. It shifted the discourse of anti-slavery and black enfranchisement from the ideological to the expedient. And it served in part to produce a political tradition in which clear ideological stances were not possible at the level of national politics.

The Democratic Party, as the main proslavery advocate, actually managed to elevate this quirk of equivocation in political debate to an equation of proslavery with nationalism itself. In response to criticism from Europe in the 1820s concerning the contradiction between a pretense to human equality and freedom and the maintenance of the slave system, the proslavery argument openly proclaimed that freedom was what made the United States great, and that freedom could only be built on servitude (Tise, 116). The more absolute the servitude, the more absolute the freedom. As a response to European attacks, these proslavery arguments made themselves the very hallmark of citizenship; they became the test of allegiance to the new nation.

In the convoluted interweavings of these political doctrines, Foner notes, debate devolved to common name-calling around white supremacy. Because the Republicans opposed slavery, albeit mainly through opposition only to its territorial extension, the Democrats called them the "black" party—meaning that the Democrats were themselves the "white man's party." The Republicans replied that they were the real white man's party because they opposed the spread of African Americans to new areas through the spread of slavery; that is, they were more dedicated to guaranteeing that those areas remain white (after the elimination of the indigenous populations, presumably) (FS, 265). Litwack quotes Greeley as saying that the Republicans, in 1859, had to present themselves as being antiblack so that the white vote would not flee to the Democrats. Today, a similar thing happens. A politician will present himself as hard on crime not because crime is on the upswing, but because crime has been racialized as black, and being "hard on crime" is code for showing that one supports whiteness. In the 1850s, by engaging in such white supremacist name-calling, both parties were tacitly admitting that the color terms they used were essentially sociopolitical categories and not descriptions of people. Furthermore, they demonstrated that beyond the mere question of the vote being subservient to racialized politics, race had become the language by which the two parties framed their own issues with respect to each other. This had nothing to do with representing black people, or establishing a democracy of all the people. The foundation of difference between the two parties had to do with what kind of white hegemony to construct, and how whiteness was to be conceived as a social structure. This is a dispute that has grounded all U.S. foreign policy during the twentieth century (after the New Deal, the two parties' roles get reversed), and it has expressed itself even in the affirmative action disputes and the building of a vast prison industry.

In effect, the question of race, as well as the language of race, became the content of a coalescence of U.S. politics around a system of two parties. The proslavery party recognized that freed slaves would align themselves with the antislavery party; thus, it opposed the franchise for black people where it could not preserve slavery. The antislavery party knew that it would get the votes of liberated black people for having opposed slavery, but it also knew it would lose white votes if it advocated black suffrage. Thus, the antislavery party vacillated on the issue of black suffrage. Indeed, the question ceased to be African-American suffrage at all, and became the ancillary question of whether one advocated it or not. That became the issue that decided the balance of power between parties. In other words, the issue shifted from the political question of extending the vote to the organizational question of what stance would lose the least white votes (NS, 88). To extricate itself from the dilemma of its vacillation, the antislavery party ultimately advanced the notion, in agreement with the proslavery party, that the black vote had to be derogated if it was not to become the swing vote in close elections or contestations of issues.

The issue of black suffrage thus became the arena in which the two movements maneuvered with respect to each other, and one of the poles around which the two-party system crystallized.[21] From the original dilemma posed by the coexistence of slavery and democratic ideals, the issue of the morality of slavery shifted first to the expediency of curtailing its extension, then to a language of political organization, and finally, returning to rhetorical sanctimony concerning democratic principles, to a concrete debate on black disfranchisement that took denigration as its basic assumption, and the endless derogation of the black consciousness as its fundamental principle. Disfranchisement was rationalized by endless warnings against the "use" of the black vote by any upcoming demagogue, and admonitions to keep black people in hand, in order to keep "them" from being "misused" by corrupt interests in a "free society." It was a version of the proslavery argument which claimed that, given the choice between slavery and a free African American population in U.S. society, the first was preferable, because the second would produce instant social chaos. The fact that these were life and death questions for millions of real people did not enter the discussion. Rather, the debate focused on an issue of law with a twisted logic, a circularity inherent in the inner contradiction of the issue. The issue of law was black enfranchisement. It was an issue of law to be decided by the citizenry about who would constitute the citizenry on the basis of law to decide issues of law. Thus, it was circular in form, self-referential in content, and indeed self-contradictory in intent.

Truly at stake was that black people had specific antisegregationist interests around which to organize their own political involvement, which had been foisted on them by the process of excluding them from suffrage and participation. More and more black people were finding their way to freedom in the North through escape, while those in the North were gradually being emancipated. Both formed community with local free black people in northern urban areas that were already becoming segregated. They sought political expression to counter the growing hostility of the surrounding white society. And they sought it within channels. The fact was that black voters tended to establish the same kind of loyalty to party organizations that whites did in those areas where no disfranchisement had occurred, such as in Massachusetts (NS, 88). In the New England states that had declined to disfranchise African Americans, no independent black political parties appeared, nor were there even black caucuses within the existing parties. Foner notes that ultimately the issue of race was less important in New England than elsewhere because there were fewer legal restrictions placed on black people (FS, 285). Had they been incorporated into the citizenry along with all others (European immigrants, for instance), they would have functioned within the evolving party system in the usual way. But instead, the familiar circle took over. They were excluded from voting because the possibility of their forming an independent black political faction was seen as a threat, while it was their exclusion that created the necessity for their becoming an independent black political force. As with the question of competition, white paranoia toward black political involvement as an alien influence created black politics as an alien influence for itself.

The argument used, in many cases, was that black suffrage would give black people the balance of power, a tie-breaking vote in close legislative contests (NS, 76–77). There were certain examples to point to. In New York, for instance, for the first few decades, the black vote was considered to have been the deciding vote between the Federalists (Hamilton's party) and the Republicans (Jefferson's). In 1821, the (Jeffersonian) Republicans gained ascendancy and, in the constitutional convention of that year, called for restricting the vote to "white male citizens" (NS, 82). The measure passed, with the proviso that African American men could vote if they could show a sizable estate in freehold. In 1851, it was estimated that there were 5,000 black voters in New York (though most African Americans had been disfranchised) and that vote swung many contests to the side of antislavery (NS, 90).

Of course, had there been no segregation, and no obsessive noticing of the "black vote," there would have been no "black vote" as such, nor counterexclusionary interests for it to express. That is, African Americans were given the necessity for an independent existence as a black vote through exclusion, hostility, and segregation, and the white obsessive need to notice black votes as different or alien. To give the "black vote" political existence means that someone not black has decided certain votes must be noticed as being black votes and not simply votes. The act of noticing that a voter is black (rather than a citizen, for instance) becomes the originary fact of the black vote being different. The black vote is produced as different by that act of noticing. Tactically, of course, once the black vote is made alien, it can be used as a pawn or bargaining chip in the political game; conversely, the threat that others will use it the same way leads back to considering it alien. Common to both tactics is the idea that the noticing of black voters and the imposed alienness upon them renders electoral politics white. The need to notice the black vote rather than how that vote was deployed as noticed is what ultimately defined party politics in the United States (given that suffrage is the ultimate question of party politics).

Though African Americans were conscious of the influence they wielded as a tie-breaker vote (where that was the case), they knew it expressed itself only at the level of voting power, as one of the keys to who got elected; it did not extend to the legislature, which would have required the organization of a third (black) political party. Indeed, this fact actually militated against the organization of an independent black political party, because the latter would have meant losing the influence they did have within the major political tendencies. For instance, when the Liberty Party was organized in 1840 out of various antislavery movements and organizations, as a third party in a still fairly fluid political arena, many African Americans hesitated to support its program. Though that program related directly to African American interests, it was thought that such support would antagonize both the Whigs and the Democrats, upon whom, as the major parties, the issues of slavery and enfranchisement really depended (NS, 88).

But those considerations did not dissuade the advocates of disfranchisement. Neither did the fact that African Americans typically rejected colonization (in either Africa or Central America) because they felt themselves to be Americans, like whites. Indeed, most African American attempts to seek stable political involvement through political organization was somehow held against them. The sentiment for disfranchisement proceeded as if white hegemony could be preserved only if no black participation were allowed (BBN, 184). Curtailment of the black franchise signified that the issues of government were to be considered white issues, and that black interests and involvement were to be derogated.[22]

Even white abolitionists in the early 1800s fell prey to the thinking that the freed slaves would pose a tremendous problem to society, because they were poor, but not just because they were poor. Abolitionists too deployed the armamentarium of white arguments, that black people were untrained in autonomous living, unprepared for free life, uncivilized (ignoring the fact that any success black people had in surviving this hostility and living an autonomous or modern life in spite of it belied that argument, and was also held against them). Many equated them with poor whites, who were seen as having inadequately internalized the norms of polite, civilized society (PSR, 304). It was a backhand way for the abolitionists to say that they too felt that black people were inferior and incapable of functioning autonomously in society.

The original abolitionist project to combat segregation and disfranchisement thus broke down in social practice, principally through an acceptance of the paradigm of "standards" which imposed the need for black people to prove something (under the aegis of "capacity for self-improvement," of being "ready for freedom," and other catchwords of gradualism). If encouragement was offered, it was only a euphemism for control. No one suggested that it was white people who needed to be improved by recognizing the criminality of their racist enterprise or the immorality of their segregationist stance. It was the victim who was at fault or lacking. Thus, even for the liberals and abolitionists, a form of control seemed necessary to substitute for enslavement, in order for society to protect itself from the liberation of the slaves. Abolitionism doubled its function as opposition to slavery and as interface and protector of the boundary between black and white society by remaining ambiguous toward black social and political participation in an "undivided" nation. Race did not serve as a threat to electoral balance or procedure for the abolitionists; rather, the issue of black participation was the obsessive racializing principle for the abolitionists' own participation.[23]

Obsessiveness means to be overwhelmed, or inundated, by imagining what another is thinking or what others are going to do. It cannot see things simply, but loses itself in imagined motives. When David Wilmot (a Democrat from Pennsylvania) made his antislavery proposal concerning the southwest territories, he said: "The negro race already occupy enough of this fair continent. Let us keep the remains for ourselves . . . for the white laborer" (RR, 116). In his imagination, and that of the political system that applauded this sentiment, the mere presence of African Americans in a locale meant they had taken over the locale, making it other than a space where white people could live. Segregation becomes a vision of self-segregation, which then becomes the rationale for segregation of the other. For the white mind, the presence of African Americans renders whites the aliens, so whites have to segregate in order not to feel alien. It is an extension of the purity concept to space, to residence, sociality, and politics, whose existence all hinge on an envisioned nonpresence of black people, rather than on any intrinsic character of their own. No intrinsic character is possible for land, society, citizenship, or politics once it is envisioned as white, because it is already enmeshed in an imagined imposition and the need to exclude an abstract African American from that terrain.[24] The allegiance to white identity and hegemony produced in this way then substituted itself for any and all immanence, which was always therefore in absence.

On the basis of this kind of thinking, the two-party system evolved, in which third-party efforts were welcomed in theory and rendered futile in practice. It is the specter that now spreads itself over all third-party efforts the moment they appear on the horizon. By monopolizing the political arena, the two predominant parties make third-party efforts inevitable, while the structural futility of those efforts and their concomitant failures are appropriated in turn by the two parties precisely to reaffirm and valorize their monopolization of the political arena. That valorization then renders their (two-party) monopoly ideologically unassailable.

We can retrace this entire process in the history of Pennsylvania. During the 1820s, the black vote was not an extant political issue. Blacks voted in some parts of Pennsylvania and not in others (NP, 171). The determining factor was generally harassment or threats by whites. In Philadelphia, with the largest black community in Pennsylvania at the time, they did not vote.[25] What brought the issue to the fore was a county election in 1837, which happened to coincide with a state constitutional convention (already empanelled, but adjourned at that particular moment). In that election, the defeated candidate (Democrat) contested the outcome on the grounds that black people had voted, giving his opponent the victory (NP, 171). The press sensationalized the story, reporting that black people had been armed and threatening, or were being incited by the abolitionists. Though the evidence was plentiful that black people had voted in many other elections without objection or problem, the court overturned the results, gave the victory to the loser, and disqualified the black vote. Thus, having been noticed by the candidate, the black vote was given determining status in the election by the court. The issue of black enfranchisement was transformed into an issue of hegemony between whites.

In making his decision, the judge referred back to an earlier ruling that held blacks to be slaves because they had been slaves before the Revolution. He concluded that because African Americans had not had the franchise in colonial Pennsylvania, they did not have it now—ignoring whatever transformation the Revolution had wrought on society (NP, 172). The judge's arguments would later appear in similar form in Supreme Court Justice Taney's decision in the Dred Scott case (NP, 170ff). The argument is basically that blacks should not have the vote because it is contrary to law, and it is contrary to law because in the past blacks have not had the vote. In thus arguing, the Pennsylvania judge encoded in Pennsylvania law the need to specifically grant black people the vote, without which they did not have it, regardless of what ideals or transformations had been expressed by the Revolution.

When the constitutional convention returned to the issue, the question debated was whether free black people already had the franchise, because not specifically barred by the earlier state constitution (of 1790), or did not have the franchise, because not specifically provided by the earlier constitution. Actually, the debate on this issue was an artificially semantic one, generated in order to derail the demand for suffrage. The Pennsylvania constitution guaranteed the vote to "freemen" but not to "free men," and the lawyers argued that there was a difference (NP, 181). Free black men were denied the vote because they were only "free men" and not "freemen." One side argued that when the state constitution said all freemen could vote, without mentioning color, it meant to exclude black men, otherwise they would have been specially mentioned. The other argued that the same language meant to include them, because they were not specially mentioned. Where one said the constitution took no notice of them, the other said that they needed no special notice (NP, 180). Discussion devolved to the question of black inferiority. Those in favor of enfranchisement denied inferiority and proclaimed justice on constitutional principle. Those opposed simply proclaimed black inferiority, while immediately contradicting that by fearing the possible political influence of the black community as an independent political force. Ultimately, white supremacy won. The new state constitution of 1838 expressly denied African Americans the franchise. That is, the constitution was interpreted as needing to take special notice of black people to include them, and it had not. In other words, it had to notice black people; noticing is everything. White supremacy depends on black people being given special existence at all social levels within the paradigm of noticing them, as the very condition for active exclusion.[26] This was the essential mechanism for establishing the government machinery as white.

While the convention was debating the new constitution, African Americans organized themselves throughout the state to petition the convention for the vote, operating in accord with all the respectable modes of expression and political influence (petitions, meetings, resolutions, broadsides and pamphlets, and memorials to the legislature). It was all in vain. Indeed, it was turned against them by whites' fear for their proprietary hold on the political system. The petitions were used as one more reason for disfranchisement. The African Americans' actions should have been a sign for whites that independent black political action was not to be feared; instead, the whites' response was a sign for African Americans that political action would not be sufficient to break through the veil of whiteness.

The burgeoning two-party system became the means of structuring white proprietary control over politics. As a domain of white allegiance, the two-party system was legitimized by the internal white solidarity produced through a traditional paranoia. It emerged as a contemporary form of intermediary control structure. In the self-referential logic of an intermediary control stratum, that structure would in turn become the center of white allegiance.

Ultimately, the issue of slavery closed the political fluidity of the early days by making ideologically oriented political participation impossible, and white supremacy closed the possibility of a multiparty political framework. Given the choice between the politics of expediency and nonrepresentation inherent in a two-party hegemony on the one hand, or on the other a multiparty system of real representation and ideological political debate, the social logic of white supremacy (requiring African American disfranchisement) drove the system toward the former. Thus, the ideology of slavery in its many variations divided whites and at the same time united them through the necessity for the nonexpression of that ideology.

But the difference between allegiance and control becomes important here. While the two-party system serves as an axis of allegiance, it does not depend on obedience. The two-party system is not something to obey. Rather it offers itself as a center of obeisance, an icon constituting one pole of national identification, a critical symbol of identity as white. To the law, one owes obedience; to an icon, one pays obeisance. In U.S. politics, allegiance and obeisance have become conflated, and the two-party system, whose organizing principle is white solidarity and whose operational coda is white nonideological consensus, is the concretization of that conflation.

In a broad historical sense, one could say that the two-party system emerged as the white supremacist solution to the problem of abolition. Though the ultimate consolidation of a two-party system as a political ethos did not occur until after the Civil War and Reconstruction, the social dynamic that determined its parameters emerged in the earlier debates on black suffrage. Had a multiparty system in which parties contended along ideological, cultural, and truly programmatic lines been possible (as opposed to electoral campaigns run on promises constructed only for the purposes of electoral campaigns), then the black interest in eliminating slavery and segregation, as well as the variety of ideological positions on slavery, would have all had a role and a voice; the black vote would have been one among many. It was for this, in fact, that black political leadership of the time was asking. That would have accorded well with the assumptions of democratic theory as they were articulated in the nineteenth century. Instead, the two-party system took hold as a process of constructing political cohesion and coherence in a nation in the process of fundamentally contradicting its own basic assumptions.

Thus, the U.S. electoral system reflected and represented the dual class structure in two ways. First, it functioned as a political means whereby white people regulated their political affairs with themselves as white. That is, it represented political differences only on how to govern white corporate society, but not questions of whether that society was to be white in its overall orientation (which can be seen in all immigration laws). It provided the means whereby whites expressed and sometimes resolved their social and political differences under an umbrella of administrative solidarity and general political consensus. Second, the electoral system became something that white people could take for granted as their political realm, the arena in which they could be united against those who were to be minoritized as outside and alien. Even today, despite the Voting Rights Act of 1965, the right to participate by people of color is still in question, something requiring ongoing struggle as opposed to something that can be culturally taken for granted, as it is by whites.[27]

In its role as an arena of allegiance, its function as a form of intermediary control stratum, and its structure as a facet of the administrative apparatus of corporate society, the two-party system absorbed the challenge which the civil rights movement offered the dual class structure. The idea that minoritization simply substituted itself for racialization is not a tenable idea by itself. It had to be contextualized within a structure designed to preserve a white consensus, a structure that had already been developed and functioned traditionally for that purpose. As long as minoritized groups thought they could actually use the electoral machinery of the United States in its two-party form to gain real political influence as a group, and to alleviate their prior marginalization, inferiorization, and segregation, they constituted no threat to corporate society; the dual class structure would remain intact. To substitute minoritization (as electoral, racialized, and ethnicized all at once) for Jim Crow was to lead the struggle against racism and the structures of racialization into a dead end.

The Judiciary

The civil rights movement and its attack on the fundamental structures of racialization were brought under control by white society through an institutionalization of the civil rights idea. This amounted to incarcerating and isolating it in legal procedures and bureaucratic agencies, installing it as the goal of political campaigns that could only be waged through a two-party system and that reduced the principle of political participation to the level of a political issue. The effect was to shift the process of racialization over to the electoral category of minority status, substituting minoritization for racialization, and deploying the two-party system as a control stratum against any serious attempts by the minoritized to either express themselves politically or gain a degree of social autonomy. This then set up the situation in which the repeal of affirmative action put an end to the civil rights era. Civil rights remained an ideal but was no longer a factor on the political landscape. The repeal of affirmative action also marked a milestone in a different, overarching political process: the government's abrogation of a sense of responsibility toward its citizens.

The alacrity with which all this happened might suggest that the civil rights movement had provided a greater shock to the foundations of this society than thought possible. Yet all three historical moments that had opened the white supremacist social structure to possible assault and transformation had ended quickly. The first, the Revolution, was never more than a mere promise, which dissolved quietly into the three-fifths clause of the Constitution and the guarantee of property ownership. The second, Reconstruction, ended when the process of reconstituting the secessionist state governments, in which black and white people worked together, was overthrown by paramilitary force.[28] State governance was returned to the landowning elite and was quickly recognized and ratified by the federal government.

The civil rights movement attacked white supremacy on a different level, one of ethos rather than structure. It reasserted the humanity of those divested of it by Jim Crow, and demanded a legitimacy in the democratic processes that Jim Crow exclusion had corrupted. It called on government to be accountable for its citizens' well-being. The vote was restored, employment was recognized as a social responsibility, and the right to education was reaffirmed. Affirmative action laws were passed to rectify the effects of past discrimination in harmony with this new ethos, and the process of breaking the "color line" on jobs, education, and housing began. To that extent, affirmative action partially dissolved the racialized class relation between white corporate society and those it had chromatically and ethnically excluded as other. But it did not criminalize white supremacy, nor its gratuitous state violence, the continual covert exclusions and the racial hostility upon which white supremacy was based. Instead, it accepted poverty as the symbol of the divide between political responsibility and past social prejudice, racism, and sexism, transforming the rectification of the democratic ethos into the distribution of money—a spigot that could be turned on or off according to strategy or political conditions. The entire process ended, and the nation returned to a familiar state of white hegemony, not through a constitution, nor by paramilitary force, but by legal repeal of a spirit of civil rights that had already been eviscerated by institutionality and the two-party system. A reconstruction of the double class structure has since unfolded through the recriminalization of race, mass incarceration, and gradual disfranchisement.

This unfolding may not be evident to white people. They are not affected by the criminalization of those racialized as black or brown, Native or immigrant, nor by the practices of racial profiling or mass incarcerations of people of color. They have less chance of ending up in court, since they are not racially profiled; they benefit from racially unbalanced court procedures and decisions, since race is precisely the axis of unbalance. As white, they will be charged with a lesser offense than would a person of color, and receive a lesser sentence if convicted. For people of color, the reproletarianization that profiling and criminalization represent is flooding their lives. At the end of 2000, one in every three black men in their twenties was in the grip of the judiciary, either on bail, in jail, or on parole. To live in the shadow of the prison-industrial complex to this extent is to face, once again, a form of the intermediary control stratum, this time composed of police, courts, prisons, and the media. The judiciary appears to have become a new interface for the racialized class structure.

To understand what this means, we need to examine the inner structure carefully. It is not enough to read the statistics on mass incarceration, racialized sentencing, or arrest records. Criminalization and the permissibility of state violence against people are cultural rather than sociological processes; for an intermediary control stratum to function, a number of other social elements, such as solidarity, consensus, and paranoia, need to operate.

Let us begin with racial profiling. The most familiar form is the traffic stop, made inordinately against people of color—for "driving while black or brown" ("DWB"). A young black man driving a car may be stopped because the police claim he fits the profile of a car thief. The traffic stop involves checking registration, searching the car, and questioning the motorist. Since the stop is made on suspicion, rather than on a perceived traffic violation, the motorist faces being detained for some time on the road or street while the police try to find something with which to charge him. This constitutes a form of harassment. The harassment is gratuitous because the profile itself is circular in construction; it is based on data that the police themselves have generated. The profile's raciality is also circular; it functions through visual perceptions of a difference (in appearance) made in the moment. But the difference perceived in that moment is only a difference from what is not profiled, and is thus inherently self-defining, a self-referential process. In short, its origin lies in the act of profiling rather than in the situation or population profiled.

But racial profiling is more than simply traffic stops. To follow people of color around in department stores, as happens routinely, is not only profiling but also a form of harassment. Subtler forms, such as redlining for bank loans, higher mortgage rates, or the refusal of a job on the basis of color, are common.[29] A young person (of color) attempting to get a job, even for unskilled work in a factory, will not be hired if his address is in the wrong neighborhood. Mortgage interest rates are automatically higher if the person is black. Patricia Williams, an African American law professor, tells the story of a mortgage loan that was approved for her at a certain rate over the phone because she was a university professor but was changed the moment she filed the papers and the bank discovered that she was black. The automaticity of the bank's response signifies that profiling resides at the social or systemic level, rather than that of individual prejudicial comportment.[30]

Ironically, a denial of service, a contract or rental transaction, or any social necessity, because of race, gets explained today as profiling (namely, that a person fits the profile of an undesirable or overly risky business prospect), while it is the profile that defines the person as undesirable or risky. Because a profile is a visual outline of general characteristics by which someone is recognized as undesirable, or as suspect, it is inherently a prejudicial act (it prejudges). It thus constitutes a contemporary form of racial prejudice. Yet it avoids that label by being systemic, by referring itself to structural or social operations (such as business or law enforcement), rather than to "race" or personal "preferences." When Jim Crow was being dismantled, the attitudes of its defenders were called prejudice in order not to admit that their racism was systemic and socially structured. Today, racialized noticing is called structural or procedural (as in standard police procedure) in order not to admit to personal racial prejudice. Prejudice and profiling work hand in hand as the personal and institutional dimensions of a single social phenomenon, one which constitutes the boundary between white corporate society and people of color outside it.

When Amadou Diallo arrived at his apartment building in the Bronx one night, he was accosted by four plainclothes police officers with guns drawn who then opened fire and killed him. They later claimed he fit the profile of a rapist they were looking for, and that they thought he was reaching for a gun when he reached for his wallet to respond to their demand that he identify himself.[31] The most frequent police rationale for killing is thinking the "suspect" had a weapon. When a white person pulls out a wallet or holds a cell phone or an address book, it is seen as a wallet or a cell phone or a book; when a black person does the same thing, it is a weapon, leading to "defensive retaliation." A presumption of violence and the violent reaction to that presumption are at the core of the process of profiling.[32] The harassment to which a motorist is subjected when stopped for DWB is only a mild form of this violence.

While profiling has come to characterize police procedure, it does not constitute legal procedure. Profiling is the inverse of law enforcement. In law enforcement, a crime is discovered and the police then look for a suspect who might possibly have committed it. Profiling means that a suspect is discovered and the police then look for a crime for the person to have possibly committed. In the first case, a criminal act is committed and the police try to apprehend the criminal. In the second, the police commit an act of suspicion and an unsuspecting person gets apprehended. In one, a person commits a crime; in the other, the police commit an act of criminalization. Law enforcement addresses people's acts in their particularity and attempts to maintain social order on a case by case basis. Profiling addresses people through a process of visual generalization and violates the social order by introducing an atmosphere of abstract harassment into it.

Visual generalization does not pertain to the people generalized, but only to those doing the generalizing. Generalization is not an empirical act with respect to people. Whatever their behavior, people always only present themselves as individuals. No generalization is objectively discernible in any individual. To see behavior as an example of a generalization implies that one already has the generalization in mind in order to see the particular person fitting it. It is to see something that does not emerge from the individual generalized, but is brought from elsewhere, prior to encounter with the person generalized, and imposed upon him or her. In effect, all generalization occurs in advance; it can only be of social origin, not flowing from the people generalized. To see a person's benign behavior as negative or criminally threatening is to have already derogated or criminalized that person in advance and, in general, prior to the encounter in question.

But precisely in that sense, as a visual procedure of noticing, profiling presents itself as wholly consistent, and even natural, in a racialized and hierarchical society; it seems a valid way to see things in a social framework that gives priority to noticing race. Above all, it presents itself as reasonable in a social milieu in which race already implies criminalization. Until the late 1990s, profiling was generally accepted by being ignored in political discourse. The assumption that judicial and enforcement procedures were proper and impartial (and colorblind) meant that the racializing aspects of those procedures would remain unexamined.

The assumptions of propriety and reason attached to profiling are allegorized by the issue of crime in the streets, to the elimination of which government, police, and media have dedicated themselves. In its present mythified form, "crime in the streets" is generally understood as black assailant and white victim. The mass incarceration of black people for victimless crimes has ironically been the main buttress for this mythification of violent crime.[33] It is another instance where profiling becomes the main foundation for the profile. Even when crime statistics drop, "crime in the streets" remains an icon for whites for the most fundamental threat to their society. That is, the threat is constructed through a system of generalizations that are provided by the process of racial profiling, while profiling then becomes the mode of apprehension of the threat. As such, it is a paranoid construct, the self-referential definition of a threat in the world in order to discover it there, generated through its ability to ignore its self-generation.

The legal concept that grounds police profiling, and which provides its juridical legitimacy, is "probable cause." "Probable cause" is a rhetorical device that allows warrantless search or arrest by a police officer. It signifies that a police officer has decided there is "cause to suspect a crime" is taking place, or has taken place. That a man "fits" the profile of a suspect being sought gives probable cause to stop and search the person (LA, 115). Should a person run away upon seeing the police, that provides probable cause for the police to think the person is guilty of something, and therefore can be chased, shot or stopped by other means, searched, and arrested. Leaving the scene upon seeing the police is profiled as being guilty of something.

A profile provides the content for "probable cause"; it legitimizes the use of an individual's appearance and behavior to stop him or her. The search and detention of persons is rendered primary over the maintenance of peace and security of social space. Such police actions become an ever present potential disruption of the social space, a low-intensity mode of social aggression by the state. Indeed, reflecting profiling's inversion of law enforcement, the profiling actions of police (as "peace officers") become what disturb the peace of those they profile. "Probable cause" does not legitimize social aggression or brutality by the police, but it rhetorically provides the space for them. Under profiling, "the peace and security of social space" becomes stratified hierarchically between those sectors of society whose peace is disturbed, and those outside the profile who are left in peace. Profiling thus creates a hierarchy of social categorizations characterized by different notions of individual liberty (LA, 122).

In the social strata profiled, the social and cultural behavior of individuals comes under the a priori purview of "probable cause" as criminalizable. Clothing, hand codes, modes of socializing (hanging out), group dynamics, as well as race, hairstyle, age, or being out late at night, are all elements of personal self-presentation or behavior that can be criminalized through profiling. When Mumia Abu-Jamal attempted to defend himself in Judge Sabo's court, his conduct and behavior were used to rule him out of order and deprive him of this constitutional right. Judge Sabo claimed that, during jury selection procedures, Mumia's demeanor and his hairstyle (he wore dreadlocks) scared one of the jurors. But the Constitution does not say a person has to act a certain way in order to have access to the right to defend himself in court. In such instances (and they are legion), the judge has set his/her standard of behavior above the non-negotiability of a right guaranteed by highest law.[34]

The power of those in certain administrative positions or in civil institutions to judge and criminalize behavior is an extension of the concept of profiling. The reality of personhood gets reduced to something that must fit a template in order to be given legal recognition or status in civil society—that is, to not be rendered beyond those legal bounds on sight. The institutional criminalization of behavior (in court or elsewhere) is not the prior condition for the legitimacy of police profiling; the criminalization of behavior is itself a form of institutionalized profiling. They reflect a common source.

To criminalize behavior, or to use profiling as "probable cause" to stop and harass, is to associate an individual with a criminalizing generalization brought from elsewhere and imposed on the individual. It is thus an operation of guilt by association. In guilt by association, it is no longer what a person does, nor even who they are, but who or what they are associated with (by others) that comes under judicial scrutiny. Guilt by association criminalizes social connections and attributes criminal meaning to an individual through his/her relations to others, or to certain concepts. Police profiling constitutes a form of guilt by association in the sense that the police officer associates a particular observed behavior or appearance with a prior concept of what that mode of behavior or appearance will have meant before being observed.

Like profiling, the association of guilt is self-referential; it is an evaluation unilaterally and arbitrarily associated by the police to a criminalizing description (of behavior or social relations, etc.) assumed by the police themselves (in effect, extra-legally).[35] Such a criminalization or derogation of behavior is not the weighing of a specific action against a legal standard of comportment; rather, it is the imposition upon a person of a prior evaluation of how a person or action already does not correspond with a prior (and even extra-legal) standard. It is the transformation of an extra-legal standard of comportment into a legal standard (without legislation) by the police. Its administrative imposition as a legal standard by the police or a judge in any encounter with an individual renders that individual guilty in advance by association with the profile because profiled, and the individual is profiled because (behaviorally) deemed guilty by association with respect to a prior extra-legal standard that is brought to bear by the administrative (or police) agent.

In effect, the police have a general ability to create legal standards that are then projected down onto actual street encounters through probable cause. But this now extends the meaning of "probable cause" a bit farther. Probable cause signifies that, for the police officer in the encounter, all the authority of the law can be brought to bear on the individual. When a police officer notices a person, he has already turned what he notices into a legal relation under "probable cause," and thus can hold the individual to standards of juridically prescribed conduct. To stop someone through profiling means to subordinate that individual to the law in the person of the police officer. Criminalized before the fact by a police officer's act of noticing, the individual becomes a captive of the legal system in the person of the police officer and is henceforth constrained to absolute obedience. "Disobeying an officer" is a crime. Refusal of or resistance to a police directive exposes a person to possible arrest or punishment (such as beating), or both. Rodney King's sin, for which he was tortured on a roadway in Los Angeles, was fleeing a traffic stop because he was afraid of what the police would do to him. Thus, having been noticed (generalized) and stopped (absorbed into the judicial system), a person is confronted by another person (the police) whose directives translate directly into law.

In the sense that a police officer's directives have the weight of law, the officer actually has the ability to make law in the moment, as well as the ability to transform the person stopped into a criminal at will, subject to arrest. To accomplish the latter, the officer has but to find a directive that an individual will resist, whether it be out of a sense of dignity or self-respect, a sense of justice, or a sense that the directive is extreme or unwarranted. Such a stance will be construed as disobedience and can be a cause for immediate arrest—often accompanied with beating, the use of painful restraints, torture with pepper spray, and charges of resisting arrest. The person can even be charged with assaulting the officer if the officer has chosen to beat the person; an officer's use of violence to make an arrest is interpreted a priori by the judicial system as self-defense, and thus evidence that the officer was threatened or assaulted. Hence, a person can be criminalized, that is, arbitrarily subject to arrest, for defense of his/her dignity or self-respect, and a defense of dignity or self-respect can be construed as an assault if the officer decides to punish that self-respect violently.

In sum, profiling and the power to criminalize behavior amount to an ability to criminalize any individual, and especially to criminalize a person's sense of justice, personal dignity, and self-respect—that is, a person's sense of his/her own humanity. Profiling and its attendant aggressiveness signify that the police have arrogated to themselves the power to determine who will be human, whose sense of themselves as human will be respected, whose autonomy and independence will go unpunished and whose not. While the immediate political import of this self-arrogation of power is a demand for obedience, its overall meaning is obeisance. Under profiling and the criminalization of dignity and self-respect, obeisance to the police is the inverse of obedience to the law—just as profiling is the inverse of law enforcement. In obedience to the law, one's humanity in society resides in the fact that one can only criminalize oneself through disobedience; obeisance to the police means that the police criminalize one as a form of willful and gratuitous dehumanization.

The political term for this is "impunity." "Impunity" signifies a hyperpolitical context in which an act (the police harass, or dehumanize, or kill someone, for instance) stands above both police regulations and legal prohibitions against torture or murder. It names the right given the police officer, as authorized by the concept of "probable cause," to brutalize or dehumanize a person at will, without accountability (since every move is justifiable within standard procedures), and against which the person so targeted has no recourse because criminalized for having been subjected to such treatment. In short, having been established, impunity functions to restratify society according to a cultural ethos of policing that presumes to determine who is human and who is not. Hence, police profiling and impunity are one way the government has allowed itself to abrogate its responsibility to its citizens in the wake of the civil rights era.

Impunity takes hold not just because a police department will stand up for its members out of organizational *esprit de corps*. It goes well beyond that. A police department is duty-bound to stand up for the impunity of each officer, since impunity is the form "upholding the law" takes under the paradigm of profiling, and "upholding the law" is their sworn duty. In effect, the police as a whole become a law unto themselves. Insofar as the law is, by definition, that to which all people are responsible, the fact that a police officer can make law in the moment implies that the officer is no longer responsible to the law. The police's responsibility to civil society is actually abrogated by the ability to make law in the moment, and their ability therefore to substitute an ethic of violence for that responsibility. To become the law means to dispense with the law. Because police directives are given the weight of law, the law becomes null.

Because these means of criminalizing are visual, they are inherently racialized, focused on those they chromatically characterize and notice as such. This does not mean that whites do not commit crimes; it means that white crime is decriminalized. Indeed, to the extent that profiling is based on a prior criminalization of people of color, it contains within itself a prior decriminalization of whites. Far from returning to or operating within a structure of racialization given by history or tradition, racial profiling is itself a process of reracialization—that is, a process of reconstitution of white consensus and white supremacy in response to a history (to the civil rights struggles that sought to dismantle the dual class structure as the social apparatus of racialization). In regeneralizing, recriminalizing, and dehumanizing those it racializes, the police constitute an intermediary control stratum, like the patrols that consolidated the slave system (or like the KKK that consolidated segregation after the overthrow of Reconstruction). Like the patrols, the police have arbitrary power to pick their targets, for which their victims have no recourse. Their operations function to divide society into those they recognize as human (the unprofiled) and those from whom they withhold that recognition—a recognition based on visual characteristics given by society to be especially noticed. There is a presumption of guilt toward those noticed which serves to set them outside the juridical protection of corporate society. A social categorization is brought about in this way, whose cultural dimensions are, like racialization, based on noticing visual aspects as a social importance, and which involve punishing (criminalizing) autonomy, humanity, resistance, or a sense of self-respect on the part of those noticed. In short, through the complex social structure of profiling (noticing, categorizing, criminalizing) and impunity, the police have constructed themselves as the boundary between (white) corporate society and those it subalterns and constrains for the sake of its own consolidation.

The social meaning of the intermediary control stratum in the present goes deeper than simply an historical analogy to the KKK. While the police system of impunity and dehumanization is congruent in form to the process of racialization, what makes it politically racializing in content is its overt and often (as Parenti calls it) theatrical violence. (One could mention the police repression of the Million Youth March or of the Dorismund funeral, the Diallo killing, Tyesha Miller's murder by the police, or that of Aaron Williams.) This overt violence is a necessary concomitant to the fact that profiling is ignorable by those outside the profiles, those who are reracialized as white by exclusion from racial profiling. Though the newspapers are full of crime stories (whose purpose is to engender fear), ordinary arrests (of both black and white) do not make news. Standard procedural police profiling, violence, and impunity all remain invisible to most white mainstream people, precisely because they themselves escape notice. One does not notice that one is not noticed by the police; this conditions one's not noticing that the police operate according to aggressive noticing.

Beyond news stories of crime, something must give the reality of police violence the ability to signify racialization. In other words, police impunity can grant humanity to some by withholding it from others only if the former are in some sense aware that this is what is being given them, and aware of the terms (of racialization) in which it is being given by being withheld from others. Deploying special modes of violence in the name of law enforcement, the police enact forms of spectacle to be noticed by those unaffected by them, and who would not otherwise notice. If the killings or police riots (such as those just mentioned above) have a function, it is to make a spectacle of what those not profiled are being given. The police are not out of control, nor reacting; they are creating a situation in which they can then claim to be reacting.

The matrix in which the police spectacle is often embedded is "quality of life" enforcing, with various "zero tolerance" strategies. The notion of a "quality of life" begs the question "Whose quality?" and "Whose life?" For instance, it is used to harass and arrest homeless people who panhandle, to clear them out of consumerist or tourist areas as a blight on the urban landscape. It aims to sweep away people and behaviors that the government decides corrode or corrupt the everyday quality of city life. At the same time, it valorizes the landlords and real estate interests which rendered those people homeless by raising rents beyond affordability. Thus, it is a class-oriented ideology. Rather than a generalization of behavior, it is a generalization of the criminalization of behavior. It overlays political repression upon those to whom society has already abrogated all responsibility and, of course, the political activists who attempt to win some justice for them (groups like Food Not Bombs, or ACT-UP). Street gangs and black social clubs, which are attempts to supplant government irresponsiveness with alternate social community, solidarity, self-defense, and self-help, have come under attack across the country (LA, 70).

Enacted by the police as an adjunct to profiling, these "quality of life" and "zero tolerance" strategies remain disguised, and thus unseen, behind "law enforcement." The theory behind "quality of life" enforcement is that if the police crack down hard on minor crimes and offenses, then major violent crime will be eliminated at the same time (LA, 71). Massive force becomes standard deployment, even against petty crimes (such as jumping over subway turnstiles), credit-card fraud, fighting, or cult activity. Rationalized as an attack on major crime, it provides the background for the routine use of brutality toward minor non-obeisance. Those not immediately obedient to police directives become offenders, to be dealt with as criminals, with systematic use of unwarranted (self-referential) violence. The zero tolerance ideology conditions and authorizes deployment of lethal weaponry and various state-sanctioned torture techniques (beatings, pepper spray, pain-inflicting restraints) as a first response, rather than as reserve (LA, 135).

Zero-tolerance strategies also represent a theory of society. They imply that an element of society has been proclaimed an enemy (profiled) whose general designation (major violent crime) becomes the veneer under which real people (certain communities) are constructed as the enemy, and "combated" through forms of low-intensity war (impunity). When someone noticed decides to run away and is shot, the officer who did the shooting is exonerated in advance by the ethos of low-intensity war. To shoot such a person is only to win a small victory in this war. Ultimately, this means that the predominant crime on which the police focus, and against which they wage their war, is the crime of being noticed by the police; those noticed become the enemy, to be engaged as such because the police have noticed them. Impunity becomes the law of this low-intensity war in which anything the police do is legitimized before the fact, the immediate extension of its operation of racialization.

The double message directed at those not profiled is, first, that the police are just doing their job to resolve an arcane problem for whose existence the operations and growth of the police are themselves the proof, and second, that they are doing more than their job by insuring the social identity of those not profiled.[36] The self-referentiality of the police operations is mirrored in the self-referentiality of the white insouciance that legitimates profiling by spectating from afar. For those not profiled, the criminality of arbitrary criminalization and impunity does not impinge, and is rarely important. What is important is their own social being, as normative in the face of the aberrant—which is what gets pointed out by the seemingly isolated instances of spectacular police violence.

In this way, the impunity enacted and the ability to ignore profiling are both given a positive meaning; it is a new sense of stratification of society noticeable to those unprofiled. As Ida Wells pointed out in the 1890s, it was the public-spectacle lynching of a black man for rape that produced the feeling of sanctity among whites and convinced them, along with the generalized demonization of black men as rapists, that Jim Crow laws were thus necessary and that the law had to be supplemented by extra-legal means to stem the tide. In similar fashion, the violence against those presumed criminal, and thrust outside societal and juridical protection thereby, signifies the sanctity of the society it is allegedly defending. Because it is blackness that is criminalized (or any of the other visibly racialized or ethnicized groups characterized in analogy to that chromatic), whiteness is decriminalized, as a dimension of social consensus and social solidarity against the "enemy" singled out by police violence. While police profiling engenders a system of social categorization (human/nonhuman), it is the white solidarity engendered by the open violence of doing so that reracializes that social categorization. The solidarity among whites with respect to spectacular police violence then constitutes for them what it means to be white. In standing behind it, they reaffirm their sense of membership in the society it reconstitutes.

In other words, the growing numbers of police murders are not coincidental, nor the work of rogue cops. They are an essential part of a larger and more complex reracialization practice, which they ritualize. It is the performance of criminalization imposed on black and brown people by the police, as an arbitrary generalization procedure, that police violence enacts. This hyperpolitical nature of police aggression signifies the role of intermediary control stratum that the police play. The police are the means by which the judiciary announces that it plays the role of interface in a reracialized dual class structure. In short, the police adopt their strategies against black or brown people (and a short list of white undesirables) so that mainstream white people can continue to be white.

Such political authorization of impunity and violence reveals a paranoia. Going all the way back to the juridical discourses rationalizing the patrols in eighteenth-century plantation society, that paranoia seems a thread that runs through all U.S. history, from the colonists' first attitudes toward the Indians, through "negro rebellion" scares, to Jim Crow, the red scare, and the Cold War. Now it is the drug war and a paranoia about terrorism. From the first construction of whiteness, police violence and impunity have produced the conditions for paranoia by terrorizing people and forcing them into stances of resistance. As before, the law of the police is arbitrary. It constitutes a domain of hyperpolitical activity for which none of the legitimate political discourses of this society offer an account. For a society beset by policing of this nature, policing that criminalizes a sector of society in the name of dealing with crime, the police themselves become the crime problem. But rather than be negatively affected, white supremacist society is (and has been historically) constructed through policing of this nature.

To recapitulate, police profiling constitutes a structure of racialization. As generalizing, it reflects within contemporary juridical space the mode by which racism constructs groups as races through its generalizations. It establishes them as groups to be noticed and differentiated through the meanings given that generalization. When police profiling singles out black and brown people, it is not their individual behavior that renders them suspect; instead, the prior criminalization of color becomes the proxy for behavior and renders their behavior suspect in advance. As criminalizing, profiling reflects the mode whereby racism excludes those it racializes; the reduction in juridical status produced for the criminalized reflects or repeats the process of inferiorization that accompanies racism's generalizations. Because the generalization of behavior becomes a euphemism for racialized generalizations, the criminalization of race gets inverted as the racialization of crime. Black behavior, whether illegal or not, becomes criminal; white racist violence, whether prosecuted or not, becomes simply behavior. Generalization, racialization, and criminalization are interwoven and inseparable in an endless reconstruction of whiteness and white supremacy, in which police procedure is today playing a major role.

Conclusion

The three elements that historically characterized the structure of racialization as produced by white supremacist society have today been reconstituted in contemporary form: the paranoia of anti–affirmative action, the allegiance of the two-party system, and the violence of racial profiling and the criminalization of race. Profiling and the criminalization of behavior are acceptable to the social (white) mainstream because they are wholly familiar in terms of prior structures of racialization. Both define themselves through some mode of violence, and both demand allegiance in the name of a social order they bring into existence as the site of their violence. The slave system was the first form this violence took. Rather than serve a hegemonic system, the enactment of violence is what brings the hegemonic group into existence. The Colonial Council brought white people into existence by giving them an identity through its violence as a state in providing and regulating slave labor. Violence then serves as the boundary of the social terrain in which membership in whiteness is constituted. The dues of membership are support for the violence. If violence is used to maintain the hegemonic structure, whether as repression, legislated disfranchisement, segregation, prejudice, or hate, the forms that violence takes serve to reconstitute the structure of hegemony according to each new set of conditions. Massive paramilitary violence against African Americans brought the post–Civil War structure of white society into existence, and maintained it in the form of Jim Crow and lynch-law spectacles. Ultimately, violence is able to constitute a structure of hegemony (white supremacy) or state power (governance) because it acts gratuitously. Through ostracism, aggression, and denigration, it reconfirms the social identity and membership of the hegemonic (white). But as gratuitous, it dispenses with responsibility to law and becomes law. Gratuitous violence becomes law because there is nothing its victim can do, once in its clutches, to avoid it. There is no recourse.

As an ancillary effect of re-establishing white solidarity as an organizational principle, the police tacitly make it a form of self-betrayal for whites to protest against injustice, whether toward themselves or toward others. Questioning the injustice of police rule or the injustice of economic exploitation will threaten to call in question their membership in whiteness. Thus, the police are doing two things: they are reconstructing whiteness for whites, and they are bringing whites under control as white by enforcing a white solidarity as the cost of that construction. Similarly, as socialist theory has pointed out, police repression serves capitalism, since it seriously hinders the ability to organize against it. But the structure by which police violence accomplishes this control is much more complex than a simple campaign of political repression or a simple divide-and-conquer strategy. It involves the constitution of a constrained identity, and enforced membership.

Because of this complexity, the word "racism" becomes a very loaded term, while at the same time it becomes impoverished. It generally refers to a hatred and segregation of nonwhites by whites; it serves to constitute whiteness through the displacement and inferiorization of people that whites chromatically designate in order to hate them. If it refers to a structure of power whose foundations are a violence that socially categorizes, then "racism" is a misnomer, since that violent and hierarchical social categorization is what produces race in the first place. If it is used with respect to the cultural complex of prejudices and discriminations whose foundations are a hierarchizing violence, then it hides behind an assumption that the concept of race to which it makes reference is real, independent of that violence. Thus, "racism" disguises the process of racialization that brings both race and racism into existence. The term falls short of referential meaning. To simply say that the police are racist ignores the fact that profiling and racial criminalization are today the basis on which white identity is constructed and white supremacy is given the role of being normative through this restructuring of racialization.

Of course, most white people would object to this. They cannot see the social dynamic of racism (as a social structure) because they already consider themselves white, and therefore merely human (meaning normative). This pretense to normativity prevents whites from noticing that racism as racialization brings into existence what it is about, namely, normativity in the form of systematic dehumanization and exclusion of others designated chromatically. This pretense to normativity preserves them from noticing that the police operate by noticing nonwhites. It allows the ancillary thought that nonwhite people are "of course" human by filtering out all the evidence that they are not treated as human. Their accession to white supremacy allows them to not notice that their own sense of being human already constitutes a social categorization that differentiates. In working-class terms, the logic of the idea that white workers seized working-class identity for themselves expresses itself in holding "class" identity against black workers. That is, the demand of black workers to be treated equally as workers gets detoured into being the demands of blacks rather than workers. This is the ghost in the working-class closet. It presents itself to all white workers in the very machinery and capital that employs them, because it employs them as white workers and not simply as workers, as long as black workers are so differentiated and excluded.

The theory that race is part of a person's innate constitution or biological being becomes essential to this structure of unawareness and pretense because it permits white people to refuse to see the difference in human difference by which they define and defend themselves. Yet, ultimately, the social construction of white blindness implies that there is no such thing as personal or individual prejudice. Many consider prejudice an individual thing, an attitude of prejudging or a derogatory action taken by one individual toward another, yet it cannot be. To have picked someone out for special notice in order to prejudicially assign a negative valuation to them, to their noticeability, implies that the importance given their appearance, and the negative valuation one assigns to it, must exist prior to the encounter. Indeed, to abstract some aspect of a person's appearance as a "characteristic," as generalized in that manner, and on which to impose a negatively valued generalization, already implies a prior social identification of it as a characteristic, pre-defined to be noticed as such. The generalization of a group is something that can only come about socially as an act of dominance. To prejudge an individual is thus to prejudge through social generalizations that are invented previously elsewhere. The terms of individual prejudice are always already given as socially instituted.[37] An instituted prejudice does not express an emotional distaste or hatred for another; it is what creates such feelings. The generalization comes first, then the segregation, then the prejudice, finally expressed as hate.

The mediation between the first step and the second is violence; between the second and the third is paranoia; each augments the other, and the momentum of the ensemble produces an allegiance to the domination that created this structure for itself, and then hates as its innermost self-generated expression.

This is seen again in the opposition to affirmative action. There were three components to the attack on affirmative action: (1) a moralism invented for the purpose (the victimology of reverse discrimination), (2) a legalism presented as a pretended norm (juridical colorblindness), and (3) a narrativization of how affirmative action is evil, deleterious to the nation (black hegemony and a biased government). The first is the mark of white violence, transformed into a rhetoric and turned against the civil rights movement in the name of civil rights. The second is a projection of the ethos of allegiance upon the exigency to preserve its normativity. The third is a resurrection of paranoia to rationalize the first and enforce the second.

Thus, white corporate society continually reconstitutes its inner structure. Majoritarian status, defining itself through the minoritization of others, demands allegiance in defense of its self-definition. The paranoia of defining others as minorities both demands allegiance and rationalizes it. The dehumanizing violence of exclusion, profiling, and arbitrariness legitimizes the paranoia. Each of these contributes to the administrative cohesion of society, which amalgamates them in turn into a sense of social identity as white. Social violence is enacted through the intermediary control stratum, the interface between that white administrative structure (the whole of white society) and those over whom it racializes itself, comprising the prison-industrial complex, the two-party system with its systems of minoritization, police violence, and the institutionalization of civil rights. These components are all totalitarian. White supremacy transforms an ideational structure into political absoluteness, social abstraction, and revised history, blocking democratic opposition by relying on exclusive claims to validity. For whites, the price of allegiance is a form of totalitarian condition called "freedom," which is given reality through obeisance to it as an idea, rather than through its exercise as citizen participation.

The genius of the ideology of freedom (as white freedom) which took hold in the United States was its location in a nation that took as its referent the nonfreedom of the nonwhite. The ideology of freedom is coded white, as the matrix in which supremacism can be promulgated. That is, obeisance to the ideology rather than the reality of freedom is the form the dues of membership in whiteness takes. All democratic opposition to white supremacy and its freedom is outflanked because it must argue the content of the issue (of whiteness and supremacy) while being engulfed in its form. White supremacists defeat antiracist whites easily because, as soon as they shift the argument back to racial terms, the white antiracists are in an impossible position as whites. Though nonwhite people escape this trap because already outside this rhetorical system, they are alone until whites learn how to effect their own escape from the trap and join with them.

CHAPTER 4

The Meanings of White Racialized Identity

Whiteness is a social structure that organizes the way most white people in the United States think of themselves, identify themselves, and in the name of which proclaim themselves members of a "white race." Despite the intentions of many of these "members," perhaps, this social structure enacts itself sociopolitically as white supremacy and seeks to attribute its origin to organic being in a biological sense. We have traced various avenues by which this social structure has instituted itself in the United States and seen that race is only intelligible as a social relation between people. Defined by whites for the purpose of encompassing all other people in subordinate racial forms, race becomes the condition, as a system of social relations, for whites to pretend to superiority and to represent themselves in a relation of domination and hierarchy. Thus, "race" is an imposition of a power relation on others, upon which white identity as white then depends. Race comes into existence as an act of definition by whites who assume the power to dominate, and it functions as a system of social categorization that the power to dominate then constructs. Biological theories only serve to disguise the tracks of this circle of power and identity constituted by the act of definition and the fact of definition.

The idea of race (as we know it) evolved in the North American English colonies along with the development of the slave system, as a way of consolidating that system socially. It did not relate "causally" to slavery, either as source or effect, but was a contingent element of slavery's process of development. It composed itself out of three cultural elements of colonial society, by which that society "racialized" itself. The first was a mandatory sense of allegiance to colonial society, and to the violence and dehumanizing enslavement of other people it required to maintain itself. The second was a sense of paranoia engendered by that violence as a fear of rebellion, resistance, or autonomy on the part of those enslaved, in the name of which its dehumanizing violence against them was rationalized. The third was a sense of "social" solidarity against this self-generated threat which concretized the paranoia and legit-imized the violence. Each of these cultural elements was generated by stages through political enactments, and given cultural reality by being both socially instituted and individually interiorized. No element of the original construction of whiteness, race, or racism proceeded without the involvement of the state.

In effect, race exists only as socially produced by such a process of racialization. Racialization is that process through which white society has constructed and co-opted differences in bodily characteristics and made them the marks of hierarchical social categorizations. It has defined body characteristics to be noticed, associated them with social categories, and transformed the characteristics associated with those categorizations (in particular, coloration) into racializing signifiers (as opposed to descriptive terms) for those social categories. In particular, chromatic terms cease being descriptive and become socially active as racially categorizing.

Racism is not the same as racialization. Racism is the system of racialized thoughts and acts by which the white supremacist system maintains itself and its hierarchy of social categorizations. Allegiance, paranoia, and a reliance on violence persist as the constituents of racism because they are primordial to it in terms of the historical process that brought race and whiteness into existence; they thus constitute the ele-ments of its continual reconstruction.

Neither racialization nor racism, whiteness nor white supremacy, can be understood without grasping the interrelatedness of their individual and institutional aspects. Racism is unintelligible as simply individual prejudice, since it relies on dimensions of social permissibility and political enactment, of white consensus and solidarity. On the one hand, prejudice expresses generalizations about a person that can only be socially constructed and socially instituted, always in advance. On the other, preju-dice enacts individually what is provided institutionally as a structure insofar as that institutional (social) structure requires that enactment for its existence. Each gives the other its social importance. If racism and white supremacy exist as social structures of the United States, it is because individual acts of violence, paranoia, and white social solidarity within a context of allegiance to whiteness institute them socially as their totalization. The inseparability of the individual and the institutional is difficult to articulate, since individual activities and social institutions are incommensurable, while each remains the indispensable condition for the existence of the other. The tenacity of racism in the United States lies in the fact of this incommensurability, whereby individuals escape rationality or responsibility by retreating into the insti-tutional, and the institutional escapes political regulation by being dispersed among a society of individuals.

The permissibility of individual white racist attitudes—condescension, ostracism, contempt, hostility, or violence—is given socially, as institutional; the variety of prej-udices, violations, and hatreds by which whites endlessly inferiorize their victims would have no claim to ethical sanction without the institutionalization of white social consensus and solidarity. Similarly, institutional racism—the variety of modes of segregation in housing, jobs, careers, education, financing and lending, the social disfranchisements incurred through gerrymandered districts and police profiling, and the ethical sanction of violence, hatred, and condescension—would not exist if not enacted continually, obsessively, and publicly by individuals.

How are the individual and the institutional, the racist act and the social structure of white racialized identity and white supremacy, to be addressed together? No movement for social justice can afford to ignore the relation between the two—the individual and the institutional—if it seeks to contest racism and racial inequality. For instance, many on the white left consider racism to be a "divide and rule" strategy, or a system of privileges accorded "white skin," as ways of maintaining social or political hegemony.[1] But to see racism as a strategy against which to counterstrategize politically, one must assume that "race" has a prior ("natural," "biological") existence that a hegemonic strategy can then grasp and wield for it own purposes. The institutional gets reduced to administrative policy (and perhaps even given democratic sanction as such), while prejudice gets reduced to individual responses to a material or "objective" reality in the world. For antiracism, the racist act and the racialized social structure become separated as problems, while their mutual affiliation with each other, or even consanguinity, remains unimpaired; antiracism then reduces itself to simply calling for an end to it all. Yet racism's tenacity, its power to withstand contestation, argument, oppositional class, or sociopolitical ideologies, belies its being a mere instrumentality in the hands of power. The question remains of how to confront them together, how to encompass together the dependence of prejudice on social discourse for its generalizations, values, and categories, and the dependence of social categorizations on acts of prejudice and violence, so that one no longer hides behind the other.

Albert Memmi takes a step toward a response by articulating a structure for racism. He enumerates four criteria: (1) "the insistence on a difference, real or imaginary" (which can be somatic, cultural, religious, or of some other characteristic), (2) the imposition of a negative valuation on the other through that difference, always accompanied by a positive valuation for the one imposing it, (3) the generalization of that negative valuation to a group, and (4) the legitimization of aggression or privilege through that difference (R, 170). For Memmi, the statement of a difference does not constitute racism; that difference has to be used negatively and as a rationalization of social aggression against the other (R, 45).

Memmi's criteriology begins to describe an interface between the individual who notices negatively or disparagingly and the institutedness that generates, totalizes, and authorizes it. But what carries the individual across that gap to the moment of aggression? Why does the individual then see that aggression as ethical? Memmi names the gap, but his criteriology stops short of insight into its form. It is a space that Memmi's language can only outline, not fill. Other theories of racism, such as the Marxist or the psychoanalytic, encounter a similar (though inverted) stopping point regarding racial ideology. They seek to explain its interiorization through various power relations (exploitation or the unconscious), but they offer no insight into why those ideologies work so well, why the cruelty and violence of racism is so irresistible. That is, they can see its form but have no account for the power of its content.

The Language of Whiteness

Let us continue along Memmi's path and examine the relation between social discourse and social aggression. Three discursive levels relating to racism can be distinguished paradigmatically: generalization, narrative, and linguistic system or sign. Race discourse defines in generality what is to be noticed about a person as racial, both physically and personally (who the person is). Physical differences exist, but they become significant only because they signify other nonphysical attributes to which they then give social import, and through which they are given social importance in turn. The act of noticing subordinates the one noticed to what must have been previously signified to be noticed as significant, that is, as of social importance. This prior signification given a person means the person has already been generalized and rendered a group.

As previously noted, because people only present themselves as individuals, generalizations about them must be brought from elsewhere. These generalizations are of social origin, rather than derivable from experience with people, and are imposed as a priori concepts upon encounter. But if a prior concept superimposes itself on the way a person is encountered, it substitutes itself for that encounter, and thus for experience of the person. That is, a generalization, because it is nonempirical and a priori, covers or effaces the generalized person's self-presentation to the encounter and substitutes itself for it. In other words, the acceptance of a generalization obviates experience of the individual on whom it is imposed. As a pretense of prior knowledge, the generalization renders other people wholly or in part unknowable. As an alibi for that unknowability, racism resorts to the ostensible "objectivity" (i.e., determinism) of biology.

Though Memmi couches his account in terms of individuals, their ability to notice a "difference" in another to which a negative valuation can be given implies a prior act of generalization of that difference, purporting a previously chosen social decision as to its negativity. A prior discourse from elsewhere (than the encounter) had to have already picked out the particular difference in question, given it social meaning, specified it for special notice, and attached an importance to it. Thus, the generalizations of race transform a bodily feature into a racial characteristic by amalgamating feature, meaning, and the social importance of noticing into that characteristic. Not only is it self-referential, because anterior to the encounter to which it pretends to make reference, but it creates the racial characteristic it pretends to notice. That is, it creates certain characteristics as "racial." In its immanent self-referentiality, the act of generalization brings into concrete existence what it is about abstractly and before the fact. A certain supremacy is already inherent in this self-arrogated power to pick out and specify a difference, define a characteristic, and give it meaning. That is, in Memmi's paradigm, a form of domination and negative valuation is already assumed for and contained in the social act of generalizing, for which the actual generalizations then provide a content self-referentially.

The imposition of generalization creates a problem, however. Those who generalize others must still encounter and interact with those the generalization renders unknowable, even if the reality of that encounter is one of utmost exploitation or hierarchy. Across the hiatus of unknowability that the supremacist generalization has constructed, an alternate knowability must be produced. The generalized "other" must be endowed with a personality, a subjectivity, a temperament and capability by which to be encountered, within the boundary of the generalization. To this purpose, white supremacy produces a vast system of narratives that reinvent personhood for those it has deprived of personhood by generalizing. These narratives become the way whites then encounter the others they generalize. This constitutes a second discursive level for racism. The specific narratives may vary from place to place or era to era, but the necessity to reinvent, to supplant and supplement generalization as a rite of superiority, is unavoidable. These narratives may begin by delineating forms of obedience and (enforceable) subservience for the other, but they eventually confabulate an entire caricature of the other for the supremacist, how the other is supposed to act. That is, they constitute a particularizing form of generalization, added in turn to those significations attached to the perceived difference.

These narratives are necessarily inferiorizing and derogatory, reflecting the power to generalize in the first place. They take the form of "I know you people like such-and-such," or "You know how they are . . ." The stereotype is both the category and the shorthand for these narratives, and they become the modular elements for the invention of more. Through these narratives, the humanity and sensitivity of the other's personal relationships, the beauty or difficulties of their love affairs, the complex cohesiveness of their families, and the varying heroics of their resistance to racism are transformed into caricatures. These narratives are always disparaging, even when complimentary, because they represent the project of speaking for the other, thereby derogating at once the other's autonomy and individuality. Whatever their content, they participate in domination. They assume generalization as their source, and they reflect the arrogated presumption to define. Their extensive and endless repetition becomes an entire realm of social discourse for many whites, at times so compulsive that all other thought becomes subordinate to both overt and veiled reference to it. But it is all self-referential. As Toni Morrison puts it, "the fabrication of an Africanist persona [for and by whites] is reflexive, an extraordinary meditation on the [white] self." Helene Cixous constructs an analogy to this structure in pointing out that patriarchy metaphorically says to women, "We're going to do your portrait so that you can begin looking like it right away."[2]

This system of narratives about the other takes on a life of its own. Because what is not renarrativized remains unseen and unknowable behind the imposed a priori generalizations, the narratives present themselves as originary. Having no other reality than themselves to represent, or to which to make reference, they assume the character of truthfulness by default. In the eyes of the supremacist, they are the reality of the other, in spite of what that other individual may do or say.[3] The other's attempt at self-presentation becomes irrelevant or insolent in the eyes that look through those narratives, not because the other is unknowable, but because the other is apprehended as known a priori. "I know more about you than you know about yourself," the supremacist will say. They may even be used as a basis for an attempt at friendship with the one racialized through them—or so the supremacist might think. It is in the name of a pretense to knowledge, against an unacknowledged unknowability, that the entire system of renarrativization and racist discourse is constructed. But it is a knowledge that is therefore also paranoid. We see in these narratives a necessity that has seemingly extant origin (in the other), and is therefore threatening (a confrontation with unknowability), while admitting of no resolution to that unknowability because it is self-generated, self-referential, and unacknowledgeable as such.

From the moment of its inception, the Virginia colony renarrativized the indigenous in generalized terms as pagan and ignorant, as always war-hungry and treacherous, especially in their friendly overtures and fair dealings. This was the tenor of the narrative dimension by which the English then interacted with them. Yet the English stood in a relation of criminal trespass to the indigenous, having come to seize the land in the interest of eventual riches, a goal to which mandatory allegiance was required, and for which in turn a narrative demonization of the indigenous was indispensable. Extending even up to the present (as testified to by the American Indian movement), the currency of these narratives is testimony to the longevity of such systems. Overlaid upon each act or possible interaction, they prevision narratively what concretely will have occurred before the fact.

Because each system of narratives constitutes the "reality" of the racialized other for whites, that is, invents the reality of each member of the generalized group, it presents itself as a linguistic system of reference to the other, a system of signs by which the other is to be spoken about by the dominating group. This system of signs is not an element of interaction between the dominant and those generalized, because those generalized did not participate in generating or inventing the signs or system. The stories that reparticularize the generalized African American (for instance) for whites have reality only for whites. Reflecting the socius and self-image of whites, they constitute discursive elements of the way whites interact with each other. These stories not only substitute for the unknowability of each generalized African American they are about, but they constitute a critical element of interaction among whites who have generated and accepted them.[4] (Similarly, masculinist men use their repertoire of stories about women not only as their understanding of women, but also as part of their language of interaction with each other as men.)

For black people who see themselves as individuals (however else they may see themselves, whether through the eyes of others or against the others' gaze), the white narrative assumptions reveal how whites see them. For some, the narratives constitute how they should appear to whites in order to be seen or to go unnoticed. But for whites, these narratives become part of how they communicate with other whites, and thus how they enter into the socius of whites. The subject of the narratives may be the character (or caricature) of black people, but their function and social meaning is to provide for white social interaction as white. By deploying these signs among themselves, white people are constantly (and obsessively) constructing themselves as white through them. In other words, this system of narratives constitutes the language

of white discourse as white. It constitutes the language through which whites understand themselves as white. The deployment of these signs of whiteness by whites with
respect to each other signifies their collective whiteness. The use of this language by
whites constitutes their participation in that collectivity as a social structure. It is the
language of a supremacist social past that provides the elements as signs for a (racialized) future, an inheritance of white racial identity in the form of a language. Simone
de Beauvoir points out that marriage is a relation between men for which women are
the means; similarly, racism is a relation between whites for which nonwhite people
are the language.

   This, then, is the domain where racialization occurs. The system of narratives and
the language they become constitute the formal milieu in which whites racialize themselves as white through having racialized (generalized) black people as black (or
Native Americans as "Indians," etc.) in the content of the narratives. It is through
abstraction from this linguistic system that the racial signifiers ("white" and "black",
for instance) get transformed from being descriptive (terms for colors) to being racialized (terms for social categories). The signifier "white" has meaning only in differential relation to other signifiers for color, and it can refer to people in a racialized
fashion only in differential relation to other racializing terms. Thus, a differential system of terms becomes necessary to refer to something invented like "race," and to
index the system of narratives by which it was invented. The social meaning given
to "black" by "whites" gets codified in the narrative signs through the system's signifying differentials, and the signs provide the social signification given to "white"
through their existence as the source of that social meaning.

   Whiteness and white identity are the meanings produced by the use of these self-
generated narratives of the other by whites, implying that these meanings remain
wholly contingent on their affirmation by other whites. White people become white
by coalescing around the language of whiteness as a symbol system, which prescribes
their identity and the identity of the group. In effect, group identification becomes
the real meaning of this "white" sign system; to speak it is to identify oneself as white,
to reconstitute one's racialization. Even when a white speaker is addressing a designated "nonwhite" person in this language, s/he is essentially speaking to other whites,
because deploying a language that is peculiar to the interrelation of whites as white.
This language becomes a white person's means of belonging; it is the membership
card in the socius of white identity. Membership is what is produced by speaking and
enacting the language that produces whites as white through a narrative system referring to another. A question that antiracist whites need to ask is, how might it be possible to speak a language other than this white (supremacist) language, and where
would such a language come from?

   The psychic violence experienced by those subjected to such conscription as a language, to being rendered the means whereby whites institutionalize their relations to
each other, remains practically indescribable. W.E.B. DuBois speaks of the double consciousness it produces, of "always looking at oneself through the eyes of others." He
extols the heroic "dogged strength" required to move on against it. To be conscripted

by a racialized language is to live a life that is at all times appropriated as a source of meaning for others (whites), who are always elsewhere yet always "here." Thus, it is a silencing as well as a psychic violence, or violation. Ironically, it is precisely because whiteness takes this structure as a sign system that racism, whose existence silences entire groups of people, is able to coexist with the Bill of Rights, to extol the right of free speech—and seek protection for itself within that right. For the racist, free speech extends only to the users of language; it does not extend to those who are a language.

To recapitulate, the racialization of whites comes about through the racialization of others. For white people to be white, they must have defined and racialized others as nonwhite, and to have defined a nonwhite in order to define and racialize themselves as white. As Ian Lopez puts it, whiteness is a double negative; it is what is not nonwhite.[5] At no time does this process unfold outside a structure of domination. A system of domination racializes itself only by racializing those dominated, through whose oppression (including exclusions and derogations) it creates the special meanings by which to do so. One could say that, in an inexorable circularity of structure, racism brings race into existence, while the concept of race so generated then becomes the content of that racism. In short, whiteness is fundamentally relational (OW, 58). At no time can it pretend to an essentiality, as an aspect of a (white) person's being. Because an other remains indispensable to its existence (even if only through a structure of invention and narrative), whiteness needs to continually redefine a "nonwhite" other in order to construct itself, its privilege, and its boundaries. All discourse between whites as whites assumes and includes the other through cliché, tone of voice, innuendo, and derogatory terms.

The other side of this coin is the necessity to exclude the other socially from the use of this language. The social structure of racialization would lose its foundation and fall apart discursively if others were able to include their own story in the social discourse, or reflect their own autonomous subjectivity in the social consciousness by which those who dominate had racialized themselves. But social and narrative exclusion is the content, and the cultural practice, that reflects and enacts the formal schema I have earlier characterized as the "purity condition." Domination would end as soon as the dominating group lost the ability to generalize those they dominate and renarrativize (hence the tradition of an exclusionary literary canon—extolled, for instance, by Allan Bloom in *The Closing of the American Mind*).

This system of meanings (called whiteness, the white race, white supremacy) constitutes an ontological paradox for white people precisely because a nonwhite other, who is given to be noticed while thrust into the distance, resides at the core of white self-definition.[6] To be white is to find the core of one's identity elsewhere, in the derogated other. The self-referentially constructed and racialized other becomes the substance of that identity. This is the source of white obsession with the nonwhite other. For whites, the nonwhite becomes at once nemesis, fascination, and self. Herein lies both the stupefying nature of racism for the "white mind" as well as the source for its necessary self-universalization. If the nonwhite other must be both excluded as other and absorbed as self in order to construct white identity, that identity can render itself coherent only through an extreme act of self-essentialization; it must universalize itself as the norm (that is, as unmarked racially) in order to consummate that absorption, and it must render abstract its sense of superiority in order to concretize its exclusion of the other (as different). That is, it must absolutize itself in order to escape from the inherent relativity of race and racialization. In the throes of this paradox, whites have only their own self-referential assumptions about whiteness to fall back on to explain themselves, and only force and violence to explain those assumptions.

The Violence of Whiteness

Real violence is inherent in the system by which whites racialize themselves as white. The nonwhite other is both placed at the center of white identity and continually evicted from it. Such absorption and rejection must be perpetrated continually to confirm one's identity as well as one's membership in whiteness. Because whiteness is a form of membership that must be continually renewed, the violence that reconstitutes it must be continually undertaken. While the modes of eviction (condescension, rejection, social exclusion, segregation) are purveyed in the narrative forms of the language of whiteness, their actual or imagined unfolding is provided by the narrative content. The narratives constitute templates of quotidian violence and hierarchy. Their enactment as brutality or hostility becomes a defrayal or payment of dues whereby white identified people affirm both membership and white consensus. One performs certain actions or speech to communicate to other members (whites) that one is still there, that one is still white; that is, one assures other whites that one is still white through those means—hence the gratuitous deployment of derogatory terms and racist violence, and toleration of them in others. Speaking the symbols, renewing the generalizing terms (as contempt, distance, objectification), and retelling or enacting the racializing narratives of violence are the various modes of performance of whiteness and white self-racialization.

This is clearly seen in the use of derogatory terms. Derogatory terms mark the quotidian operations of all domination. Recently called "hate speech" or "slurs," they exemplify the constant and gratuitous desire by the dominant to hurt the other. Although derogatory terms are words, they are not signifiers. They do not refer to or contain meaning outside their use, which is always to disparage. They signify only as derogatory acts rather than as signifiers—as form without content. As self-generative acts, their purpose is not to provide meaning but to harm, to categorize, to impose a negative valuation, to generalize individuals without referring to them, all at once. In effect, derogatory terms do not constitute speech but forms of assault, in verbal though not in linguistic form. As self-referential and gratuitous assault, they are self-legitimizing. They assault the existence of the other in order to render that existence assailable, and to regenerate that facet of white intentionality that assails.

Derogatory terms rely on a power hierarchy for effect. They constitute a form of interface between the individual enactment of racism and its institutional or instituted existence. As a metaphor for the physical violence always in actual or potential presence as the eviction of the other from individual white identity, they encapsulate the necessity of violence to the institutionalization of white identity. In all its forms—the prenarrativization of the other, the continual denigration and its affect of aggressiveness, the templates of violence always suggested in the content of white language, and the forms of white language that ostracize and segregate the other they take as their materiality—violence constitutes the connection between the individual and the institutedness of racism. That institutedness embodies the inner demands and rules of the white socius, of membership in whiteness.

In short, derogatory terms call upon a hierarchical authorization that is dependent on a complex structure of violence, and is perforce not available to those denigrated. This is why the counter-use of derogatory terms by the subjugated or subaltern remains an idle gesture, though perhaps one of resistance and autonomy. However, it is not only derogation's reliance on a hierarchy of domination but also its pseudosemiotic character that renders it unanswerable in kind. Response or counterviolence in self-defense cannot be similarly derogatory, since that is already circumscribed by the fact of hierarchy, and would have to be truly semiotic, an attempt to deploy a real meaning. Though the dominant may take umbrage at being the target of what pretends to be derogatory, it would only be at the act of rebellion or resistance contained in the fact of response. Indeed, response is doubly proscribed, since self-defense by the subordinated is outlawed by definition as a fact of hierarchy. Self-defense is labeled aggression and criminalized, in which terms the original aggression of the dominant takes on the retroactive aura of self-defense for itself.

If derogatory terms are a means of assault, then their continual use in white speech positions the speaker in an attitude, an affective state, of continual aggressiveness. The animus that drives such an attitude has nothing to do with the persons assaulted. It is their existence rather than their acts or agency that is assaulted. Because the performance is self-referential, without the involvement or provocation of those it is about (how they ultimately respond to it notwithstanding), and gratuitous as an attitude of aggressivity, it is always redundant, being addressed to both the (real or imagined) target of derogation and to other whites from whom the speaker seeks approbation. It is white consensus that requires this animus as the quotidian performance of white solidarity. The person assaulted, whether present or not, is both a pretext and a moment of white self-affirmation through this animus. White solidarity thus conditions the repetition of self-affirmation that is required by the utmost dependence whites have placed at the center of their identity. Independence and autonomy are least possible for whites as white, which explains their inability to abide the thought of autonomy or independence in the racialized other.

This need for autonomy, and its impossibility in terms of dependence on the other for one's identity, explains the obsessive repetition of derogation. This can even take the form of consciously signifying implicitly or explicitly that one is withholding the act of derogation, in order that the derogation withheld be recognized by one's listeners as "there" in absentia. The obsessiveness opens a virtual space to be filled by recognition, by other whites who hold the key to a necessitated future, a promised destiny to be recalled in the present. As obsessive, it presents itself as excess—an excess of hegemony, a hyperhegemonic enactment for its own sake. White identity cannot do without this gratuitous and excessive self-replication. It is its primary source of self-legitimation as supremacist, to compensate for its dependency on the other. Through this complex of redundancy, obsessiveness, and gratuitousness—the analogue, on the plane of the individual, of social allegiance, paranoia, and violence—one maintains one's standing, one's identity, as white.

What is most threatening about racism or white supremacy is the gratuitousness of its actions. The secretly recognized but unacknowledged power of gratuitous violence is its inescapability, the inability to install defenses against it. It does not provide a handle by which to grasp its logic, or against which to form battle lines and prepare for defense. To formulate a defense, there has to be a discernible motive for the coming aggression. But when that is wholly self-referential, with nothing extant to grasp as motive, the entire world becomes an arena of ambush. Thus, as a modus operandi, gratuitous violence terrorizes in its constant potential for appearing unexpectedly. No model of preparedness will guarantee safety. If the victims acquiesce, they lose; if they resist or attempt to ward off the violence, they only provide the assailant with a material (rather than self-referential) reason to attack. In other words, it is the nature of gratuitous violence that both resistance and nonresistance provide validation for it.

This inability to fit the gratuitous into any form of social rationale is what makes it so venomous and evil. Gratuitous violence would be a form of scapegoating if it involved community ritual, but it does not. It simply resides at the core of an individual's sense of membership, deficient in morality because subordinated to that self-referential goal. It distinguishes itself from scapegoating insofar as it is extemporaneous, beyond ritual, though ritualistic. Finally, it cannot be discussed with whites since a discussion of gratuitousness would highlight the inherent irrationality in their identifications and their actions, and hence be unintelligible to them. The despair to which this leads their victims is known and desired, a motivated result. It sets racism beyond the purview of reasoned or experience-based argument or opposition.

Here, a second level of violence emerges: the provocation of resistance or opposition. Because white identity can be affirmed only through gratuitous violence (whether direct or by proxy, whether physical or psychic) against the other—a violence both prescribed and appropriated by "white language"—an instigated response that can be deemed violent itself, and thus a rationale for violence in response, becomes desirable. The provocation of resistance becomes a form of metaviolence, a way of creating a situation in which the violence essential to white supremacy can be promulgated. This is a secondary motivation for the gratuitous hostility to which those racialized by whites are subjected, and the material substrate for racism's various "blame the victim" strategies (in masculinist ideology, it goes: "She brought it on herself"). The daily moments of white hostility, which have for centuries amounted to terrorism, though denied through an evocation of history, evolution, and attempts at reform and education, all signify conscious purpose and a conscious desire, for which an elaborate discursive technology has been constructed. While many excuses for gratuitous behavior can be offered, its source lies in the structure and meanings of white racialized identity.

Whiteness as a Politics

The operations of white racism take on a tinge that could be characterized as fascist in the sense that Walter Benjamin articulated fascism, as an estheticization of politics. This means that an esthetic dimension is given to power, to its deeds, even to the violence and tyranny by which it rules, and through that esthetic dimension, a sense of belonging and of membership is created.[7] People can express themselves through the esthetic dimension, so they feel as if they are participating in a social process, while the real political processes and the structures of power remain uneffected. That is, a means of political expression is constituted for people that both continues and hides their real sociopolitical powerlessness. This is not an idle analogy to white supremacy. Fascism is not only a form of capitalist tyranny, as the Marxists analyze it, but a gratuitous use of terror to constitute control for its own sake, sometimes even over capital.[8] What it always requires is the establishment of a boundary between a coherent inside group (nation, race, or party) and an outside held in subjection through organized and excessive violence and dehumanization. If, inside that boundary, a modicum of democratic structure is possible, it only continues the facade covering the raw power by which the "other" is dominated.

There is an inherent esthetic dimension to the politics of whiteness that is more than just boundaries positioned along black/white or chromatic lines. The estheticization of racial politics revolves more centrally around the discursive nature of the narrative, as well as the focus on what is to be noticed about others, signifying access to who they are. The social importance generated by that act of noticing belongs to the esthetic realm, and dictates the coordinates by which the racist responds with a distaste or negative valuation to the other who is noticed. This does not belong to an ethics but borders on it, and rationalizes racist violence as ethical. What is perceived as ethical becomes dependent on and reflective of this esthetic structure.

For white supremacy, the narrativity of "white language" gives descriptive life to what is indispensable to whiteness; it becomes a mode of expression of being white, without giving the whites who use it any greater power over their situation. They simply gain the personal feeling of aggressiveness, which is valorized again as membership. In effect, the system of narratives that lies at the core of racism is both a structure of power and the content of its politics. It is both the content of white solidarity (as belonging, power, and control) and the formalization of whiteness as a politics itself.

In that sense, whiteness as a political structure becomes a form of state, a mode of governance, and its dealing with black or brown people is the substance of its state concerns. Even when black people are out of sight or absent from the area, governance goes on in the discourse among white people as white. When that discourse reaches a point where it needs an action in order to make itself feel real, perhaps because of something in the newspaper or a rumor passing around a neighborhood, then whites go looking for a black person to exercise their state power on. The dragging death of Donald Byrd, the drive-by shooting of a black man walking down a railroad track by two white hunters who had come home empty-handed, the Howard Beach attacks, and a hazing through a viciousness in language are considered ethical by their perpetrators because they have an esthetic base that gives permissibility to these acts as acts of entitlement. These acts are lived as entitlement, and their legitimacy lies in the structure of governance that they represent. The violence regenerates a sense of citizenship; that is, citizenship is based upon a sense of violence.

The structure of racialization provides a boundary for such a state, and delimits its operations. Throughout U.S. history, racialist ideology has authorized gratuitous and generalized local violence from which transformed means of governing have emerged. The overthrow of Reconstruction, the epidemic of lynchings that ushered in Jim Crow, the mass murders of indigenous toward which the early settlers established American mythologies of pride, and contemporary police brutality and impunity are all examples. The overall political effect has at these times been transformative, and new structures of power have emerged from the violence. For the perpetrators, however, their participation in the power they engendered was illusory, a form of patronage at best. As an estheticization of U.S. politics, color has been the mark, and white identity has been the language.

White-identified people cannot escape the effect of these structures of violence: to first tolerate, then notice, then enjoy, and finally to desire the derogations and violations heaped upon the designated nonwhite other at the center of white identity. Identification of oneself as white puts one in complicity with the entire structure—and thus with all the criminality and dehumanization that lie behind it, with all the racializing definitions and objectifications by which the social structure of whiteness was engendered—precisely because it is a social structure and not an element of personal choice. One cannot escape the implication that the psychic violence produced by the structures of racialization was designed for that purpose, for that complicity. It is not possible to identify oneself as white and be antiracist at the same time. To identify oneself as white is to accept all the racism and violence that reside at the foundation of that identity, as well as the narrative language that engendered whiteness as an identity in the first place, within which racism ineluctably resides.

Concretely, the discourse of race (with its biologist theorizations, its reliance on derogatory terminologies, and the interior narrative structure of its significations) is a projection onto common language of the social categorizations that whiteness produces through its racialization of society. It becomes another circular process; the racialization of society is perceived and understood through the discourses of race that the structures of racialization produced. Similarly, racial categorization, which both transcends and participates in producing class difference, gets explained in class terms as produced by class relations. It thus blinds one to a fundamental aspect of capitalism, namely that capitalism constructs itself using the differences between people that it finds useful, and conditions its own historical trajectory through the character of those differences. To assume that class relations are fundamental, as does Marxism, means to blind oneself to their contingency on cultural systems of social categorization. Because the hyperoperations of racialization are more than simply tactics of oppression, they can transcend social norms and render certain actions normative that would otherwise be considered alien to social coherence or ethics (such as lynching, racial profiling, racial disfranchisement and segregation, and police murders). The "useful" social differences that capitalism exploits constitute a social coherence beyond the terms of capitalist exploitation, whose development in turn hides the fact that class organization and class exploitation are themselves instrumentalities—in the United States built upon whiteness and in Europe upon nationality.

The structures of racialization are not monolithic, however. Against the violent operations of white identity, there is a liberal version. It is just as obsessive, and violent in a different, more subtle way. Liberalism seeks to reject white supremacy by adopting the effects of white racism as a project. It seeks to alleviate the distress of racism's "victims." It feels it has to "help these people," who are seen as caught in a bad, if not hopeless, situation. But as hegemonic, liberalism is actually threatened by the autonomy or reconstitution of subjectivity that would represent real self-determination by the subordinated. In seeking to focus on the effects of racial oppression, liberalism leaves the objectifying structure of whiteness intact, and thus continues the designated "other's" objectification. Even when speaking of autonomy (black or Native American, for instance), liberalism prenarrativizes that autonomy, ready to point out that "You are going too far." (Too far for whom?) In using the effects of white racism to establish a different form of hegemony, liberal antiracism reifies the structures of racialization and derogation it seeks to alleviate. Thus, while white liberalism attempts to be antiracist, its continued residence in the language and hegemony of whiteness remains complicitly racist since it unwittingly preempts and obviates the autonomy or subjectivity of the racialized other. To the extent that liberal antiracism has not contested the language, narrativity, and social solidarity of whiteness, it will only have reinscribed white identity in what already forms the core and mortar of white supremacy. Its often attempted separation of whiteness from white supremacy is an empty gesture.

This problematic extends to oppositional (reform) movements and organizations at all levels of U.S. society. Labor union solidarity may momentarily overcome racial antagonism by bringing people together for a common struggle, but in remaining unaware of how white hegemony has conditioned class structures and, in particular, labor union organization itself, it continually reinscribes white solidarity into its every economic and cultural act. In general, when oppositional political movements call for solidarity and unity today, they assume those who would unite belong to the same economic structure and are not incommensurably divided. They ignore what has made racism work so well, what has been used with such alacrity: the foundational nature of white supremacy to all levels of social activity, even opposition politics. A call for unity that does not recognize the dual class structure thus assumes a unity from a white perspective (even in its calls against racism).

Unity from an antiracist perspective, or a deracializing project that sought to end the operations and legitimacy of white structures of racialization, would have to begin with a recognition of the existence of the structures of racialization, even within oppositional movements. That is, a call for unity cannot be made that requires black or brown people to cross over into white corporate society if they are to join. (Many people of color attempt to cross that boundary, but it is not generally as part of oppositional political movements.) Such a call would remain white supremacist. In particular, because there is a class distinction between white and black workers, not to have taken steps to overthrow that class relation within its own class organizations renders labor union calls for class solidarity more rhetorical than real, more hegemonic than solidarist. It is part of the double bind of white supremacy that an oppositional call to unity would have to be a call to whites to break their solidarity as whites. Even in the women's movement, white women centered leadership in themselves and then wondered why black women, who had different issues (one of which was white hegemony) and gave different meanings to aspects of women's conditions in this society, did not come around, or felt excluded from the deliberations, critiques, programs, and leadership.[9] Despite good intentions, the white people in these movements did not see the relation between standing opposed to racism as an ideology (which only scratches the surface) and standing within the operations of the hegemonic mind, which governed their own words and actions. The hegemonic mind is not something one escapes just by dedicating oneself to antiracism.

In short, while the white supremacist accentuates exclusion and alterity as a form of appropriation, white liberalism accentuates inclusion or absorption as a form of reified alterity. To the extent that both identify themselves as white, they both deploy the designated (nonwhite) other as a meaning for themselves. The designated other is reduced to a form of nonpersonhood; the supremacist does it through ostracism, and the liberal does it by "speaking for." Both do this consciously in adopting their respective positions and linking their actions to the standards of society around them; that is, they see their conduct as focused (not redundant), called for by their situations (not obsessive), and properly contextualized (not gratuitous)—in a word, not violence, neither as assault nor as objectification.

In effect, there is a common bond between the white liberal and the white supremacist: their dependence on those defined and designated as nonwhite. The bond is partially given; whiteness refers to one's belonging to the white corporate state, not because one joined but because one had been joined to it by the operation of corporate society itself. But it is partially intentional in the sense that one recognizes and accepts what is given. The supremacist accepts that membership and its supremacy, both ignoring and valorizing the injustices and inequities of it, while the liberal accepts that membership and its supremacy while trying to render that supremacy just and equitable against the supremacist. Neither seeks to cancel membership, nor live their lives in a way that respects others as different without defining and appropriating that difference for themselves. Both have preserved the structure of noticing others as different (for their own identity and membership), rather than respecting others as different, while transforming that noticed difference into different forms of importance for themselves. Neither foregoes that social importance. At the same time, both claim simply to be human, but their active membership in the social institution of whiteness means their claim to mere humanness is in bad faith. By belonging to the institution of whiteness, their humanness is rendered a white humanness. For white people to become human would imply more than simply adopting a stance of colorblindness (which is a stance that again centers whiteness). To no longer be in bad faith, they would have to dismember that institution.

The institutedness of racism exists as the totality of actions of white individuals that it valorizes—as a social "institution"—before the fact. The enactments of whiteness (as white supremacy, racial violence, or white skin privilege) by those individuals are what constitute that institution. One belongs to the institution only in order to enact it through enacting one's whiteness, while one can enact one's whiteness only because one belongs to the institution. One cannot speak of one without the other (even though we do not have a language that permits us to speak of both at the same time). The institution has no buildings, constitution, or by-laws; it is to be found only in the discourses that describe aspects of it. Yet in the United States it is more real than any other political or cultural institution because it resides at the foundation of them all.

White Skin Privilege

In the quotidian world, the hegemonic mind terrorizes because it acts gratuitously, in response to self-referential motivations. The operation of the hegemonic mind, the excess of hegemony marked by gratuitous acts of violence, goes unnoticed for two reasons. First, it is taken as a natural entitlement by whites, as simply the way things are; second, its effects transcend articulation insofar as they are excessive. This is what makes it terrorizing for those subjected to its ambushes—which can occur in any and all social spaces, even reform or oppositional movements where it is especially insupportable. There is nothing one can do, by either act or comportment, to avoid it. Within oppositional political movements, hegemony creates a space of silence across which one as "other" remains unheard; what one says in that space is seen as unhelpful, beside the point, the source of unnecessary distinctions or disputes, of not acceding in all simplicity to what leadership is trying to organize. There are rare persons who can fight through the muck of white domination in reform or oppositional movements and still maintain a focus on the organization's reform goals. But most people do not have the time to waste.[10]

This excess of hegemony has been referred to by radical antiracists as "white skin privilege." The theorization of white skin privilege and the call for whites to abandon it have become the essence of an antiracist project. Traditional liberalism sees racism as ignorance or as a moral question and attempts to eliminate it by focusing on its effects (segregation, impoverishment). The theorists of white skin privilege focus on the perpetrator of racist acts and structures, the "white race." They critique the self-arrogated and self-aggrandizing hegemony that provides whites with unearned and unwarranted privilege in society and social interactions, which is withheld from others. It is the white race as white, and not simply as a race, that has to understand itself and its actions in order to put an end to racism. The white skin privilege idea points out the way all whites benefit from the structures of racism. Racism is an exclusion of those chromatically characterized from participation in society. Whites are called upon to see the privilege they have arrogated to themselves through that exclusion, and to stop that privileged arrogation. The critique of white skin privilege is thus a response to the disclaimers so often heard from whites: "I haven't hurt anyone"; "I don't owe anybody anything"; "I never enslaved anyone."

Yet when a movement seeking to end both personal and institutional racism as exclusion, ostracism, or gratuitous negative valuation issues a call for social deprivileging, it ironically inverts itself. It sounds as if whites should give something up, that they should reduce themselves to the level to which they have reduced others. It seems neither to alleviate the condition of the oppressed nor contest the normativity of whiteness, which remains the standard from which the notion of "reduction" is to be measured.

What whites "have," however, is a sense of citizenship and social entitlement. Rather than privileges, these appear as elements of social being that simply go without saying. Indeed, they refuse articulation as belonging only to white skin (the purity concept is omitted from the articulation of social being). It is difficult for whites who self-identify as whites to see wherein their privilege lies, and how it is socially given from elsewhere. Indeed, working-class whites or white women, subordinated as they are to capitalist wealth and patriarchal institutions, see themselves as deprivileged by their own subordination.

In fact, abandoning white skin privilege would not mean giving up something. When antiracists attempt to spell out what white skin privilege means, they produce long lists of conditions that whites do not confront, but that black or brown people do as matters of daily concern. For instance, Peggy McIntosh enumerates her sense of white skin privilege in a famous article called "White Privilege: Unpacking the Invisible Knapsack."[11] The most banal things become elements of "privilege." One does not have to worry if one will be served in a public establishment or in public accommodations. One can travel alone or with one's family without expecting embarrassment or hostility from those one encounters. One does not have to fear being mistreated. One can go shopping in supermarkets or department stores without being followed or harassed. One's speech is respected. When one speaks to a group, one's race is not put on trial, nor is one considered to be speaking for one's racial group. One's everyday acts, such as doing something well or not, dressing in old clothes, or being late for a meeting, are not attributed to one's race. One can participate in social or political organizations relevant to one's life and feel connected rather than isolated, out of place, feared, outnumbered, unheard, or held at a distance. One can be sure that needed legal or medical help will not be withheld or questioned because of one's race. One can consider one's social, political, imaginative, or professional options with equanimity, without wondering if one will be accepted or allowed to pursue them. In short, white skin privilege appears as a system of absences. To be white in this society means to feel welcome and "normal" in ordinary public life, free of the necessity to anticipate the possibility of hostility, free of the fear or anxiety of being treated as an unwanted alien. What is absent goes unnoticed, or can be taken for granted. Conversely, in the absence of that "privilege" of being unnoticed, the most banal aspects of life become sources of confrontation. While whites can take their civil rights or liberties as a basic assumption of cultural existence, nonwhites cannot; for them, civil rights inhabits a domain of continual political struggle.

Understandably, normal opportunities and possibilities may appear as privileges in the eyes of those denied them. But the notion of privilege exists only in a situation of disparity between denial and nondenial that should not exist in the first place. The normal opportunities and possibilities that appear as privilege for those denied them define a circle. People of color are first inferiorized in order to deny them social access, and then denied social access in order to further inferiorize them. Indeed, whites' inferiorization of people of color is essential to their blindness to the system of denial that appears to others as privilege. Unfortunately, none of this is contested by the idea of abandoning white skin privilege. Rather, the structure is sidestepped by simply calling for its abandonment.

Actually, many whites will admit they have certain privileges because they live a situation given to them by society from which people of color are wholly or partially excluded. But for them, the social givenness of their situation implies it is out of their hands as individuals—an attitude which plays individual action and institutional sanction against each other. Most whites, and especially openly racist whites, will not admit that their identifying as white participates in an actual structure of impoverishment, destitution, and death foisted on others. It is not intelligible to them that, by identifying as white, they are actually hindering others from enjoying life, or buttressing a structure that impoverishes others. At the same time, they are speaking from a position of entitlement, ignoring the contradiction between what entitlement implies and their denial of participation in impoverishment.

This engenders a kind of twistedness or narrowness in the white skin privilege idea. While privilege can be understood as social, the accompanying notion of benefit is often measured economically. In such terms, the call to abandon white skin privilege shunts the problem of racism over to a form of social economy and enmeshes it in the political ideology of entitlement. Economic entitlement becomes what is withheld from nonwhites, while nonwhite equalization becomes antithetical to white entitlement. Antiracism calls for equalized economic entitlement, and white supremacy responds from a defense of white entitlement. If the demand for racial equality couches white entitlement in economic terms, then the antiracism of equal social entitlement becomes economically antiwhite. The assumption of white social entitlement is co-opted by whites as an opportunity to contest equality as (antiwhite) racism, and to recontextualize antiracism as white economic disentitlement. But it is whiteness that constitutes the substance of white entitlement, not economic entitlement, and white entitlement can exist only if there are others to whom comparable entitlement is denied. The call to abandon white skin privilege avoids the idea that whiteness itself as entitlement must be abandoned, rather than simply economic entitlement for whites; it would mean abandoning the identity of whiteness, and the identification with whiteness that grounds it.

Here, we must recall that the white race is not a race in the same sense that others are. Whites constituted whiteness through a purity concept that divided them from others they designated chromatically, against whom and through whom they then defined whiteness. It was a double process instituted for self-racializing purposes, to define themselves as white and the others metaracially as "races." The social conditions that establish race and whiteness, and through which whites differentiate themselves from other peoples as races, are things that whites have done as white. Where white self-racialization is the source of the concept of race and a hierarchical racial system, white racialized consciousness sees race itself as the origin, with the white race as one of its products. Race and racism become unintelligible for whites because they appear to be a result of the existence of race, while white self-racialization actually functions structurally as prior to and generative of race.

The privilege of being white arises from the disparity between what whites have generated and how they see themselves produced by race originally as just one race among many. It expresses itself in black or brown people being noticed and profiled everywhere they go while this remains something that does not happen to whites. But the two conditions are mutually conditioning. Not being noticed means not being subjected to daily harassment or aggression, which comes from whites who notice and are not themselves noticed in either their being or their noticing. It is not simply the police, or certain groups of extreme racists, who do the noticing and harassing. For those whom whites metaracialize and designate chromatically, every white becomes someone who notices, and becomes a potential agent of harassment; to be white means to chromatically designate others, to attach a negative social importance to that, and then to notice a person through that importance. This is the general context in which all whites inarticulately legitimize unending hostility and harassment, by their silence and acquiescence if by no other means.

To those whose identification as white "goes without saying," the injustice of inequity, with its attendant travesties, remains a normal landscape. If that reflects a dependency that whites cannot afford to see (as white), it reveals the real white skin privilege of blindness to the shape of that social landscape, the privilege of not seeing, of not having to see, what is being done in small everyday actions and attitudes of derogation, what they as whites do that makes the societal machinery of racialization work. Each white-identified white person is not only a machine operator with respect to the machinery of white supremacy, but part of the machine, insofar as s/he identifies as an "operator."

When whites consciously rather than inarticulately act through daily hostilities or harassments, they tacitly become participants in a form of intermediary control stratum. If all whites, by identifying themselves as white, participate in the discursive framework that guides this control stratum, that directs its attentions and aggressions, then all whites become part of a contemporary control stratum. It does not matter whether they actually enact any control functions or not. To simply take for granted their humanity and their constitutionally guaranteed rights within a social stratum that withholds those through a variety of control functions from people whom whites designate chromatically as other is to participate implicitly in barring people from inclusion. Whether from a liberal or a supremacist point of view, what is taken for granted only reveals the white obsession with noticing everything that black people do and are, while not noticing what they themselves do and are, especially in the act of noticing. It is an abstract negative privilege.

We must understand white skin privilege as the tacit functioning of a control stratum which proactively establishes a social structure, and not simply as the benefits or privileges of being white which then present themselves as absence. The absences that get listed silhouette a hierarchy, a hyperhegemonic relation that conditions control without actually being articulated as such. The absences, to which attention need not be given because taken for granted, are a dimension of all structures of hegemony. To understand white antiblack racism, it is wholly insufficient to point out that there is such a thing as white skin privilege, since that goes without saying, while also going unheard. Though it may be the most basic thing for whites, a conscious realization of it escapes behind the discourses of biological or inherent racialization. We again confront the masking relation of racialization, its metaracial nature as that which is bypassed by the white skin privilege critique. Yet because it is fundamental, it must be the starting point, rather than a programmatic culmination, for antiracism.

If white skin privilege is really about being left alone, allowed to function socially in a normal, welcomed, peaceful, and sociable manner, free of constant political battles (political for one side, identity confirming for the other), then for whites it is not a question of abandoning anything but of stepping outside a social hierarchy and freeing themselves from the need for that form of identity confirmation. It is not a question of granting others these rights (of being left alone, or taking civil rights for granted), since the act of "granting" would only conserve the relation of white hegemony. It is rather a question of recognizing that others already have those rights, and ceasing all hindrance to them—of constructing a nonhindering and undependent identity for oneself. It is not a question of abandonment, but of self-liberation from the obsession that expresses white dependence on the other for self-confirmation. Part of the obsessive construction of whiteness is that such a cessation of noticing and of acting on one's noticing, as the essence of one's self-identification as white, would be a really difficult thing for a white person to do.

The call to abandon white skin privilege is thus misdirected. In contenting itself with the demand that whites stop denying normality and citizenship to those they metaracialize, it reduces to liberal antiracism—namely, that racism is a set of ethical or ideological choices that whites need simply be educated about in order to make better choices. In assuming a certain essentiality or objectivity for race, both the white skin privilege idea and liberalism ask if we can get the different races relating to each

other better, on a basis of equality. As an ethical choice, however, the notion of abandoning privilege also reduces racism to a thing one can pick up or put down, add or
subtract from whiteness, rather than as inherent in the structure of social relations and
categorizations that define and construct whiteness for itself in the first place. The idea
of abandoning white skin privilege thus remains embedded in the process of racialization, and even participates in it, because it does not contest the structure of racialization. Indeed, it does not even differentiate between the racialized use of the term
"white" and its descriptive use.

Unfortunately, the white skin privilege idea dovetails with the age-old liberal notion
and rhetoric that "Negroes have made progress." As McIntosh suggests, no one says
that whites who are lacking in education and morality are examples of their race. No
one suggests that white skin privilege is a disguise for a moral failure (racism), a lack
of culture (bigotry), a spiritual inferiority (obsessiveness) which can be made to seem
positive only through the use of force (racial violence). Indeed, no one suggests that
white skin privilege is itself a moral failure. To do so would mean that emancipation
implied a prior moral fault by whites. It would mean that whites are the ones who
need "to make progress." It would mean that nineteenth-century whites needed to
listen to their former slaves in order to find out what knowledge they had (especially
of whites) that whites did not have, for which they had fallen into such egregious
moral failure. This would then have to be extended to all other realms. On the issue
of the franchise, one would have to say, "They (blacks) more than anyone should
speak." The unjustly incarcerated prisoner, when released, should have his say, to tell
of his experience and be respected for that knowledge, and have his proposals for
change acted on. It would be a wholly humane thing to do, but it would admit that
there were prisoners who had been incarcerated unjustly. The logic of such a view
would be that black people should have the franchise, while that of whites be
restricted until they had shown that they could be moral rather than hypocritical
toward others—until they had shown that they could "progress" to the point of being
able to live up to their own ideals. For the white skin privilege critique to leave out
that black and brown people should become the real judges of how racism is to be
judged leaves it in the camp of whites, unable to abandon their hegemony.

More to the point, the notion of abandoning white skin privilege actually regenerates the structure of racialization by assuming that whites must pay a social cost to
establish racial equality and social justice and to make common cause with black people. But this "cost" implies that there is a real inferiority in being black, rather than
an inferiorization of blacks by white self-enactment. That is, it assumes that if whites
gave up their supremacy, they would be actually losing something, rather than regain-
ing a modicum of lost humanity and moral standing. However, there is not any cost.
Rather, if black people are continually reduced in status in order to establish white
skin privilege, it is an admission that the status they are reduced from, in being made
black, is the crux of the matter. Their inherently equal status (their humanity) has to
be denied them again and again, each day, and is reconfirmed each day by the alleged
necessity of whites to deny it (and again, to deny that denial in refusing to see the

acts of hostility and segregation that constitute the structure of race). Black (and brown) people come into the world without such denial. Their blackness is given to them afterwards, at which point the process of producing reduced status begins. It is black and brown people who must stop having to pay the social cost for whites being white.

(Of course, this would also mean ending excessive profitability and racist immigration laws; it would mean equating the right to live equally with the right to earn a living, the right to a job; in other words, it would mean an end to corporate capitalism.)

The implication is that whiteness and privilege are not strictly distinguishable from each other. White people become white because certain things do not happen to them. White skin privilege is based on what is ignorable by whites, and it resides in that very ignorability and the social violence it entitles. It means not having to think about those structures of racialization by which one becomes white. In that sense, the notion of "white skin privilege" is essentially redundant. Whiteness has already assumed the privilege of the power to define, the privilege of the ability to hierarchize and to maintain hegemony in that hierarchy, as inherent (tautologically) in the process of defining oneself as white. To give up the privilege of defining and generalizing others, to give up the privilege of blindness to one's actions, cannot be anything less than abandoning the whiteness given by that abandoned social machinery.

Abandoning white skin privilege does not do this. To give up privilege is not to establish entitlement in the other from whom it had been withheld. It cannot because white entitlement is self-referential. If it calls on whites to question white entitlement, it calls on them as whites. There is no abstract racial entitlement to which whites among other races had simply laid claim. There were no "other races" except through the construction of whiteness and an attendant social racialization by whites of others. Self-entitlement is one of the aspects of the construction of whiteness by which that occurred. Thus, white skin privilege undermines its own attempt to deracialize white supremacist society in centering itself in whiteness again; to that extent, it leaves unquestioned the idea that whiteness means entitlement, and hence privilege. Abandoning white skin privilege does not dismantle the structure of whiteness. At most, it might suggest that white superiority is a pretense. But neither promoting inclusion of black people in white society nor giving up white skin privilege will mean giving up being white, or dismantling the structures of whiteness either as an institutedness or as an identity.

Indeed, any gesture of inclusion by whites assumes white hegemony, since it is made from within white corporate society. It relies on, rather than contests, the structure of racialization from which that hegemony emerges. It is thus always already racially corrupt, a form of reracialization, deigning inclusion in an uncontested structure built through exclusion. The possibility of exclusion, and of proletarianization of those of color, remains inherent in the very gesture of unity. As long as white people do not see themselves as hegemonic within opposition political movements, and do not contest the racialization that gives them hegemony in order to dismantle it, no unity will be possible for them. But contesting their own hegemony would only be a first step. A second step must be that of recognizing the autonomy of black and brown communities and identities, and guaranteeing their sovereignty, as the very condition of unity, sovereign with sovereign—that is, subordinating the terms of unity to a mutual sovereignty, and a mutual recognition of sovereignty. To the hegemonic mind, this would appear to be a reverse hegemony, rather than a confluence of mutually respected sovereignties; that would be the test of its hegemonic self-contestation. Yet this is what would be entailed in a deracialization procedure. For whites to make common cause with black and brown people, it is not colorblindness that is the question, but a self-deracialization through dissolution of the structures of racialization.

Conversely, white people cannot individually abandon whiteness in order to abjure their white skin privilege, because they do not produce that whiteness; it is bestowed on them by its social institutedness in white society. It will be continually reimposed by the social institutions that preserve and reconstitute it, as well as by all others one encounters in society. The issue in question in whites giving up ostracizing, condescending to, or harassing those they are obsessed with is that they stop being white as a social paradigm. That would mean putting an end to their obsessiveness and noticing, hostility, and exclusion, and deconstructing the social machinery of whiteness. It would mean contesting and resisting white corporate society, which would be nothing less than abandoning being white and dismantling the structures of white supremacy as the content of white corporate society.

In effect, dismantling whiteness or deracializing society will not imply simply a re-empowerment of black or brown people. If against the unintelligibility of racism a re-empowerment of blackness (for instance) must be engendered, it will have to be a blackness defined by black people, and not by whites, an empowerment of black people that emerges from black people's experience, and not from that of whites. That is, to abandon being white will also mean to stop imposing a white-defined concept of blackness on black people, or Nativeness on Native Americans (or femininity on women in the masculinist paradigm). The re-empowerment of blackness has to be understood as founded upon an autonomy and a self-re-empowerment within a context of respect and acceptance for what black people have constructed for themselves socially in the face of white supremacy—of what they have made of themselves out of what had been made of them by white supremacy. The necessity to deal with white supremacy is a problem that black people have faced which white people have not. Whether black people have or have not embraced a notion of community autonomy, have or have not deployed it for survival, resistance, positive self-definition, or political solidarity, or any other mode of autonomy and self-expression against white supremacy, all must be respected by whites, a priori.

For all these reasons, the programmatic notion of abandoning white skin privilege remains unintelligible, especially to the racist whites at whom it is aimed. Many antiracist whites accept and propound the idea because it offers a more concrete focus than other antiracist ideologies. But it is of limited practical value, especially since how one is to abandon privileges that are given in the ordinary course of events has so far escaped description. Antiracist whites who call upon other whites to give up their white skin privilege are essentially crying in the wilderness. Not only are they ignoring the inferiorizing violence that is the real referent of what is called white skin privilege, but they are refusing to recognize the self-referentiality of whiteness. As such, the ability to issue a call to give up white skin privilege is part of white skin privilege.

To Dismantle the Structure of Whiteness

To call upon whites to stop doing what they do to be white, and to stop identifying with what constructs them as white, would mean a tremendous conceptual leap, because to be white means to inhabit a conceptual circle that continually reconstructs itself. That circle has the following form: the meaning of whiteness is already supremacy, the meaning of supremacy is already privilege, and the meaning of privilege is already whiteness. As a circle, it is hermetic, and self-insulating against argument, experience, or critiques such as that of white skin privilege. At whichever point antiracism addresses racism on the circle, there is a preceding point for racism to fall back on that then directly regenerates the substance of the point on the circle attacked by antiracism. The insularity of this circle is precisely its resistance to argument; that is, its form as a circle is an essential dimension of its conceptual presence in the world.

We return to the notion that it is not possible to identify oneself as white and be antiracist at the same time, except in the most superficially ideological sense. A white antiracism, in not requiring one to abandon one's whiteness, contains a cognitive dissonance. One's identification with whiteness constitutes acceptance of the violence, both physical and discursive, social and narrative, that forms the foundation of a racist identity in the midst of a rhetorical antiracism. One positions oneself in collaboration with white consensus without the recognition that whiteness is given to one socially, and thus without the means of deconstructing one's social role or of contesting the corporate social hierarchy that maintains it. If whiteness is given socially, it can only be "given back" socially or collectively. Here again one encounters the double bind inescapably inherent in white identification. Though one cannot identify oneself as white and be antiracist at the same time, white identity cannot simply be discarded. (And it is not a question of identifying with a nonwhite group, made what it is by whiteness and its structures of racialization, since a white person will not have lived the life of racialization at the hands of whites, and thus would not understand what membership in such a group would entail.)

The double bind injects a fundamental unintelligibility into all questions of contestation of white racism. But the double bind cannot be explained; it can only be reproduced. It is the basis upon which white supremacy and white racism explain themselves and make their thinking hermetic or insular. It blocks out the power of reason by being what constitutes the foundation of reason for racism. Racism traps antiracist whites in the double bind of Manichean thinking. It attacks black people for anything not in accord with white values, having defined black people as already and irrevocably people who are not in accord with white values. A white person who takes an antiracist stance is required to either agree to the propriety of subordinating black people, or defend whatever practices the racist has singled out as inimical to white values (real or imaginary). The antiracist white person is given the choice of either being antiblack or being antiwhite because problack, shifting the discourse to race rather than social structure.[12]

Ultimately, however irrational the double bind may be, it cannot be seen by those who live its structures because it is the way they see the world in the first place. For white racism, the double bind is what is universal, effecting a boundary for the thinking of both racism and antiracism. For black people, racism is an impossible dilemma, a no-exit situation. For white supremacists, the illogicality of racism is the logic of the world, the key to citizenship. For white antiracists, there is only the Manichean choice that racism leaves them with: to be white, thus undermining all efforts to be antiracist, or to be antiracist, and thus perforce to abandon whiteness altogether.

To deconstruct the notion of race, the circle by means of which it continually regenerates itself must be addressed as its central conception, its central signifier, whose meanings are the social structure, the identity, and the violence against which antiracism attempts to throw itself. That circle has taken many forms in this discussion. One is the circularity of supremacy, whiteness, and privilege. Another is the circularity of allegiance, violence, and paranoia. There is the circle of class relations, an intermediary control stratum, and white solidarity, as a sociological concretization of the preceding. A third is the circle of minoritization composed of exclusion, inferiorization, and the generation of special interests. Another is the circle of noticing, negative valuation, and the social importance of noticing. These circles are all variations of the same social structure, operating at different levels of social discourse or social organization. Each is circular because each element generates the next as its content or meaning, endlessly, the last in each list returning to the first. If the first circle refers to the operation of white supremacy itself, and the second circle to the structure of racialization, the third is that of political participation, and the fourth of individual racism.

There is yet another circle, a mutual engendering of forms of violence. The first form of racializing violence was that of the state in founding the patrols as an intermediary control stratum. This established the ground for all subsequent forms of racialized violence, whether harassment, segregation, renarrativization, or the form of murder known as lynching. But these other forms of violence emerge after the generation of the racialized state has consolidated itself, and becomes the arena of permissibility of "popular" violence from ostracism to murder. Thus, a state structure, even one of liberal democracy such as characterizes the United States, concretizes a second form of violence, that of institutional and instituted violence. This has taken a variety of forms, from early disfranchisement to Jim Crow to the prison-industrial complex. The liberal democratic state is not averse to state violence; indeed, it is founded on it. Liberal democracy is the state form that capitalism deploys for itself, and it thus depends on the existence of capitalism for its foundation. Capitalism is a form of violence insofar as it must maintain a population in a form of impoverishment in order that they will work for it. Thus, liberal democracy depends on the existence of insti-tutionalized forms of impoverishment for its very existence. Finally, on top of insti-tutional violence in the maintenance of the state, there is the vast system of gratuitous violence that is the daily operation of the racism in white society. Constituting vio-lence, institutional violence, and gratuitous violence form a circle, constantly regen-erating each other.

What must white people do to stop being white, to dismantle the social structures of whiteness altogether? White people individually attempting to escape white cor-porate society would not put an end to white supremacy, just as a prison guard quit-ting his job would not change the nature of the prison system, nor eliminate the incar-ceration ethic of the United States. It would be an empty gesture meaning nothing. In the wake of his resignation, the guard would just go home, or become an inmate. Instead, the structure, rationalizations, and forms of power that rely on the racializ-ing (or prison) system would have to be dismantled.

The primary political question with respect to white hegemonics and supremacism is how to transform society and culture insofar as it is white. The problematic of antiracism for whites becomes how to invent a deracializing movement and a dera-cializing identity for themselves for which "whiteness" would in turn be rendered an otherness, without opportuning on others for whom whiteness is already other (a white-identified person could not reidentify with some other group or ethnos with-out being appropriative, or opportunist), and without leaving the institutions and dis-courses of whiteness intact or uncontested. In other words, if whiteness renders all others an otherness for itself, objects through which it constructs itself as a social structure and an identity, and racializes itself and its others through that process, then a movement is needed that would render whiteness an object for itself as other, and would deracialize itself and all of whiteness's others through that process.

Such a dissolution of the social relationships that racism and racialization consti-tute for a white person would require a mass resignation from the intermediary con-trol strata, in whatever forms they took. An entire segment of white society would have to step outside the white class structure and become, in some unforeseeable sense, ex-white. Ceasing to be white (or becoming ex-white) would mean losing class identity, becoming racially identityless, stepping outside the two-party system polit-ically, and acting to dissolve the boundary between the two class systems, the white and the racialized. One of the arenas in which such a movement could develop would be that of affirmative action. But it would be necessary to recognize that affirmative action is actually a form of class war within the dual class structure of the United States. The kind of class war one would then have to fight within the racialized class structure against white corporate society is something for which there is no histori-cal precedent. As long as the structure of white supremacy exists to give white peo-ple their whiteness over and over again, they, in their whiteness, will again and again enact the social categorizations, the gratuitous superiorizations and inferiorizations that constitute reracialization over and over again—with each derogatory term, each act of noticing, each act of hostility against those noticed.

Conclusion

The question of class identity and class solidarity in the United States cannot be understood through the European experience. Europe does not provide a template for the double class system in the United States, in which an entire corporate society functions as the "ruling class" in a racialized class system. Reform in the white class system (including labor-movement victories) amounts to an administrative restructuring within that ruling class, leaving unchanged the racialized relations of exploitation on which it depends for its identity and its inner social cohesion and consensus. A restructuring of the (white) administrative apparatus does not change the racialized (proletarianized) status of people of color. Unionization and third-party campaigns in the white class system are things people of color have little stake in, with little reason to valorize or make common cause. Many do so because they live and work contiguously with white society, though always separated by a veil of intermediary control strata, sometimes subtly, sometimes not. But anarchist movements against transnational corporations, or white environmentalism, for instance, leave the racialized class system intact. An antiracializing environmentalism could not content itself with "noticing" environmental racism; it would have to call in question the white state's support for industrial production itself, the sense of the world as nothing more than a resource, and the resulting act of industrially polluting as an inherent aspect of the structure of whiteness.

In a dual class structure, the question of working-class solidarity is in principle irresolvable. White class politics in the white class system leave all relations of racialized (proletarianized) people of color unrepresented. Whites may expect people of color to participate in the white system, but it would be according to white rules, to which black or brown interests would be incommensurable. White workers generally understand solidarity as workers of color being in solidarity with white. To invert this would mean joining black workers against white corporate society, out of class solidarity, and standing in opposition to themselves as part of that white society. Their whiteness constitutes an obstacle to real solidarity because it places them in a class opposition to black people, not through privilege but rather through the identity and property that produce privilege for itself.

When people of color organize (as people of color, autonomously, rather than under white leadership or white hegemony), it necessarily constitutes a mode of confrontation with white (corporate) society—the proletarianized against racialization. Some whites may see this as a radical necessity for people of color, but as ancillary to their lives as white. Others will see it as antiwhite, and therefore a critical threat. But deep inside even the white antiracism that seeks to make common cause as white, there is a preservation of that "proletarianization" against a demand of deracialization, meaning an end to whiteness and the white corporate state.

The white left faces two main problems today. The first is how to understand its own inability to deal with the United States, having had no nonsuperficial understanding of the racialization upon which it is founded. The second is what to do as an opposition movement in the world's main superpower, for which there are no checks or balances. The United States emerged from World War II as the only unscathed capitalist power. As powerful anti-imperialist movements in both the capitalist countries and the colonies emerged, the suppression of these movements became the hallmark of U.S. operations. If this process, a war of the capitalist world against the socialist and the anticolonial movements for national liberation, constituted World War III (as Subcommandante Marcos of the EZLN in Chiapas has said), then in the wake of becoming the single superpower, the United States has entered World War IV, between itself and the people of the world.

The situation of the left in the United States has three misunderstood dimensions. First, it is pitted against a superpower from within while thinking that it is simply dealing with a standard model of capitalist class. Second, it has benefited from imperialism, because it is part of a society that has benefited as a whole, accepting the twisted thinking of a society in which a "free labor ideology" makes sense. Third, it has operated within the purview of a radicalism that does not fit the United States historically, because derived from a (European) capitalism that was not founded upon racialization. The operation of the United States in the world has mirrored its internal operations, in the sense of being based on the reduction of status of those over whom the United States is an intermediary control stratum, and toward whom it can act with impunity. The left was not equipped to see the process of institutionalization of U.S. impunity as an ethic.

If the United States has become the administrative means of guaranteeing the continuation of corporate economics in the world, then it ceases to be a political government for its own people. To fight the government is to fight an administrative institution working for economic institutions that are no longer grounded in the United States as a corporate (white) class structure. To fight those economic institutions means to be faced with the U.S. government operating under international treaties, deploying modes of police impunity as its own political nature. To fight that political structure means to be faced with economic power that one has no structural connection to, because it now operates transnationally, behind the United States as its control stratum. To struggle on the economic plane nationally means to be blindsided politically on the international by treaty regulations; to struggle politically against the state nationally means to be blindsided by economic processes that belong to the multinational arena. The people in the United States are caught between a rhetoric of democracy and a state that operates by police impunity.

At the present time, people of color—the proletarianized of the contemporary racialized class system—find themselves without allies in the white class system. Especially grievous is this lack among Marxists, who remain non-allies to the extent they continue to adopt a white point of view. Yet they cannot call that in question as long as they prioritize the white working class, ignoring its role in the white corporate society it is instrumental in producing. The Marxist acceptance of a European working-class theory sets them in collaboration with capital in the United States.

Marxism is a white ideological system, part of the social structure of whiteness that has swept the Euro-American world as a necessary adjunct to colonialism.[13] It may understand class relations and how to change them, but it does not have a sense of how to change a cultural structure (like whiteness or white supremacy). Without racializing itself, or repositioning itself within the racialized class structure, Marxism reduces itself to liberal reform. This can be seen with respect to the prison system. In understanding the workers (guards) in the prison administration as part of the working class, Marxism sees no further than a form of prison reform movement. It has no sense of how the "inmate" population (whether of the racialized class structure or of the prison-industrial complex) constitutes a juridically different working class in the United States. Indeed, the homology between the prison structure and racialization suggest that racialization and the incarceration ethic of white society stand or fall together. But what an abolition of prisons might mean in the dual class structure is a question that is as yet unaddressed.

What would a transformation of a cultural structure entail? An answer to this is suggested by the "apology" made by the Bureau of Indian Affairs in 2000 for its traditional treatment of Native Americans. Such an apology is hypocritical as long as it does nothing to rectify the historical results of its operations. For whites, such a rectification is unthinkable; it would mean the proverbial "giving the land back to the Indians." But this reflects and repeats the discourse and ideology that "took" the land in the first place. It is incommensurable with the alternate discourse to which an apology should point—an incommensurability of discursive structures that haunts all aspects of white–indigenous relations. When the whites who own the land say, "They can't take this away from me; I own it," they are making a statement that is meaningless for Native Americans, because the question of land itself is not addressed. Such a statement only addresses the question of property.

The land was not "taken" in any objective sense; it is still there. It was instead juridically transformed into an "object" it could not actually be (an imaginary object) in order to be "take-able" (in an imaginary and military sense). That transformation constituted its taking. It was transformed from being the earthly surface of a living community to a virtual reality composed of papers and juridical property lines— from sustenance to profitability, from a realm of living to an economic resource. To restore the land to the state of being place and source, rather than value and resource, would mean devirtualizing the land, and retransforming society from a governance of property to a nonproperty-oriented government of people. To make restitution, to rectify the past crime of land seizure, would mean eliminating the concept of property in land altogether. In other words, for the Bureau of Indian Affairs apology to be sincere, it would have to be accompanied by an entire transformation of the bases of white society. This would not remove it to some form of the tribal, but it would render it nonhegemonic and, above all, no longer a white corporate state. Similarly, for people of color, any program of social justice within white society and the white class system would be hypocritical if it did not move toward eliminating the racialized class system, that is, deracializing white corporate society. Not even changing the class in power in the white class system (socialism) would do that.

To put this a different way, in the United States, a liberatory idea would have to address, first and foremost, the liberation from proletarianization of those within the racialized class system. The "prison guards" (the white working class) would have to embrace the idea of "decriminalizing" (deproletarianizing) the "inmates" (people of color) and walking off the "job"—that is, opening the prison doors and dispensing with their "jobs" altogether. Unfortunately, the notion that whites would have to dismantle the concept of "criminalization" is not really a metaphor. From the inception of race and whiteness based on an original outlaw (noncontractual) status through the paranoia and violence of all subsequent racializations, the criminalization of people of color is what white identity has always depended on.

For this reason, the prison system is at the core of social cohesion in the United States, and imprisonment has become the central motif of dealing with social problems. The prison system is not only the defense of whiteness but its icon and metaphor at the same time. The ability of the political right to mobilize populist energy for programs of inequality, mass imprisonment, and injustice in the name of justice and social equity springs not from its speaking to what white people want, but to who they are. Tapping the wellsprings of whiteness, it has gained the initiative over the left not only by invoking a betrayal of the "white nation," but also profiting from the left's thinking that one can be nonracist and still identify oneself as white.[14] What gives the right its hegemony is precisely what hamstrings the white left. To contest the right within this structure of populism is to accept its language, and to lose oneself in it. Yet this is part and parcel of the left's entanglement in the state. Though the left opposes the state as fostering inequality and injustice, it goes to the state to rectify racial abuse and discrimination, to obtain equality and justice. It opposes racism from within the racializing function of the state, thereby betraying itself to that racializing function.

What the left requires, if it wishes to develop movements of opposition to oppression (in general), is a strategy to unravel the cultural framework, to invent a corrosive alternative to the white identity that is woven into and constitutes it. It would need strategies that would call for an end to the property entitlement of whiteness, and thus the property basis of society itself. To break down the racialized class structure and put an end to racism, the entire structure of racialization, meaning the social structure of whiteness and the white corporate state that concretizes it, would have to be demolished. To do this, an alternate politics and political culture would have to evolve in the United States—one that stands outside the white corporate state and makes possible a distance from the systems of narratives by which people have been racialized, so that they can be rethought and reencountered again as people and not as generalizations.

Notes

Introduction

1. Affirmative action programs were implemented in response to the various movements by African Americans, women's groups, Chicanos and Latinos, Native Americans, and others seeking equality, sovereignty, and civil rights. In organizing movements, these groups sought to change a history of discrimination. People of color had been segregated by neighborhood, by law, by exclusion from participation in social and political processes. Women of color had been excluded as women and segregated as people of color. White women had been excluded while living in the midst of the included. The demands to end discrimination cut across class lines. While affirmative action programs are about race and gender discrimination, the other side of the dispute, the anti–affirmative action movement, is about race.

2. An example of the dilemma this distortion of language produced occurred during one of the hearings of President Clinton's Commission on Race Relations, a body of experts empanelled in 1997 and led by John Hope Franklin, an eminent African American historian. To conduct a national dialogue on the problem, the commission held meetings in many cities. In San Jose, a number of poor and working-class black people claimed the problem was not race relations but racism, and accused the panel of excluding those who most suffered from it. A white man accused the entire project of "white bashing" and said that the problem was not white racism, but the racism of those who blame everything on the white race. Clearly, a dialogue between these two sides would be very difficult. Racism and the language of race mean one thing to black, Native American, or other people of color who have had to defend themselves against discrimination and the truncation of their lives by white supremacy; they mean something else to whites whose lives are truncated by having to defend whiteness when they would prefer it went without saying or notice. One side seeks to call attention to a hierarchical system of racialization; the other side seeks to deny the existence of racial hierarchy. The white eye sees its world as one of unracialized equality, of the merely human, in which the charge of discrimination is unintelligible. The others inhabit a racialized world in which they find themselves given lesser status in the name of that (white) equality. Though both sides live their respective racializations as social coloration, it is as if they spoke different languages.

3. For a critique of "colorblindness" at the constitutional level, see Neil Gotanda, "A Critique of 'Our Constitution Is Color-Blind,'" *Stanford Law Review*, 44(1), November 1991.

4. W.E.B. DuBois, *Black Reconstruction in America, 1860–1880* (New York: Atheneum, 1975), p. 283. Hereafter BR.

5. Jefferson goes further and says, in *Notes on the State of Virginia,* ch. 14: "I advance it therefore as a suspicion only, that the blacks, whether originally a distinct race, or made distinct by time and circumstances, are inferior to the whites in the endowments both of body and mind. It is not against experience to suppose, that different species of the same genus, or varieties of the same species, may possess different qualifications. Will not a lover of natural history then, one who views the gradations in all the races of animals with the eye of philosophy, excuse an effort to keep those in the department of man as distinct as nature has formed them?" Is he speaking about a probability of inferiority? Is this a form of Pascalian reasoning, then, for juridical purposes? He seems to be saying that it would be safer to assume inferiority and be wrong than to assume equality and be wrong—whatever would constitute "being wrong" or how such a thing would be decidable.

6. A familiar example of this phenomenon is the use of Manichean logic, where an issue is dealt with structurally as all or nothing—either you agree fully or you are on the other side. For instance, a Manichean response to a person who says he does not believe in god would be, "Don't you believe in anything?" This is a structural response that catches the person in a choice between saying yes or no, with the yes answer requiring self-explanation, effectively switching the subject from the issue of god or religion to one's status as friend or enemy. Nationalism works the same way, in terms of its demonization of those it decides to establish as its enemies. Any attempt to rehumanize the other, in an effort to preserve international peace, elicits the Manichean response, "Oh, you think they're good guys, huh? Why don't you go live with them." That is not the issue, but in order to deal with the issue (peace), one has to understand one is confronting a structural response and not logic or reasoning.

7. Bernard Bailyn, *The Origins of American Politics* (New York: Knopf, 1968). See, in particular, ch. 3. Hereafter OAP.

8. With over two million prisoners in its prison system, the United States leads the world in numbers and in per capita rates. While the crime rate goes up and down, the prison population doubled over a twenty-year period, while the nation's population increased only 4 percent. More people are arrested for minor offenses in the United States than elsewhere, more are prosecuted, and more are given lengthy sentences out of proportion to the offense. Blacks are more likely than whites to be arrested and convicted, and they are given longer sentences for the same offenses. Vince Beiset, "How We Got to Two Million," *Mother Jones,* July 10, 2001.

9. Mike Davis, *The City of Quartz* (New York: Vintage, 1992). See, in particular, ch. 4, "Fortress L.A."

10. Simone de Beauvoir, *The Ethics of Ambiguity* (New York: Citadel Press, 1964), p. 83.

11. Frantz Fanon, *The Wretched of the Earth* (New York: Grove Press, 1963), pp. 54ff.

12. Leon Litwack, *North of Slavery: The Negro in the Free States, 1790–1860* (Chicago: Univ. of Chicago Press, 1961), p. 34. Hereafter NS. See also Edward R. Turner, *The Negro in Pennsylvania* (Washington, DC: American Historical Assoc., 1912), p. 191. Hereafter NP.

13. Cedric Robinson, *Black Marxism: The Making of the Black Radical Tradition* (London: Zed Press, 1983), p. 176. Hereafter CR.

14. Karl Marx, *Capital* (Moscow: Foreign Languages Pub. House), vol. 1, pp. 717–760.

15. Eric Williams, *Capitalism and Slavery* (New York: Capricorn Books, 1966), p. 52. Hereafter CS.

16. Cf. Frank Wilderson, *The Indifference of Marxism to the Black Subject;* <http://www.ocf.berkeley.edu/~marto/paradigm/wilderson.htm>. Oliver Cox, *Capitalism as a System* (New York: Monthly Review Press, 1964), pp. 213–214.

17. Charles Mills, *The Racial Contract* (Ithaca, NY: Cornell Univ. Press, 1997), p. 11. Hereafter RC.

18. One could list a number of thinkers: Toure, Nkrumah, Cabral, Fanon, Memmi, Means, Banks, Trudell, Ward, Churchill, Senghor, Cesaire, Guevara, Castro, Marighela, G. Jackson, Malcolm X, Robert Williams, Carmichael, Morrison, and entire movements of Chicano arts, Black Arts, Latin American literature, and African philosophy. The issues were political and cultural, but their discourses called in question the white western generalizations of person-hood, subjectivity, and the definition of culture, affirming in their stead the questions of sovereignty, autonomy, alternate political structures, and the retrieval of a suppressed history. Many black writers have directly addressed the white radical tradition as a target for their critiques. George Padmore, Harold Cruse, and Oliver Cox have traded political polemics with white Marxists. DuBois has produced extensive treatments of this problem, mostly through his own reanalysis of the American scene.

19. In part, it is in response to such distortions, to the fact that the necessities of opposition to racialized oppression appeared unintelligible to class-based thinking, that novels like *Invisible Man* by Ralph Ellison, *The Outsider* by Richard Wright, or *Dark Princess* by W.E.B. DuBois were written. These thinkers used the novel form to investigate possibilities of discourse and thinking not opened to ideological polemic or philosophical critique. In polemic, one has to adopt the language of the discourse one is attacking. In critique, though one addresses the discourse, one also places under scrutiny the language of that discourse, and thus inhabits an alternate language, and an alternate dimensionality of thinking. Though both polemic and critique offer direct access to political programmatics, they are at the same time self-limiting in the generality they assume as discourses. The novel, on the other hand, deals with human activity and thought in its particularity. It can map out for itself a domain, as a lived space, that is beyond that of the discourse under criticism. One can propose alternative actions directly, without having first to free one's language from that of the programmatics one calls in question. In *The Outsider,* for instance, Wright's main character theorizes about himself and black consciousness directly, in the face of the law, without having to set aside a place in which to do that. His polemic against Marxism comes in the form of the actions of Marxists and his direct responses. His language begins and remains his own. In *Dark Princess,* DuBois constructs a powerful insight into the inner dynamics of politics in the black community, and articulates the relative inability of Marxism to relate to that. Its irrelevance is highlighted in a few short, almost dispensable scenes. The novels of Chester Himes and Ernest Gaines directly address white violence, presenting the possibilities of counterviolence as a necessary survival mechanism and a mode of reconstruction of autonomous subjective and cultural being in the world.

20. Paul Baran, *The Political Economy of Growth* (New York: Monthly Review Press, 1957) deals with this phenomenon in the case of India when colonized by the British in the eighteenth and nineteenth centuries. The most recent example is that of Chiapas, whose uncommodified land economy had supported the indigenous population and had been guaranteed by the Mexican Constitution of 1914. That aspect was eliminated in order for Mexico to sign NAFTA, spelling disaster for the indigenous communities of Chiapas, Guerrero, Oaxaca, and other areas. Cf. George Collier, *BASTA: Land and the Zapaista Rebellion in Chiapas* (Oakland, Calif: Food First, 1994); John Ross, *Rebellion from the Roots: Indian Uprising in Chiapas* (Monroe, Me.: Common Courage Press, 1995); Teresa Ortiz, *Never Again a World Without Us* (Washington, D.C.: EPICA, 2001).

21. There are four main aspects to the Structural Adjustment Programs: (1) privatization of social services and government operations and agencies; (2) capital market liberalization, which

means repeal of labor and environmental legislation that reduces profitability, and adoption of open investment policies toward "foreign" (transnational) capital; (3) market-based pricing, meaning the elimination of price controls on necessary commodities and of government subsidies to local economies; (4) free trade, meaning the elimination of any tariff protection for domestic investment, industry, or economic activity. Gregory Palast, "The IMF's Four Steps to Damnation," an interview with Joseph Stiglitz, former chief economist for the World Bank and a 2001 winner of the Nobel Prize in economics, in *Z Magazine*, August 24, 2001; reprinted in the *London Observer*, October 10, 2001.

22. Implied in this omission is the operation of the variable capital cycle, as one of the cycles Marx identifies in the capitalist production of surplus value. On Marx's theory of value, the wage represents the value of commodities needed to maintain and reproduce the labor force. Worker consumption functions as a vital aspect of local markets on which capital, in its local development, relies as a system. He sees the inability of the slave to function as a consumer as breaking this process, rather than simply reducing the variable capital cycle to its utmost minimum. Cf. Robinson, *Black Marxism*, p. 442.

23. In particular, there is no connection demonstrable between physicobiological characteristics and social or cultural propensities. This idea was first given extensive treatment by Ashley Montagu, *The Idea of Race* (Lincoln: Univ. of Nebraska Press, 1965). See also Ashley Montagu, ed., *The Concept of Race* (New York: Free Press, 1964), and J. Richard, *Intelligence and Class Structure in American Life* (New York: Free Press, 1994).

24. Barbara Fields tells the following story. When a U.S. journalist once asked Duvalier, the dictator of Haiti, what percentage of Haiti was white, Duvalier answered, "Ninety-eight percent." After recovering from his initial shock, the reporter asked, "How do you define white?" Duvalier responded, "How do you define black in your country?" The reporter replied that anyone with any black blood was considered black. Duvalier said, "Well, that's the way we define white in my country." Paraphrased from *Region, Race, and Reconstruction*, ed. J. Morgan Kousser and James M. McPherson (Oxford: Oxford Univ. Press, 1982), p. 146. Hereafter RRR.

25. Cf. Naomi Zack, *Race and Mixed Race* (Philadelphia: Temple Univ. Press, 1993).

26. The term "race" has been used in different ways in European history. During the late middle ages, in northern Europe, it signified those peoples or elements of a society who could trace their lineage back to before the Roman invasions. That is, it referred to a sense of local legitimacy, as well as noncompliance with Roman imperialism, and became a mark of prerogative or birthright to governance. Thus, the medieval European use of the term "race" was on a cultural rather than a physical basis. It concerned histories and lineage, rather than socially defined categorizations. Cf. Jacques Barzun, *The French Race: Theories of its Origins* (Port Washington, N.Y.: Kennikat Press, 1966) and George Mosse, *Toward the Final Solution* (New York: H. Fertig, 1978). Similarly, the Spanish developed a sense of race, which they referred to as "blood," at the time of the Reconquista. Those families that had resisted intermixing with Moorish families were ordained to rule the new society as having been superior in their resistance to the Moors. Both instances bordered on a purity concept insofar as intermarriage or its absence was a criterion. The Reconquista families of Spain had not passed antimiscegenation laws, however; purity of blood was to be a sign of historical or contemporary merit, religious sanction, and political dominance, and could be bestowed by political fiat or favor. (Cf. Albert Memmi, *Racism*). In some cases, dispensations to marry cross-culturally were given, if a political purpose was served. The case of the English colonies on the American continent developed very differently. "Race" is, in all cases, a form of social identity and internal social organization with respect to an exclusion of others as different.

27. The idea that the United States is a "white nation" has been affirmed by many people in many different forms, from rabid chauvinists such as Jedidiah Morse (in "American Geography," 1789) to liberal theoreticians of the republic, such as John Jay (in the First Federalist Paper). Benjamin Franklin had projected it as the preferable character of his foreseen society in 1751 ("Observations Concerning the Increase in Mankind"). And it was written into the first Naturalization Law of March 1790, which permitted citizenship only to "free white persons." James Madison implies it as the only possibility in a number of letters (cf. James Madison, *Letters and Writings of James Madison,* vol. 3, pp. 134, 239–240, 542. It appears again in the Dred Scott decision; and Andrew Johnson states it openly (the United States is a "white man's government") when campaigning for Vice President in Nashville, in January 1864 (BR, 244).

28. William Greider, *Who Will Tell the People: The Betrayal of American Democracy* (New York: Simon and Schuster, 1992); *One World, Ready or Not: The Manic Logic of Global Capitalism* (New York: Simon and Schuster, 1997); and Richard Barnet and John Cavanagh, *Global Dreams: Imperial Corporations and the New World Order* (New York: Simon and Schuster, 1994). It is not simply that the people's relation to government may have become vestigial. Under a global government, such as that constructed around the World Trade Organization and the World Bank, the United States will face the same reduction to administrative duties as other nations, though the United States, as the most powerful military nation, will be the police, keeping the others in line, pursuant to "foreign policy" over which no voters will have any influence.

Chapter One

1. Yehudi Webster lays out the problem in its generality by describing what racially oriented historians have done, which passes for a history of race. "As the theory was developed over the last two centuries, not only slavery but also ancient history and, indeed, the whole human past is racially interpreted. Archeological findings are examined for racial implications. Egyptian, Asian, Greek, and Western civilizations are scrutinized for racial configurations. However, these discovered configurations are not part of the ancient past but rather a modern practice of describing persons as 'whites' and 'blacks' and tracing their ancestors through racial bloodlines. Thus, the racialization of the past is a backward extension of a contemporary practice, for scholars allocate persons to racial groups, then claim that history is an unfolding of relations between races." Yehudi Webster, *The Racialization of America* (New York: St. Martin's, 1992), p. 3.

2. Alden T. Vaughan, "Blacks in Virginia, the First Decade," *Roots of American Racism* (Oxford: Oxford Univ. Press, 1995). Hereafter RAR.

3. In order to speak about the seventeenth century without imposing a twentieth-century racialization upon it, we need a different terminology. In particular, when speaking of the seventeenth century, and the Virginia colony, I will refer to all Africans and African Americans simply as Africans. By the end of the century, many of the people referred to generally by the colonists as "Negro" and who would soon be racialized as "black" had been born in the colonies and thus were really American. But the notion of being an American was just coming into existence through these very processes. During the seventeenth century, the English colonists referred to themselves as either English or Christian. Thus, to give a form of nonracialized parity to my reference to those torn out of Africa and held in the colonies in captivity, I will use the term "African." When speaking of the eighteenth century or later, I will change this.

4. I will at times use color designations for races, since other physical traits associated with color are all overgeneral, stereotypical, and indefinite. In any population, all traits vary over a

fairly wide spectrum. On the characteristic division of races, there are the famous five: white, yellow, red, brown, and black (Tomas Almaguer, *Racial Fault Lines* [Berkeley: Univ. of California Press, 1994]). Because this racialization of humanity was produced by European colonialism and given scientific form (if not content) by European anthropology, in the process of Europeans racializing themselves as white, the focus of this critique will be the structuring of whiteness and white supremacy through their racialization of others.

5. Winthrop Jordan, *White over Black: American Attitudes toward the Negro, 1550–1812* (New York: Norton, 1977). Hereafter BW.

6. Vaughan makes the same assumptions as Jordan, that prejudice against black people was general (universal) among the English, as a product of "color," and was not the result of social process (RAR, 162). What both ignore is the idea that race has to be made a discourse first, from which rules of social structure and comportment can be derived.

7. Theodore Allen, *The Invention of the White Race* (New York: Verso, 1997), vol. 2. Hereafter IWR.

8. Michelle Fine, "Witnessing Whiteness," in *Off White: Readings on Race, Power, and Society,* ed. Michelle Fine, Linda Powell, Lois Weis, and L. Mun Wong (New York: Routledge, 1997), p. 58. Hereafter OW.

9. In *Roots of American Racism,* Vaughan discusses Godwyn, who wrote in 1685, and Tryon, who wrote in 1684. In Vaughan's account, Godwyn complains that Christian conversion was insufficiently pursued, the main obstacle being the Christians themselves, and he articulates the difference between the Christians and the non-Christians as being one between humans (us) and "them" (ostensibly nonhumans). The implication of subhumanity had been broached, but within a religious or cultural dimension; the difference had not yet been articulated as one of race. It is an interesting datum for the proposition that the development of the structure of slavery slightly preceded the concomitant development of a racialized difference, the mediation between these being the attribution of subhumanity as a step in the production of race. Ostensibly, then, the terms for color were still being used (by Godwyn) as descriptive, and the situation of the slave still Aristotelian rather than racialized.

Tryon confirms this to the extent he refers to black and white as hues, giving them a certain parity as colors. He too is opting for a Christian basis for society and attempts to refute both the color coding and the Christian/heathen dichotomy, in order to argue for a "Christian bargain" between master and slave. Tryon actually ventriloquizes the African slave resisting slavery, and through that understands the "bargain" to be a version of allegiance, an instance of the superiority/inferiority paradigm on which slavery was being constructed. For him, the humanity of the slave is not a question. But this only points out that subhumanity becomes a sort of intermediary moment between the evolution of slavery and the racialization of the social-class hierarchy it establishes.

10. Toni Morrison, *Playing in the Dark: Whiteness and the Literary Imagination* (Cambridge, MA: Harvard Univ. Press, 1992), p. 11. Hereafter PD.

11. Kenneth Stampp, *The Peculiar Institution* (New York: Vintage Books, 1956), p. 21. Hereafter PI.

12. Columbus, in his diaries, gives the underlying rationale by which this process of genocide was legitimized. On his first voyage, he is taken by the beauty of the island people. He does not speak the language, but this never hinders him from deciding on his own what they think, who they are, and what they feel. His November entries contain references to the Taino as "devout," who should therefore be readily convertible to Christianity. But his procedure is to take a number of Taino prisoner in order to convert them, suggesting in practice that cap-

tivity is necessary to the process. Indeed, Columbus meditates on this, affirming that his captives need to be held, in order to come to the awareness that the Spanish are indeed the emissaries of the true religion. He addresses his meditation to Isabel, suggesting that she take this into account, as opposed to simply destroying those who do not convert or confess. But within his affirmation, conversion becomes signifier for the fact that destruction of those who do not convert is the alternative, through which (and to which) conversion makes reference. In the background of such an ethos, destroying the islanders who did not convert, and who did not deliver a predetermined quota of gold, would be a matter of small moment for the Spanish.

13. Howard Zinn, *A People's History of the United States* (New York: Harper and Row, 1980), p. 24.

14. For the colonists, the Algonquin's refusal to work for them was equated with a refusal of Christianity. As a result, few attempts were made to convert them, and those attempts met with little success while the Indians remained in a free state. Their refusal to work for the colony also got translated into a refusal to engage in agriculture, which in turn became the rationale for seizing their land. This idea of refusal to engage in agriculture became a permanent element in white derogation of the native peoples. For the treaty of Ghent in 1815, which concluded the War of 1812 with the British, John Quincy Adams argued, in his prototype discourse on Manifest Destiny, that the United States would distinguish between those Indians who planted and those who did not, respecting the rights and lives of the former but not of the latter. But though the Cherokee in Georgia had built a large and extensive agricultural practice, the United States ignored this, allowed Georgia to attack and seize their land, and eventually marched them to Oklahoma in the terrible Trail of Tears.

15. Quoted in Joseph Boskin, *Into Slavery: Racial Decisions in the Virginia Colony* (Washington, DC: University Press of America, 1979), p. 9. Hereafter IS.

16. Throughout the colonial period, a succession of charters with different kings all contained clauses demanding allegiance and defining the conditions of its administration. Cf. William W. Hening, ed., *Statutes at Large: A Collection of All the Laws of Virginia . . .* (Richmond, 1809), vol. 1: p. 105; vol. 2: pp. 94, 485. Hereafter SL.

17. Hector St. John de Crèvecoeur, *Letters from an American Farmer* (New York: Penguin Books, 1981), p. 214. Two indigenous tribes lived within the territory of the Virginia colony for a while, incorporated there by the settlers to make them tributary and trading partners, as well as spy on other tribes.

18. Indeed, it amounted to a form of political paranoia, such as will appear later. Richard Godbeer articulates it this way, when summing up the literature about earlier colonial rejection of intermarriage with the Native people: "Forced to rely on Indian food supplies and advice as they struggled to survive in a new environment, the colonists sought to shore up their battered sense of superiority by maintaining a self-conscious boundary between the 'savage' natives and their 'civilized' selves; Anglo-Indian marriage threatened that strategy both physically and symbolically. On a more practical level, colonists harbored suspicions that the Indians might use intermarriage as a way to infiltrate colonial settlements. They were also concerned that Anglo-Indian unions might give rise to native male jealousy. . . . Marriage to native women, then, endangered the colonists' sense of cultural supremacy as well as their mores, safety, and health." Godbeer, "Eroticizing the Middle Ground: Anglo-Indian Sexual Relations, in *Sex, Love, Race*, ed. Martha Hodes (NYU Press, 1999), p. 92.

What is astounding in this passage is its identifying the connection between exclusion of others and the fantasy that they want to infiltrate and dominate. The reversal of onus in this is obvious, especially given Crèvecoeur's later sentiments.

19. Pierre Bourdieu, *Language and Symbolic Power* (Cambridge, MA: Howard Press, 1991), p. 336. Quoted in Fine (OW, 58).

20. Cf. Boskin (IS, 14). The "bond-laborer" is one who is bound to labor under contract or by captivity for a certain period of time to pay off a debt, generally for passage or subsistence. Historically, this form of holding laborers has been abused by making the conditions of remuneration for labor and repayment of the debt such that the debt can never be repaid; in such cases, it becomes what is called "bond-slavery." This was the condition imposed on many of the freed slaves who attempted to survive agriculturally after Reconstruction in the South.

21. James Curtis Ballagh, *A History of Slavery in Virginia* (Baltimore: Johns Hopkins Press, 1902), ch. 2, p. 45. Hereafter HS.

22. This problem holds for wage labor as well. Though Marx theorized labor as a commodity that an employer buys and uses instrumentally, he left out the enforcement problem, except through the threat of firing the worker and hiring another. But the mere fact that you commodify labor, and hire it, does not insure that it will do what you say. An entire infrastructure of economic duress, social ethics, class honor, as well as an unemployment problem, is necessary to get the laborer to do what he is hired to do in the time the employer wishes it done. This problem is both magnified and simplified in the case of slave labor.

23. For accounts of the slave trade, its profitability, and its relationship to industrialization of the Atlantic economy, see in particular Oliver Cox, *Capitalism as a System,* Eric Williams, *Capitalism and Slavery,* and Daniel Mannix and Malcolm Cowley, *Black Cargoes: A History of the Atlantic Slave Trade.*

24. Eugene Genovese, *The Political Economy of Slavery* (New York: Pantheon, 1966), pp. 15ff. Basically Genovese argues that slavery was not a form of capitalism because its forms of irrationality were different from those of capitalism. Slavery structured reinvestment differently and had lower rates of profit and a greater need to expand territorially. (The North's ability to limit that expansion put plantation society into severe crisis, which it could meet only through secession and war.) While capitalism develops and innovates by investing in new and often different plant and equipment, plantations reinvest in land and labor, and thus do not develop. The plantation system impeded industrialization because it provided an insufficient local market from produced goods (p. 23). It made supervision of labor expensive and impeded technological progress (p. 26). All this is true but does not imply that plantation slavery is not a capitalist system. Indeed, it proves that it is one, since it sought profit to accumulate and had the ability to shift its capital investment from one area (territory) to another, however slowly it did that.

All Genovese has shown is that the slave plantation system fulfilled very poorly the economic necessities thrust on it by its capitalist structure, but not that it was not of that structure. For instance, Genovese points out that the plantation economy needed always to move to new land, as plantation agriculture continually depleted the land it used (p. 26). But he does not follow the logic of this. The plantation depleted the land because it was tied to a form of commodity production, as an industry, that was in contradiction with the notion of agriculture. Agriculture grows stuffs that are socially needed on the basis of a stable location of production, and supplies its own food and means of subsistence alongside what it produces for cash value. That is, it can escape an inner pressure toward subsistence operations, usually involving small-scale self-sufficient farming and systematic crop rotation, only through capitalization and focused commodity production. This was the nature of the colonial economy from its inception. Its degree of capitalization may have been unwieldy and wholly inefficient, but its structure was one that brought it up against those inefficiencies, and not others. It was simply a poor form of capitalism, more adapted to the world economy of the seventeenth and eighteenth centuries than to that of the nineteenth century.

25. W. J. Cash, *The Mind of the South* (New York: Vintage Books, 1941).

26. Eva Saks, "Representing Miscegenation Law," *Raritan*, 8, no. 1 (1988): 48. Hereafter Saks.

27. William J. Wilson, *The Declining Significance of Race* (Chicago: Univ. of Chicago Press, 1978). Hereafter DSR.

28. Daniel Mannix and Malcolm Cowley, *Black Cargoes: A History of the Atlantic Slave Trade* (New York: Viking, 1962). Hereafter BC. The first American slave ship was launched in 1638, in New England, with routes between the Caribbean and the tobacco colonies. The first American slave ship to Africa was 1645. Dutch slave ships operated out of New York from 1625 to 1650, carrying Africans to Brazil, Curacao, and New York. The Royal Africa Co. was chartered by the king in 1672.

29. Martha Hodes, ed., *Sex, Love, Race* (New York: NYU Press, 1999), p. 92. Hereafter SLR. Many commentators on the colonial period interpret the antimiscegenation laws as symptomatic of early "antipathy" toward Africans, on the basis of which they argue that racism produced enslavement of Africans (e.g., Boskin and Vaughan). In the context of the colonial development of the slave system, the statutes are seen as reflecting social mores. Bardaglio states: "Contrary to some historians, who discount the value of statutes for revealing the character of society, [I will argue] that statutory law is an important source of evidence for assessing white sexual anxiety about black men. . . . statutory law does tell us a great deal about the hopes and fears of society" (SLR, 112). He adds, "Public feeling about miscegenation was potent enough to make its way into the statute books of many colonies" (in particular, Virginia and Maryland in the 1660s) (SLR, 114). He assumes, along with the historians he debates, that the society he addresses is a democracy, and that statutory law reflects the feelings or will of the people. But if that is not the case, then the law reflects the political desires of elite lawmakers, who create statutes to sculpt a political order for themselves in the space between their desire for autocracy and what will be culturally in context. As with the tenets of race, an historical investigation such as Bardaglio summarizes would have to be careful not to impose twentieth-century anxieties on the men and women of the seventeenth century, white or black. If mixed couples were not a source of social instability, as they were to be in the nineteenth century, then the probability is that the statutes reflect an elite desire to create anxieties and fears in pursuit of its own interests. In general, people do not have to make something taboo if it is not prevalent (cf. SLR, 119). It is the need to reduce the incidence of an act that calls for legislation, not the need to prohibit something that is nonexistent.

30. Quoted in Jonathan Alpert, "The Origin of Slavery in the United States—The Maryland Precedent," *American Journal of Legal History* 14 (1970): 195, 209.

31. In point of fact, the first rebellion in the Virginia colony occurred less than a year after the passage of this first antimiscegenation statute, and it is interesting to speculate that the two events were connected in some way. The historical documents concerning the rebellion are sparse. They indicate that it was fought by veterans of Cromwell's army, sent as transported prison labor shortly after the Restoration (1660). But no records of the causes or demands of the rebellion have been preserved (SSS, 123). Yet an influx of prisoners of war would have upset whatever gender balance there may have been in the colony, and the newly arrived men would not yet have been subjected to the demonization of the native peoples that formed the core of English allegiance to the colony. Given the factors of natural attraction between people (in the

absence of social denigrations), along with the masculinist feelings of sexual entitlement prevalent among soldiers, and finally the rebel background of those who fought for Cromwell, one might expect these newly arrived bond-laborers to pay serious attention to both native and African women bond-laborers. Rape probably became prevalent, and it was not yet prohibited. Indeed, women in the colony who complained of violation were punished for their sexuality. The statute banned both mixed marriage and mixed sexual relations as such.

32. Here especially, on this issue, the lens of contemporary racialization "colors" one's historical perception of the process that produced that focus (and dependence) on coloration in the first place. Bardaglio, in an otherwise perceptive essay, says: "Recognizing that only the reproduction of 'pure white' children by white women could maintain the fiction of a biracial society, the legal system was particularly determined to keep white women from interracial sexual unions" (SLR, 115). This is true in the wake of racialization but misses the role of the purity concept to which it makes reference in generating the structure that (bi)racialized society in the first place.

33. The statute (Act 12, December 1662) reads: "Whereas some doubts have arrisen whether children got by any Englishman upon a negro woman should be slave or ffree, Be it therefore enacted and declared by this present grand assembly, that all children borne in this country shal be held bond or free only according to the condition of the mother, And that if any christian shall committ ffornication with a negro man or woman, hee or shee soe offending shall pay double the ffines imposed by the former act."

34. Betty Wood, *The Origins of American Slavery* (New York: Hill and Wang, 1997), p. 114. Hereafter Wood.

35. Vaughan argues that the physical characteristics of black people led to slavery and prejudice. He speaks about "pigmentation and its implication" (RAR, 156). Allen undermines that argument by showing that the structure of oppression of the Irish in Ireland was congruent to that of Africans in the colonies while being independent of pigmentation. But Vaughan goes on to claim that among historians of the period, "there is even agreement that before the 1660s white Virginians harbored some degree of prejudice . . . toward blacks" (RAR, 156) because of manners, language difference, and behavior. But he has already addressed a number (Breen, Handlin, Allen, Morgan) who would disagree with this, since prejudice would not, for them, be independent of class.

36. Albert Memmi, *Racism,* trans. Steve Martinot (Minneapolis: Univ. of Minnesota Press, 2000). Hereafter R. Memmi's structural model for racism contains four elements. The first is the existence of a difference, whether of body, culture, ethics, religion, and whether real or imaginary. To that difference a valuation is given; one group negatively evaluates the other through that difference, and by imposing that negative valuation then valorizes itself. Finally, self-valorization through derogation of the other is used to prepare hostility, social ostracism, hate, and aggression. This process is always concomitant to a system of colonialist oppression, which begins as territorial aggression and finds racist aggression the most direct mode of continuation. As a structure, Memmi's model is instructive, and explanatory. It assumes the power, or social cohesion, in the hands of one group capable of doing this to another group—that is, the power to define, to impose the definition in practice, and to make it concrete for itself through its own violence and brutality.

37. Cf. T. H. Breen, "A Changing Labor Force and Race Relations in Virginia, 1660–1710," and Bernard Bailyn, "Politics and Social Structure in Virginia," in *SSS.* The nature of Bacon's rebellion has been widely debated among historians. Much has been written about it, including nov-

els, diatribes, and careful researches. The account I give is a rough composite of several interpretations from Breen, but including accounts from Washburn and Zinn. Cf. Wilcomb Washburn,
The Governor and the Rebel (Chapel Hill: Univ. of North Carolina Press, 1957); Zinn, *People's History*. Two accounts from the period by Ann Cotton and Thomas Burwell (pro and contra) are
printed in Peter Force, ed., *Tracts and Other Papers* (Washington, 1836). Hereafter Tracts.

38. This is echoed in what Bailyn calls the ideology of U.S. conservatism: the desire not to
incur upheaval as the utmost evil in and of itself. It is a fear and rejection of such things as
mass strikes, rebellion, or other forms of political uprisings. The Colonial Council seems to have
concocted just such a conservatism in the colony in its attempt to prevent further opposition
to itself. Bailyn, *Ideological Origins.*

39. Bailyn argues that, for Jefferson and Tucker for instance, the resistance of whites to antislavery was a resistance to rebellion and was used to rationalize whiteness as destiny, as a civilizing mission. Rebellion was seen as an act of savagery, and indicated a need for accultura-
tion, which only the whites could bring. Reginald Horsman adds that slavery was seen as
continuing the English civilizing mission. The American Revolution was not seen as a rebellion, but as an independence movement, as a way to continue what the English had started,
for which the king became an obstacle. Cf. Reginald Horsman, *Race and Manifest Destiny* (Cambridge, MA: Harvard Univ. Press, 1981), p. 115. Hereafter RMD.

40. David Brion Davis, *The Slave Power Conspiracy and the Paranoid Style* (Baton Rouge:
Louisiana State Univ. Press, 1969), p. 4. See also Richard Hofstadter, *The Paranoid Style in American Politics* (New York: Knopf, 1966).

41. For instance, in a statute of October 1670, it says: "Whereas it hath beene questioned
whither Indians or negroes manumited, or otherwise free, could be capable of purchasing
christian servants, It is enacted that noe negroe or Indian though baptised and enjoyed their
owne ffreedome shall be capable of any such purchase of christians, but yet not debarred from
buying any of their owne nation." The reference to "nation" is interesting in confirming that
"Negro," as well as "English" and "Christian," were seen as comparable, and that the term
"nation" referred to place of origin.

42. Interestingly, the construction of an intermediary control stratum as the form of transformed allegiance closely follows John Locke's views on social organization. As Betty Wood
points out, Locke had referred to slavery as a form of war (Wood, 63). This does not refer to
the idea that archaically slaves were the spoils of war in the form of captured enemy personnel. In Locke's meaning, the war is to get labor to perform the tasks required of it, without control over those tasks.

Betty Wood's account of racialization differs from that of Jordan or Genovese. She sees race
developing out of slavery, rather than slavery reflecting a consciousness of race. What she is
looking at is the way a difference is raised to the level of an essentiality, a concrete differentiation, which is then used to create social, cultural, and political disparity, not as social value,
but as "natural" worth (Wood, 101). The identification with whiteness, which then spread to
Europe, only recapitulated the process of invention of racialization. Anthropology, for instance,
which sought to investigate the differences of races and ethnicities, was therefore itself a result
of the process of racialization (Wood, 104). But Wood does not present an account of the medi-
ations or control structures that participate in this process.

43. Karl Marx, *Capital,* vol. 1, chapters on primitive accumulation.

44. The idea that class lines and class relations can be politically constructed might be as hard
a concept to grasp as that of the invention of race. For instance, Bowser and Hunt, in *The Impact*

of Racism on Whites, have trouble freeing themselves from the assumption that class boundaries were always easily discernible. At one point, they briefly introduce the historical idea that the term "white . . . designated European unity across class and nationality" (xxiv). They mention that the process of forging this unity was accomplished in great part through the passage of laws that lowered African status and raised that of European labor. They recognize that racial differentiation occurred neither automatically nor without juridical definition and sanction. But if the juridical lies at the core of the construction of whiteness (while not subsuming it), and one assumes that the forging of white unity operated across class lines from the beginning, then those class lines had to have been already defined. But then, against whom or what is that white unity forged if it marked the moment of racialization? Cf. Benjamin Bowser and Raymond Hunt, eds., *Impacts of Racism on White Americans* (Beverly Hills: Sage, 1981).

It is characteristic of a corporate structure that class boundaries are not well defined within it, even for the elite. For example, one does not speak of class relations in an army, though a wide gap separates officers and troops. The relation of officers to soldiers (who may come from different classes) is not considered a class relation. While the colony may have inherited a class structure (with social and juridical practices) from England, the economic roles of those in the nonelite were themselves changeable and often fluid.

45. That it is still the conceptual core of whiteness is obvious. Even after the dismantling of Jim Crow, antimiscegenation remains the calling card for a defense of racism. The extreme invocation of the purity of white southern women provided the strength of the false rape charges against black men used to pass Jim Crow laws throughout the South in the 1890s. Cf. Grace Hale, *Making Whiteness: The Culture of Segregation in the South, 1890–1940* (New York: Pantheon Books, 1998). During Reconstruction, when black legislators attempted to promote the value of marriage and the home, calling for the legalization of interracial marriage but the outlawing of concubinage, the majority white legislators passed a bill outlawing interracial marriage and decriminalizing concubinage (Saks, 54). Only white marriage was to receive sanction.

46. This only highlights the role of the literary in the process of racialization, which Jordan focuses on. The fifteenth- and sixteenth-century literary descriptions he cites provide intermediary moments between self-identification as English and identification as white. Even before the establishment of the colonies, travelers from European countries had attempted to explain the existence of darker peoples. The predominant hypothesis during the sixteenth century among the Portuguese and English adventurers around the Atlantic was climatic, that the sun of the tropics had the effect of darkening the skin. Second to this was the apocryphal story of the punishment of Ham, who ridiculed his father Noah's drunken nakedness. For this offense, Ham's progeny were cursed and condemned to be the servants of the progeny of Ham's brothers Shem and Japheth. Ham's son was Canaan, so the curse becomes the curse of Canaan, into whose lands Moses led the Jews when they left Egypt. Apparently, the story has its origin in rabbinical thinking of the tenth or eleventh century. It is not found in the Bible; in Genesis, Ham insults Noah by looking at him naked, but no curse is pronounced. But the very appearance of literary explanations for the existence of dark peoples is testimony that the concept of race did not yet exist. As literary, these texts create their subject matter against a social framework that does not already contain them as such. The literary accepts prior social categorizations only as a context for its own transcendence of them. It is as transcendence that it uses the descriptive terms (such as white and black) that it does. Otherwise, it would not focus on them but use them as social context. The passages that Jordan quotes construct descriptions poetically, as yet unshifted from the descriptive to the categorizing. On the other hand, from

where else could the content of such an ideological notion as race come than from the literary? From where other than the poetic and the fanciful would a language of categorization and racialization emerge? Indeed, the purity concept itself is a literary development. The juridical incorporation of such descriptions is an intermediary phase in creating a cultural relation.

47. Paul Gilroy, *Black Atlantic: Modernity and Double Consciousness* (Cambridge, MA: Harvard Univ. Press, 1993), p. 118.

48. David Brion Davis, *The Problem of Slavery in the Age of Revolution, 1770–1823* (Ithaca, NY: Cornell Univ. Press, 1975), p. 262. Hereafter PSR.

49. Eric Schlosser, "The Prison-Industrial Complex", *Atlantic Monthly*, December 1999, p. 77.

Chapter Two

1. This is the specific context in which the word "race" will be and can be understood in the United States. Though the word has been around a long time, it has meant different things in different places and contexts. Here, it will only refer to the system of social categorizations that have been produced, and are continually reproduced, by specific processes in the United States—though it has spread, through the emergence of U.S. hegemony in the world, to Europe and to its other colonized areas.

2. Eugene Genovese, *Roll, Jordan, Roll: The World the Slaves Made* (New York: Vintage Books, 1976), p. 619. Hereafter RJR.

3. Genovese notes that while this paternalism gave the slaves a measure of humanity against a system that sought to remove it from them entirely, it also made solidarity among the slaves harder, since it established a complex system of individual relationships between the owners and the individual bond-laborers.

4. The Panic of 1741 in New York City offers an example of both systems. A slave conspiracy was imagined which pushed a coterie of shop-owning and professional whites into the limelight, and to which the poorer populace of the city lent its active support in terrorizing black people in general. The panic started when a serious of unexplainable fires broke out. No evidence pointed to any particular suspects, or even to arson. But Mary Burton, an Irish servant of a white innkeeper, came forward and accused her employer of being involved in a plot with a vast network of slaves to take over the city and make concubines of all the white women. The bar association refused to defend any of the arrested slaves, and the prosecutor used a convicted white thief to give testimony to confessions made to him by those arrested (presumably to save his own life, since theft was a capital crime). Burton's employer and those black people she accused as ringleaders were put to death, and a vast movement of whites got involved in accusations, bringing people to court, and attending the executions. During the summer of 1741, at least two people were executed each week, with an enthusiastic mob as audience. Burton became a fairly powerful person in the city, and the panic ended only after her stories exceeded all bounds and the entire structure of conspiracy she had concocted collapsed. The principle of economic profit and the importance of belonging (allegiance), to which the poor and middle-class whites clung, were both directly reflected in the invention of the conspiracy. Approbation was given to those who came forward to defend society against the threat, and the issue was used to settle personal scores. Like Bacon's rebellion, it constituted an opportunist attack on the nonwhite to reaffirm white solidarity toward poor or marginal whites in the name of a responsibility to defend the society. Cf. Edgar McManus, *Black Bondage in the North* (Syracuse, NY: Syracuse Univ. Press, 1973), pp. 133ff. Hereafter BBN.

5. Larry Tise, *Proslavery: A History of the Defense of Slavery in America, 1701–1840* (Athens: Univ. of Georgia Press, 1987), pp. 192–193. Hereafter Tise.

6. David Brion Davis discusses the effect of this in terms of bipolar paranoia following the Revolution. The abolitionists and the southern elite looked at each other as a subversive conspiracy involving foreign or alien powers. For Davis, it is a Hofstadterian paranoia style, but to the extent it revolves around the issues of the structures of whiteness, it can be seen as more fundamental, a form of social paranoia.

7. Larry Tise explains the way the proslavery argument was transformed into the central tenet of U.S. nationalism. The charge by European nations against the United States that it could not be a nation founded on freedom as long as it had slavery was turned around. Because Europe attacked the United States on this basis, allegiance to the United States, as the core of its nationalism, required that one defend its institutions. Indeed, within the framework of nationalism, the proslavery advocates claimed that slavery was the way in which whites had attained freedom, that servitude was the necessary condition for democracy, and that nonfreedom was the necessary condition for freedom.

8. Eric Foner, *Free Soil, Free Labor, Free Men* (Ithaca, NY: Cornell Univ. Press, 1970), p. 12. Hereafter FS.

9. Wilmot, Democratic representative from Pennsylvania, authored the Wilmot Proviso as an amendment to the resolution for annexation of Mexican territories (New Mexico). It stated that the new territories should bar slavery. Although the House passed it, the Senate did not. Slavery thus could be said to have controlled a majority of the states but not a majority of the votes.

10. John Mayfield, *Rehearsal for Republicanism: Free Soil and the Politics of Antislavery* (Port Washington, NY: Kennikat Press, 1980), p. 10. Hereafter RR.

11. Alexander Saxton, *The Indispensable Enemy* (Berkeley: Univ. of California Press, 1971), p. 22. Hereafter IE. Saxton argues that the white working class in northern California established its identity as a class through the anti-Chinese campaign. It also acted to bar black workers from California. While corporate capital turned to the Chinese for cheaper labor, the white working class united against Chinese labor in its fight for recognition as the working class, and for access to the middle class. Ultimately, free African Americans were not excluded from California, but they were excluded from Illinois, Indiana, and Oregon by constitutional provision in the 1850s (NS, 70). In California, white workers refused to admit black workers into their craft and political organizations, while welcoming newly arrived white workers. Chinese workers were segregated as unskilled labor and disfranchised. Black workers remained sparse in California because of the hostility they met. That is, race functioned as a primary factor in the determination of class. Tomas Almaguer says, concerning California in the mid-nineteenth century: "Who gained access to land, owned businesses, became skilled workers, and, more generally, was subjectively placed in either a 'free' wage-labor market or an 'unfree' labor system was fundamentally determined on the basis of race" (Tomas Almaguer, *Racial Fault Lines* [Berkeley: Univ. of California Press, 1994], p. 13; hereafter RFL). In short, race is part of a political process whereby class membership was assigned and class identity constructed.

12. Timothy Messer-Kruse, *The Yankee International* (Chapel Hill: Univ. of North Carolina Press, 1998), pp. 207–216. Hereafter YI. See also Alexander Saxton, *The Rise and Fall of the White Republic* (London: Verso, 1990), ch. 13.

13. On this score, Tomas Almaguer's treatment of the different ways whites constructed their white identity in California in establishing dominance over the various people they

encountered there—Indians, Mexicans, Asians, and African Americans—is instructive. While he details the social and political processes by which whites subjugated each different group, he suggests that their identity as white, which they brought with them, contained within it as a template their relation to black people, as those through whom white identity had been constructed in the first place in the East. In this sense—housing a black/white binary within their white identity as the mode by which it had been constructed in the first place—white supremacy and the structures of racialization constitute something essential to the society the United States founded in each new territory it conquered or occupied (RFL).

14. Saxton describes the forms this populism took in California as a confluence of the operation of socialist and labor-oriented political organizations, but engaged in general in social movements. As political movements, focusing on exclusion of Asian labor, they sought to win recognition for themselves by the California industrial elite. But that populism was as far as it was able to go. Working-class movements against oligopoly and its political hegemony in California remained a demand for parity, which meant recognition rather than economic equality.

15. David Roediger, *The Wages of Whiteness* (New York: Verso, 1991)

16. Robert Starobin, *Industrial Slavery in the Old South* (Oxford: Oxford Univ. Press, 1970), pp. 16ff. Hereafter ISS.

17. See McManus, *Black Bondage,* pp. 36ff. See also Frederick Douglass, *Narrative of the Life of Frederick Douglass* (New York: Signet, 1968), p. 103.

18. For a cry of outrage against this desperation, see David Walker, *Appeal to the Colored Citizens of the World* (New York: Hill and Wang, 1965).

19. Arthur Zilversmit, *The First Emancipation: The Abolition of Slavery in the North* (Chicago: Univ. of Chicago Press, 1967), p. 113. Hereafter Z.

20. These admissions and others emerged in large part in debates over the desirability of black colonization of Africa. The African colonization scheme was proposed as a resolution of the contradiction between slavery as property and the ideals of the Revolution in the Declaration of Independence. Rather than a moral or political stand, the instinctive response seems to have been to simply move people elsewhere, and thereby eliminate the problem they posed— as people. Ultimately, the government turned against the idea of African colonization, but only because it would eliminate the possibility of white people not having to do the menial work. See Litwack, *North of Slavery.*

21. DuBois recognized this racialized relation as a class relation when he counterposed as polar opposites the notions of black workers and white profits, meaning both economic and social (BR, 30). It suggests that class relations do not have a single center in the United States, but at least two centers.

22. As an addendum to this position by the Republican Party, Foner provides an insight into their thinking in an anecdote concerning the 1860 Convention. In the 1850s, the issue of black colonization (that is, the exiling of black people from the United States, an early idea of ethnic cleansing) was widely discussed. A proposal to include it in the Republican platform of the 1860 election was made. Its authors prepared their case, given indications that it would be adopted without significant opposition. But it was neither proposed at the convention nor included in the platform. Foner suggests that this happened because those who favored the idea thought it needed to be adopted "without objection," that is, without debate. That is, it depended intimately on white unanimity.

23. John R. Commons et al., *Documentary History of American Industrial Society* (A. H. Clark, 1910), vol. 9, p. 145. Hereafter CA.

24. Mike Davis, *Prisoners of the American Dream* (London: Verso, 1986), pp. 36ff.

25. Today, immigrants from Latin America who seek work are disparaged as taking jobs from native (white) Americans; those who do not seek or cannot find work are disparaged as coming to the United States to live off welfare. Today, as 180 years earlier, the immigrants are thrown back upon communities of similar immigrants which become gradually more and more impoverished and must develop internal and insular economies in order to survive.

26. This same double bind appears in the political process of abolition in Pennsylvania. The first Pennsylvania constitution (1790) declared that all men were born equally free and independent. The abolitionists went to court with this juridical fact in an effort to free those still enslaved in the state. The court ruled (1803) that black people were "legally" slaves because they had been slaves before the state constitution of 1790 was drawn up. In other words, on such an issue, the court refused to recognize that the Revolution had wrought an entire social transformation in law, jurisprudence, and sovereignty. This conflation of what had been overthrown with what the Revolution had instituted persisted in U.S. jurisprudence and later became the basis for the Dred Scott decision in 1857. In Pennsylvania, while these cases were still on their way to the state's highest court, the abolitionist movement proposed a bill to accomplish the task legislatively. The bill was considered in 1796 and thrown out by a state assembly committee (1797) because, the committee held, slavery was not in accordance with the constitution of 1790, and hence a law abolishing it was not needed (NP, 84). The fact that slavery still existed in the state was apparently immaterial. The bill was to give the freed slaves full political as well as civil rights, namely the franchise. When the court ruled that slavery was indeed legal, the assembly let the issue die there.

27. During the Civil War, violence against black communities became an ongoing pogrom. The attacks became so disruptive that even Lincoln stepped in, showing that he had a greater class consciousness than those white workers. In 1864, he made his famous statement that "the strongest bond of human sympathy, outside of the family relation, should be one uniting all working people, of all nations, and tongues, and kindreds" (BR, 216). While the ruling classes were settling their internal differences by military means, the working classes were exacerbating theirs by paramilitary means. Indeed, until the civil rights movement won some important victories, there was no time when violence did not occur against black communities in the United States.

28. The entire history of lynching, publicly accepted and given media approbation and publicity, is further testimony to this idea. Cf. Ida B. Wells, *On Lynchings: Southern Horrors* (New York: Arno Press, 1969). In one case from the 1920s, a black man was arrested in a southern state, and the word went around that he was going to be lynched. This was announced in the newspapers of the region, a date was given, and the railroad put on extra trains to that town for that day. An estimated 1,500 people showed up and composed the mob that took the man out of jail and killed him. Grace E. Hale, *Making Whiteness* (New York: Pantheon Books, 1998).

29. Today, the corporate form perfuses U.S. society from top to bottom. Townships, towns, and counties are incorporated areas. The modern corporation, born in nineteenth-century capitalism, was first given its juridical standing as a "person" in the United States. Though the Virginia Company went bankrupt in 1624, its style of rule was sustained by the Virginia Colonial Council, which exercised similar controls on production, land use, and the disposition and control of labor—which has persisted and grown up to the present.

30. These social substructures are common to all industrialized countries, but the social meanings they bestow on one's self-identification or positionality differ from one country to

another. In France, to say one is a machinist is not a form of identification. Social identification begins with the corporation one works for, and the union or political party one belongs to. Those who work in small shops have a different place on the social scale from those who work in big plants, since one's political relation to the society is different. It implies one has not fought the class struggles the others have, and that one's union participation and party activity have been different. In the United States, people who identify themselves by saying "I am a worker" are immediately known to be members of either some leftist or rightwing patriotic group (cf. the ideology in some of Merle Haggard's songs, for instance). In France, it is common to hear "Je suis un ouvrier" as a form of self-identification.

31. My thanks to Dylan Rodriguez for contributing to this analysis in conversation and unpublished work.

32. Cf. William Hayward, *Bill Hayward's Book* (New York: International Publishers, 1958), for an account of these methods of breaking strikes throughout the Rocky Mountains from 1894 to 1920.

33. This fact of American history has produced a number of versions of an American exceptionalism thesis, which holds that the United States is an exception to the dynamics of other capitalisms because it is democratic at its core, has no feudal antecedents or traditions, and had a frontier that could insure the possibility of class and upward social mobility. The thrust of the American exceptionalist thesis was to explain why the U.S. working class had not produced a class consciousness or revolutionary movement. One could mention Mike Davis's thesis, in *Prisoners of the American Dream*, and Earl Browder's, which he put before the Communist Party of the United States in the 1940s.

34. Dan Georgakis, *Detroit, I Do Mind Dying* (New York: St. Martin's Press, 1975).

35. It is the same conflict and program that Frank Norris weaves through his account of railroad takeover of land in California in *The Octopus*. The same sense of being thrown away by more powerful economic forces led ranchers like Jesse James and the Dalton brothers to form their gangs to do battle against the railroads in the Midwest.

36. David Harvey, Jack Ruggio, and Greg Meyerson are Marxist writers who still see racism as primarily a capitalist instrumentality, a tactic to divide the working class and maintain control.

37. Timothy Messer-Kruse, *The Yankee International* (Chapel Hill: Univ. of North Carolina Press, 1998). Even this attitude faded rapidly after the Civil War. The official representatives of Marx in the United States, led by Friedrich Sorge, gave up the notion of a racially united working-class movement when the NLU did. Their theory was that the Irish and German workers should be organized, to lead the charge against the wages system. They felt that to advocate an integrated movement would split the white workers. They were the one's upon which the Marxists concentrated (pp. 189ff). Marx says, in a letter to Engels of December 2, 1864, that slavery had to be destroyed to allow for the historical advancement of the white working class (p. 54). He felt that with the end of slavery, black people would just be swept aside. In his own support for northern white workers against black, he was actually supporting the organization of the intermediary control stratum, as an incipient form of working-class organization in the United States. This was tantamount to supporting the patrols in the South for the same reason.

38. Harry Haywood, *Negro Liberation* (New York: International Publishers, 1948). Haywood posits the black belt as a region of black culture and thus of African American nationality. But in the party platforms of the CPUSA, or any of the Marxist parties of the 1960s, black workers are seen as the most exploited sector of the working class, and racism a tactic of capital to divide

workers. The idea that race might be more fundamental than class in the United States does not compute for Marxist thinking.

Chapter Three

1. As socially categorizing, race shorthands itself as color, while color makes itself a proxy for reracialization. Though the mainstream understanding of race is that it is already color, and vice versa, this is insufficient. If race is a social categorization, it cannot be understood as a bodily characteristic; it can only be what is signified by bodily characteristics. Though an individual's body may be subject to unconscionable violence through its characteristics, it is subjected to that violence because of its social categorization, for which the bodily characteristic has been conscripted as signifier by the hegemonic (white supremacy). The difference between bodies and social categories must be kept in mind.

2. The notion of being "chromatically characterized" contains a double racialization: chromatic differentiation has become the social (as opposed to geographic or anthropological) iconic mode of racial reference, while the very notion of "characteristic" is already racialized in the sense that a racializing discourse has to have picked out and individuated definable concepts to be noticed as existing and racializing. (My thanks to Jared Sexton for pointing this out and reasoning it through with me.) To the extent that "race" is a generalizing and disparaging way for whites to define themselves through others, the specification of chromatic terms and of "characteristics" as a category to which the chromatic belongs refers to the white point of view. The very subsumption of chromatics in the category of "nonwhite" specifies the "white" point of view and centers the designation to which all "nonwhite" people are related. The focus on color is something whites have done, not a necessary social condition. For people of color, color does not "characterize" them but participates in the system of social categorization given by whites. People of color and whites may use the same chromatic terms, but the terms do not mean the same. The chromatic terms (black, brown, red, etc.) are terms of dissolution and exclusion in the speech of whites, but for people of color they become terms of cohesion and belonging (for instance, as seen in the name of the Native American organization Women of All Red Nations, WARN).

3. Racism continually escapes information. Lani Guinier recounts the story of white people who oppose welfare costs because they are too high. When they are shown the facts, that welfare is a small part of the overall budget and that the military is the largest part, they change their minds and say that the military costs should be reduced. But on a different issue, they will return to the notion that welfare costs are too high, as if the racist coding of that issue overshadows all information about it.

4. For useful surveys of contending theories on the corporate state, see Howard Wiarda, *An Introduction to Comparative Politics: Concepts and Processes* (Belmont, CA: Wadsworth, 1993), and *Corporatism and Comparative Politics* (Armonk, NY: Sharpe, 1997). Hereafter CCW. See also Peter J. Williamson, *Corporatism in Perspective: An Introductory Guide to Corporatist Theory* (London: Sage, 1989), and *Varieties of Corporatism: A Conceptual Discussion* (New York: Cambridge Univ. Press, 1985). Hereafter VC. See as well Norman Birnbaum, *Crisis of Industrial Society* (London: Oxford Univ. Press, 1969). Hereafter CIS. Birnbaum's theme is the nature of power, administration, and social movements in industrial society. What he sees as corporate power in the United States is in general congruent to the ontological character of white society that I have been analyzing here.

5. Although the corporate state can take on the trappings of individualist democratic procedures, it would stand in antithesis to proportional representation in terms of social conflict resolution (VC, 76). For the corporatist, irresolvable social conflicts are referred to higher executive authority, because higher bodies have greater power over lower bodies and interests. In proportional representation, authority would come from the electorate, in its relative strengths, and conflicts between groups would be resolved in the halls of legislatures, at higher levels, taking their authority from the lower levels. The idea of the state would be the working out of political and economic conflicts democratically, rather than as a body for the governance of society above those conflicts.

6. What has become ever clearer in the United States since the Vietnam War is that the executive branch has been acting ever more independently of Congress, though not out of relationship to "corporate" interests. Its military adventures (Grenada, Panama, Iraq, Somalia, Yugoslavia), its demand for consensus, the failure to institute health care, the dismantling of the social safety net, the restriction and dismantling of affirmative action, the militarization of the police, and the prioritizing of weapons over education all signify an abandonment of executive responsibility to the electorate and a breaking of ties of responsibility to Congress or civil society.

7. U.S. foreign policy has used demonization to establish its enemies and its domestic paranoia with respect to them, whether directed to nonwhite people such as Iraqis or Grenadans, or ostensibly white people such as Serbians. Thus, the mechanism for generating patriotism in the United States is homologous to that for generating white solidarity internally.

8. For corporatism, representation needs to be based on more than voting; an inner voter–representative relationship must exist, as continuity and familiarity, for example (VC, 65). Corporatism also requires that its organizational framework have been given state legitimacy. Thus, corporatism provides an insight into representation theory as well as into the social problematic of multicultural representation. When U.S. theorists assume that a black representative constitutes the representation of blacks, or a woman of women, they are advancing a corporatist argument. It seems a natural argument because corporatism has been at the center of U.S. government organization for its entire history. The historical subtext to this is how the corporations have themselves achieved representation, or been given it. That is a more specialized discussion than is warranted here.

9. For instance, the WTO has established rules on government procurement. In the U.S. case, this amounts to over a trillion dollars in federal, state, and local spending together, and can be used to reduce environmental damage, create jobs, assist women-owned and minority-owned businesses, and promote fair labor practices. "Dozens of cities and counties, have local ordinances banning purchase of products made in sweatshops. . . . Citizens can use government purchasing policy to guide their regional economy onto the path most likely to improve their quality of life . . . [and] to impose human values on their local and regional economy." The WTO rules, which are made by corporate lawyers who are not elected and are not responsible to any citizenry, nevertheless constitute an enforceable commercial code governing markets and trade at the national level, because it has treaty-level authority (the same as the Constitution). Its rules set in the Government Procurement Agreement say that "governments can set standards for the *performance* of purchased materials but cannot set standards based on *methods of production.* Therefore, government purchasing policies cannot discriminate against materials produced by child labor or slave labor, . . . [nor require] that items be manufactured from recycled materials." Cf. "Steps Toward a Corporate State," *Rachel's Environment and Health Weekly,* No. 694, April 27, 2000, Environmental Research Foundation.

10. An interesting experiment was undertaken by a college student in Philadelphia that indicates the extent and depth of this disparity between modes of life, racialized and racializing. A white person, he had his skinned darkened chemically, as had John Griffin, the author of *Black Like Me*. It was, in fact, a direct retake of Griffin's sojourn across the color line. What is astounding about it is that the student lasted only a few days before calling an end to the experiment. He reported that the experience was horrendous; he could not stand the hate and the continual disrespect. (Joshua Solomon, "Skin Deep; Reliving 'Black Like Me,'" *The Washington Post*, 30 October 1994, p. c-1)

11. W.E.B. DuBois, *The Souls of Black Folk* (New York: Vintage Books, 1990), pp. 107ff.

12. It is worthwhile pointing out that these anti-Reconstruction tactics are still in vogue. Debt servitude, for instance, has become the main form of reducing a nation to subservience to globalized corporations and globalized production. The IMF facilitates this economically by imposing Structural Adjustment Programs that dissolve a nation's native economic traditions in privatization regulations and subordinate that nation's economic resources to debt service (some countries are now forced to allocate between 40 and 60 percent of their gross domestic product to debt service to the IMF). Nations that refuse the loans are embargoed from major areas of international trade. The issue of paramilitary groups is also germane to the present. A primary tactic in use today against popular democratic or revolutionary movements is low-intensity warfare through the organization of paramilitary groups or "death squads." Assassination is a favorite tactic, as are terror raids on small towns or villages, with indiscriminate killing of citizens. These paramilitary groups play the same role that the KKK did in undermining the Reconstruction governments. The use of paramilitary groups sidesteps international law and human rights codes because they ostensibly operate outside the law, though in most cases they are connected to the military of the government against which the popular democratic movements pose a threat. They have been used extensively in East Timor, Chiapas, Angola, Colombia, and El Salvador.

13. William J. Wilson, *When Work Disappears: The World of the New Urban Poor* (New York: Knopf, 1996).

14. See Douglas Massey and Nancy Denton, *American Apartheid: Segregation and the Making of the Underclass* (Cambridge, MA: Harvard Univ. Press, 1993). The authors go over various dimensions of the persistence and maintenance of social segregation in the United States since the civil rights movement, and they analyze the ways in which separation and prejudice cyclically and endlessly engender and reinforce each other.

15. The tactic of criminalization is fairly common. It is often promulgated by using criminal violence itself to criminalize a group that is in reality its victim. The process involves criminalizing the problem, which then gives the problem the aura of being a domain of criminals. It can then be resolved as a crime problem; that is, the people who were targeted as the problem can then be dealt with through police actions and imprisonment. (Eric Schlosser, "The Prison-Industrial Complex", *Atlantic Monthly*, December 1999, p. 77). A town in Colorado in the late 1970s decided to eliminate a bohemian and street-oriented population. The police permitted a gang of teenagers to harass and beat "street people" under cover of night. These actions became a source of popular discussion, because a number of street people were getting seriously injured. The local newspaper conducted a survey that asked if citizens felt threatened by the street people, though they had not been the source of any violence. Thus, they were given the onus for the violence, under the cover of which the police arrested and ejected them from the town.

16. With respect to women, there was a combined effect of competition and minoritization in which they were played off against each other. Though all women had been discriminated against, and thus were theoretically minorities, white women were not racialized as a minority. They remained "women," and were separated from women of color within the affirmative action programs, since women of color were primarily classified with racial minorities. The competition that white women offered within the institutionalized framework of civil rights disguised its ability to call upon white solidarity, while white women could do so only up to the point where it seemed to contest elements of patriarchal control of economic and political domains. The institutionality of affirmative action for women mapped out a domain for them between the white interface with minorities and the glass ceiling in organizational promotions. In a sense, this was a replay of the divisions created in the women's suffrage movement of the 1890s. White women eventually were given the vote in exchange for support for segregation; the bargain was that they would turn their back on black women and abandon support for the movement of black people that sought to block the growing segregationist structures of Jim Crow.

17. Another dimension of this can be seen in white responses to ghetto rebellions. Ghetto rebellions are explosive reactions to this same subtext of entitlement. While they generally represent mass outrage at social betrayal, they are rarely seen by whites as responses to broken promises of fairness, because the white sense of fairness equates to white entitlement. The white sense of fairness lies within the white bargain of solidarity. The issues that lead to ghetto rebellions are thus issues in which a white sense of fairness has not been betrayed. Conversely, when whites do feel betrayed, it does not lead to solidarity with people of color, because people of color are a priori implicated in any sense of a loss of entitlement by whites as whites.

18. The NAACP held public hearings immediately after the 2000 election among the people affected, mainly in West Palm Beach, Leon and Hillsboro counties, and other predominantly black areas, and collected data and affidavits on harassment of voters, prevention of voting, unreasonable demands for identification, lost ballot boxes, and mysterious disappearances of names from the registration rolls. All these had occurred frequently and were all illegal. The NAACP has issued a report on their findings and filed suit in Florida against the state for violation of the Voting Rights Act of 1965. Laura Flanders, "A Racist Elephant in Our Living Room," ZNet / Z Magazine, December 13, 2000. According to CBS News (August 17, 2001), the state of Florida requested that the suit proceedings be delayed pending findings by the federal government in a previously initiated investigation into five counties in Florida for discrimination under the Voting Rights Act.

19. The two-party system is possible only on the basis of winner-take-all districts. It was not established by the Constitution but evolved out of the operation of white supremacy, as will be seen later in this chapter. It cannot provide representation for diversity, whether of multiple classes, or cultural, social, and identity interests. Cumulative voting would be a step, but only a step, toward proportional representation, since it preserves the old form of district. Instant Runoff Voting does nothing to contest the two-party system as a structure; it only makes more efficient its dispensing with a plurality of candidates. Proportional representation would require multirepresentative districts with different parties representing different interests, getting representation according to their voting strength, and resolving the conflicts of interest among the people within the halls of government through real debate on content and program—something single-delegate, winner-take-all districts prohibit. Cf. Robert Ritchie and Steven Hill, *Reflecting All of Us: The Case for Proportional Representation* (Boston: Beacon Press, 1999). Also see Lani Guinier, *The Tyranny of the Majority* (New York: Free Press, 1994).

20. Major industries have the ability to hold a district or group of districts hostage to their particular interests because they provide employment and investment. They can threaten to move if their political interests are not met by the legislative representatives. This threatens the well-being of the district and the reelection of the representative. Major corporations, acting in concert, can determine the success or failure of legislation by severally making the same threat to the representatives of the various districts in which they function. Proportional representation would serve as a buffer to this power. In multirepresentative districts, the council of representatives could provide real political leadership in the creation of alternatives and prohibitions to this form of corporate blackmail.

21. As an example of class relations on this issue, a suffrage amendment was proposed for the New York State constitution. It was wholly opposed by Democrats, while the majority of Republicans supported it. It was defeated on the strength of the Republican antisuffrage opposition to the proposal. The Republican districts that opposed the amendment were mostly around New York City, mostly working class (at the time, New York City was mainly Democratic). The white working class of both parties opposed black suffrage, while black suffrage itself would have swung the vote the other way (FS, 285).

22. A wave of disfranchisements swept the North from 1807 (in New Jersey) to 1837 (in Pennsylvania). "From the admission of Maine in 1819 until the end of the Civil War, every new state restricted the suffrage to whites in its constitution" (NS, 79). Thus, the actual issue debated in the 1840s was whether to reenfranchise or not, to overturn what had become a general disfranchisement.

23. The unassailability of white hegemony extended itself into the ranks of the abolitionist movement and came to the fore in the split between Garrison and Douglass. The main thrust of white abolitionist ideology was a moral appeal to other whites, that liberty could not coexist with slavery (a form of moral "free labor" position). The conceptual issue that Garrison foregrounded, in carrying his moral absolutism to its logical conclusion, was disunion, the need to break the United States into two nations because the Constitution was a proslavery document. For Garrison, this meant opening the possibility of starting the United States over again. He argued that the South could not stand as an autonomous region and would collapse with disunion, whereas continued union meant the northern states sustained slavery's existence in the South. He refused to recognize that disunion, in jettisoning the South, would mean abandoning the people held in thrall there.

The focus of black abolitionists lay elsewhere, in the question of independent organization. One position advocated abandoning independent organization and uniting with "white friends" against segregation. A more radical position saw antiblack prejudice, even among white abolitionists, as unavoidable, and faced the need to resist it. It proposed independent organizing and action to facilitate that resistance.

Though Douglass counted himself a loyal Garrisonian, his thinking began to shift in 1850 from a moral to a political activist stance. When Garrison sought to win Democratic and Whig representatives over to antislavery in Congress, assuming the luxury of playing with administrative possibilities within the white corporate state, Douglass could assume no such luxury. Located within the racialized class structure rather than in the white class structure, with different options, Douglass had to be more circumspect. While Garrison could assume his human and citizenship status within his abstract moral stand, Douglass had to wrestle with the questions of how to accomplish (human) being, (national) belonging, and (political) citizenship all in one move, even against Garrison. Rather than jettison the South, he reasoned, new networks in the South, conjoining resistance in both regions, should be developed. He included the possibility of violence to finally eliminate slavery. For this, Garrison attacked him as a traitor to the cause, and Douglass faced metaphoric excommunication (in Stowe's term) at Garrison's hands. The conflict divided black antislavery forces between Garrisonian moral persuasion and Douglass's call for independent black political action.

Garrison's concept was not wholly coherent, if seen from Douglass's point of view. If a massive political action at the federal level would be needed to bring about disunion, why would not such a political movement be sufficient to bring about federal abolition of slavery? When Garrison proclaimed the right to repeal the union constitutionally, he was calling for enactment of a higher law while grounding the statement of that higher law in the structure of the lower law (the Constitution) which he sought to render inoperative through that transcendence. Cf. Aileen Kraditor, *Means and Ends in American Abolitionism* (Chicago: Dee Publishers, 1989), p. 198. It is a confusion akin to the conception of freedom Garrison was employing when he sought to require abolitionist allegiance to his particular ideology, in effect restricting black abolitionists from thinking and acting independently of the white. By reserving for himself the role of the movement's primary ideologue, Garrison positioned himself above the struggle, in what amounted to a racialized stance between the self-liberation of the slaves and the paradigm of white hegemony. He became a moral resistor within the white class system, while at the same time an administrative participant in white control over the racialized class system. In that sense his moral stance became a purity condition, rather than a rehumanization against racialization.

24. This is allied to what Toni Morrison refers to as an Africanist presence in American thinking and literature. Cf. *Playing in the Dark*. The issue here is obsessiveness, even as witnessed in Wilmot's proposal to reserve the land for whites.

25. African Americans had indeed voted during the previous thirty years in Pennsylvania; in general, those who paid county taxes were allowed to vote. In Philadelphia, however, no African Americans had voted because the city had "purposely failed to assess them for taxes" (NP, 185). This is, of course, an admission by the Philadelphia government that African Americans had the right to vote upon meeting this one simple requirement. In effect, the white need to prevent African Americans from voting was pressing to the point of sacrificing significant revenue.

26. In general, the arguments against black suffrage were that it would disrupt the regulation of governmental affairs by the white parties. Black suffrage was labeled anarchy, corruption, and the "Jacobin" within. A Rhode Island committee exclaimed in 1844 that "the whole frame and character of our institutions [would be] changed forever" (NS, 76). Then too there was a fear that the freed slaves would engage in factionalism out of "secret animosity" were they given suffrage. George Tucker, Virginia, 1801; in Gary Nash, *Race and Revolution* (Madison Wis.: Madison House, 1990), p. 163.

27. The 2000 election shows that the black vote is still used as a pawn in the two-party game. Though the harassment and disqualification of black voters in Florida violated the law, neither party saw fit to bring any criminal charges against those responsible. Under the Voting Rights Act of 1965, preventing a vote from being counted constitutes a crime, but the Supreme Court chose to ignore that and stop the Florida recount. Both parties acceded to that, though it gave the election to Bush, who tacitly admitted, by seeking to stop the recount, that it would have gone against him. Both parties knew in advance that the black vote was key to a Democratic victory, and the election was decided, as it was in Bucks County, Pennsylvania, in 1837, through a disqualification of the black vote. That is, the election was decided by an act of disfranchisement.

28. Lerone Bennett, *Black Power: The Human Side of Reconstruction 1867–1877* (Baltimore: Penguin, 1969), gives a comprehensive account of the rise and fall of Reconstruction in each southern state. See, in particular, ch. 8 for a summation of forms of white terror against the Reconstruction state governments.

29. Massey and Denton, *American Apartheid,* pp. 51ff.

30. Patricia Williams, *Seeing a Color-Blind Future: The Paradox of Race* (New York: Noonday, 1998), p. 38.

31. The Diallo case became famous for the related popular uprising against profiling and police violence in New York City. The four police officers were at first exonerated but then indicted because of the public protests, in which thousands were arrested. The officers were tried and acquitted. The next day, the police killed another black man, Malcolm Fergusan, a few blocks from where Diallo had been murdered. A few weeks later, Patrick Dorismund was killed by an undercover officer, and several thousand people marched at his funeral. Many were injured and hospitalized after police charged into the march. The protest against police violence seemed to exacerbate it rather than cause city government to bring it under control.

32. See Christian Parenti, *Lockdown America: Police and Prisons in the Age of Crisis* (New York: Verso, 1999), p. 54. Hereafter LA. This is an important investigation of the forms of police violence that developed during the last quarter of the twentieth century. Parenti argues that the growth of police and prisons was a response to a classical Marxian overaccumulation crisis in the 1970s, when the economy got caught between a profit squeeze and a strong labor movement (LA, 32). But he goes no further than such an historical materialist explanation, namely that police repression is only to stem an economic and political crisis (perceived as hyperdemocratic) and return political control to the capitalist elite. Cf. Samuel Huntington, "The Crisis in Democracy," in *The Crisis of Democracy: Report on the Governability of Democracies,* ed. Michael Crozier (New York: New York Univ. Press, 1976). The social meaning of police power cannot be gleaned from endless stories of police abuse, however. Anecdotal accounts represent the general nature and effect of police operations (LA, 111), but one has to go behind the histories to excavate their meaning. The ideological relevance of brutality and dehumanization must be examined. Parenti counsels that when the police "abuse of power" overflows into white and middle-class communities and threatens the "safety and security" of the mainstream, then political protest will have political weight. But this misses the idea of the constitution of the mainstream precisely through police violence against nonwhite people.

33. The ramifications of this are endless. One could surmise that in a democracy, where people had a say in how they were to be dealt with by the government, and thus were not simply things thrown about by political processes, there would be less crime. Such is not the case for the United States. Popular opinion has no way of expressing itself in content; it is created rather than represented by opinion polls. Thus, when representatives base their actions on public opinion as expressed in the polls, it is an empty gesture. The prison boom is an example. According to Eric Schlosser, in 1970, drugs were considered an illness, not a crime. Popular opinion was against building new prisons, and mandatory minimums were eliminated. In 1973, Rockefeller proposed new prisons and a reinstitution of mandatory minimums, and all of a sudden, there was a crime scare. Prisons then were built to house the overpopulation resulting from the minimum sentences, and the boom was on. The people had no say in it and were simply used as tax fodder, and as a sounding board for the propaganda of the government. One could say that there is a high crime rate because democracy is very limited.

34. A similar paradigm holds for psychiatric hospitals. The psychiatric industry is based on the same hyperconstitutional principle; if one's behavior strays sufficiently from an unlegis-

lated "norm," then one can be deprived of one's freedom without due process, by means of an ostensibly medical decision. Cf. Thomas Szasz, *Ideology and Insanity* (Garden City: Anchor Books, 1970). Szasz focuses on the notion that psychiatry can incarcerate a person because his or her behavior is embarrassing to or uncomfortable for others. In fact, psychiatric treatment is closely linked to criminalization; a psychiatric record will ensconce one ever deeper into the juridical machinery, in a subtle form of pseudocriminalization.

35. An example is the Juvenile Crime Bill in California, which criminalizes teenagers in the name of street-gang management. Under current juvenile statutes, if one associates with others whom the police have labeled gang members (with neither a hearing nor accountability), one commits a crime. Clothes, gestures, or other behaviors that have been listed as signs signifying gang status establish the guilt of people who use them by association. Again, a visual means of generalizing people is associated with past events that have been adjudged (whether by the police, judges, or politicians) to be criminal, thus establishing a priori guilt. The unconstitutionality of the practice is evident, while its acceptability can be adjudged a corollary to the white supremacist ethos of U.S. society.

Guilt by association carries profiling and institutional criminalization one step further. In profiling, the police commit an act of suspicion that generalizes a person; in guilt by association, the police commit a judgment of association, and apprehend the individual as already convicted through the generalized signifier of that association. The most twisted form of guilt by association, in which guilt is assumed and innocence must be proven, occurs in asset forfeiture. Asset forfeiture attributes behavior to things themselves, as a way of getting around constitutionality. Though the Fifth Amendment establishes that property cannot be seized without due process, assets can be seized arbitrarily if the police decide that such assets can be used in the commission of a crime, again through probable cause that the person associated with the assets might be a criminal. Thus, asset forfeiture is not a seizure of someone's property, but a preventive detention of property to obviate facilitating a crime. The forfeiture treats the assets as suspect, and apprehensible (detainable) as such, while the person associated with the assets then becomes guilty by association with them. The assets are guilty by association with the suspect, and the person is suspect by association with the assets.

36. At the core of this ethos is the social phenomenon that police or military action seems to legitimize what it does in the act of doing it. That is, military action valorizes military action. It is self-justifying. There is a congruence between that and the way whiteness sanctifies or legitimizes whatever white society as white does to affirm its sanctity. This is the obverse side of the ability of racist hegemony to hold against its victims what it does to them, and to interpret the other's self-defense as aggression. In social terms, the political prisoner sits at the boundary of this phenomenon. A political prisoner is someone who has risen against the state, or racial hegemony, or the discourses of state power, or whom the state considers to have risen against it in some fashion, and who is then suppressed through juridical means (that is, criminalized) for having committed a crime, or been framed for the purposes of incarceration. Political prisoners are the archetype of the person who responds to oppressive conditions and is therefore transformed into the extreme aggressor. Under criminalization, if the state frames an activist or inflates the seriousness of a crime with the activist's radicalism, this action is seen as just, as is the torture to which the political prisoner is subjected through the psychological adjuncts to criminalization, such as super-max prisons, death-row sentences, or simply the knowledge of unjust treatment.

37. Turner, in his treatise on racism in Pennsylvania, associates four factors with the increase of prejudice and discrimination against black people from 1800 to 1860: the influx from the South,

a deterioration of character, an increase in crime, and the rising pretensions of black people (NP, 251). If we were to translate these into social terms, rather than leave them simply as things for white people to notice and evaluate negatively, they would appear thus: The influx of people seeking freedom was noticed as numbers that offered competition. Were these people white, they would probably have found jobs and eventually acquired property. But they were discriminated against, which made their numbers noticeable as a desperate and alien population, rather than simply as population gain. A "deterioration of character" becomes a social mode of naming and reifying the alienness already imposed by the policy of segregation, as poverty is engendered by exclusion from employment in the name of competition. An increase in crime is then logical in the face of poverty and privation. Being the one aspect that can be given statistical foundation, however, crime gets separated sociologically as a factor from other effects of discrimination and is perceived as associated with black people as such, as a continuation of noticing. Any attempt by a black person at self-respect in opposition to this process of criminalization would be seen as stepping out of line, exhibiting improper attitudes and pretensions.

Chapter Four

1. In the same sense that one can speak of a white left, one could speak of a "nonwhite left"— a "left of color" that conjoins black, brown, Native American, and Asian American in a project that could pretend to an ideal unity in the same way that the white left does. But each racialized group has a different relation to white supremacy, and each has been used by whites to redefine themselves in different ways, according to the logic of the situation. (Cf. Tomas Almaguer, *Racial Fault Lines.*) Thus, each has different necessities to meet to facilitate its program, as well as a different program derived from its different self-constituted cultural trajectory— including its tradition, its specific history, its relation to white society through which it had been racialized in the first place, and the competitions into which it has been thrust by white supremacist control of civil rights. In effect, difference is a necessary starting point for grounding resistance in a social and cultural reality that is never separable from the structures of racialization. If the nonwhite right has generally been an attempt at organized or individual accession to white domination, an opportunism with respect to a view of its inevitability ("We might as well get used to it and learn to live with it"), the nonwhite left may be understood as anyone who rejects that idea and dreams of human dignity, self-respect, and a future in which relations of domination and the identities produced by them have been eliminated (including all forms of accession). What each nonwhite racialized people does to resist, to develop a politics and a cultural infrastructure for themselves or in conjunction with others, has to be respected a priori insofar as it founds itself on whatever autonomy is possible.

2. Toni Morrison, *Playing in the Dark,* p. 17. Helene Cixous, "The Laugh of Medusa," *Signs,* I, no. 4 (Summer 1976), p. 892.

3. All colonialism has depended on such a system of narratives; it is what Edward Said analyzed as European "orientalism," by which Europe rationalized the colonial domination of Asia. Edward Said, *Orientalism* (New York: Vintage, 1979).

4. Many whites will complain that black people generalize whites as well. The feelings black people develop toward whites (often anger, rage, hate, pity, contempt, distance, circumspection) occur on an individual basis; each black person must decide for himself or herself how to navigate an experience with whites in this white supremacist society. Different black peo-

ple will evaluate their past experience in different ways. It is not a group phenomenon, because the group does not have the power to impose a definition or generalization on whites. Instead, a group sense of solidarity, not filtered through a paranoia, is more germane. But the question is also a source of debate among blacks, that is, how to survive the constant derogations of white society, of which the white complaint about blacks generalizing is an example. Similarly, when black people prefer the company of blacks rather than whites, many whites complain that this is a form of self-segregation. For blacks, however, this is most often an attempt to free themselves from having to deal with the unending renarrativizations to which whites subject them.

5. Ian Lopez, "White by Law," in *Critical Race Theory*, ed. Richard Delgado (Philadelphia: Temple Univ. Press, 1995), p. 547. Ironically, Lopez advances this notion of the double negative in a critique of the apparent ongoing need for a juridical definition of race.

6. Since whiteness is constructed discursively and it constructs all other races in the process, one could say that all other races are also only systems of meanings and narratives. However, all other racialized people have had to defend themselves from the onslaught of whites in the forms of enslavement, colonialism, segregation, second-class citizenship in their own native lands, and plain racism; the cultural, community, and identity structures they have had to build in resistance—to reconstruct themselves and their social infrastructures in the very midst of oppression—may have greater import for them than the being of a discursive system, whatever its origin. Concrete cultural being would take on an existence and a cultural importance as the signification to which the signifiers of race then make reference, which would not be true of whites as such.

7. Walter Benjamin, "The Work of Art in the Age of Mechanical Reproduction," in *Illuminations*, trans. Harry Zohn (New York: Schocken Books, 1969), p. 245.

8. Alfred Sohn-Rachel, *The Economy and Class Structures of German Fascism*, trans. Martin Rethel (London: Free Association, 1987).

9. A critique of this attitude was levied by a collective of women of color, as part of an extended struggle with the white hegemonic mind that had assumed leadership of women's groups. Cf. "A Black Feminist Statement" by the Combahee River Collective, in *This Bridge Called My Back*, ed. Cherrie Moraga and Gloria Anzaldúa (New York: Kitchen Table Press, 1983).

10. Women felt the same way in male-dominated organizations and formed women's organizations. The men's sense of entitlement was homologous. It took a while before white women began to see that they were expressing a similar hegemonic thinking in the women's movement with respect to women of color—in the name of women's unity.

11. Peggy McIntosh, "White Privilege: Unpacking the Hidden Knapsack," published in the Winter 1990 issue of *Independent School*; it was extracted from Working Paper 189 of the Wellesley College Center for Research on Women. I have extracted a number of items from the article here, quoted some, paraphrased others, and changed the order in which McIntosh presents them. See also Nelson Rodríguez and Leila Villaverde, eds., *Dismantling White Privilege: Pedagogy, Politics, and Whiteness* in vol. 73 of *Counterpoints* (New York: P. Lang, 2000); and George Lipsitz, *The Possessive Investment in Whiteness: How White People Profit from Identity Politics* (Philadelphia: Temple Univ. Press, 1998).

12. A similar Manicheanism, or double bind, is clearly illustrated as the effect of colonialism in Chinua Achebe's *Things Fall Apart*. In the novel, the son of the main character turns to the Christianity of the colonialist missionaries, for which the father curses him and then commits suicide. The father dies both because the new religion spells the end of the native culture,

on which all people rely to live, and because he has cursed his son and thus can no longer live under the old social framework. What colonialism brought into being was a disruption of the traditional social framework of the African community by an alternate ethics that preached life but meant death because it disrupted that framework. Colonialism kills through its church and its ethics as much as through its bullets. With no discussion of the meaning of the colonized community's traditional practices, the self-proclaimed ethical stand of the colonialist church derogates that community as a culture simply by being hegemonic. Those who live in the traditional culture are given a Manichean choice to either accede to derogation or defend the entire culture. An African might accept the idea that certain practices were not good, but he or she would be placed in a position where to defend the culture means to defend those practices, and where to agree that the practices might be bad means to attack the entire culture and thus betray the community. To advocate reform of these practices would thus place one in complicity with colonialism's ends of destroying the culture and taking it over. Such a person is trapped by colonial hegemony between surrender and the defense of the unethical, between betrayal and dogma.

13. One thing Marxism unfortunately has in common with white supremacy is its desire and tendency to speak for others. The Marxian theoretic leads its practitioners to adopt the position of a vanguard, as savants empowered to estimate the popular will and its thought processes, decide what the working class is thinking, and speak for it. That this propensity has been the source of failed revolutions goes unquestioned in the annals of Marxist self-criticism. (The failure of the revolution is interpreted as "the masses are not ready.") This propensity is also the source of Marxist theorizing on apathy as passive disengagement, rather than see it as an active process of disengagement requiring great energy, but of greater benefit to the individual than involvement. In minimal form, the propensity appears as hypothesizing the "lowest common denominator," by which the political activist gives in to and reduces his or her thinking to the level of popular culture and media propaganda. But speaking for others is an act of the hegemonic mind; it is part of the way people turn other people into a language for themselves. In that sense, Marxism is culturally connected to colonialism and white supremacy, though it attempts to stand in opposition to both.

14. Sara Diamond, *Roads to Dominion* (New York: Guilford Press, 1995), pp. 261–270.

Index